CW00686066

CORNELIUS COLLETT AND THE
SUFFOLK YEOMANRY
1794–1820

CORNELIUS COLLETT AND THE SUFFOLK YEOMANRY

1794–1820

Defending Suffolk against the French

Edited by
MARGARET THOMAS

General Editor
JANE FISKE

The Boydell Press

Suffolk Records Society
VOLUME LXIII

A Suffolk Records Society publication
First published 2020
The Boydell Press, Woodbridge

ISBN   978-1-78327-493-2

Issued to subscribing members for the year 2020

The Boydell Press is an imprint of Boydell & Brewer Ltd
PO Box 9, Woodbridge, Suffolk IP12 3DF, UK
and of Boydell & Brewer Inc.
668 Mt Hope Avenue, Rochester, NY 14620–2731, USA
website: www.boydellandbrewer.com

The publisher has no responsibility for the continued existence or accuracy of
URLs for external or third-party internet websites referred to in this book, and
does not guarantee that any content on such websites is, or will remain, accurate
or appropriate

A catalogue record for this book is available
from the British Library

This publication is printed on acid-free paper

Printed and bound in Great Britain by TJ International Ltd, Padstow, Cornwall

CONTENTS

ILLUSTRATIONS

The editor and publishers are grateful to all the institutions and persons listed for permission to reproduce the materials in which they hold copyright. Every effort has been made to trace the copyright holders; apologies are offered for any omissions, and the publishers will be pleased to add any necessary acknowledgement in subsequent editions.

ACKNOWLEDGEMENTS

I was first introduced to Cornelius Collett and his three volumes when starting to research material for a history of the Suffolk Yeomanry, which was published in 2012. He has therefore been a part of my life for a number of years. In writing that history it was apparent that Collett's volumes contained a wealth of contemporary observation that deserved to be more widely known and that they covered a subject which had received little attention in Suffolk. I am therefore grateful to the Suffolk Records Society for agreeing to make Collett's volumes the subject of one of its annual publications.

I am grateful to the Suffolk and Norfolk Yeomanry Museum Trust for giving me their agreement to publish Collett's volumes, and in particular to Major Gary Walker MBE, whose interest and help has been much appreciated, as it was during the writing of the history of the Yeomanry. I am also grateful to the Suffolk Record Office for allowing me to use maps, prints and photographs in this book, and to the staff of the Ipswich branch for their willing assistance during my many visits to the Record Office.

My thanks are also due to Gloucestershire Archives for permission to reproduce the Hollesley Bay Defence map and to Val Dudley for alerting me to its existence. Similarly, I am grateful to Jo Rothery for sharing with me William Goodwin's Diary. I am grateful to the Duke of Grafton for allowing me to reproduce the portrait of Lord Euston.

I would like to thank my general editor, Dr Jane Fiske, for her interest and encouragement. Her two volumes of the Oakes Diaries, 1778–1827, volumes 32 and 33 of the Suffolk Records Society's series, have provided valuable cross-references for Collett. Many thanks must also go to Mike Durrant for his photographic expertise and for drawing the maps.

Most of all I would like to thank my family, Harold, Harriet and Charles, for living so long with Cornelius Collett and for all their patience, help, support, encouragement and technical expertise, without which this book would never have been finished.

The Suffolk Records Society is grateful to the trustees of the Suffolk and Norfolk Yeomanry Collection for a grant towards the cost of printing this publication.

Margaret Thomas
Little Horkesley, March 2019

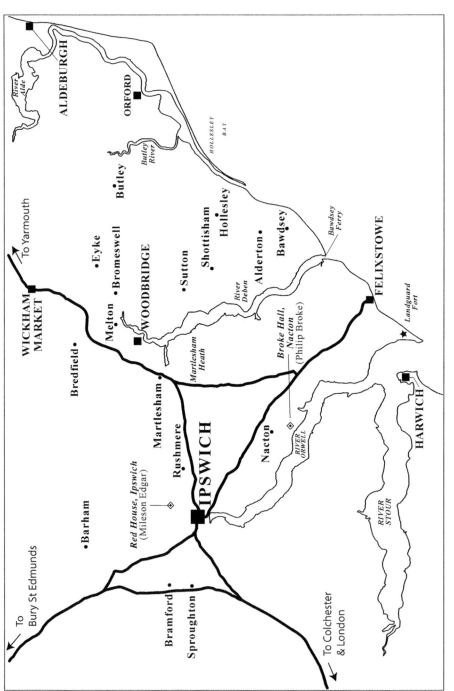

Plate 1. Places mentioned in the text and their relationship to Woodbridge and the coast. Drawn by Mike Durrant

INTRODUCTION

Cornelius Collett and his book

The efforts of a volunteer force of Suffolk gentlemen and farmers to provide a defence for the county against threatened invasion are the subject of this book, set against the context of twenty years of war against France between 1793 and 1815. While most volunteers of the period trained as infantry units, this force was one of cavalry, known as the Loyal Suffolk Yeomanry Cavalry. Somewhat akin to the concept of the Home Guard, members attended training sessions, inspections and reviews, but continued with their ordinary lives for the rest of the time. The book is a transcription of three volumes of records of their activities written by Cornelius Collett, a member of one of the Yeomanry's Troops. His declared aim was to give 'An Account of the cause and institution of the Yeomanry Cavalry in the County of Suffolk, with minutes made at sundry times of the occurrences in the 2nd Troop, by Cornelius Collett of Woodbridge who installed himself a member thereof at the commencement of the Institution in 1794.'

Cornelius Collett lived in Woodbridge, a market town and port on the river Deben, nine miles from Ipswich (Plate 1). In 1801 Woodbridge had a population of 3,020, which had swollen to 4,332 by 1811 because of the regular army troops stationed there (Plate 2).[1] Well-known and respected in the town, he was referred to as Cornelius Collett of Woodbridge or Cornelius Collett, Banker. Collett was a common local name,[2] and as the family was very extensive in the area, he probably acquired the soubriquet Banker rather than Esq. to differentiate him from other members of the family. He opened the Woodbridge Bank on 24 June 1791,[3] and by 1804 he had gone into partnership with the prominent Alexander family of Ipswich to form the Alexander and Collett Bank.[4] Collett was also a landowner, with holdings that included 63 acres of the Deadman's Estate and the Farlingay Hall land as well as Drybridge Marsh.[5] He bought the parade ground at the barracks when it became obsolete at the end of the French wars (Plate 2).

The son of Anthony Collett and Mary née May, Cornelius was baptised on 27 March 1748 in Eyke. His father was lord of the manor of Eyke and owned extensive lands in the area, while his uncle, another Cornelius, was lord of the manor of

---

[1] For an account of army regiments and other forces in the general area during this period, see J. Foynes, *East Anglia against the Tricolour, 1789–1815* (Cromer, 2016).

[2] There was another Cornelius Collett who was later a quartermaster in the same Corps of Yeomanry.

[3] SROI HD365/1–3. The Diary of William Goodwin of Earl Soham 1785–1810 records that on 24 June 1791 the bank was opened 'under the firm of Francis Brooke, Philip Riches and Cornelius Collett. Their Notes are Cashed at Mr Riches's and at Messrs. Thorton, Down and Frees in London.' By 1797 it was known as Brookes and Co.

[4] The building still stands at the bottom of Church Street. For many years, Bernard Barton, the Quaker poet, was the bank's branch manager. J. Fiske, ed., *The Oakes Diaries: Business, Politics and the Family in Bury St Edmunds 1778–1827*, Suffolk Records Society, Volumes 32 and 33, Volume II, 1990, p. 367.

[5] SROI HD11/475/2405. He commissioned Isaac Johnson to draw him a sketch map of the area.

Plate 2. Map of Woodbridge Barracks in 1804, built for the regular army stationed in the town, and close to the turnpike road for fast reaction. The fifty acre site lay to the west of the town. After the army had left, part of it was bought by Collett in 1814 and used for Yeomanry exercises. © SROI, P630/1. Photograph by Mike Durrant

Westerfield. Cornelius was twenty-five years old when he married Susanna Page on 2 December 1773, and they had six children.[6] Only two of them, Cornelius and Mary, were still alive when he made his will on 21 February 1816, together with a grandson George Daniel Curling, son of Elizabeth.[7] He left his estate to his wife Susanna in her lifetime, but she predeceased him, dying on 4 February 1818.[8]

---

6   Cornelius (baptised 20 July 1774, but who died shortly afterwards); Susanna (baptised 2 July 1775); Cornelius (baptised 24 August 1776); Lucy (baptised 9 January 1778, but who died in infancy); Elizabeth (baptised 11 December 1778) and Mary (baptised 25 July 1780).
7   PROB 11/17/1748, the will of Cornelius Collett proved in London on 17 December 1828.
8   *Bury and Norwich Post* 4 February 1818.

Collett left instructions that after her death everything he owned was to be left in trust to his friends Dykes Alexander and Samuel Alexander the Younger, to be sold as soon as possible by private or public sale, with the proceeds divided between his son, daughter and grandson.

Collett was a wealthy and educated man who had the resources to finance his interests. The auction of his effects held after his death, expected to attract 'the Nobility, Gentry and Connoisseurs in the Fine Arts', clearly illustrates the quality of his possessions and the breadth of his interests, from a large library of antiquarian books, prints and engravings, maps and charts, to plate and thirty-three-year-old bottles of port.[9] His astronomical instruments included 'a curious Mile Wheel, (late the property of J. Kirby Esq., supposed to be the one with which he surveyed the county of Suffolk in 1735)'. He was a regular client of Isaac Johnson, who provided maps and illustrations for him, ranging from plates of cavalry belts and trooper mounts to maps of his land in Woodbridge.[10] One particularly curious acquisition was an exceptional and very fine cupboard, dated 1509, with an unusual carving of the Tree of Jesse, which possibly belonged to the Holy Roman Emperor. He engaged Johnson to draw illustrations of it and had them framed and placed near it, presumably to be able to see the carvings more clearly.[11]

Collett was also very active in the community and did much for the town and surrounding area. He was a churchwarden at St Mary's,[12] and served on numerous committees from acting as a trustee of the Turnpike Trust for Eye[13] and investigating a bridge over the Deben, to chairing a meeting of inhabitants to consider the effect the proposed navigation between Bungay and Diss would have on the port of Woodbridge.[14] He was elected as the county representative on the Grand Jury at the Suffolk Lent Assizes in 1819.[15]

Collett volunteered for the Woodbridge Troop of the Suffolk Yeomanry Cavalry on its inception in July 1794 and was appointed its quartermaster. He was commissioned as cornet (the lowest rank of commissioned officer) in October 1801 and as second lieutenant in May 1803. He became a captain when the original Troop of 150 men was divided into a Corps of three Troops in September 1803.[16] He served as such until he resigned in October 1820, aged 72. He died on 20 November 1828 after 'a long affliction bourne with great fortitude' and was buried at Eyke.[17]

Collett's three volumes arrived at the West Suffolk Record Office at Bury St Edmunds in 1953 after the yeomanry regiment of the period, the 358th, purchased them, in conjunction with the archivist, Martin Statham.[18] After Collett's death, the

---

[9] *Ipswich Journal* 3 January 1829, 21 February 1829, 18 April 1829. Catalogues of the sale were available as far away as London, Norwich and Chelmsford.

[10] J. Blatchly, *Isaac Johnson of Woodbridge: Georgian Surveyor and Artist* (Dorchester, 2014), p. 55.

[11] See Blatchly, *Isaac Johnson* for further information on its intriguing history and an illustration on p. 55. It was later bought by Lord Fairhaven and is now at Anglesey Abbey.

[12] Blatchly, *Isaac Johnson*, p. 55.

[13] *Ipswich Journal* 2 March 1822.

[14] *Ipswich Journal* 11 July 1818 and 14 March 1818.

[15] *Bury and Norwich Post* 31 March 1819.

[16] Rather confusingly, Collett became captain of the 2nd Troop of the 2nd Woodbridge Corps of Suffolk Yeomanry Cavalry.

[17] *Ipswich Journal* 29 November 1828 and *Bury and Norwich Post* 3 December 1828.

[18] A price of £60 is pencilled inside the cover. Major (later Lieutenant Colonel) Champness, a great enthusiast of Suffolk Yeomanry history who did much work on the subject, was instrumental in the purchase of the books from a London dealer.

volumes became separated.[19] One was eventually acquired by Reade and Barrett, booksellers of 31 Cornhill, Ipswich, who on 8 February 1878 offered it to F. C. Brook, for whom they were in the practice of acquiring antiquarian books: 'We also send you for your approval a copy of Coopers Winchelsea which we have at length found, bound up together with a rather curious MS History of the Suffolk Yeomanry. The price of this last is 10 shillings.'[20] Realising it was one of a set, Brook asked them to advertise for the other two.[21] George Booth, printer, bookseller, stationer, general newspaper and advertisement agent, Woodbridge, apparently found the two volumes: a postscript, added to his receipt for the payment of six pounds by Captain Brooke of Ufford Place, noted 'The owner of the 2 Vols was greatly disappointed last night, he did not think they could have been purchased, he cannot think how he came to let me have them. He reluctantly took the six pounds as if I could get the books back.' They are now in the Suffolk Record Office, Ipswich.[22]

Collett wrote his account in three handsome matching volumes, bound in rough calf, with marbled inside covers and very good-quality plain paper, each 15 by 9 inches. Written in ink, the three volumes had hand-pencilled lines carefully ruled to aid the writer. Spacing varied according to the subject matter (Plate 3).[23] The pages were written on both sides. Volume A had 359 written pages, Volume B, 348 and Volume C, 116. The last had been pre-ruled for several pages ahead although it was left incomplete with only about half the book used. Each page was carefully numbered. Collett, as well as being the author, transcribed the documents in all three volumes himself: the handwriting is consistent throughout and covered the years 1794 to 1820. It is well-written in a neat, legible hand by an educated man, with mostly consistent modern spelling, although with an over-abundance of capital letters and a lack of punctuation.[24] There are few illegible words, alterations or crossings out.

Collett's volumes are unique both in their nature and content. They were not written as a continuous prose, but were a collection of fascinating and wide-ranging material. The war against France was central to the text, and provides the contextual background throughout, apart from the last few years. The descriptions of the activities of his Yeomanry Troop, such as general musters, inspections, reviews, shared celebrations and general administration, were written by Collett himself, creating a recurring pattern as might be expected of such a force. However, a significant part of the book is his transcription of a very wide variety of documents, including letters to and from commanding officers, the lord lieutenant and central government, defence evacuation plans, government instructions, acts of parliament and

---

19 Collett's will required his executors to sell all his possessions so his volumes may have been split up very soon after his death. The Suffolk Yeomanry had been disbanded in 1827, the year before he died, so there was therefore no official body to recognise the importance of Collett's work and claim the history of the Regiment. In 1830, when the government, recognising its mistake, reinstated the Yeomanry, it was in effect a new institution based in different areas of Suffolk.

20 This loose letter was found in Volume B from Reade and Barrett addressed to F. C. Brook.

21 The advertisement from the *Ipswich Journal* is stuck inside the front cover of Volume B: 'Suffolk Yeomanry Cavalry Any person in possession of Volume B and C of the details of the Woodbridge Troop, established 1794, would oblige the advertiser by communicating with Messrs. Reade and Barrett booksellers, Ipswich. The volume is probably about 15 inches high and bound in rough calf.'

22 SROI HD80/3/1, 2, 3.

23 They varied according to the subject; for example, when he was copying long newspaper accounts of national events, the handwriting was smaller and the lines much closer together.

24 A few words are consistently wrong such as se for see and where for were.

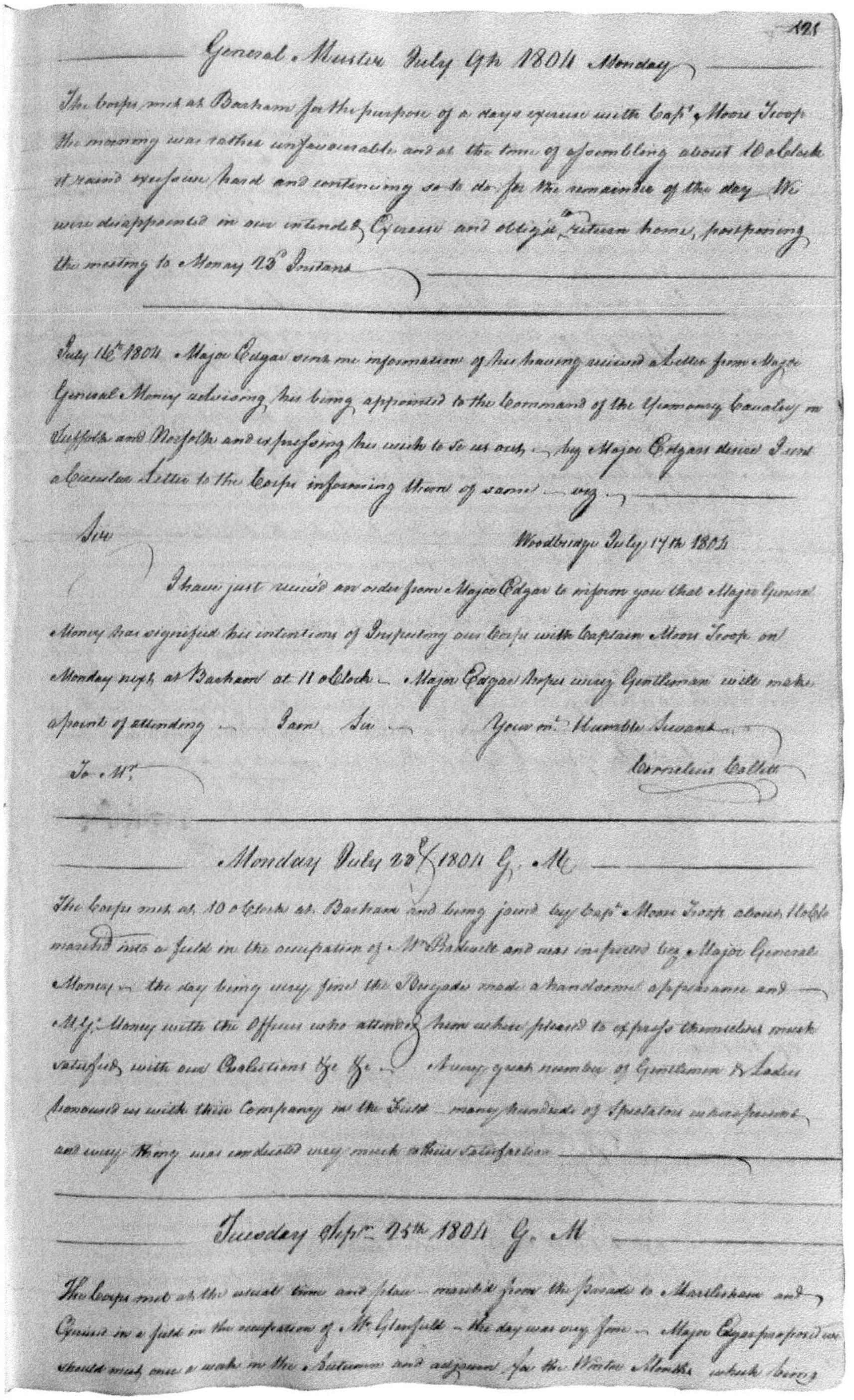

General Muster July 9th 1804 Monday

The Corps met at Barham for the purpose of a days exercise with Capt. Moore Troop the morning was rather unfavourable and at the time of assembling about 10 oClock it raind exceeding hard and continuing so to do for the remainder of the day. We were disappointed in our intended Exercise and oblig'd return home, postponing the meeting to Monday 23d Instant —

July 16th 1804. Major Edgar sent me information of his having received a Letter from Major General Money advising his being appointed to the Command of the Yeomanry Cavalry in Suffolk and Norfolk and is pressing his wishes to see us &c. — by Major Edgar desire I sent a circular Letter to the Corps informing them of same — viz —

Sir   Woodbridge July 17th 1804

I have just receiv'd an order from Major Edgar to inform you that Major General Money has signified his intentions of Inspecting our Corps with Captain Moore Troop on Monday next at Barham at 11 oClock. Major Edgar hopes every Gentleman will make a point of attending — I am Sir — Your most Humble Servant —

To Mr.   Cornelius Collett

Monday July 20th 1804 G. M.

The Corps met at 10 oClock at Barham and being join'd by Capt. Moore Troop about 11 oClo marched into a field in the occupation of Mr. Bastwell and was inspected by Major General Money — the day being very fine the Brigade made a handsome appearance and M.G. Money with the Officers who attended him where pleas'd to express themselves much satisfied with our Evolutions &c &c. — A very great number of Gentlemen & Ladies favoured us with their Company in the Field — many hundred of Spectators where present and every thing was indeed very much admired satisfaction —

Tuesday Sept. 25th 1804 G. M.

The Corps met at the usual time and place — marched from the parade to Martlesham and Exercise in a field in the occupation of Mr. Glanfield — the day was very fine — Major Edgar proposed we should meet once a week in the Autumn and adjourn for the Winter Months which being

Plate 3. A typical page from Collett's book showing entries recording general musters in 1804. © Suffolk and Norfolk Yeomanry Museum Trust. Photograph by Charles Thomas

newspaper entries. Collett was also concerned to provide the national context for the Suffolk scene, and sizeable sections of the volumes were devoted to copies he made from the *London Gazette Extraordinary* reporting important battles and celebrations, which are not included in this edition since they cover national rather than local events.

In many ways Collett would seem to have conceived his enterprise as a whole. From the start he had the intention of moulding it into the appearance of a conventional book, complete with page numbers, cross references and indices. Yet the book is not what it at first appears to be, an account written as events happened, recorded on a regular basis, much like a diary, which it has often been called, but a much more complex compilation. Although the text adopts a chronological approach, starting in 1794 in Volume A and tailing off after May 1818 in Volume C, this is misleading in terms of when it was written. The actual order of creation remains much of an enigma, as it would appear that a considerable part of his text was not written contemporaneously with the events they described. Collett himself made several references to the order. He began with Volume B, with its inside front cover pasted with coloured illustrations of earlier cavalry forces (Plate II). This ran from August 1803 to May 1814. However, he explains that at some later date, he acquired the minutes of the committee of subscribers for the internal defence of Suffolk, who established the Suffolk Yeomanry Cavalry in 1794, which had not been included before, because they were not in his possession. These he copied into Volume A. After the minutes, he finally got to the subject of his book, the 2nd Woodbridge Troop of Loyal Suffolk Yeomanry Cavalry, and starting in 1794, made great efforts to fill in the years he had missed. His treatment of events, such as musters, is far less detailed than in the other two volumes. He acknowledged that he had filled the rest of the volume with transcriptions of national events from the *London Gazette*. Collett used less than half of Volume C. He started with his usual entries, which ran from July 1814 until 7 May 1818, when they end abruptly. A few unfinished entries followed and finally petered out in 1820 with no explanation, although the pages had been ruled and numbered beyond this date. The last entry in 1820 was a list of the members of the Troop of which he was captain.

Collett's reasons for embarking on this huge undertaking were never explained. It was his personal project and was not written for publication. It may be assumed that he wanted the activities of the Suffolk Yeomanry Cavalry, an institution of which he and all the officers and men were so proud to be members, and to which they and he had devoted so much time and effort over a protracted period of war, to be in some way recorded, and their commitment, dedication and patriotism remembered. Collett could have written a straightforward account of the activities of the Troop. However, what emerges is a much more detailed and in-depth account of the period. In order to achieve this, he must have had some sort of official authority to use such a wide range of archives: correspondence between the Lord Lieutenant, Philip Broke and Mileson Edgar, the War Office and ministers, material concerning the administration of the yeomanry, which normally would not have reached the public eye.[25] The other Troops of Yeomanry Cavalry in Suffolk would have received many of the same documents as those that Collett recorded. However, very few archives

---

[25] This would have been facilitated by Collett's position in the Troop as quartermaster and by his social and professional status.

survive for these other Troops;[26] nor do the originals of most of what he transcribed, apart from some recorded in the Letter Book of the Lord Lieutenant for a few years, a few in Mileson Edgar's papers and others published in the local newspapers.

Collett was not concerned with his own part in events: this was no extrovert performance. His voice is not heard: his was not an active presence. He acted as a recorder of events, with little attempt to interpret, comment or express his opinion on the documents or their contents, even when he, as a banker, must have been in a position to comment. He reproduced the documents accurately and in their entirety.[27] Where they were letters or orders, often between social equals in a quasi-military environment, the mode of address and conclusion was always included, and provides an interesting insight into the social and political mores of the period. As such, they have been retained in this volume. Nor is there any evidence that this was a personal selection of evidence. Collett reported with a detached voice throughout, and rarely are there signs of emotional involvement. This was perhaps most notice-able in 1803, 1804 and 1805 when the crisis of a French invasion was thought to be imminent. However, these years were probably written up some years later, and he was not tempted to comment using hindsight, but left the authentic contemporary reaction of the county to speak through the documents themselves.

The threat from France and the formation of the Suffolk Yeomanry Cavalry

The context for Collett's book was the war against the French and the resultant need to provide a defence of the country, and of Suffolk in particular. Britain was accustomed to fighting the French, since for long periods in the eighteenth century, she had been at war. But protected by the power of the Royal Navy such wars had relatively little impact at home. When war between France and Britain was declared at the end of January 1793, it soon became obvious that this time it was to be a very different kind of war and that invasion had become a real possibility. The introduction of the *levée en masse* of French citizens in August 1793[28] created huge new armies, and with them, very different fighting strategies from those of small professional armies. War had become 'the business of the people'.[29] The new armies soon moved outside traditional French boundaries and, after a series of victorious campaigns, annexed what is now Belgium and embarked on a successful campaign against the United Provinces, now Holland. Once these coastlines were in French hands, they threatened British control of the English Channel, and Suffolk, with its open and vulnerable coastline, now came within reach and an attempted invasion became a possibility.

Given such a threat, the available options for defence open to the government were limited. Reliant for centuries on the power of her navy, Britain, with its fear of standing armies,[30] had only a small professional army, and this would be needed to

---

[26] A few survive for the 1st Blything Troop in the papers of Lord Rous, their captain. SROI Rous Catalogue HA11.

[27] Apart from the minutes of the subscribers' committee, which were sometimes reordered and some details not applicable to the Yeomanry, were omitted.

[28] This was conscription in all but name: all unmarried, able-bodied men between 18 and 25 were called to fight for their country. It became official in 1798.

[29] Clauswitz, quoted in L. Colley, *Britons* (London, 1992), p. 283.

[30] This was a permanent professional army not disbanded in peacetime and was feared because of issues arising from the Civil War and James II.

join with allies in a coalition to fight the European threat abroad. Home defence was traditionally in the hands of the militia. This was made up of able-bodied men aged between 18 and 45 from each parish, whose names were drawn in a much-hated compulsory ballot. Their numbers were established from a county quota, which was then divided between hundreds and parishes. This was a feared and highly unpopular system. Those unlucky in the ballot then attended a meeting when their fitness and individual circumstances to serve were examined.[31] If considered suitable, they had to join the local county militia regiment, unless they could pay for a substitute. They were then trained to be a home defence force. In peacetime this amounted to attendance for only twenty-eight days' training a year. In wartime, however, when they were called up (embodied), they were subject to martial law and although paid, had to leave their homes and families to serve for five years because militias were rarely based in their home county.[32] It was not an inspiring force to provide the main defence of the country against any invading French army.

By 1794 the King and the government under William Pitt were faced with a crisis.[33] Having resisted the idea of using volunteers since the outbreak of war they now became convinced that change was urgently needed. They were forced to contemplate the need for additional defence forces, although plans were also put in place to enlarge and augment the militia. There were certainly many people throughout the country ready and willing to answer a patriotic appeal. However, Britain was in the throes of the world's first industrial revolution and the social and economic problems resulting from it, which together with a rapidly increasing population, had caused major popular protest, unrest and rioting in the areas most affected by change. Appalling living and working conditions encouraged the spread of the radical ideas engendered by the French Revolution and the government feared revolution at home. Pitt was frightened and reluctant to consider an appeal, since to arm volunteers was considered a dangerous option when such arms might be used against the government. This was the dilemma that had to be faced. How far would patriotic duty triumph over radical ideals if the French landed?

One solution to the problem was the suggestion that a yeomanry cavalry might be formed. It was put forward, or so he later suggested, by Arthur Young, the famous Suffolk agriculturalist and friend of the King who was himself very interested in farming.[34] Young suggested a volunteer cavalry made up of landowners, farmers and yeomanry, people who, since they held a stake in the country, would not only be willing to defend it against the French but could be totally relied upon at other times.[35] They would be prepared to deal with riot and tumult at home should the need arise, and the government could fall back on them should other volunteer infantry groups prove untrustworthy. Accordingly, early in 1794, the decision was made to ask volunteers to come forward and also to encourage local fund-raising

---

[31] James Oakes served on one such committee and makes numerous references to attending meetings describing the process in practice. *Oakes Diaries*, Volume I, pp. 339–41, 362; Volume II, pp. 35–6.

[32] This was because it was feared that they might be tempted to join the very protestors they were there to stop.

[33] William Pitt the Younger had been Prime Minister since December 1783. Once France descended into extremist terror after the Revolution, Pitt considered this would occupy them internally and they would be no threat to the rest of Europe for some time. He was soon disillusioned.

[34] A. Young, 'Annals of Agriculture', Volume XVII, in M. Bethem Edwards, ed., *Autobiography of Arthur Young* (London, 1898).

[35] There was also a fear that recruiting volunteer forces would reduce the number of people available to join the militia and regular army.

efforts to support groups so raised. A volunteer yeomanry cavalry was to be one of the important outcomes.

On 14 March 1794 the government proposed that citizens could assist in the creation of new forces by raising voluntary financial contributions, which could be used for the formation of new fencible units or independent volunteer corps, as well as providing bounties for the augmentation of the militia.[36] Official legislation authorising this and the acceptance of volunteers was rapidly passed.[37] Once it had been accepted that volunteer forces were necessary, the huge undertaking needed to be organised as quickly as possible. Because central government bureaucracy at that date was minimal with only very limited resources, it was therefore structured on a county basis.

Collett opened his Volume A with an account of Suffolk's response to these proposals and how the government's nebulous ideas were put quickly into practical application: within months, the first Troops of the Loyal Suffolk Yeomanry Cavalry were in being.[38] This was achieved using the Crown's representative in charge of each county, the Lord Lieutenant.[39] Henry Dundas, the Home Secretary, wrote to the Lord Lieutenant of Suffolk, Lord Euston, son of the 4th Duke of Grafton, with suggestions for how this might be accomplished. The letter coincided with the meeting of the Grand Jury for the Suffolk Assizes at Bury St Edmunds,[40] and Euston was therefore able to involve the High Sheriff, Sir Charles Bunbury, and other influential members of Suffolk society, who had collected in Bury for the Assizes. Such a group could be relied upon to quickly expedite Dundas's suggestions and also had the money to launch a subscription to put them into practice. The speed and efficiency with which the whole operation was carried out also reflects their concern over the general situation, both at home and abroad.

Plans were immediately put in place to organise such a subscription and arrangements made for its collection and management. A meeting of subscribers was soon arranged and a committee formed.[41] Collett copied the minutes of the subscribers' committee meetings, which clearly outlined the process that led to the formation of the Suffolk Yeomanry Cavalry. The first meeting took place on 3 April at the White Hart Inn, Stowmarket, under the chairmanship of Sir John Rous, and soon agreed how the money already raised would be used. It was decided that the best way of strengthening the county's internal defence against an invading enemy was to set up a fencible cavalry, consisting of nobility, gentry, yeomanry, farmers, tradesmen and others, and men were asked to come forward to join the new volunteer cavalry. By 11 April the subscription already amounted to £4,300. It was agreed that the

---

[36] Fencible units were corps made up of men enlisted for home service only in wartime.

[37] I. F. W. Beckett, *Britain's Part-time Soldiers: The Amateur Military Tradition 1558–1945*, 2nd edn (Barnsley, 2011), p. 73.

[38] He managed to do this by acquiring access to the minutes of the meetings of the subscribers' committee for the internal defence of Suffolk. See Collett's opening to Volume A.

[39] The Lord Lieutenant was the King's personal representative in each county. He was also responsible for the militia.

[40] The Grand Jury heard potential criminal cases to determine whether there was a case to be heard at the Assizes.

[41] James Oakes, attending the Grand Jury, subscribed £20 on 21 March. He was present at the opening meetings at Stowmarket, together with the subdivision meeting for the hundred of Thedwastre and Thingoe on 14 May. His diary provides a more personal view of the process than Collett. *Oakes Diaries*, Volume I, pp. 298–301. The local newspapers also reported the meetings, often publishing the minutes almost verbatim.

subscription could support four cavalry Troops of 60 privates. An augmentation of the militia was also agreed, together with two companies to man the coastal batteries. When insufficient volunteers were forthcoming to man the batteries, the number of cavalry Troops was raised to five.[42] There was also some limited support for volunteer infantry Troops.

The subscription eventually amounted to £7,109 15s. Collett included the list of subscribers and the amount they subscribed, made up of people from a wide section of Suffolk society who gave what they could afford (see Appendix 1). Amounts ranged from £200 from the Earl of Bristol to a shilling from Widow Sherman. Besides individual contributions, sums were raised by eight parishes. One surprising subscriber was the Duc de Liancourt, the former grandmaster of the wardrobe at the court of Louis XVI.[43] In total over 630 people subscribed, clearly illustrating the patriotism of many people in Suffolk and their fear of the French.

The subscribers' committee ensured that the whole process for strengthening the internal defence of Suffolk was organised quickly and efficiently. By July two Troops of cavalry had mustered, with others underway. The committee set out the parameters within which the volunteer yeomanry was to operate, establishing a secure basis for their operations for the twenty years covered by Collett. Names of volunteers had been collected, Troops established, officers chosen and commissioned, basic rules laid down, uniforms selected and paid for, arms and accoutrements supplied, all achieved very swiftly in the face of what the county considered an escalating threat that required a solid defence force. Since no immediate plan for substantial financial support from the government was put in place, the support of the committee was crucial for the Yeomanry Cavalry in the first two years.

The social make-up of the men volunteering for the Yeomanry was determined by the fact that they were joining cavalry units. To become a member two things were necessary: to own or have access to at least one horse, and to be free to attend musters during the week, which, with travel, might take up a whole day. The bulk of the membership, therefore, both rank and file as well as officers, came from the wealthier and better-off sections of Suffolk society, made up of some gentry but mostly farmers, with a few well-off artisans, shopkeepers and professionals such as Collett himself.

It is important to see their Yeomanry involvement and activity as they themselves must have seen it, as an integral part of their ordinary lives, with their families and social life, their houses and estates, their parks and gardens, their farms and their crops and their jobs. Collett included many references throughout the text, albeit often brief ones, to issues such as the weather and farming conditions, illustrating their importance to their farming lives: musters were arranged to fit in with the farming year to ensure a good attendance. It was to protect these things that they had chosen to volunteer. The motto of the Suffolk Yeomanry was 'Liberty, Loyalty

---

[42] The question of whether six could be supported was suggested but it was decided the cost was not feasible.

[43] He had been living in Bury for two years as an émigré at this date. He was the father of Francois de La Rochefoucauld, who wrote a lively, detailed and amusing account of Suffolk life, its society, customs and agriculture after spending a year in Bury in 1784. This was only ten years before the start of Collett's account and reflects the life led by some members of the Yeomanry. See N. Scarfe, ed., *A Frenchman's Year in Suffolk: French Impressions of Suffolk Life in 1784*, Suffolk Records Society, Volume 30, 1988, pp. xxxiv–v.

and Property', which sums up very clearly the reason for their commitment, while two additional ones on the tokens of the 1st and 3rd Troop further encapsulate their reasons: 'For King and Constitution' and *Pro Aris et Focis* (For Home and Hearth) (Plates 4 and 5). For many of the membership who served for a very long time, the Yeomanry became an integral part of their lives.

Collett's transcript of the subscribers' minutes outlined the establishment of the Suffolk Yeomanry by the committee. It was created as a number of separate Troops, spread across the county, loosely based on the boundaries of a hundred or groups

Plate 4. A token of the 1st Troop of Loyal Suffolk Yeomanry Cavalry, recruited from the Blything hundred, depicting a member in the uniform of the 1790s. The badge and motto of the Yeomanry Cavalry are on the reverse: LIBERTY LOYALTY PROPERTY. Within the cartouche the keep resembles that of the Suffolk Regiment's, which refers to the keep of Gibraltar where the regiment played a prominent part during the siege of 1779–83; 1794 relates to the date of the formation of the Troop and not the date of the production of the token. Diam. 30 mm. Private collection. Photograph by Mike Durrant

Plate 5. A token of the 3rd Troop of Loyal Suffolk Yeomanry Cavalry, which drew its membership from the hundreds of Hoxne and Hartismere. It shows an early representation of a member of the Suffolk Yeomanry Cavalry with the motto PRO ARIS ET FOCIS, 'For Hearth and Home'. The Troop was raised early in 1795, the date on the token. Diam. 30 mm. Private collection. Photograph by Mike Durrant

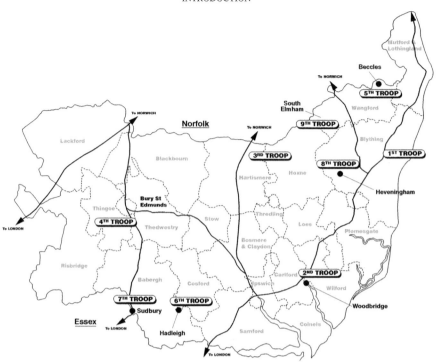

Plate 6. Map to show the position of the Troops of the Suffolk Yeomanry during the French Wars and the hundreds from which they were recruited. Drawn by Mike Durrant

of hundreds, where enough people came forward to form a Troop (Plate 6). Two Troops were quickly set up in 1794. The first was based on Blything hundred, while the second centred on Woodbridge.[44] It was not until the following year that two more Troops were formed, one for Hoxne and Hartismere hundreds and the other for Bury St Edmunds with Thedwastry and Thingoe.[45] A fifth Yeomanry Troop, based at Beccles, followed. Each of the Troops was formed as an independent unit under the command of their captain. No commanding officer was appointed in overall command of the Loyal Suffolk Yeomanry, although the committee thought that they would, if embodied and called into actual service, form one regiment under the command of a colonel. Each chose their own officers,[46] although as a new institution and given the rather uncertain situation in which they found themselves, it was natural for those of social standing and experienced in leadership, to be selected

---

44 The division of Woodbridge included the hundreds of Wilford, Loes, Plomesgate, Colneis, Carlford and Thredling.

45 Horatio Churchill was commissioned in 1794 to captain a Bury Troop, but it did not materialise until Lord Brome took over early in 1795. This would indicate that Brome had no previously existing troops to bring into the Suffolk Yeomanry framework. His supposed command of an earlier Troop in 1793 is usually quoted by the Yeomanry as the reason for the date 1793 on their later badge.

46 Officers' commissions could not be purchased as in the regular army, and all promotions were decided within the Troop, until the official formation of a regiment in 1814.

– people such as Sir John Rous,[47] Lord Brome,[48] and in the case of the 2nd Wood-bridge Troop, Philip Bowes Broke of Broke Hall, Nacton.

The subscription money was not used to pay the volunteers but to encourage them by giving them an allowance for each attendance at musters, thereby helping to reduce the expenses of rank and file members. They were allowed 2s. a day for every day of exercise for the use of their horse, and since the numbers of musters was high during the early months when volunteers were being trained to become an efficient force, the demands on the subscription were considerable. Money was also provided for their uniforms. Commanding officers were eventually allowed £12 for each man: £4 for the uniform, £1 for the helmet, £1 18s. for the great coat and £2 2s. for saddlery and accoutrements.[49]

All this caused a heavy drain on finances even though officers received no money, providing their own uniform.[50] Eventually, by March 1796, it was reported that the subscription fund was running out. The committee seems to have assumed that the Yeomanry would disband if there were no funds although this was far from true.[51] An attempt to raise a new subscription produced only enough to pay the arrears that were owing to the officers and others for expenses they had already paid out. Finally, on 20 April 1797 with all money gone, information was received that the government was finally about to adopt a plan to properly support the Yeomanry and other volunteer groups, which was, indeed, soon introduced.

The organisation of the Suffolk Yeomanry Cavalry

The Troops of the Loyal Suffolk Yeomanry were numbered in the order of their completion. In 1794 two Troops were formed. The first was that of Blything hundred (1st Troop), led by Sir John Rous of Henham Hall. The second was the Wood-bridge Troop. The third and fourth, in 1795, were the Hoxne and Hartismere Troop captained by Thomas Maynard, and the Bury Troop (Thingoe and Thedwastry), led by Charles Cornwallis, Lord Brome. An extra Troop was agreed by the subscribers' committee when volunteers to man the coastal batteries were not forthcoming. This was based at Beccles captained by Robert Sparrow and recruited from the hundreds of Wangford, Mutford and Lothingland.

In the early summer of 1794 sixty men from the hundreds around Woodbridge volunteered to serve in the 2nd Troop. Collett began his account of the Woodbridge Troop with a list of the conditions under which they agreed to serve, as specified for all Troops by the subscribing committee. He then included a copy of the King's commissions for the three officers of the Troop: its captain, Philip Bowes Broke of Broke Hall, Nacton, its lieutenant, Francis Brooke of The Abbey, Woodbridge[52] and its cornet, Mileson Edgar of the Red House, Ipswich.[53] Cornelius Collett was

---

[47] Sir John Rous of Henham Hall.
[48] Lord Brome was the eldest son of Marquess Cornwallis of Culford Hall; he resigned as captain when he succeeded his father in 1805.
[49] Collett, p. 20.
[50] Collett, p. 14. The committee's subscription also funded the augmentation of the militia, which amounted to seven men per company, in total 42 in the Western Regiment and 56 in the Eastern Regiment.
[51] Collett finished this section with the information that the Woodbridge Troop had met on 7 November 1797 and voted to continue their services without future pay. Collett, p. 24.
[52] This was probably the man with whom Collett started a bank. See footnote 3.
[53] A cornet was the lowest rank of commissioned officer.

appointed quartermaster. His detailed account of their activities began with their first muster, which took place on 20 July 1794. The first one on horseback was on 26 August, although it was not until 2 December that they first appeared in uniform.

While all the volunteers would have been able horsemen, the conversion of sixty gentlemen into a disciplined force in late 1794 and early 1795 was no easy undertaking since few of them, if any, had any military knowledge. It would have been impossible without someone with experience. The government was concerned that the volunteers should be properly trained in performing the formal evolutions and movements required of an effective cavalry unit and moulded into a force capable of supporting regular forces if needed. From the beginning they were therefore willing to pay experienced personnel trained in the regular army to teach the Troops. Government funds were provided to pay for a sergeant to join the Troop and train it, together with a corporal, replaced by the Yeomanry with a trumpeter to sound the orders. These two were the only paid members of the Troop, although much later there was a paid farrier.

The uniform for the first five Troops was the same, as it was organised and paid for by the subscription committee. The Troops needed to be uniformed as quickly as possible, and the fastest way was to have patterns of the jacket ready to copy. Collett, in the committee minutes he transcribed, included details of how this was achieved. Alterations had to be made to the proposed pattern before it was given official permission, the first time to please the Yeomanry, and the second, the government, since it had to meet military conventions.[54] The one finally agreed was a scarlet coat, lined with white, with dark blue military cape and cuffs, scarlet and blue chain epaulettes, white waistcoat, leather breeches, high top boots, round hat with bearskin, feather and cockade and white plated buttons with the crown and garter of the order with the words 'Loyal Suffolk Yeomanry' inscribed on the garter (Plate III). The first Troop to be raised, and accepted by the Lord Lieutenant to be complete, bore No. 1 on the buttons, and the other Troops the number according to the order of acceptance of their completion. The only contemporary representation of this early uniform is to be found on the tokens produced by the 1st and 3rd Troops (Plates 4 and 5).[55] The uniform of the Woodbridge Troop was renewed in the summer of 1802, but since there was little discussion about it and it was organised quickly, it would seem probable it was little changed from the original. In 1809, however, when the uniform was again in need of replacement, the Troop chose a very different one, with red jackets replaced by blue, chosen without reference to the other Troops, although they again had to obtain War Office permission.[56] When the Troops were formed into a regiment in 1814, it was this uniform that was adopted: new uniforms were in the process of manufacture when peace was declared.

The Troops shared the same badge, which was adapted from that of the Suffolk Regiment. Collett recorded no discussion by the committee or by the Woodbridge Troop about what the Yeomanry badge was to be, so presumably they wished to associate themselves with the regular forces of the Suffolk Regiment. The central

[54] Collett, p. 16.

[55] The government withdrew all copper coinage of low denomination because of the huge amount of counterfeiting. Great hardship was suffered by the poor, who only dealt in low-value coins. It was eventually agreed that respected institutions in society could be licensed to produce their own to meet the need, using copper from a Welsh mine. The 1st and 3rd Yeomanry Troops were two such groups and produced coinage in the form of tokens.

[56] Collett, pp. 208–10.

cartouche copied that of the regiment, with its Gibraltar keep surmounted by a crown, while round the cartouche was the motto of the Suffolk Yeomanry Cavalry, 'Liberty, Loyalty, Property' (Plates 4 and 5).[57]

Members in the Suffolk Yeomanry were addressed as gentlemen, and the Troop must have become, for many serving over such a long period, rather like a gentlemen's club.[58] For them service in the Yeomanry was a long-term commitment. Dedicated, loyal and hardworking men, committed to the defence of their county, they were the antithesis of the stereotypical picture of the Yeomanry so often portrayed, especially later in the nineteenth century.[59] Members needed to fit into the ethos of the Troop, and new members therefore had to be recommended or approved by the membership. They sensibly treated each other with politeness and respect, given their time spent in the Yeomanry was only a small fraction of their civilian lives, to which they had to return after musters.[60] It is a good example of how tightly knit were the social circles in Suffolk at the time and indeed many of the fellow members were neighbours. This is particularly noticeable in the wording and tone of the correspondence, especially in the early years, when handwritten orders were sent out to members, requesting their attendance at musters or meetings, many of them composed by Collett himself as quartermaster of the Troop. The way such letters were addressed, concluded and generally worded, was often a reflection of the recipients' civilian lives rather than their part-time military position.[61]

General musters were central to the life and activities of any Troop of Yeomanry Cavalry, and throughout Collett's book provide a recurrent and repetitive pattern of entries (Plate 3).[62] A general muster was a meeting of the whole Troop where it practised the evolutions, massed movements and other exercises necessary to ensure it acquired and maintained the high standard expected of an efficient and effective cavalry unit.[63] Collett usually chose to write short individual reports of each meeting. They all followed the same basic formula, which included the date and place of assembly, the field and its owner where they exercised, and what they practised (Plate 3). Recording of such information was a requirement of govern-

---

[57] The date of 1793 on the Yeomanry badge was later adopted. It is unclear how this happened since it is not the date of the formation of the Suffolk Yeomanry. It may have occurred after 1830 when the Yeomanry was re-established. Having been disbanded in 1827, the new Troops had few, if any, links with the original ones, and were concentrated more in the western part of the county. Many of the original members who would have known about the origins of the Yeomanry would have died by this time. See M. Thomas and N. Sign, *The Loyal Suffolk Hussars: The History of the Suffolk Yeomanry 1794–1967* (Solihull, 2012), pp. 33–5.

[58] As far as an associated social side to their Yeomanry activities is concerned, that of the Woodbridge Troop would appear to be limited to shared Troop dinners. A rather different picture of the Yeomanry emerges of the Bury Troop from James Oakes, whose son Orbel was a cornet in that Troop. *Oakes Diaries*, Volume I, pp. 186, 312–13 and 316.

[59] Thomas and Sign, *Loyal Suffolk Hussars*, Chapter 2.

[60] Interestingly, this was completely understood even by the War Office. Collett, p. 160: 'Regulations for the preservation of good order to be adopted in case of actual invasion in each county of Great Britain.'

[61] The difference in language between the Army and the Yeomanry for the orders for the mock battle is noticeable. Collett, p. 65.

[62] Since many of the entries of general musters repeat the same formula they have been omitted from the text. A full list of their dates of meeting is recorded in Appendix 2.

[63] For Collett's most detailed reference to what these actually entailed, see his description on 28 February 1804. Collett, p. 144.

ment, as was the keeping of a record of attendance in the muster roll (Plate 7).[64] Collett often added some comment about the weather, which was of such major importance to them as farmers and owners of estates, as well as the chance of holding a successful muster. Notices to members alerting or reminding them of the dates of general musters were in the form of letters in the early days, replaced later by cards printed with their dates and eventually by advertisements in the local newspaper, the *Ipswich Journal.*

Regular attendance at general musters was a requisite of membership because a sizeable body of horsemen was needed to practise the complicated cavalry evolutions effectively. The number of general musters held each year tended to vary from time to time, according to the perceived threat from the French and state of the war abroad (see Appendix 2). Exemptions from the ballot to serve in the militia, from taxes such as the one on hair powder, and from the duty paid on keeping a cavalry horse, were offered by the government to encourage volunteers.[65] In order to gain such exemption the number of musters that volunteers had to attend was strictly enforced. This created a dilemma for the captain of a Troop who was required on his honour to say that the members had in fact attended the requisite number of musters.[66] Each time, when a certain number of members had not attended, he felt compelled to arrange extra meetings for them to ensure they complied. While this was welcomed by many members, it tended to lessen the numbers at official musters because some members, knowing that extra musters would be arranged, might not make every effort to attend the ordinary musters. Personal or family illness, accompanied by a medical certificate, and the lameness of one's horse, were the only acceptable reasons for non-attendance.[67]

The Troop drew from a wide radius of Woodbridge for its membership, and many members travelled considerable distances to their designated place of assembly, the Market Square in the centre of Woodbridge (Plate 8). From parade they marched to a field where the actual exercise took place and then back home again afterwards (Appendix 3 and Plate 1). Captain Edgar referred to some members having to travel from ten to twelve miles, perhaps just to have their name recorded if the weather became too bad to continue with their training. The condition of a horse was all-important, especially if some members might only own one animal. Many members, however, given their social status, had more than one, which might include a troop horse or charger as well as a riding horse. The inability to keep a horse was sometimes given as a reason for withdrawing from the Troop.[68]

---

64 In other parts of the country, where there was considerable protest, it was necessary to be able to differentiate between official musters and those meeting to organise unrest and riot.

65 Beckett, *Britain's Part-time Soldiers*, p. 84. The government first offered the militia exemptions in 1794, but they became general in 1798, together with exemption from the tax on hair powder and keeping a horse for personal use.

66 Mileson Edgar's letter to the Troop, just after he had taken over on 3 December 1801. Collett, p. 90.

67 Collett actually includes a copy of a medical certificate for John Field who, although an officer, had not appeared for over a year. He was old and suffering ill health, but could not bring himself to resign. Collett, p. 232, 30 December 1813.

68 Collett recorded the names of those who joined the Yeomanry between 1794 and 1820, and noted their reasons for leaving. About 400 names are listed: 57 on the first day of muster on 30 July 1794 and 102 during 1803 at the height of the French threat. In addition to death, illness or old age, the main reasons for leaving included moving away from the area, failure in business or having no horse, and the reduced threat owing to the ending of the war. A few were expelled, including Nathaniel Bunn from Wickham Market, a member of the Yeomanry for seven years, whom Collett records as 'bankrupt and a most infamous villain'.

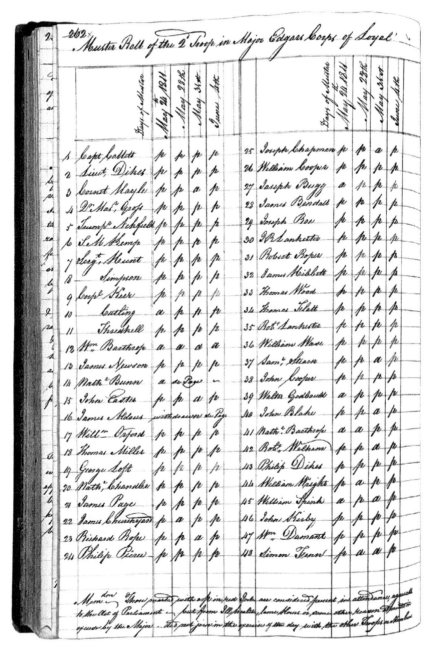

Plate 7. *A typical muster roll recording the attendance of Collett's 2nd Troop in the Woodbridge Corps. © Suffolk and Norfolk Yeomanry Museum Trust. Photograph by Mike Durrant*

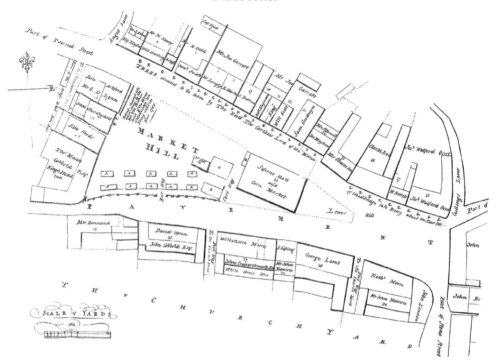

Plate 8. Plan of Market Hill, Woodbridge, in 1814 surveyed by R. Blythe. The Woodbridge Troop, later Corps, assembled and paraded here for each general muster, before moving off to fields where there was more room to practise their cavalry exercises. The Market Hall had the Sessions Hall, where Quarter Sessions were held, on the first floor, while the ground floor served as the Corn Market, very important given the high price of corn during the French wars. This was the scene of the unrest reported by Collett. © SROI, V5/9/6.3. Photograph by Mike Durrant

The Troop was divided into a number of smaller units known as divisions, which grouped members according to where they lived. They were organised to enable practices to be attended by members on a more regular basis than general musters. Collett made few references to the divisions, except to list the membership of the one he led at Eyke, together with, for a very short time only, the dates of their meeting, but they obviously were held on a regular basis throughout the period.[69] On 21 June 1803 with the crisis at its height, Collett recorded that musters were being held every Tuesday fortnight and practices in division twice weekly.[70] If there was a landing by the French, or indeed civil disturbance, the time taken to assemble the Troop might be critical, especially as many lived some distance from Woodbridge, their designated place of assembly. A plan was therefore drawn up to overcome the problem. Orderlies were appointed who lived in Woodbridge, with each given a list of people who resided in the same area, to whom they were to pass orders if an

---

[69] Collett lived at Woodbridge but Eyke, a distance of over four miles, was his family home.
[70] See Collett, p. 103.

emergency arose. Collett included the plan for his Troop, with the added instructions that the messenger was not to ride more than eight miles an hour and should not ride his troop horse nor be in uniform, in order not to cause panic as he rode.[71] Experiments to see how fast they could muster without prior notice being given also took place, as at Woodbridge on 23 September 1803 and again in 1805 at Barham.

In 1794 the Suffolk Yeomanry Cavalry was a new institution.[72] There was no existing military establishment for it to join, no existing military hierarchy to impose control over its actions, no military conventions, rules or regulations it had to adopt, except those that ensured its effectiveness and utility as a military unit in the field. No regular army officer could give it orders and members were not subject to martial law and army discipline unless called out and embodied. Collett records a clear example of this independence when on 29 July 1813 Major Edgar was accused by the general commanding the Woodbridge garrison of failing to give notice of the Troop being in town. Edgar, protective of the Yeomanry's position, objected to the highest authority when thus attacked and the general was forced to give him an abject apology.[73]

Since there was no overall commanding officer of the Suffolk Yeomanry until 1814 when it became a regiment, the Troop operated as an independent unit and was therefore in charge of its own discipline. It was only when disciplinary issues concerned a commissioned officer that the War Office and Lord Lieutenant became involved.[74] The Troop, therefore, had to devise its own solutions. Its members had to formulate and to reach a consensus on a set of self-governing rules and regulations by which they would be happy to operate. It was not until January 1804, when increased membership the previous year led to the formation of a Corps of three Troops, that Major Edgar suggested the setting up of a formal committee of thirteen to decide if new regulations were needed.[75]

Collett charted their attempts to deal with problems as they arose, recording the great care which they took over the details of disciplinary actions in order to achieve a fair conclusion.[76] If disputes arose these could have been difficult as many members were well-known to each other in civilian life and shared the same social circles. The dynamics of a volunteer group of Suffolk gentlemen and farmers, from a variety of prosperous backgrounds, in their struggle to uphold their regulations and maintain the Troop as a contented and well-ordered one, is an interesting theme running through Collett's account.

While the Troop had created its own regulations with the agreement of the whole membership, enforceable methods of ensuring these were adhered to were more problematic. Since they were all volunteers they were not obliged to serve and could withdraw whenever they wished. A recurrent difficulty reported by Collett, and one that caused most contention within the Troop, was that of non-attendance. The failure of members to attend general musters was important because, without a good turn-out, it was impossible to practise effectively the required cavalry evolu-

---

[71] See Collett, pp. 115–16.

[72] It was new because it was an institution of volunteers but supported by the government. Troops of volunteers had been raised before but were totally funded by the wealthy local gentry who formed and often captained them.

[73] Collett, pp. 222–3, transcribed the correspondence.

[74] The situation was clearly stated by the Lord Lieutenant when the Troop appealed for guidance over the non-attendance of Mr Mitchell. See Collett, p. 80.

[75] Collett, p. 139.

[76] William Kell's court martial, see page xxviii.

tions. The one acceptable method of trying to resolve such disciplinary problems was the use of fines. These were agreed by the whole Troop for non-attendance without a medical certificate, with the hope that peer pressure would ensure their payment. In fact, fines often created yet more issues over enforcement of their payment. Throughout the whole period covered by Collett the issue of non-payment was a continual concern: new fines would be introduced, work for a short time, be dropped and then be reimposed.[77]

Most disciplinary issues could be settled in this way or by members being quietly encouraged or allowed to resign. Serious breaches of discipline were rare. There were, however, a few examples of extreme indiscipline, which led to dismissal. Two of the most serious detailed by Collett concerned members of the Troop who were not volunteers, but paid from government funds.[78] On 24 June 1796 Trumpeter Kell drew his sword against John Slack, a sergeant major of the Queen's Bays, and grossly insulted him. The Troop held its own court, setting up an investigation, which led to a court martial, with the jury being chosen in a quite unconventional way.[79] The other was the bizarre incident when the Woodbridge Corps chose a new uniform, which the three Trumpeters refused to wear because it did not have enough silver braid. They were dismissed.[80]

By far the most unpleasant incident was that of Tollemache Cole, who had served as a member of the Troop since its formation but had obviously been an annoyance to many in the Corps, being rude, obstreperous and often absent. When he rudely resigned without giving a reason, on 5 November 1803, a time of heightened tension, the case was one of the very rare occasions when such incidents were badly handled.[81] Instead of being allowed to resign quietly, his dismissal became an acrimonious and unpleasant episode, fought out in full public view through letters in the two local newspapers.[82] It did little to enhance the reputation of the Yeomanry, but was a good example of the Troop's huge support and regard for its major, Mileson Edgar.

Central to the organisation of the 2nd Troop, the other Yeomanry Troops and indeed the whole volunteer movement in Suffolk, was one man, Lord Euston, the Lord Lieutenant (Plate 9). Suffolk was extremely fortunate that someone of his calibre happened to fill the position at such a critical time in the county's history, other counties being far less well-served.[83] He was the key person around whom the whole of the volunteer movement in the county revolved and without whom it could not have functioned so efficiently. The number of his letters transcribed by Collett clearly illustrated Euston's importance and key position. Appointed by the

---

[77] Collett, p. 37.

[78] The government was willing to pay for a sergeant and trumpeter to help train each Troop.

[79] Collett, p. 35.

[80] The three trumpeters involved had other occupations. They were Spencer Leek who was a basket maker, Spencer Leek junior, a miller, and Thomas Symonds, a surgeon. They were each paid nine guineas for Yeomanry duties that were neither time-consuming nor onerous given the number of musters each year. Collett, p. 210.

[81] Collett, pp. 131–4. Cole was the only member of the Troop to be so treated. The problem probably arose because Colonel M'Leroth, newly appointed inspecting field officer, interfered, when it should have been left for the Troop alone to sort out quietly, without the unwelcome publicity.

[82] *Ipswich Journal* 19 November 1803; *Bury and Norwich Post* 20 November 1803. Collett, pp. 132–4.

[83] The Earl of Euston had been appointed as Lord Lieutenant of Suffolk in 1790. It is noteworthy that it was he rather than his father, the 3rd Duke of Grafton, who held the position. Grafton had briefly been Prime Minister between 1768 and 1770, but had been more interested in his horses than affairs of state. Lord Euston succeeded his father as 4th Duke in 1811.

Plate 9. Portrait of Lord Euston, Lord Lieutenant of Suffolk, later 4th Duke of Grafton, by John Hoppner (1758–1810). Reproduced by kind permission of the Duke of Grafton, Euston Hall

crown, he was the King's representative in the county. Working with a number of deputy lieutenants,[84] the clerk of the peace and the justices of the peace, he had a huge number of duties, including overall responsibility for the volunteer groups in Suffolk, as well as the militia.

Working unpaid, the enormous amount of time Euston devoted to public service illustrates his strong devotion and patriotism. He was the central hub of the administration and organisation of the volunteer effort in general and the running of the Yeomanry in particular. He was the funnel through which most of the correspondence to and from central government flowed, much of the time directly. One letter to him would then be copied and passed to relevant recipients across the county.[85] The system also worked in reverse when queries from forces in the county could also be funnelled through him to central government. Many of the letters that he sent to the Woodbridge Troop and Collett copied in his volumes would also have been the same as those sent to the other four, and eventually nine, Troops of Suffolk Yeomanry, for whom few archives have survived. The grasp of detail, the down-to-earth approach and the calm common sense displayed in Euston's letters ensured well-run volunteer forces, which must have been very reassuring in the years when invasion was said to be imminent. Even when in Torrington in Devon, commanding the West Suffolk Militia, the tone remains the same.[86]

---

[84] One of whom was Mileson Edgar who was also a justice of the peace.

[85] SROI P454. A copy of his Letter Book survives for the period September 1801–May 1807.

[86] Euston had received his commission as colonel of the West Suffolk Militia Regiment as early as 1786. It was stationed at Torrington in Devon for a period during the war, militia units not usually serving in their home county.

The recipients of many of the Lord Lieutenant's letters were equally as patriotic, hardworking and devoted to public service as the Lord Lieutenant, namely the captains of each of the Troops. As commanding officers of each Troop of Suffolk Yeomanry, they were all-important. They had the overall responsibility for every aspect of their Troop, from military direction to general administration, dealing with everything required for an effective and happy force. If members were unhappy and attendance dropped, the captain would be forced to resign, as was the case when Captain Moore of the Babergh Troop stepped down for this very reason.

Philip Bowes Broke of Broke Hall, Nacton, captained the Woodbridge Troop from its formation in 1794 (Plate 1). He was a successful commanding officer establishing high standards for the Troop from the beginning, and providing inspirational leadership. He sadly died suddenly on 23 August 1801, aged 52. He was buried in Nacton church. His son refused the offer of a burial with military honours, which the Troop would have liked since he had been a much-loved and respected captain.[87] The *Ipswich Journal* of 29 August 1801, reporting his death, said he was a gentleman replete with those amiable qualifications that endeared him to all who had the pleasure of his acquaintance and by whom his death is most sincerely regretted. Those who stood in need of his assistance were sure to experience the marks of his favour and protection and the poor inhabitants of Nacton will long have reason to lament his loss.[88]

The Troop was fortunate that Mileson Edgar was the lieutenant of the Troop and therefore his successor. He lived at the Red House on the northern edge of Ipswich where he owned a sizeable family estate (Plate 1). He was a justice of the peace and deputy lieutenant, and thus well known to Lord Euston. He became a successful and effective cavalry captain. Building on the high standards already established, he converted the Troop into the most successful one in the Suffolk Yeomanry. They were always highly commended when inspected, both by regular army officers and inspecting field officers.[89] Other Suffolk Yeomanry Troops were willing to follow Edgar's leadership on the rare occasions they came together for permanent duty. He was regarded with such esteem and gratitude that on 25 September 1804 the Troop presented him with a fifty-guinea sword. The Troop was a popular one, attracting such large numbers that on 8 September 1803, with 150 members, it divided into three Troops and became a Corps.[90] Edgar was promoted to major and later lieutenant colonel, and was to remain in the Yeomanry until the government dispensed with its services late in 1827. He died on 16 June 1830.[91]

Since each Troop of the Suffolk Yeomanry Cavalry had been set up as an independent unit, their captain was their commanding officer. For the first few years of operation, each worked hard to improve the standard of their men and there was

---

[87] See Collett, pp. 85–6.

[88] There was an Incorporated House of Industry at Nacton serving the parishes in the hundreds of Carlford and Colneis.

[89] This was not always the case. There was much discussion about the standard of volunteer forces, with the regular army often critical of the volunteers' military effectiveness; nor were relations between volunteers and inspectors always cordial.

[90] See Collett, pp. 113–14. The only other Troop to become a Corps in the Suffolk Yeomanry was the Bury Troop for a short time before its numbers declined and it lost its officers. Several others, which were large enough to divide, chose to remain as one large Troop.

[91] *Ipswich Journal* 19 June 1830.

obviously some friendly rivalry among the Troops themselves.[92] Only on one occasion did all the Troops of the Suffolk Yeomanry Cavalry appear together, when they were reviewed on Rushmere Heath on 28 August 1803 by the Duke of York, commanding the army, who was making a military tour of the Eastern District.[93] Their relationship with the regular army appears largely limited to celebrations and reviews, although occasionally officers did appear at a yeomanry inspection muster, presumably to assess the standard of the volunteer Troops. Their first inspection by army officers was on 22 June 1797.[94] Collett recorded only one example of a shared exercise between regular and voluntary forces. This was a mock battle fought along the Martlesham valley with Captain Broke's Troop acting as a body of French cavalry.[95]

It was not until the autumn of 1803, with the crisis deepening, that the government finally strengthened the structure, and therefore effectiveness, of the volunteer forces. The Duke of York persuaded it to make a key appointment to improve standards among the Yeomanry and volunteer units in general. This was the establishment of inspecting field officers in each military district.[96] As regular army officers, they could officially only advise units, but their job was to improve the Troops' performance and ensure it reached the standard necessary to be able to support the regular forces.[97] They were to inspect and review both volunteer cavalry and infantry units, evaluating their capabilities and advising on improvements. Regular inspections would ensure that standards were maintained. On 16 October 1803 Colonel M'Leroth was appointed Suffolk's first inspecting field officer, stationed at Bury St Edmunds. Four months later, in 1804, Lieutenant Colonel Sharpe was also appointed inspecting field officer, based at Ipswich to help and advise volunteer cavalry and infantry units in east Suffolk. Collett recorded the close relationship that the Woodbridge Troop built up with him. A basic higher command system was put in place, and should the Yeomanry Cavalry be embodied if an invasion happened, the inspecting field officers would serve as brigade staff.[98] Although many of the government's orders and some of the paperwork still continued to be funnelled through the Lord Lieutenant, the inspecting field officers took over some of the administration.[99] In July 1804 another important appointment was that of Major General Money who was given command of the Yeomanry Cavalry in Suffolk and Norfolk, for the first time providing overall co-ordination.[100] As links with central government improved, systems became more formalised and increased support

---

[92] Collett, p. 33, 19 December 1795. Captain Broke had visited three other Yeomanry Troops to assess their standards.

[93] Collett, p. 113, 28 August 1803, Duke of York's Review. The Suffolk Yeomanry then was made up of seven Troops and 639 members.

[94] Collett, p. 41.

[95] This took place on 8 October 1798 and was the only account of a realistic exercise for the Yeomanry. Collett, pp. 65–6.

[96] The country was divided into military divisions. Suffolk and Norfolk were in the Eastern one, together with Essex, Cambridgeshire, Lincolnshire and Hertfordshire. These divisions, in turn, were divided into districts: Suffolk had two, east and west.

[97] As regular army, they could not give orders to volunteer forces, but such forces would be ill-advised to ignore their advice.

[98] Beckett, *Britain's Part-time Soldiers*, p. 106. The Duke of York instituted a brigade system for Yeomanry and volunteers in May 1804 in the event of embodiment.

[99] Collett, p. 126. Lieutenant Colonel Gordon, assistant adjutant general, through M'Leroth, sent out a Letter of Instructions to officers of Voluntary Corps on 28 October 1803.

[100] Collett, p. 161.

brought increased levels of bureaucracy. Collett included hand-drawn copies of some of the basic forms that had to be completed.

As the threat of invasion became even more critical, increased numbers of volunteers were encouraged to join, and they signed up under different conditions under different Acts of Parliament.[101] When Major Edgar expanded his Troop, he failed to fill in the right form before the right date, perhaps not realising there was any urgency to do so, because he knew the country needed as many volunteers as possible. The government refused to pay allowances for the extra seventy-seven new recruits.[102] Even after intervention and appeals by Edgar himself and Lord Euston,[103] the War Office still refused to give way, although it was a time of great crisis. Collett reported on the reaction of the Troop when it was left with a very considerable debt and forced to borrow the money, which it took some years to pay off.

In March 1804, it was suggested that Troops of Yeomanry Cavalry might like to have a period of permanent duty, for a number of consecutive days away from their usual base.[104] This would permit them to have a longer and continuous period of training, allowing better understanding and practice of the field movements while also improving discipline. For this they would be embodied, and since they would then become an official part of the armed forces, subject to martial law, they would be paid for their days away. It was also suggested that several Troops could be embodied in the same place and practise together as a larger unit. It was agreed by the Woodbridge Corps at the end of April, and by the middle of May their first permanent duty took place. With billets for the men and quarters for the horses, and food for both arranged, they were quartered in Bury St Edmunds for sixteen days including travel.[105] The 7th Babergh Troop under Captain Moore of Kentwell Hall asked to join them for exercises, which were so successful that they asked to join the Woodbridge Corps on a permanent basis. The Woodbridge Corps also met the 4th Bury Troop[106] and the 6th Cosford (Hadleigh) Troop[107] for exercises on Thurston Plains under the command of Major Edgar, where, as Light Dragoons, they practised various mounted and dismounted evolutions and sword exercises. When offered the chance to go on permanent duty the following year,[108] however, the Woodbridge Corps decided to refuse the offer, giving as an excuse that their size already allowed them to practise evolutions in large enough numbers, and the expense, given that they were having to repay their sizeable loan.

---

[101] Beckett, *Britain's Part-time Soldiers*, p. 92. In 1802 and 1803, 21 different Acts were passed, each offering different terms of service.

[102] Collett, pp. 170–2, 10 December 1804.

[103] SROI P454. The Letter Book contains copies of letters Lord Euston sent to the War Office on Edgar's behalf.

[104] Beckett, *Britain's Part-time Soldiers*, p. 106. This was first offered to maritime counties in October 1803. However, by June the following year, 100,000 volunteers had taken it up.

[105] Although billeted in inns in the first instance, these periods of permanent duty evolved into the famous annual camps that became such an important feature of the Yeomanry's social calendar in the later nineteenth century. See Thomas and Sign, *Loyal Suffolk Hussars*, pp. 35–53. Collett, pp. 154–6.

[106] The 4th Bury Troop were stationed at Stowmarket for four weeks.

[107] They were also stationed at Stowmarket for three weeks, but not in conjunction with the 4th Troop.

[108] Beckett, *Britain's Part-time Soldiers*, p. 101. The Consolidation Act of 5 June 1804, which had consolidated all previous legislation, established that attendance for twelve days on permanent duty training exercises would exempt members from the militia ballot and that of the army of reserve.

The plans for the defence of Suffolk

The Yeomanry and other volunteer infantry forces had been instituted to defend the county should the expected French invasion take place in Suffolk. As Collett recorded, the first years of the war were spent acquiring the skills necessary for them to be able to play an active part in the defence of their county and to support regular forces if necessary. A very sizeable number of professional troops were stationed in Woodbridge, Ipswich, Colchester and other towns in the area, throughout the war, depending on the degree of danger and the need for professional troops to serve abroad. This part of Suffolk and north Essex became a fortified camp, with large barracks being built to house the troops, such as those in Woodbridge, which occupied the western part of the town (Plate 2).[109] Militia regiments from different parts of the country were also stationed there. It was not only the number of army forces in the area but also the functions of the regiments chosen to be stationed there that indicated the concern of central government to defend this part of Suffolk. Collett's account of the great review of the garrisons of Woodbridge and Ipswich by the Duke of York held on 12 November 1805 reported that there were as many as 8,000 men from various regiments including detachments of Royal Horse Artillery and Light Dragoons.

From the start of Collett's account in 1794 there was a general assumption and an underlying fear that percolated through the various documents that he transcribed, that the French would invade. However, what had been a general fear of invasion very quickly reached fever pitch when that threat became a reality: four times in two years, the French did try to invade. Not having command of the Channel, the French attempted landings in unexpected places in Ireland and in Wales, where they anticipated support from disaffected groups. The first, at the very end of 1796, could have been serious: General Hoche and 15,000 French veterans, aboard a fleet of 43 ships, tried to land at Bantry Bay in support of Wolfe Tone and disaffected United Irishmen,[110] and were only prevented by bad seamanship and the weather.[111] Captain Broke, addressing the Troop about this attempted landing, warned it to be ready for any emergency.[112] This was followed, two months later, by a landing near Fishguard, Pembrokeshire, by Colonel Tate and the Legion Noire, and it was two days before they were forced to surrender.[113]

News of the Welsh landing, so soon after the near-escape in Ireland, created fear and panic throughout the country including Suffolk. This led to a financial crisis,[114] and in Bury St Edmunds, for example, two of the three banks failed, with

---

[109] SROI P630/1. Map of the army barracks in Woodbridge.

[110] They supported militant Irish republicanism, established with French assistance.

[111] The fleet avoided the British fleet, and sailed along the coast for two weeks waiting for their commander to arrive. Terrible storms prevented the landing, before the fleet limped back to Brest. Collett copied newspaper reports of the landings.

[112] Collett, p. 39. Letter 7 January 1797.

[113] Bristol was said to have been their destination. Despite the fact that half the force were convicts who deserted and got drunk on landing, Tate had managed to penetrate two miles inland before surrendering on 24 February 1797.

[114] Goodwin's Diary, Monday 27 February 1797: 'The Bank of England this day stopped paying in cash. The greatest consternation has taken place – an immense concourse of people, crowded with their notes for payment but were refused.' People panicked because they wanted to withdraw their money in coin not paper.

Oakes just managing to save his own.[115] Collett, as a banker, would have appreciated the seriousness of the situation, although interestingly made no comment in
his text. The country, at last, united in its opposition to the French, and people of
all classes flocked to join volunteer troops, both cavalry and infantry.[116] Tension
and an air of impending doom were further intensified when news came of two
more French attempts at invasion in 1798, both in Ireland. In August, a landing
in County Mayo by General Humbert and 1,000 veterans had some initial success
when joined by United Irish forces, but it had come too late. The main rising had
already been defeated two months earlier and Humbert was forced to surrender
in early September. Six weeks later, another French attempt was made in County
Donegal by an invasion force of nine ships with 3,000 men on board, but was
prevented from landing after a short naval battle. Collett and the Troop celebrated
the victory with a *feu de joye* on 26 October 1798. The same year there was worse
news when a French invasion army was stationed at Boulogne and along the French,
and what is now the Belgian, coast and the threat of imminent invasion became
visible just across the Channel.

With the threat now so close to home, definite defence plans emerged and were
instigated in 1798. While the army could be relied upon to deal with the French
forces once they met, the concern lay in the reaction of the local inhabitants in
the villages and surrounding countryside to a landing and its immediate aftermath,
before such forces arrived. If panic, chaos and instant flight were to be avoided, plans
needed to be put in place to reassure the local population and involve them in their
defence. The key element of the crisis plan, known as 'Driving the country', adopted
a scorched-earth approach. It envisaged the removal inland of population, crops and
livestock – anything in fact that might help the enemy and supply them with food and
transport. This would obviously necessitate the full co-operation and involvement of
everyone in the threatened area if it were to be successfully implemented.

The Woodbridge Troop was given an important role to play. It was made responsible, if an emergency occurred, for supervising the removal of livestock from a
large area of land at a key strategic point, which Collett described in considerable
detail.[117] The area lay between Ipswich and the sea, and between the Stour to the
Butley River, in the hundreds of Samford, Colneis and Wilford (Plate 1 and Plate 6).
The animals were to be driven inland to a point where the Bury Yeomanry Troop
would take over and move them yet further away from the danger zone.[118]

Collett also recorded the task that the Woodbridge Troop was given, two weeks
later, of surveying the area from the Butley River to Bawdsey Ferry and inspecting
each of the passes from the marshes to the uplands in some considerable detail.[119]
In an emergency, these would provide alternative routes for evacuation of animals,
avoiding the main roads altogether or, at worst, entailing a quick crossing of
them. Collett included the reports written by Captain Broke and Lieutenant Edgar
describing the location of lanes, driftways and tracks that might be used, together

---

[115] James Oakes gives an account of the collapse of the two banks in Bury and reported on how his own
bank was saved. *Oakes Diaries*, Volume I, pp. 79–80.

[116] Goodwin's Diary, February 1797: 'Twenty tons of hard biscuits were lodged at Framlingham, more
at Ipswich, Bury, Colchester and other towns, as are cannon and all war-like stores, to be in readiness
to defend the country.'

[117] Collett, pp. 84–5, 13 July 1801.

[118] Collett, pp. 84–5. Routes were prepared for the Troop to take, but were only to be released if the
emergency occurred.

[119] Collett, p. 82.

with the names of the landowners. This was an area considered to be particularly at risk, which was why General Sir Eyre Coote, two years later, was asked by the government to provide a defence plan for it (Plate IV).

The Defence of the Realm Act, passed in April 1798, complemented the 'Driving the country' plan by imposing the collection of enough detailed information from each parish to ensure it could be put into operation. Forms required each parish to count the number of able-bodied men between 15 and 60, together with the number of cattle, horses, livestock, waggons, carts, dead stock, ovens, corn or other mills and malt among others. The number of boats, barges and small craft on the rivers was also to be included.[120] The information was sent to the Lord Lieutenant to collate and the totals sent to the government and the army.

The letter of Dundas, the Secretary of War, to the Lord Lieutenant, copied by Collett, recognised that in order to ensure success the whole population needed to be involved, and in particular as large a percentage of the male able-bodied population as possible.[121] Dundas wanted able-bodied men aged 16–60 in the countryside, not already in a volunteer force, to join units, rather like equivalent infantry groups in the towns, and to attend training sessions. The men were asked to become pioneers, conductors, waggon drivers or guides. They were to be organised into companies of between twenty-five and seventy-five with a leader or captain, but to what extent this actually took place is unclear. Armed with any weapon to hand, from pitchforks and spades to axes and bill hooks, it was expected that they would be vigilant and observant at all times. If the French managed to land, a chosen few would remain in their village for as long as possible, watching the movements of the enemy to alert the army when they arrived.

The exercise awakened Suffolk villages to the reality of what invasion might involve. Arrangements were made and places of assembly agreed, while carts and waggons were prepared for evacuation. Fears were at their height through the spring and early summer of 1801. The Yeomanry asked farmers with cattle on marshes near the sea between Hollesley and Bawdsey to move them inland.[122] However, on 13 July, Collett recorded a change of government: Pitt was replaced by Addington, who opened peace negotiations. Preliminaries for peace were signed on 1 October 1801, becoming a formal peace with the Treaty of Amiens on 27 March 1802. This clearly had implications for the Yeomanry. Collett describes the agreement that the Woodbridge Troop made to remain in being, forming a society or club to meet for musters, although the government did in fact decide to continue with yeomanry services. However, the Treaty of Amiens gave only a temporary respite: it had in fact allowed the French to strengthen their position.

---

[120] Collett, pp. 56–7. Copies of these forms survive for a few parishes, including Haughley. SROI FB220/A7/3. They illustrate the exceptionally detailed nature of the information and the amount of planning and organisation undertaken by individual parishes. Names of individuals were provided of those appointed to oversee the removal of cattle, those doing the same for sheep and other livestock, and those appointed to remove horses and waggons to convey such persons as were unable to move themselves. Nine men were willing to be pioneers, armed with seven felling axes, two picks, ten spades, nine bill hooks and one saw. Four men volunteered to be guides, and four conductors and fifteen men were willing to act as servants with the teams. John Longe records a parish meeting at Coddenham where the same process was organised. M. Stone, ed., *The Diary of John Longe, Vicar of Coddenham, 1765–1834*, Suffolk Records Society, Volume 51, 2008, p. 36. If all parishes were so well-organised, it becomes possible to consider that the Yeomanry's job of 'Driving the country' might actually have been possible.
[121] Collett, p. 55. Dundas's important letter laying out the plan.
[122] Collett, p. 84.

When war was renewed in May 1803, Britain stood alone without allies, and the country faced one of the most serious threats it had ever faced or was to face, that of imminent invasion. Suffolk and the Yeomanry were on full alert. 'The Proposals for rendering the body of the people instrumental to the general defence in case of invasion' was a rewording of the 1798 plan.[123] It was accompanied in June with another Defence Act, which again obliged the Lord Lieutenant and the parishes to repeat the earlier exercise, with more details of their able-bodied men, this time, between 15 and 60, and distinguishing those already serving, those willing to serve and those ineligible for service.[124] The number of livestock and carts had to be updated, and millers and bakers added.

The policy of 'Driving the country' had met strong opposition as well as support in the country and created much confusion. Lord Euston, while recognising the divided opinions, thought that the most sensible approach would be to remove only horses and draft cattle, as this would cause little delay. He remarked that the 1798 plan was 'too much in my opinion in minute detail to have been found practicable'.[125] General Sir Eyre Coote in his recommendations for the defence of Hollesley Bay in 1803 reiterated the same thoughts:

In the event of a debarkation, that is as soon as it is clearly ascertained where the enemy is going to land, the inhabitants of the adjoining country must be hastened in withdrawing their horses and draft cattle etc according to the arrangements previously made for the purpose. Parties of Yeomanry must be sent in different directions to enforce the execution of this essential service. In these removals, horses and draft or horned cattle must be our first object, as without these the enemy cannot make use of either cavalry or artillery. And besides in a moment of confusion as the above must invariably be, I am clearly of the opinion that it would be utterly impracticable to drive away sheep, hogs or the like and often dangerous to attempt it.[126]

Later, in November 1803, the plan was effectively dropped although its basic premise, to remove the horses and draft cattle, remained.[127]

In 1803, with invasion seemingly imminent, all over the country there was another huge rush to volunteer, including many in Suffolk. The volunteers came from a wider social base than earlier and formed infantry Troops in their villages and small towns. Rooted in their local communities, they were armed and trained. Collett included the full list of volunteer Troops in Suffolk, both infantry and cavalry.[128] To these must be added the pioneers, conductors and guides in the countryside. The organisation of these groups throughout the country overwhelmed central government, and for a time arms and uniforms were in short supply.[129] There was also an

---

[123] SROI HA11/B2/3, the 1803 version of 'Driving the country'.

[124] Colley, *Britons*, pp. 291–3 and 378–81. By 1804 the Act had revealed that of those parishes who filled in the returns (the vast majority) the number of male inhabitants in Suffolk aged between 17 and 55 was 37,452. Of these 11,217 were serving in volunteer units while 2,195 were already in uniform. Thirty-six per cent of the possible age-range in Suffolk, therefore, was already under arms. Beckett, *Britain's Part-time Soldiers*, p. 95 gives the ages of able-bodied men required under the Defence Act of 1803 as 15 to 60.

[125] Letter Book, p. 7, 16 June 1803.

[126] Gloucestershire Archives D421/X19, General Sir Eyre Coote's Defence of Hollesley Bay.

[127] Beckett, *Britain's Part-time Soldiers*, p. 94.

[128] Collett, pp. 122–5.

[129] Beckett, *Britain's Part-time Soldiers*, pp. 103–4. By January 1804 the number of volunteers and Yeomanry reached 342,000, but the previous September it had been estimated that the Ordnance Office, responsible for issuing arms and equipment, had only enough arms for 5,000 to 6,000 men.

influx of volunteers to join the Yeomanry. The Suffolk Yeomanry Cavalry grew to nine Troops, with new cavalry Troops formed at Heveningham and South Elmham. The expansion of the Woodbridge Troop led to the establishment of a Corps of three Troops in September. Because of its strategic position, Suffolk became a training ground not only for its own volunteer units but also for the many units of the regular army and militia regiments that were now stationed in the county.

Although Collett made no personal comments about the crisis he included a unique collection of documents issued at the time – by the government, the inspecting field officer and others – in an attempt to impose at least the semblance of order on a situation that had the potential for total breakdown if the French ever did arrive. The urgency of the state of affairs permeates the documents. The concern of their authors to offer reassurance and instil confidence, to ensure that panic and terror did not take hold, is palpable. It is through these directives that the seriousness of the position and the sense of impending crisis that loomed over society at the time can really be appreciated. One of the most important documents included by Collett was the assistant adjutant general's instructions to officers commanding volunteer troops, sent to Colonel M'Leroth, inspecting field officer, for circulation to officers of the Yeomanry and the other volunteer troops. This gave detailed instructions as to exactly what to do if the French landed in their vicinity.[130] It was an evocative and remarkably thoughtful directive. The sensitivity shown was impressive, revealing a real understanding of the position in which volunteers such as the Yeomanry and others might find themselves. The advice: 'Don't be afraid to cover yourself with trees and stones' and watch the enemy, rather than act as a hero and be killed unnecessarily, was typical of the type of instruction.

If a landing was successful, its obvious objective would have been to capture London, and, as a result, interest came to focus on the Suffolk coast. It had been concluded that while the whole coastline between Yarmouth in the north to Selsey Bay in the south was vulnerable, parts of the Suffolk coastline were areas most at risk. While one likely landing zone was on the English south coast around Hastings and between Pevensey Bay and Beachy Head, the second considered most likely was Hollesley Bay, with its shingle beaches, together with the area between the Deben and the Orwell, and Harwich and Clacton.[131]

Hollesley Bay was considered of primary importance since it had all the requisites needed for a landing: relatively easy access to London, an isolated position, a secure and capacious bay and deep water that reached to the high shingle beach for landing. The area was considered so important that General Sir Eyre Coote, who was seemingly used by the army for drawing up defence plans,[132] was commissioned to supply one such plan for the area. His recommendations were extremely detailed: as well as suggesting works that would prevent the French landing in the first place (Plate IV), he included possible locations of defensive lines that could be held, if forces were driven back by the French, as far as the edge of Ipswich.[133] Hollesley Bay's importance was also highlighted by the presence of Commodore Sir Sidney

---

[130] Collett, pp. 126–30, 28 October 1803.
[131] K. W. Maurice-Jones, *The History of Coast Artillery in the British Army* (Uckfield, 2009, first published 1959), p. 93. Such areas, being much closer to London, unlike the earlier landings in Ireland and Wales, would require a much more immediate response.
[132] William L. Clements Library, University of Michigan, Eyre Coote Papers. After Hollesley Bay, Coote went on to draw up plans for the defence of Galway Bay.
[133] Gloucestershire Archives, D421/X19.

Smith, stationed offshore in command of a small flotilla. This was made up of his own ship the *Antelope* of 50 guns, the *Romulus* of 32 guns fitted as a floating battery or block ship and three or four flat or gun boats.[134] Collett described a visit by him from his ship to inspect the Woodbridge Troop early in May 1803 and later a review and a dinner he shared with them.[135]

Collett reported in October that the Yeomanry had been asked to form as large a force as possible to watch the most critical points on the coast and offer protection to the most exposed situations, on a rotation of short periods, at places that offered quarters for them.[136] The original intention of the subscribers' committee in 1794 had been to give support to volunteer companies to man batteries built to protect the coast. However, insufficient volunteers were forthcoming.[137] In response to the new appeal, the Woodbridge Troop, together with the other maritime Yeomanry Troops along the Suffolk coast, volunteered, but given the time of year it was decided they were not needed.[138]

The critical periods in 1804 and 1805 when invasion was said to be imminent saw a major increase in the activities of the Woodbridge Troop. Detailed instructions were issued as to what they were to have packed, ready at a minute's notice, should the call come in case of emergency. More musters were held: one took place without prior notice, to gauge how many of the Troop could react quickly, with excellent results.[139] Tension built up particularly during the critical months in 1804 and 1805 when the tides and weather were conducive to an invasion, but the threat was ever-present and pervasive.

After so many years of threats of imminent invasion, tension and crisis, in the event, all the plans and preparations were not needed. Late in August 1805, the vast army of invasion based along the French coastline melted away, as Napoleon was forced to withdraw and move his army to deal with the threat from the Austrians.[140] Perhaps one of the most intriguing puzzles of the whole of Collett's account is the anticlimax at this key point in his book, when the Yeomanry, the county and the country in general had so much to celebrate.[141] It is unclear how long it would have taken for news of the withdrawal to filter through to the public, although it must have taken some time for it to be reliably confirmed that the danger was over. Collett

---

[134] Commodore Sir Sidney Smith was one of the most flamboyant sailors of his day, famous for victories such as the breaking of Napoleon's siege of Acre. However, many of his victories were achieved while he held independent commissions, and because of his individual and unorthodox methods, he was out of favour with Nelson and the navy. The fact that such a successful officer was at Hollesley Bay clearly indicates that the government judged it to be an exceptionally vulnerable and dangerous spot.

[135] Collett, p. 99.

[136] This avoided the necessity of having to withdraw regular troops from other areas, but shows how important the area was considered to be.

[137] J. Millward, *An Assessment of East Coast Martello Towers* (London, 2007). The 1790s batteries, of a curved triangular shape in plan, were open at the back with guns mounted on a firing platform to fire over the parapet (*en barbette*). These early batteries formed the forward batteries of some of the new Martello Towers when construction began on the east coast in 1808.

[138] Collett, p. 137, 25 October 1803. Details of the offer from other Troops appeared in the local newspapers: 3rd Troop *Ipswich Journal* 3 November 1803; 5th Troop *Bury and Norwich Post* 7 December 1803; 9th Troop *Bury and Norwich Post* 30 November 1803.

[139] Collett, p. 178, 13 August 1805.

[140] After standing alone, Pitt had managed to arrange a third coalition with Russia and Austria in 1805. Napoleon was forced to face the threat from the Austrians. He withdrew his Army of England from the coast, which was transformed into his Grand Army, which would fight and defeat the Austrians.

[141] Particularly as Collett was still writing retrospectively at this date.

made no entries between the muster at Barham on 13 August and the next on 16 October except notification of the date of that meeting. For the country as a whole, the threat of invasion was removed when news arrived of Nelson's comprehensive defeat of the French and Spanish fleet at Trafalgar on 21 October, in celebration of which the Woodbridge Corps fired a *feu de joye* on 12 November. This was recorded by Collett, albeit in a very muted response, considering the huge celebrations to such glorious news, even if it was somewhat dimmed by Nelson's death. Trafalgar certainly blunted the French threat, but since Napoleon was so successful in Europe, defeating the Austrians at the battle of Ulm in October and the Austro-Hungarian armies at Austerlitz on 1 December 1805, the war continued, and therefore the need for defence and the Yeomanry remained.

The role of the Suffolk Yeomanry after 1805

The government wanted the Suffolk Yeomanry Cavalry to continue, and Collett records that its pattern of musters continued much as before, but with rather less frequency. Pitt's death at the beginning of 1806 led to a change of government and a new Secretary of State for War and the Colonies, William Windham. He was hostile to the use of volunteer forces and dispensed with the services of many of the volunteer troops of infantry, although the Yeomanry survived.[142] Inspecting field officers were abolished, and Collett described the dismay felt by the Woodbridge Corps at the withdrawal of Lieutenant Colonel Sharpe.[143] A further change of government in March 1807 saw the appointment of Castlereagh, a much more able secretary of state, who restored proper funding, at least for the volunteer cavalry.

The King, worried about the decline in morale, and the government seeing the drop in numbers, allowed the return of the inspecting field officers.[144] Sharpe was reappointed, and the Woodbridge Corps welcomed him back at his first inspection of them in June 1807. He held the position until March 1812 when he was promoted to general.[145] Such was the respect and thanks for his help and friendship that all the Troops, in what by January of 1814 had become the Suffolk Yeomanry Regiment, presented him with a magnificent silver epergne of which Collett included a sketch and description.[146]

Since 1794, the individual Troops had been proud members of the Loyal Suffolk Yeomanry Cavalry, but it had not been created as a regiment with a commanding officer. As the war progressed, the number of Troops increased from the original five to seven in 1803, and to nine by 1805, with the addition of the 6th (Cosford) Troop commanded by Captain Gooch, 7th (Babergh) Troop under Captain Moore, 8th Troop at Heveningham under Captain Vanneck and 9th Troop at South Elmham commanded by Captain Adair (Plate 6). They each continued to operate as an independent Troop. The appointment of Major General Money in overall command of the Yeomanry Cavalry in Suffolk and Norfolk on 14 July 1804 was an important

---

[142] Windham, himself a volunteer force commander, was famous for saying that volunteers were 'painted cherries which none but simple birds would take for fruit'. Quoted in Beckett, *Britain's Part-time Soldiers*, p. 104.

[143] Collett, p. 184, 13 June 1806. Sharpe's goodbye letter to the Troop.

[144] Collett, p. 188, 25 April 1807. Beckett, *Britain's Part-time Soldiers*, p. 108. The King's views were expressed in a letter from Hawksbury, the Home Secretary (later Lord Liverpool).

[145] Collett, p. 218, 26 March 1812.

[146] Collett, p. 237 and footnote Volume B 175.

step, which, together with the appointment of inspecting field officers, ensured that the same practices and standards were applied to all members of the Suffolk Yeomanry.[147] Their meetings to exercise and train together when on permanent duty brought them even closer together.

The first suggestion that the formation of a regiment might become a reality came during the 2nd Corps' first spell of permanent duty, when several Troops trained together under the command of Major Edgar. Following this, on 23 October 1804, two of them, the 7th Babergh Troop and the 6th Cosford, asked to join the Woodbridge Corps. Such numbers would have been of sufficient size to allow the formation of a Suffolk Yeomanry Regiment, and expectations were raised. Collett referred to a regiment as if it had been formed at this date.[148] However the 6th Troop withdrew their offer to join soon afterwards. Although the Babergh Troop chose to remain with the Woodbridge Corps to form a Corps of four Troops, the formation of a regiment had to wait.

It was to take until 1813 before a regiment was formally established. Addington, the Home Secretary, announced new plans at the end of October to reorganise the Yeomanry nationwide into county regiments of not fewer than six Troops to make them more efficient and effective in the field.[149] Each regiment would be expected to undertake at least twelve days of annual training, receiving regular cavalry pay while on exercises, and would be subject to formal inspection.[150] This would hopefully ensure that the Yeomanry Cavalry would become a cohesive and integrated force, serving as a reserve and, perhaps more importantly for Addington, proving useful in dealing with riots and tumults should the need arise.

On 10 December 1813 a large meeting with representatives from several of the Suffolk Yeomanry Troops took place in Ipswich to determine which wanted to join the new regiment. Captain Wythe of the 3rd Troop asked to be part of the new regiment, together with the 4th Bury Troop, which at that point totally lacked officers and were represented only by their quartermaster.[151] Eventually in the coming months after many complications, all the surviving Troops joined and the new regiment was formed. It was left to Major Edgar and the Lord Lieutenant to determine the final details and numbers, which proved to be a complex operation, well described in the letters copied by Collett.[152] The new regiment, when numbers were eventually sorted out, was to have nine Troops with 415 men and commanded by Mileson Edgar.[153]

However, as the reorganisation was being implemented and new uniforms ordered so they would all be clothed alike, the news came that they had waited so long to hear, that Napoleon had abdicated on 11 April 1814. In all the joy and relief came

---

[147] Collett, p. 161.

[148] Collett, p. 168, 6 November 1804.

[149] Collett, p. 225, 29 October 1813.

[150] Beckett, *Britain's Part-time Soldiers*, p. 120.

[151] It is unclear how this arose. Since 1805 Major Fowkes had commanded the successful Bury Corps of three Troops until his retirement early in 1810. The *Bury and Norwich Post* of 7 February reported on a sumptuous retirement dinner and presentation of an elegant silver cup. Captain Shillitoe then took command, but within three years numbers had greatly reduced to one Troop with no officers.

[152] Collett, p. 239, 7 February 1814. The numbers and ranks of personnel in the old Troops did not fit the new prescribed ones. For example, the number of sergeants allowed was fewer than they had had before, and some therefore had to become privates.

[153] Collett, p. 250. The nine Troops were the four Troops of the 2nd Corps (which included the 7th Babergh Troop) and the 1st, 3rd, 4th, 5th and 6th Troops, since the 8th (Heveningham) and 9th (South Elmham) were no longer in existence.

Plate 10. Undated photograph from the east of the Market Hall, also known locally as the Town Hall and the Shire Hall. It was the headquarters of the Woodbridge Troop, later Corps, where they held their meetings and kept their magazine. It was their place of assembly in an emergency. © SROI, K681/1/513/198. Photograph by Mike Durrant

one particular worry for Edgar: in expectation that the government would no longer need the Yeomanry, could the order for new uniforms be stopped?[154] In the event the government was clear it wished to continue with the Yeomanry and the new regiment went ahead, under the command of the newly promoted Lieutenant Colonel Edgar. However, the planned reorganisation was never completely implemented and full integration was never achieved: while all the Troops remained under the overall command of Lieutenant Colonel Edgar, a considerable degree of independence was retained by individual Troops, holding independent musters and attending their own permanent duty.[155] In 1818, they finally agreed to hold permanent duty together and exercise as a regiment; this then became a regular practice.

Each Troop of the Suffolk Yeomanry Cavalry played an important role in boosting the morale of Suffolk throughout the long war years, and especially at times of the greatest threat. For Woodbridge, as a garrison town during the war, soldiers were a common sight, though not always ones that were wanted, but the Yeomanry troops were a welcome addition for the townspeople.[156] For each general muster, the Woodbridge Troop, later Corps, assembled for parade on the market square in the centre of the town (Plate 8) and had their headquarters at the Town Hall there (Plate 10). The sight of such a large force, on horseback, in their smart uniforms or even their practice gear, must have been a very reassuring sight for the town, or at least such of

---

[154] Collett, p. 251.

[155] Collett did record some of the dates of the musters to be held by other Troops, but they have not been included here.

[156] V. Harrup, 'Woodbridge Barracks during the War with Napoleon', Part 1, *Suffolk Review* (Autumn 2013), pp. 35–41 and Part 2, *Suffolk Review* (Spring 2015), pp. 21–6.

the community as Collett always described as 'respectable'. The members travelling the considerable distances through the countryside from their homes to Woodbridge were also a very visible symbol of confident authority in the Suffolk countryside, especially in the later years of the war and afterwards at a time of major unrest.

The Woodbridge Troop took part in celebrations local to the town, such as the dedication of its own royal standard at St Mary's, and the return of the new bells to the church (Plate 11, p. 30). Very large crowds flocked to watch inspections of the Troop. Collett reported on the national celebrations in which the Troop participated, particularly when news of naval or military victories finally filtered through, providing a great boost to local morale. He was always careful to mention the presence of spectators whenever the Yeomanry turned out in force, whether for an inspection, formal review or the King's birthday in June, which was always celebrated as an act of loyalty and patriotism. The firing of a *feu de joye* was the usual way of celebrating. At times of heightened tension, the celebrations were huge, both those taking part in the reviews and the crowds that flocked to see them turning out to watch and be reassured.[157] The celebrations held in Woodbridge 1805, at a time when everyone thought invasion imminent, were spectacular.[158]

Social unrest with riot and tumult

When the Yeomanry was formed in 1794, it had a dual function: defence of the county against invasion and support of the civil powers in dealing with unrest. By 1815, its first task was complete, but its second function began to assume much greater importance. There was major social unrest in many parts of the country caused by underlying economic issues. The country's already serious social and economic problems had been further exacerbated by the huge escalation in the price of corn and therefore of bread, caused by the war and the interruption of trade, the result of Napoleon's Berlin Decrees and resultant Continental System.[159] A rapidly growing population added to the problem.[160] The Yeomanry in other parts of the country was often called out to deal with the unrest. Edgar's unpleasant interchange with the new commander of the Woodbridge garrison was caused at least in part because Major General Hawker had been stationed in an area where such unrest was common and relations with the local populace fragile.[161]

The early incidents recorded by Collett, when the Woodbridge Troop was called out in cases of threatened unrest, were reported in a straightforward, unbiased manner, with no personal comments or opinions expressed, except a general relief

---

[157] Collett was always careful to mention the names of Troops attending, whether regular army, militia or volunteer cavalry, infantry and sea fencibles, giving a detailed picture of the forces available in the area at any one time.

[158] Collett limited his descriptions of celebrations to the Yeomanry's involvement. For a more detailed account, see V. Norrington, 'Peace at Last: Celebrations of Peace and Victories during and after the Napoleonic Wars', *Suffolk Review* (Spring 2003), pp. 17–33.

[159] Napoleon's Berlin Decree of 1806 and the Continental System attempted to close the European coastline to British trade, which resulted in a trade war. Britain's retaliation involved demands being made over neutral shipping and trade, which eventually brought about war with America in 1812. By 1811 interruptions in trade were causing very serious problems at home, worsening the economic situation and leading to protests and unrest.

[160] The population of Suffolk in 1801 at the time of the first census was 210,431; by 1821 it had risen to 270,542.

[161] Collett, pp. 222–3, 29 July 1813.

that no bloodshed had occurred. Just the very presence of the Yeomanry often acted as a deterrent, especially as members of the Yeomanry would have known some of those about to protest, and this prevented any serious trouble. The first incident, on 3 July 1795, was caused by large groups of labourers assembling to demand a reduction in the price of corn and other provisions. The Troop was called out and, on being very publicly issued with 18 rounds of ball cartridge, held a field day at Bromeswell, where there was a regular army camp, and skirmishing parties in Sutton and Hollesley. No trouble was encountered, but Collett reported there was much agitation when the ammunition was distributed.[162] On 18 January 1796 a serious attack was suspected on the House of Industry at Melton, just outside Woodbridge. The Troop, on being again called upon by the magistrate, assembled and searched the neighbourhood for miles around, dispersing anyone likely to cause trouble. The involvement of the Yeomanry again averted what could have been an unpleasant incident.[163]

The Yeomanry was also mustered to deal with a protest in Woodbridge itself. Food prices increased rapidly during the war, more than many people could afford. On 17 September 1800 people arriving to sell their produce were intercepted as they arrived on the outskirts of the town. They were offered what the interceptors considered a fair price that they could afford, far below the market price. The next day, being market day, a serious situation developed, but the local magistrate, forewarned by Collett, called out the Woodbridge Troop (Plate 12, p. 77). Its presence and careful handling of the situation restored law and order without the use of force.[164]

The situation deteriorated rapidly as the war ended, Suffolk being one of the counties that suffered most from the economic recession. The Yeomanry, many of whom were farmers in their civilian lives, were as affected and concerned as their neighbours. The county was in the throes of the final phase of major agricultural change from a largely dairying area to one dominated by arable farming, which during the war had allowed farmers to maximise their profits from the high wheat prices. Despite the attempt by the government to protect the interests of the landed classes after the war by passing the Corn Laws in 1815, the price of wheat dropped very considerably, and many farmers found themselves in financial difficulties.[165] Those who had invested or borrowed money to convert land to grow arable crops, especially by the enclosure and ploughing up of the large commons that had still survived in Suffolk, were also in trouble.[166] Farmers were forced to lay off their workforce and unemployment became rife. Even those in work found their weekly wage reduced, with some incomes as low as six shillings a week.[167] At the same time the war had seen the end of the spinning of wool for the yarn trade, which had

[162] Collett, p. 31.

[163] Collett, p. 33.

[164] Collett, pp. 76–7, 17 September 1800. A similar but much more serious incident occurred some years earlier in the market at Bury on 25 April 1795. *Oakes Diaries*, Volume I, pp. 311–12.

[165] The Corn Laws passed on 3 March 1815 were introduced by a government of landowners to protect landowners by not allowing the import of foreign corn until the price at home reached eighty shillings a quarter.

[166] Many independent smallholders who until this point had survived because of their grazing rights on the commons, were, after their enclosure, driven to seek paid employment. See David Dymond, ed., *Hodskinson's Map of Suffolk in 1783*, Suffolk Records Society, Volume 15, 1972, for the extent of the commons, tyes and greens in Suffolk at this period.

[167] Farmers often paid such low wages knowing they would be supplemented by the poor law overseers, after such a practice was introduced in 1795, depending on the price of corn and the size of the family.

allowed women at home to earn money to supplement the family income.[168] It has been estimated that a third of the Suffolk working population was unemployed.[169] Reliance on poor law relief became so widespread that the rates, which were paid largely by the rate-payers, namely farmers, who were themselves in difficulties, rose to unprecedented levels.[170] Collett, as a banker, showed his understanding of the situation in his brief but masterly synopsis of the issues in May 1816.[171]

Suffolk saw a transformation from one of the wealthiest counties to one of the poorest. With no vote or any other form of legitimate protest, widespread poverty, desperate deprivation and hardship caused protests, riots, demonstrations and outrages. Suffolk was on the verge of a rural war in 1815.[172] Sporadic outbreaks of incendiarism, when barns and hay ricks were set on fire at night and threshing machines attacked, created fear throughout the farming community. The following year, 1816, was particularly bad when the 'Bread or Blood' riots shocked the country as East Anglia erupted in agrarian outrages.[173] So serious was the situation that the Prince of Wales offered a reward of £100 to try to catch the perpetrators; Collett transcribed the offer from the *London Gazette*.[174] Riots broke out all over the county,[175] with those in Bury and Hadleigh of particular concern to the Lord Lieutenant (Plate I).[176] Collett recorded that at musters the Woodbridge Corps practised the best way to control a mob, and that Edgar made very clear what they could do in such a situation.[177] The Corps was put on immediate alert should the Lord Lieutenant or the magistrates need to call it out, but in the event, it was not required. The Yeomanry remained vigilant the following year since the harvest of 1816 was so poor and the latest Collett ever remembered, with no-one having finished harvesting by the beginning of October and some still cutting their crop at the end of the month.[178] Many other serious outbreaks of unrest took place, but are barely mentioned by Collett because the Yeomanry was not called out to deal with them. His account stopped in May 1818, but the unrest and outrages continued in Suffolk and were to worsen in future years.[179]

---

[168] *Oakes Diaries*, Volume I, p. 33.

[169] D. Dymond and P. Northeast, *A History of Suffolk* (Chichester, 1995), p. 97.

[170] In 1802 the cost in Suffolk of poor law relief per head was 11s. 4d., but by 1821 it had risen to 17s., with 13 per cent of the population claiming poor law relief as early as 1802–3. R. Smith and M. Satchel, 'Malthus, Poverty and Population Change in Suffolk 1780–1834', *Proceedings of the Suffolk Institute of Archaeology and History*, Volume 44 (2018), pp. 256–69.

[171] Collett, p. 264.

[172] For an overview, see J. E. Archer, 'Rural Protest 1815–1851', in D. Dymond and E. Martin, eds, *An Historical Atlas of Suffolk* (Ipswich, 1999), pp. 124–5.

[173] The best known were the Littleport and Ely riots, but there were many others scattered across the region. See A. J. Peacock, *Bread or Blood: The Agrarian Riots in East Anglia 1816* (London, 1965). The most feared weapon was incendiarism. Rioters made much use of night attacks to fire barns and hay ricks, and to attack machinery, especially the first threshing machines, which were just becoming more generally used and deprived labourers of much-needed winter work hand-threshing the corn. See S. Wade-Martins and T. Williamson, *Roots of Change* (Exeter, 1999), p. 118.

[174] Collett, p. 266.

[175] For the riots in Suffolk see Peacock, *Bread or Blood*, pp. 72–82.

[176] In the *Oakes Diaries*, Volume II, pp. 202–4, James Oakes gives a detailed and personal account of the Bury unrest and how it was dealt with.

[177] Collett, p. 265.

[178] Collett, p. 267.

[179] Outrages such as the Swing Riots of 1830 continued until better economic conditions in the 1850s brought relief, at least in the short term, with the so-called Golden Age of Agriculture. Sadly for

Patriotism in action

Patriotism lay at the central core of Collett's account, which covered over twenty years. In recording the activities of the Woodbridge Troop, he also recorded an account of their commitment to defending their King and country, and particularly their county. From the beginning, their motto 'Liberty, Loyalty and Property' encapsulated their aims. It was also inscribed on the tokens: those of the 1st Troop had around the edge 'God save King and Constitution', while those of the 3rd Troop also emphasised this commitment: '*Pro Aris et Focis*' (For Home and Hearth). There were obviously other important reasons for their service: loyalty to the Troop, duty, commitment, service and friendship must also have played their part. For many of the membership who served for many years, such as Collett himself, the Yeomanry must have become a central part of their lives.

There has been much discussion about the nature of patriotism and the emergence of popular identity during this period. When war was first declared, the country was undergoing a period of enormous stress, creating serious and extensive social, economic and political unrest in many areas. This led the government to question the commitment and patriotism of sections of the population.[180] How far could popular patriotism be relied upon? The answer came in 1797 and 1798 with French landings and attempted invasions: the country flooded to volunteer and the government was forced to change its mind and trust in patriotism. Although some volunteers joined the Yeomanry, the great majority formed infantry troops. Most were supported by the government, but a few were raised and funded by local gentry who commanded them, such as Sir John Henniker-Major's Worlingworth Volunteers in Suffolk.[181] Efforts were also made to ensure that there was even unofficial mobilisation of the whole population for the defence of the country with the organisation of pioneers, conductors, drivers and guides in rural areas.[182]

In 1803, following the failure of the Truce of Amiens, a further great wave of volunteering swept the country. There was a huge outpouring of patriotism as invasion fears intensified and continued until 1805. Nothing reflected its extent more than the large numbers that Collett recorded in the volunteer units, both infantry and cavalry, formed in towns and villages throughout Suffolk.[183] This amounted to the largest volunteer mobilisation of the civilian population that the country had known. Where the balance lay between patriotic duty and those encouraged by exemption from the militia ballot,[184] is obviously unknown and unimportant. What is important is that when the country faced the most serious threat of invasion it had ever faced, or would face again until the Second World War, people from all over the country came forward in huge numbers to volunteer to serve and defend their country.

Suffolk, the subsequent agricultural depression of the 1870s was to last well into the twentieth century.

[180] Because of the increased political awareness in England engendered by the French Revolution, Pitt saw the disturbances in a political rather than a social and economic context and feared revolution in England.

[181] G. Robinson, 'The Loyal Worlingworth Volunteers', *Suffolk Review* (Autumn 2015), pp. 20–31.

[182] Defence of the Realm Acts of 1798 and 1803.

[183] Collett, pp. 122–5, giving a list of all official volunteer groups in Suffolk in 1803, both Yeomanry Cavalry and infantry.

[184] The government chose to offer militia ballot exemption as an inducement, together with exemption from other supplementary forces introduced by the government at the time.

xlv

Collett's dedication and commitment

After the enormous amount of hard work over many years that Collett had devoted to his great enterprise of recording the activities of the Woodbridge Troop, it was left with no conclusive ending. His entries for 1817 were as usual, if rather short, but there were only three entries for 1818, the last on 7 May being a typical account of a muster. Collett then stopped abruptly, making no more normal entries, although there were several more pages ruled for use, some with headings or unfinished indications as to what he had intended to put on the page. The very last entry in the volume jumped to 1820 when he added a list of the names of his Troop. He offered no explanations for leaving his work unfinished: perhaps if he was writing retrospectively he simply had insufficient time for completion and was unable to catch up; or perhaps he just did not feel he wanted to finish it.

Collett remained as captain and his Troop continued to operate in the usual way until at least June 1820.[185] He resigned in October, together with two other captains, Couperthwaite and Wythe.[186] Entered against his name in the muster roll of the dates of members joining and leaving the Corps was the reason for his resignation: deafness and infirmity of age,[187] not altogether surprising considering he had served his Yeomanry Troop for so long and was seventy-four years old (Plate 13, p. 193). When Collett retired in 1820, a few of the original members who joined the Troop in the first year of its formation were still serving twenty-seven years later: Isaac Churchyard, Philip Dikes, J. M. Theobald, William Pearson and Mileson Edgar. Collett did, however, remain active, both in his bank and in his involvement in local committees and trusts. He died in 1828 in his eighty-first year after a long illness.

Cornelius Collett's volumes stand as a unique record of a group of Suffolk gentry, farmers and others, doing their patriotic duty in service of their King and country and in defence of their much-loved county.[188] His account is a very clear tribute to the dedication and patriotism of the Yeomanry, exhibiting his determination to record their enormous commitment over such a long period. The volumes are also a testament to Collett's own dedication and commitment to the Woodbridge Troop of Loyal Suffolk Yeomanry Cavalry – and indeed to his own patriotism.

---

[185] *Ipswich Journal* 15 June 1820.

[186] *Ipswich Journal* 28 March 1821. The entry merely announced the resignations and the names of the new officers replacing them.

[187] Captain Couperthwaite resigned because of gout and infirmity of age.

[188] The Yeomanry continued under the command of Mileson Edgar until the end of 1827, when the government suddenly dispensed with its services (*Ipswich Journal* 8 December 1827). Edgar died in 1830, the year the government was forced to reinstate the Yeomanry to help deal with the deteriorating social problems with their resultant protests and riots. It was, however, a very different type of Yeomanry Cavalry that emerged, more socially exclusive, drawn from different parts of Suffolk, serving for different reasons, with different aims and values, from those held by the men who had served so long and patriotically in the defence of their county. See Thomas and Sign, *Loyal Suffolk Hussars*, pp. 33–5.

EDITORIAL PRACTICE

The text of Collett's three volumes is very long and comprehensive. It has, therefore, been edited and reduced to allow for a manageable publication. The cuts
mainly relate to two subject areas. The first concerns the repetitive accounts of
general musters, many of which have not been included in the main text, although
a complete list of their dates between 1794 and 1820 is to be found in Appendix 2.
The second relates to the reports that Collett transcribed from the *London Gazette
Extraordinary* of the national events of the war against France: naval battles, invasion attempts and celebrations of great victories. Some of them are very long, and
they have been excluded both because of their length and also because of their lack
of local associations. Their presence in the text is, however, acknowledged by a
footnote indicating the subject of the report, the number being found on the line
separating the entries.

Collett was writing his book over many years, and occasionally lost or mislaid
documents he wished to include. When finding them months or years later, he copied
them at the point he had just reached. Most have been moved to the appropriate
chronological position, with their original position shown in a footnote. Collett's
own page numbers have been indicated in the text as small, bold font, with the
volume letter preceding the page number, as well as in footnotes where pages have
been omitted.

Collett's practice of using lines to separate entries has been retained, but the
dates of entries have been highlighted in bold for ease of reference. For the same
reason, the original layout has been adapted by consolidating the formatting. Original spelling and the idiosyncratic capitalisation so typical of the period has been
retained, as has the punctuation, other than the addition of an occasional full stop.
Abbreviations within Collett's book have, however, been expanded for clarity.

The Suffolk Record Office, Ipswich, is abbreviated as SROI.

CORNELIUS COLLETT'S BOOK

Suffolk Record Office, Ipswich

HD80/3/1, 2 and 3

VOLUME A

An Account of the Cause and Institution of the Yeomanry Cavalry in the County of Suffolk, with minutes made at sundry times of the occurrances in the Second Troop, by Cornelius Collett of Woodbridge who enrolled himself a member thereof at the Commencement of the Institution 1794[1]

The first part, or for the proceedings of the Lord Lieutenant and of the Committees appointed at a meeting of the County at Stowmarket prior and after raising the sundry Troops of Cavalry not before entered in this Book on account of their not being in C Colletts possession[2]

A25 Institution of the Yeomanry Cavalry
Bury St Edmunds   March 21st 1794

At a Meeting of the Grand Juries for the County of Suffolk,[3] a letter having been submitted to their consideration, by Sir Charles Bunbury,[4] which he had received from the Earl of Euston, Lord Lieutenant of this County,[5] recommending an augmentation of the internal forces and proposing various plans which had been transmitted to him by the Secretary of State, a Subscription was agreed to, for a fund to be applied to strengthen the internal defence of the County of Suffolk, in case the bill now pending for the augmentation of the militia, should be passed into law.

Resolved, That the Lord Lieutenant of this County be requested to appoint a meeting of Subscribers, and of such other persons as are desirous of supporting the measure, to be held at Stowmarket[6] on an early day, as the present crisis seem to require a speedy and vigorous increase of the internal defence.[7]

---

[1]   The first twenty-four pages of Volume A are taken up with muster rolls and indices. The opening page has a brief index of the book's main contents. Recorded on A1–22 is the muster roll of members of the 2nd Troop Loyal Suffolk Yeomanry Cavalry from July 1794 to September 1803, followed by the muster roll of the Division of the Troop commanded by Collett, meeting at Eyke, from 29 July to 16 September 1803. An index of the main events in Volume A appears on A24. All are omitted here.

[2]   The meetings were reported in great detail in editions of the local newspapers, the *Ipswich Journal* and *The Bury and Norwich Post*. SROI HD79/B1 is a bound but incomplete copy of the minutes. Both show that Collett did not always copy the minutes verbatim: some material was moved, added to or occasionally omitted.

[3]   The Grand Jury, made up of important local citizens, heard potential criminal cases to determine whether there was a case to be heard to go forward to the Assizes.

[4]   Sir Charles Bunbury lived at Barton Hall, Great Barton, near Bury St Edmunds and was MP for Suffolk, 1761–84 and 1790–1812.

[5]   Lord Euston was the son of the Duke of Grafton at Euston. He was one of the two MPs for the University of Cambridge, the other of whom was his friend William Pitt. As Lord Lieutenant of Suffolk, he was in charge of the Militia and Volunteer forces in the county and played a key role in organising the defence of Suffolk.

[6]   Stowmarket was considered the most central meeting place in the county.

[7]   The present crisis was caused by the escalation of the war, as the French had successfully attacked the United Provinces (now Holland), and the British army under the Duke of York, together with its allies, was driven back, unable to stop the invasion.

That copies of the resolutions be left with the Bankers, in Ipswich, Bury St Edmunds and the several other market towns in the county; and subscriptions be received by the said Bankers who are desired to send, to the next meeting, a list of such persons as have subscribed at their various houses. That the High Sheriff be requested to cause these proceedings to be inserted in the Ipswich and Bury papers.[8]
Signed Thomas Maynard

For Charles Purvis Esq Sheriff

Conduit Street   March 26th 1794

A Liberal Subscription having been made at the Assizes at Bury[9] last week, for the internal defence of the kingdom, and of the county of Suffolk in particular, the application of which, as well as of any further subscriptions that may be added Being still unsettled, I do in consequence of a request arrived this day from the gentlemen of the Grand Juries, desire the attendance of the Subscribers and others desirous of supporting the measure, at the White Hart Inn, at Stowmarket on Thursday the 3rd day of April, at 12 oclock.

Signed Euston

Stowmarket Suffolk   April 3rd 1794

At a meeting of the Subscribers for strengthening the internal defence of the County, held here this day, in pursuance of an advertisement from the Lord Lieutenant, at the request of the Grand Juries assembled at the last Assizes.

Resolved, That this Meeting do now form itself into a general and open Committee for all the Subscribers.

A26 That fencible cavalry, consisting of the Gentry, Yeomanry, Tradesmen, and others; companies for manning batteries on the coast; together with an augmentation of the militia, appear to this committee to be the models best adapted to the circumstances of the situation of the County for strengthening the internal defence against an invading enemy, providing such modes of internal defence do meet the sanction of parliament.[10]

That the specific number of each force be referred to the next Committee, which the Lord Lieutenant is requested to appoint to be holden on Thursday the 27th instant at Stowmarket at 12 oclock at noon.

That such of the Nobility, Gentry, Clergy, Landholders and other persons, as are desirous of subscribing before the next meeting, in defence of the county, against the designs of an ancient and inveterate foe, will, it is hoped, leave their names with the respective bankers, in such market towns in this county, who are advised to send in a state of the subscriptions to the next meeting.[11]

That the thanks of the meeting be given to the Lord Lieutenant, for his polite and ready attention to the wishes of the County, and for his animated support of the business of the day.

---

8   Such was the power and influence of this circle of people that they were able to see how this could be achieved and organise how it should be done, at just one meeting.

9   The County Assizes were always held at Bury and tried the serious offences that had not been filtered out by the Grand Juries.

10   The Yeomanry headed the list for what was considered by the meeting to be the most urgent need for the defence of the county.

11   The range of people that in fact subscribed was much wider than this.

That the thanks of the meeting be given to the High Sheriff, for his very active and proper conduct on this occasion.

That the Lord Lieutenant be requested to sign these resolutions and the High Sheriff to cause them to be inserted in the Ipswich and Bury Papers.[12]   Signed   Euston

Stowmarket   April 17th 1794

At a General Meeting of the Subscribers for strengthening the internal defence of the County of Suffolk held here this day, pursuant to appointment by the Lord Lieutenant, according to the resolution passed by a meeting held the 3rd instant. Sir John Rous in the Chair.[13] The state of the Subscription was reported to amount to £4,300.[14]

Resolved, That Fencible Cavalry, consisting of the Nobility, Gentry, Yeomanry, Farmers, Tradesmen and others; companies for manning batteries on the coast; together with an augmentation of the militia, appear to this meeting to be the modes best adapted to the circumstances of the situation of this county, for strengthening its internal defence against an invading enemy, provided such mode of internal defence do meet the sanction of parliament, but as such a plan can only be carried into execution by the exertion of individuals within the County; that any such persons who shall associate in their respective districts or neighbourhoods, for the purpose of forming a troop of cavalry, shall give in the names of such officers as they shall have agreed upon to the Lord Lieutenant who, on being approved by him, A27 under authority from His Majesty, shall receive temporary rank, according to their commissions.[15]

These troops of cavalry to serve during the war, to consist of gentlemen and yeomanry, and such persons as they shall bring forward, to be approved by the Lord Lieutenant under authority from His Majesty. The Officers to receive temporary commissions from the Lord Lieutenant, and the muster rolls to be approved of by him, at periods to be fixed. Numbers of officers and non-commissioned officers to be the same as usual in cavalry.

To have no levy money, to have no pay unless called out and embodied; to find their own horses and cloathing;

government to provide arms and accoutrements, as usually allowed to cavalry;

government to allow pay for one sergeant and corporal per troop; the sergeants and corporals and their horses to be billeted at such places within the county as the Lord Lieutenant shall appoint. The horses for them to be provided by government and the clothing at the expense of the subscription;

to be exercised only at such times and places as shall be fixed with the approbation of the Lord Lieutenant, to be embodied on appearance of invasion of the county; a certain part to be called out of the county by special directions from His Majesty or by the Lord Lieutenant, or by the Sheriff of the County, for the suppression of riots or tumults within the county or any adjoining county and in aid of any Corps which may be raised for the defence and security of the same; in either case, when

---

[12] The *Ipswich Journal* 19 April 1794 reported this meeting in such detail that it appeared to be from a copy of the minutes.

[13] Sir John Rous of Henham Hall became the captain of the 1st Troop of Yeomanry Cavalry recruited from the Blything hundred.

[14] The size of the subscription and the very short time it took to raise this amount illustrated the concern and fear felt in the county.

[15] The volunteers chose their own officers from those volunteering, usually large landowners well known to them.

actually in service, to receive the pay of dragoons and to be liable to the provisions of the mutiny bill.

As it is probable that several persons who for reasons cannot serve themselves may be desirous of rendering every assistance in their power towards formation of these troops, and several Gentlemen may wish to furnish men and horses besides serving themselves, it is resolved to accept of men and substitutes under the following restrictions; That they shall be men of good character and that they shall have been accustomed to riding; that they shall have fixed residence in the County, of course menial servants must be deemed improper; that they shall not be persons whose situations make it at all probable that they would enlist in the army or navy or militia, and that they shall be approved of by the commanding officer of the troop in which they serve. These men and substitutes to be equipped in the same manner as those who serve themselves and at the expense of those persons in whose place they serve, and by whom they are furnished.

That companies of infantry, for manning batteries on the coast, do consist of the Nobility, Gentry, Yeomanry and Farmers, Tradesmen, and other persons whom they may bring forward to be approved of by the Lord Lieutenant under authority from His Majesty. The Officers to be recommended by the Lord Lieutenant but to have commissions from the King. To assemble two days in each week to practise. The Officers to be allowed [no] pay, and the non commissioned officers and privates men each, one Shilling, per day, for the days they are to exercise; **A28** to have cloathing given by government, that they may be all in uniform, not to be removed more than five miles from home unless ordered by His Majesty on the appearance of an invasion, when they are to be called out, and paid like other militia, but not to be removed out of the county, to be under the provisions of the Mutiny Bill when embodied and under the command of a general officer.

That the subscription be applied to the following purposes under the direction of a Committee of subscribers;

1st to defray the expenses which may occur in the equipment, formation or continuance of the above mentioned troops;

2nd to augment the Militia by volunteers;

3rd to raise companies of infantry for manning batteries on the coast;

4th To assist in providing for the general defence of the county by the modes above specified, in such manner as the committee shall think expedient, with approbation of government and under the sanction of Parliament.

That the specific number of each force together with plans for raising companies for manning batteries to be referred to the next general meeting, to be holden at Stowmarket, on Thursday, the first day of May next, subject to further adjournment by the Chairman, in case the Volunteer Corps Bill be not passed into a law, previous to the first of May aforesaid.

Copies of the resolutions passed at this and the preceeding meetings; together with the names of the Subscribers, be printed and sent to the respective Bankers, and left at the inns in the usual market towns in this county, in order to give such persons as are unable to attend the General Meeting an opportunity of Subscribing.

The Chairman do sign these resolutions and the High Sheriff be requested to cause them be inserted in the Ipswich and Bury papers.

Signed   John Rous Chairman

That the thanks of this meeting be given to the Chairman for his attendance at this meeting and impartial conduct in the Chair.

Signed   William Pearson Under Sheriff

6

Copy of An Act of Parliament for encouraging and disciplining such corps or companies of men, as shall voluntarily inroll themselves for the defence of their counties, towns, or coasts, or for the general defence of the kingdom, during the war.[16]

April 17th 1794

Whereas the utmost exertions are now requisite for increasing the military force in this kingdom; be it enacted by the King's most excellent majesty, by and with the advice consent of the lords spiritual and temporal and commons, in this present parliament assembled, and by the authors of the same, That any corps or companies of Volunteers who now are, or shall hereafter be formed, in any countries or towns in Great Britain, during the continuance of the present war, under officers having commissions from his Majesty, or from the lieutenants of counties, or others who may be specially authorised by his Majesty for that purpose, and who shall at any time, on being called upon by special direction of his Majesty, in case of actual invasion, or appearance of invasion, voluntarily march out of their respective countries or towns, or shall voluntarily assemble within the same to repel such invasion, or who shall voluntarily march on being called upon in pursuance of an order from his Majesty or from the lord lieutenant or sheriff of the County, to act within the county or the adjacent counties for the suppression of mobs or tumults, shall in such cases be entitled to receive pay in such manner, or at such rates of the officers and soldiers of his Majestys regular forces do now receive; and shall, during the time of their being continued in such service, and so receiving pay as above, be subject to military discipline as the rest of his Majesty's regular and militia Troops; provided always, That no officer or soldier of any volunteer corps shall be liable to be tried or punished by any court martial at any time, unless such court martial be composed entirely of officers serving in volunteer corps, formed as aforesaid such court martial, be composed entirely of officers serving in the volunteer corps, formed as aforesaid, such court martial to be assembled by warrant under his Majesty's signed manual, or by warrant from some general or other officer duly authorised to hold court martials.

2nd And be it further enacted, That it shall be lawfull for all mayors, bailiffs, constables, tithingmen, headboroughs, and other chief magistrates and officers of cities, towns, parishes, tithings and places, and (in their default or absence) for any one Justice of the peace inhabiting with or near any such city, town, parish, tithing or place (but for no others); and they or he are or is hereby required to quarter and billet the sergeants corporals and drummers, of such troops and companies as aforesaid, and their horses, in inns, livery stables, alehouses, victualling houses, and all houses of persons selling brandy, strong waters, cyder, wine or metheglin, by retail, upon application made to any mayors, bailiffs, constables, tithingmen, headboroughs, or other chief magistrates or officers by his Majesty's lieutenant, or by the officer commanding such corps or companies.

---

[16] Collett copied this Act of Parliament authorising volunteers on B218–219, presumably having found it some time after completing contemporaneous sections. It has been inserted here for clarity.

3th And be it further enacted by the authority aforesaid That if the officer commanding any such corps or company as aforesaid shall discharge from such corps or company any persons who shall have been inlisted or inrolled aforesaid; and if such person shall refuse or neglect on being required by such commanding officer, to deliver up any arms, accoutrements or cloathing, which shall have been intrusted to his custody, every person on refusing or neglecting shall, on being convicted thereof, before any justice of the peace of the County within which such corps or company shall have been formed, forfeit and pay the sum of ten pounds, to be Levied by distress and sale of the offenders goods and chattels by warrant under the hand and seal of such justice rendering the overplus (if any) on demand, after deducting the charges of such distress and sale to the person whose goods and chattels shall have been distrained and sold; and for want of sufficient distress, such Justice is hereby required to commit such offender to the common gaol of the county, riding or place, where the offence shall have been committed, for any time not exceeding one Month; and the monies arising by such penalty shall be paid to the treasurer of the county, riding or place where such offence shall have been committed; to be applied as part of the stock of such county, riding, or place.

4th And be it further enacted by the authority aforesaid, That all commissioned officers of the said corps, who shall be disabled in actual service, shall be entitled to half pay; and all non-commissioned officers and soldiers so disabled to the benefit of the Chelsea hospital; and the widows of commissioned officers killed in the service to a pension for life.

5th And be it further inacted by the authority aforesaid, That no person who shall be inlisted or inrolled in any corps or company of volunteers as aforesaid shall, during the time that he is serving in the said corps or company, be liable to serve personally, or provide a substitute to serve in the militia, provided he shall produce to the deputy lieutenants, assembled at the subdivision meetings, holden in the several counties, for the purpose of hearing appeals against the militia list returned from each parish, an affidavit of his having been inrolled as foresaid, and a certificate that he has for the space of six weeks, immediate proceeding such sub-division meeting, punctually attended at all times and places, as may have been agreed upon for the exercise of such corps or company.[17]

6th Provided always, and be it enacted, That this Act shall have continuance during the present war and no longer.

Signed by the commanding officer of the said corps or company.

Stowmarket May 1st 1794

At a General Meeting of the Subscribers for strengthening the internal defence of the county of Suffolk held This day, pursuant to adjournment.

Thomas Maynard in the Chair.

The state of the subscription was reported to amount to £5,100.

---

[17] This clause, which gave exemption to volunteers from their liability to serve in the militia, was to become increasingly important. There has been much discussion as to its influence on motivation, particularly where the division lay between self-interest and patriotism.

Resolved, That the urgency of the present crisis under the immediate exertions of everyone necessary, as well individually as collectively, in order to provide the best means of repelling the hostile attempts of France against this kingdom, and of maintaining the security of this county in particular.[18]

A29 That of the three modes of increasing the internal defence, agreed to at our last meeting, as best adapted to the circumstances and situation in the County, the following be the proportion, viz

Four Troops of Fencible Cavalry consisting of 50 privates each.

Two Companies of Infantry for manning Batteries on the Coast, consisting of sixty privates, One Captain, two Lieutenants, three Sergeants, three Corporals and two drummers each.

An augmentation of seven men per Company to the two Battalions of Militia.

But as such a plan can only be carried into execution by the exertion of individuals within the County, Resolved, That any persons who shall associate in their respective districts or neighbourhoods for the purpose of forming a Troop of Cavalry, shall give in the name of such officers as they shall have agreed upon to the Lord Lieutenant, who, on being approved by him, under authority from His Majesty, shall receive temporary rank, according to their commissions. These Troops of Cavalry to serve during the war, to consist of the gentleman and yeoman, and such persons as they shall bring forward, to be approved by the Lord Lieutenant, under authority from his Majesty. The Officers to receive temporary commissions from the Lord Lieutenant, and the muster rolls to be approved of by him, at periods to be fixed, Number of officers and non-commissioned officers to be the same as usual in cavalry.

To have no levy money; to have no pay unless called out and embodied; to find their own Horses and Cloathing; government to provide accoutrements, as usually allowed to cavalry; government to allow pay for one sergeant and corporal per troop, the sergeants and corporals and their horses to be billeted at such places within the county as the Lord Lieutenant shall appoint. The horses for them to be provided by government, and the cloathing at the expense of the subscription; to be exercised only at such times and places as shall be fixed, with the approbation of the Lord Lieutenant; to be liable to be embodied on appearance of the invasion of the county, and to be called upon by order of his Majesty or by the Lord Lieutenant or the Sheriff of the county, for the suppression of riots and tumults within the county; one fourth to be liable to be called out of the county by special direction of his Majesty, in case of the actual invasion of any adjoining county, or for the suppression of riots and tumults therein, in aid of any corps which may be raised for the defence and security of the same; in either case, when actually in exercise, to receive pay as dragoons, and be liable to the provisions of the mutiny bill.

As it is probable that several persons (who for various reasons cannot serve themselves) may be desirous of rendering every assistance in their power towards the formation of these troops, and several gentlemen may wish to furnish men and horse besides serving A30 themselves, it is resolved to accept men and substitutes under the following restrictions; That they shall be men of good character, and that they shall have been accustomed to riding; that they shall have a fixed residence in the County, of course menial servants must be deemed improper; that they shall not be persons whose situations make it at all probable that they would enlist in the army,

---

[18] The minutes of this meeting repeat sections of the previous one but have been retained as new decisions were reached, developing or amending former ones.

or navy or militia, and that they shall be approved of by the commanding officer of the troop in which they serve. These men and substitutes to be equipped in the same manner as those who serve themselves, and at the expense of those persons in whose place they serve, and by whom they are furnished.

Every person acting as a private, to be allowed out of the fund of the subscription two shillings per day, for every day of exercise, for the use of his horse, if required. The places and days of exercise to be approved by the Lord Lieutenant;

the places of rendezvous, when called out, and embodied, to be fixed by the Lord Lieutenant, High Sheriff or General commanding the district. Such Troops, when called out on actual service, to form One Regiment, under the command of a Colonel.[19] These Troops to muster at Bury and Ipswich as herein after directed, and then subdivide for exercise in their respective hundreds or districts. The companies of infantry to assemble Two days in a week for practice.[20] The officers to be allowed [no] pay and the non commissioned officers and men each one shilling per day from government, for the days they are to exercise, to have clothing given by government, not to be removed more than five miles from home, unless ordered by his Majesty, on the appearance of an invasion, when they are to be called out and paid like other militia, but not to be removed out of the county, to be under military law when embodied, and under the command of a General Officer. The officers to be recommended by the Lord Lieutenant, but to have commissions from the King. Officers on half pay will be accepted if recommended, privates to be further allowed one shilling per day out of the subscription.

That six Guineas and a Half be allowed for every volunteer militia man certified by the Colonels of the two batteries as approved and accepted[21] and that the sum of four hundred pounds be lodged with Mr Spink of Bury St Edmunds, Banker, to be drawn for and applied by the Colonel of the Western Regiment; and that the sum of four hundred pounds be lodged with Messrs. Cricket and Co. of Ipswich, bankers, to be drawn and applied for by the Colonel of the Eastern Regiment for the above purpose, and for enlisting corporals. That a state of the money so applied, together with the number of volunteers raised, and the corporals enlisted, be sent signed by the Commanding Officer of each battalion, to every general Committee of the Subscribers and that such volunteers and corporals be single men.

A31 That Subdivision Committees be formed by the subscribers of each hundred,[22] to receive on muster rolls the names of such persons as are willing to enrol themselves for the respective service, into which they choose to enter; and that such committees do meet in the principal towns in the respective hundreds, or any adjoining one in another hundred or division on Wednesday the 14th day of May instant at 12 at noon, and adjourn as they see fit, the several Muster Rolls, signed in and for the respective hundreds, and towns, be sent to the two principal Sub-division Meetings hereby appointed, to be holden at the Angel Bury St Edmunds on Wednesday the 21 May instant and the other at Ipswich in the Moot Hall there, on Saturday the

---

[19] The clear intention was that the separate Troops of the Loyal Suffolk Yeomanry Cavalry would form a regiment under a unified command if actually embodied and called out to face an invasion.

[20] The following section refers to infantry not cavalry.

[21] Lord Euston was in charge of the county militia. In Suffolk it was divided into two regiments, west and east, and both were to be augmented by volunteers paid for by the subscription. Lord Euston himself commanded the West Suffolk Militia when the invasion crisis was at its height.

[22] It is interesting that the committee reverted to the old hundred division of the county as the organisational base for the new force.

24th May instant at Twelve at noon respectively, in order that the said muster rolls may be transmitted to the Lord Lieutenant for his approbation, that the officers may receive commissions under authority from His Majesty.[23]

That the Subscribers inform the sub-division Committee for the several Hundreds and that Three be a Quorum. And that every Committee shall have a power to add to their Numbers, other Subscribers.

That a parchment Muster Roll be provided by every Committee and the following preamble be and is hereby recommended: We do hereby inroll ourselves to serve during the war in the yeomanry cavalry, or in companies for manning batteries in the county of Suffolk, under the following conditions "which conditions are to be agreeable to the Resolutions of the General Committee, passed at Stowmarket this day respecting the fencible cavalry and companies of infantry, and further we hereby pledge ourselves to attend in person or by our substitute duly enrolled. In case of non attendance, without sufficient cause, upon occasion of the Corps being called out and embodied in the actual service, we agree to subject ourselves to the forfeiture of fifty pounds to be added to the general subscription, and to be expelled the Corps; the cause of such non-attendance to be judged of by the majority of volunteers serving in person."

That a general Committee of all the Subscribers, or any seven of them, do for bringing the above resolutions into execution, meet at The White Hart, Stowmarket on Wednesday the 28th May instant at Twelve at noon, and adjourn from time to time as they see fit, not exceeding Twelve weeks, between each and every adjournment; the High Sheriff, the Lord Lieutenant, the Representatives for the County, the Clergy and persons being subscribers, who have served as officers in the Army, Militia or Navy, together with the Chairman of the several sub-divisions Committees (to report the receipt and expenditure passed before this between each General Meeting) be and are hereby particularly requested to attend the Committee.

A32 That the Volunteers enrolling themselves for the respective hundreds do muster at the Angel, Bury, on Thursday, the fifth day of June next, and at Ipswich, in the Moot Hall there on Saturday the 7th day of June next at Twelve at noon, as may be most convenient for their respective situations.

That the Under Sheriff be appointed Secretary to the General Committee,

That Messrs Spink and Cass of Bury St. Edmunds, bankers; Messrs Crickett and Co of Ipswich, bankers, to be Treasurers to this Subscription and that the several sums subscribed be paid to the said Treasurers, on or before Saturday the 10th of May instant.

That copies of resolutions passed at this and proceeding meetings, together with the names of subscribers, be printed, and sent to the respective bankers, and left at the inns in the several market towns in this county, in order to give such persons as are unable to attend the General Meeting an opportunity of subscribing.

That the Lord Lieutenant be requested to appoint an Agent in London to make application for arms and accoutrements etc

That the subscription be applied to the following purposes, under the direction of a Committee of subscribers;

1st To defray the expenses which may occur in the equipment formation of the above mentioned Troops

---

[23] Sub-division meetings in each hundred were a more efficient way of administering and encouraging new subscribers and volunteers.

2ndly To augment the militia by volunteers,

3rdly To raise companies of infantry for manning batteries on the coast

4thly To assist in providing for the general defence of the county, by the modes above specified, in such manner as the Committee shall think most expedient, with the approbation of Government and under the sanction of Parliament; and to pay the expenses of printing and distributing the Resolutions and all other expenses relating to conducting the object and intent of the subscription.

The Chairman do sign the resolutions, and the High Sheriff be requested to cause them to be inserted in the Ipswich and Bury papers and in the St James' Chronicle.

That the thanks of this meeting be given to Philip Bowes Broke Esq for his unabated zeal in the service of his country on every occasion and more particularly on the present.

Signed Thomas Maynard Esq for Charles Purvis Esq High Sheriff

That the thanks of this Committee be given to the Chairman, for his polite and candid attention to the business of the day.   Signed William Pearson Secretary

---

A33 Stowmarket Suffolk May 28th 1794

At a General meeting of the Subscribers for strengthening the defence of the County of Suffolk, held here this day pursuant to the adjournment.

Philip Bowes Broke Esq in the Chair.[24]

That the state of the subscription was reported to amount to £6075 1s 6d.

The Muster rolls for the Yeomanry Cavalry and Infantry, were returned to this Meeting; from the following towns and hundreds; Thedwastry and Thingoe with Bury St Edmunds, Bosmere and Claydon, Risbridge, Colneis, Carlford, Loes, Wilford, Plomesgate and Thredling, Ipswich and Samford, Babergh, Blackbourn, Stow and Cosford.

Ordered that copies of the signatures of the volunteers to the several muster rolls together with the recommendations for commissions, be sent to the Lord Lieutenant for his approbation.

That the following passage on the preamble recommended by the resolution passed at the General Meeting on the 1st Instant for the muster rolls, viz 'In case of non attendance without sufficient cause, upon occasion of the corps being called out and embodied for actual service, we agree to subject ourselves to the forfeiture of £50 to be judged by the majority of Volunteers serving in person', be expunged.[25]

That the muster rolls be returned to the Chairman of the last Hundred Committee Meeting to remain with them, to receive the signatures of such person as may be willing to sign their names; which muster rolls are to be returned to the General Meetings hereafter appointed; and that the preamble to the said muster rolls be amended according to the resolutions of this day, relating thereto.

That, for the convenience of the Yeomanry, the Lord Lieutenant be requested to appoint such days of exercise (not more than one in a week) and at such places

---

[24] Philip Bowes Broke became captain of the 2nd Troop of Yeomanry Cavalry. He lived at Broke Hall, Nacton, by the River Orwell, just outside Ipswich on the Woodbridge side, where he owned a sizeable estate.

[25] This must have been the result of feedback from volunteers because £50 was a huge sum and would deter men from volunteering. Requirements laid down at one meeting were sometimes expunged or rescinded at the next when their full implications were realised or the volunteers objected. This was inevitable given the speed with which so much was achieved in so short a time by a group of Suffolk gentry and others unused to military detail, but against a background of growing crisis.

for that purpose (not exceeding six miles from their respective homes)[26] as shall be recommended by the volunteers, forming themselves in their respective districts, in a troop or part of a troop; and that in the month of July and August no attendance be required, more than once a fortnight.[27]

That it is expedient to explain to many persons well inclined to enter themselves in the Yeomanry Cavalry, and Infantry for manning batteries on the Coast, that the act of the 17th day of April last for encouraging companies of men voluntarily A34 inrolling themselves for the defence of their counties, and provides that every man shall be left to act voluntarily on such occasions as his service may be therein required, according to the said Act, viz 'That any corps or companies of volunteers who shall at any time, on being called upon by special direction of his Majesty, in case of actual invasion or appearance of invasion, voluntarily march out of their respective counties or towns, or shall voluntarily assemble within the same, to repel such invasion, or who shall voluntarily march being called upon, in pursuance of an order from his Majesty, or from the Lord Lieutenant or Sheriff of the county etc That an alphabetical list of all persons who have subscribed or may subscribe to this plan of internal defence, on or before the last day of June next, shall be published and dispersed throughout the County; by which time the Committee apprehend and hope, that all persons disposed to support so useful and laudable a measure, will come forward with their subscriptions; and that such printed list shall be transmitted by the Secretary to the Lord Lieutenant, requesting him to give directions to the Clerk of the Peace, that the same list may be deposited amongst the records of the county.

That the days appointed on the 1st instant for the volunteers to muster, be adjourned to the 19th of June next, for their appearance at The Angel at Bury St Edmunds, and the 21st June instant, at the Town Hall in Ipswich, as may be most convenient for their respective situations, before the Lord Lieutenant, or the members appointed for the several Hundred Committees, or any three of them;

That the Uniform of the Yeomanry Cavalry be a dark blue Coat faced with yellow, cape and cuffs, yellow shoulder straps, white waistcoat, leather breeches, high top boots, round hat with feather and cockade, white buttons, with the letters SY (Suffolk Yeomanry)[28] and that a pattern of the uniform coat, be left with Spink and Cass, Bury; Crickett and Co, Ipswich; Mr. Hilliard, Stowmarket; Reeve and Co, Beccles; Jermyn and White, Halesworth.

That the sum of three guineas be allowed to every man enrolling himself and appearing at the general muster, before appointed, to serve the Yeomanry Cavalry, towards a uniform, if required.[29]

That the sum of 12 shillings a man, being allowed for accoutrements, to the seven men per company, for the augmentation of the militia.

---

[26] The six-mile limit is of interest, given the total distance to be travelled by horse, in addition to the practice of exhausting evolutions at the muster.

[27] Many of the volunteers were farmers and this reassurance over harvest time would have been welcome.

[28] Initially, there was clearly one uniform for all the Troops of the Suffolk Yeomanry Cavalry.

[29] It is sometimes claimed that the cost of the uniform deterred men from volunteering but it is clear that in Suffolk the cost was paid out of the subscription, except those of officers who met the cost themselves.

That copies of these resolutions be printed and sent to the representative Bankers, and left at the inns in the several market towns in this county, in order to give such persons, as are unable to attend at a General Meeting, an opportunity of subscribing; and that the same be inserted in the Ipswich and Bury papers.

That the Committee be adjourned to Thursday the 12th day of June next, A35 at 12 o'clock at noon to be here holden.

The thanks of this Meeting were most unanimously and cordially voted to the Chairman, for his very impartial conduct in the chair, and for his very zealous attendance to the business of this day, and also for the several measures which he has from time to time taken since the last meeting, towards promoting the plan for the internal defence of the county.

Signed William Pearson Secretary

Stowmarket, Suffolk June 12th 1794

At a General Meeting of the Subscribers for strengthening the internal defence of the county of Suffolk, held here this day pursuant to adjournment. Philip Bowes Broke Esq in the Chair.

The state of the subscription was reported to amount to £6439.

The Volunteers enlisted for the augmentation of the Militia, were returned to be as follows, For the Western Regiment 42, for the Eastern Regiment 52 Privates and 4 Corporals.

The Muster Rolls for the Yeomanry Cavalry and Infantry, were returned to this meeting from the following towns and hundreds: Thedwastry and Thingoe with Bury St Edmunds, Bosmere and Claydon, Babergh, Stow, Ipswich and Samford, Loes, Wilford, Plomesgate, Colneis, Carlford and Thredling; Blackbourn, Blything and Cosford.

Ordered that copies of the additional signatures of the volunteers to the several muster rolls, together with the recommendations thereon by this meeting, for the commissions to be sent to the Lord Lieutenant for his approbation.

That the muster rolls be returned to the Chairman, of the last Hundred Committee Meetings, in order to receive the signatures of such persons as may be willing to sign their names, at the Committees for the several hundreds (appointed on 1st May last and now by this Meeting required to assemble again, at the several places where they were before held, in each hundred or division) on or before the 18th instant at 12 oclock at noon, and adjourn from time to time as they shall see fit; such muster rolls to be returned to the General Meeting herein after appointed.

That the four Troops of Fencible Cavalry, consisting of 50 privates each, agreed on the 1st day of May last, to form a part of the force for the internal defence of this county, be Independent troops, and under the command of their respective officers;[30] but subject to the other regulations before adopted except that they may not be liable to march to any adjoining county, for the suppression of riots and tumults therein, in aid of any corps A36 which may be raised for the defence and security of the same, unless a mutual agreement shall have been entered into with the corps so raised in any adjoining county, mutually to assist each other.

That a list of all persons who have inrolled themselves, or may enrol, to serve for the internal defence of the county, in their respective corps, before the last day of

---

[30] The decision to have independent Troops helped mould them into effective units, both as an efficient military force and as a satisfactory, happy and coherent entity.

14

this present month of June, shall be published and dispersed through the County; and that such list shall be transmitted, by the Secretary, to the Lord Lieutenant, requesting him to give directions to the Clerk of the Peace, that the same list may be deposited amongst the records of the county.

That the resolution of 28th May last, appointing Ipswich and Bury for the place of general muster be rescinded; and that such musters be instead thereof, held for each troop, in each market town or place, as is most convenient for that purpose, for the volunteers inrolled for their respective districts, and with the approbation of the Commanding Officer of each troop, in order to be inspected by him, and that such Commanding Officer do certify to the Lord Lieutenant, that the volunteers whose names appear on the different lists, did actually answer to them on the day of muster.

A pattern of the uniform of Yeomanry Cavalry, resolved at the last meeting, having been produced and it being represented to this General Committee that such uniform does not meet the approval of the Yeomanry. Ordered, That the uniform be as follows viz A Scarlet Coat, lined with white, with dark blue military cape and cuffs, scarlet and blue chain epaulettes, white waistcoat, leather breeches, high top boots round hat with bearskin, feather and cockade, white plated button with the Crown and Garter of the Order, the words "Loyal Suffolk Yeomanry" to be inscribed on the Garter, and that the first troop raised, and accepted by the Lord Lieutenant to be complete, bear "No. 1" on the button; and that other troops to bear the number according to the order of the return of their acceptance as complete.

That for a great coat of dark blue lined with white, and uniform buttons, one guinea to be allowed out of the subscription to every volunteer.

That the Commanding Officer of each troop be allowed to draw for £6 1s 0d for the accoutrements, sadlery and great coats of each volunteer in his troop, when he shall report such troop to be complete to the Lord Lieutenant; and that such accoutrements, sadlery and great coats, be ordered by the Commanding Officer of each troop only, in order to prevent any inconvenience that must otherwise arise to the volunteers individually from not knowing where to apply for such articles of equipment. That a pattern of the uniform coat be left with Spink and Co Bury, Crickett and Co Ipswich, A37 Mr. Hilliard Stowmarket, Rede and Co Beccles, Jermyn and Co Halesworth.[31]

That the following gentlemen be and are recommended by this meeting to the Lord Lieutenant for commissions viz Sir John Rous, Bart, to be captain, George Doughty Esq lieutenant, John Claydon Esq cornet,[32] Philip Bowes Broke Esq captain, Francis Brooke Esq lieutenant, Mileson Edgar Esq cornet,[33] Charles Maitland Barclay Esq captain in the army, to be captain, Charles Berners Junior Esq lieutenant, John Meadows Theobald cornet,[34] Horatio Churchill Esq captain in the Army, to be captain, Edward Pryor Esq lieutenant, Orbell Ray Oakes Esq cornet.[35]

---

[31] J. Laver, *British Military Uniforms* (London, 1948), p. 29, Military Tailors Pattern Book *c.*1800.

[32] These were the commissions for the officers of the Blything Troop of Loyal Suffolk Yeomanry Cavalry, the first one to complete.

[33] The officers' commissions for the Woodbridge Troop, the second to complete.

[34] It is unclear which Troop had chosen these men as officers.

[35] This was intended to be the 4th (Bury) Troop but it was not in fact formed until early in the following year and then under the leadership of Lord Brome. Orbell Oakes, the cornet, was the son of James Oakes whose diaries recorded several early meetings of the Troop.

The Reverend J G Smith, the Reverend Dr. Frank and the Reverend John Higgs inrolled themselves at this meeting, to serve in the Yeomanry Cavalry, by their respective substitutes.[36]

That copies of the resolutions be printed, and sent to the respective Bankers (who are requested to continue to receive subscriptions and transmit a list of names to the Secretary of the General Meeting) and left at the Inns in the several market towns in the county, in order to give such persons, as are unable to attend at the General Meeting, an opportunity of subscribing: and that the same be inserted in the Ipswich and Bury papers.

That this Committee be adjourned to Thursday 10th day of July next, to be holden at Twelve oclock at noon.

That the thanks of this meeting be given to the chairman, for his polite attention to the business of the day.   Signed William Pearson Secretary

---

Stowmarket July 10th 1794

At a General meeting of the Subscribers for strengthening the internal defence of the county of Suffolk held here this day pursuant to adjournment.

                    Charles Purvis Esq High Sheriff in the Chair.

The state of the subscription was reported to amount to £6800 15s[37]

That in consequence of a note from the War Office communicated to this meeting signifying that dark blue facings are not allowed to any but Royal Regiments, light sky blue be adopted for the facings instead thereof according to the pattern uniform now produced, And it is recommended to volunteers of each corps, not to order their uniform till after the first day of muster of each troop; and that patterns of the uniform A39 be left with Crickett and Co Ipswich, Spink and Co Bury, Mr Hilliard Stowmarket, Read and Co Beccles, Jermyn and Co Halesworth.

That the Captain of each troop shall make a list of every article of arms and accoutrements that shall have been intrusted to the custody of each volunteer (and of clothing of such volunteers as may not provide themselves), and that each volunteer shall enter into an engagement to return the same on being required by such Captain, or forfeit and pay the sum of Ten Pounds, according to the act for raising volunteer corps.

That it appears to this Meeting, that no privates have inrolled themselves for manning batteries on the coast, and that the amount of the subscription this day returned will admit of an increase of the plan adopted for internal defence; therefore, in lieu of the infantry companies for manning batteries, that Two Independent Troops of Yeomanry Cavalry be added to the Four determined upon by the Committee on the 12th day of June last.

Bury August 11th 1794

At a General meeting of the Subscribers for strengthening the internal defence of the county of Suffolk held here this day pursuant to adjournment

   Philip Bowes Broke Esq for Charles Purvis Esq High Sheriff, in the Chair.

The state of the subscription was reported to amount to £6824 11s 6d

---

[36] The Revd Dr Frank himself became the chaplain of the Woodbridge Troop as well as providing a substitute.

[37] It is obvious that the format, content and language of the minutes of the Subscribers' Committee quickly became very repetitive and although Collett conscientiously copied them out, the following entries omit much of the repetition and only contain new material.

The muster rolls for the Yeomanry Cavalry were returned to this meeting, from the following Towns and Hundreds viz the same as those specified 10th July, the rolls were returned complete, and the respective troops to have mustered for exercise A41 That the Subscribers who have not yet paid their respective subscriptions be and are most earnestly requested to leave the amount at the Treasurers, Spink and Co or Crickett and Co before the 4th day of September next, in order that the full and correct state of the efficient fund, be prepared against the next General Meeting to which the said Treasurers are desired to make their returns.

That it is and most pressingly recommended to the Chairman of the Hundred Committees to attend the next general meeting with their Muster Rolls that the number of volunteers may be clearly ascertained when it is hoped that such persons as are inclined to offer their services in raising a troop or troops, will deliver in their names and lists, the strong emergency of the present crisis requiring the utmost exertions for increasing the internal defence of the kingdom, and of the counties upon the coast in particular.

That these resolutions be published in the Ipswich and Bury papers;

That this Committee be adjourned to Thursday 11th September next, to be holden at the White Hart Inn in Stowmarket at Twelve o'Clock at noon, when the attendance of all subscribers is particularly required on special business.

That the thanks of this meeting be given to the Chairman for his very zealous attention to the business of the day. (Signed) William Pearson Secretary

Stowmarket September 11th 1794

At a General meeting of the Subscribers for strengthening the internal defence of the county of Suffolk held here this day pursuant to adjournment.

Philip B Broke Esq in the chair.

The state of the subscription was reported to amount to £6867 13s 6d.

The muster rolls of the Yeomanry Cavalry were returned to this meeting from the following Towns and Hundreds viz Thedwastry and Thingoe with Bury St Edmunds, Ipswich and Samford, and from the hundreds of Blything and division of Woodbridge, including Loes, Wilford, Plomesgate, Colneis, Carlford and Thredling.[38] The rolls were reported complete, and the respective troops to have mustered for exercise.[39]

Ordered That the muster rolls be returned to the Chairman of the last Hundred Committee Meetings, in order to receive the signatures of such persons as may be willing A42, to sign their names at the several places (appointed on the 1st of May last, and now by this meeting required to assemble again, at the several places where they were before held, and after mentioned, in each hundred or division) and adjourn from time to time, as they shall se fit; such muster rolls to be returned to the General Meeting herein after appointed;

Blything Hundred Angel Hotel Halesworth; Bosmere and Claydon Crown Claydon; Risbridge Half Moon Clare; Colnies, Carlford, Loes, Wilford, Plomesgate and Thredling Shire Hall Woodbridge; Lackford Bell Mildenhall; Blackbourne Pickerell Ixworth; Stow White Hart Stowmarket; Cosford White Lion Hadleigh; Thedwastry and Thingoe Angel Inn Bury; Hoxne and Hartsmere White Lion Eye; Ipswich and

---

[38] This was the area from which the members of the 2nd Woodbridge Troop were drawn.

[39] This is unclear since in fact the Bury Troop was the fourth one to be completed but only early in 1795. There never was a Troop of Loyal Suffolk Yeomanry Cavalry at Ipswich although a Troop of Provisional Cavalry was later formed there.

Samford Town Hall Ipswich; Babergh Black Lyon Melford; Wangford Kings Head Beccles; Mutford and Lothingland, Crown Lowestoft.

That the Captain of each troop shall make a list of every article of arms and accoutrements that shall have been entrusted to the custody of each volunteer (and cloathing of such volunteers as may not provide themselves), and that each volunteer shall enter into an agreement to return the same, on being required by such Captain, or forfeit and pay the sum of ten pounds according to the act for raising volunteer corps.

That the Treasurers do make out, and return to the next General Meeting, a list of such subscribers as shall have paid their respective subscriptions; and that those subscribers who have not paid their subscriptions, be and are most earnestly requested to leave the amount at the Treasurers immediately, in order that a full and correct state of the official Fund, be prepared against such next General Meeting.

A43 That it be and is most pressingly recommended to the Chairman of the Hundred Committees to attend the next General Meeting, with their muster rolls, that the number of volunteers inrolled may be clearly ascertained; when it is hoped that such persons as are inclined to offer their services in raising a troop or troops, will deliver in their names and lists; the strong emergency of the present crisis requiring the utmost exertion for increasing the internal defence of the kingdom, and the counties on the coast in particular.[40]

The muster rolls from the Hundreds of Bosmere and Claydon, Hoxne, Hartismere, Risbridge, Lackford, Babergh, Blackbourn, Stow, Wangford, Cosford, Mutford, and Lothingland not being returned, the number of volunteers inrolled for the Yeomanry Cavalry in their respective Hundreds cannot be ascertained; but this Committee consider it their duty to represent, that letters of service were received from the Hundred of Wangford purporting that two Companies of Infantry are ready to be embodied whenever the General Committee shall determine such mode of increasing the Internal Defence of this County, shall constitute a part of its forces.[41]

That these resolutions be published in the Ipswich and Bury Papers.

That the Committee be adjourned to Thursday the 25th of September instant to be here holden at Twelve o'clock at noon when a full meeting of Subscribers will be particularly requisite to take into consideration the raising of Companies of Infantry in such towns as have or may offer, in case it does not appear to such meeting, that the Troops of Yeomanry Cavalry not yet filled, are likely to be soon completed.[42]

That the thanks of this meeting be given to the Chairman for his attention to the business of the day.

(Signed) William Pearson Secretary

---

[40] This is yet another indication of the heavy weight of public conviction that a crisis was imminent, which pervaded the contents of many of the documents included by Collett, both personal and official, reflecting the opinion of much of the country.

[41] Although it was not included in Collett's copy of the minutes, the handwritten minutes show that at least one Volunteer Infantry Troop in Ipswich was supported to the sum of £50, and that two Wangford ones, at Bungay and Beccles, were not supported at the time because they gave no indication of how much money they needed. The committee appeared unwilling to commit to long-term support of the infantry, in the same way they did the yeomanry and militia.

[42] Some towns obviously had some volunteers for the cavalry but not enough for a full Troop. It would be interesting to know which they were.

Stowmarket September 25th 1794

At a General Meeting of Subscribers for the internal defence of the county of Suffolk, held here this day, pursuant to an adjournment, Edward Tyrell Esq in the Chair.

The state of the subscription was reported to amount to £7067 13s 6d.

A44 A45 That this Committee be adjourned to Thursday the 9th day of October to be here holden at twelve oClock at noon when a full meeting of Subscribers will be particularly requiste.

Stowmarket 9th October 1794

At a General Meeting of Subscribers for the internal defence of the county of Suffolk, held here   Sir John Rous in the Chair.

The state of the subscription was reported to amount to £7064 11s 6d.

It being the opinion of the Committee that the allowing of clothing to Infantry would induce many persons to enrol who are not within the description of respectable householders and might be detrimental to the service of the army or Militia, ordered that the expense of accoutrements, clothing and pay of sergeants and drummers of any corps of infantry to be raised within the county be allowed out of the subscription when the officers shall have received their commissions.

That this Committee be adjourned to Thursday the 6th day of November to be here holden at twelve o'clock at noon.

A47 Stowmarket 6th November 1794

At a General Meeting of Subscribers for the internal defence of the county of Suffolk.

                 Philip Bowes Broke in the Chair.

The state of the subscription was reported to amount to £7109 15s.

That Thomas Maynard Esq be recommended to Right Honorable the Earl of Euston Lord Lieutenant of the County to be Captain of a Troop of Yeomanry Cavalry to be raised in the Hundred of Hoxne and adjoining Hundreds; George Smith Esq, late lieutenant in 15th Regiment of Light Dragoons to be Lieutenant and Francis Gilbert Yaxley Luke Esq to be Cornet.[43]

A48 Stowmarket 8th January 1795

At a General Meeting of the subscribers for the internal defence of the county of Suffolk.

                 Philip Bowes Broke in the Chair.

The state of the subscription was reported to amount to £7130.

That the following noblemen and gentlemen be, and are, recommended to the Right Honourable the Earl of Euston Lord Lieutenant of the county for commissions, viz the Right Honourable Charles Cornwallis Lord Brome, to be Captain of a Troop to be raised in the Hundreds of Thedwastry and Thingoe, and adjoining hundreds, and William Fowkes Esq to be Lieutenant;[44] Robert Sparrow Esq to be Captain of a Troop, to be raised in the hundred of Wangford, Mutford and Lothingland and adjoining hundreds; Robert Rede Esq to be Lieutenant, and George Brown Bohun Esq to be Cornet.[45]

---

[43] This was the 3rd Hoxne and Hartismere Troop.

[44] These are the officers of the 4th Bury Troop.

[45] The 5th Troop was the last to be supported out of the Subscription.

That the resolution passed at the General Meeting on 12th day of June last, impowering the Captain of each Troop to draw for the county allowance, when he shall report to the Lord Lieutenant his Troop to be complete, be rescinded, and that he shall, and is hereby impowered, to draw for the said allowance when twenty names shall appear on his roll, and for every additional five names until his Troop shall be complete.

That the resolution passed at the General Meeting held here on the 28th of May **A50** and 12th of June respectively the county allowance for the Yeomanry Cavalry, be rescinded; and that in lieu of such allowance, the Commanding Officer be allowed to draw for the sum of Twelve Pounds for each Volunteer, for the uniform, helmet, great coat, sadlery and accoutrements for each troop, in the following proportions, viz £4 for the uniform, £1 for the helmet, £1 18s for the great coat and £2 2s for sadlery and accoutrements.

That the Resolution passed at a General Meeting held here on 10th of July last, for raising two additional Troops be rescinded, and that it appears to this meeting, upon a review of the state of the fund, and estimates of the expenses for raising each troop, that the subscription is not competent to furnish more than five troops. A List of such Subscribers to the Plan for the Internal Defence of the County of Suffolk as have paid in their Subscriptions, published in pursuance of a Resolution passed at a General Meeting, held at Stowmarket on the 8th January instant.[46]

Stowmarket March 12th 1795

At a General Meeting for the internal defence of the county of Suffolk.

Philip Bowes Broke in the Chair.

The subscription is £7109 15s.

A56 May 7th 1795

At a General Meeting of subscribers   Richard Ray in the Chair.
The subscription is £7109 15s.[47]

A58 March 31st 1796 Stowmarket

At a General Meeting of subscribers   Philip Bowes Broke in the Chair.

It is resolved that this Committee do adjourn to Thursday 16th day of June next, to be then here holden, at Twelve o'clock at noon; when and where a General Meeting of subscribers to the Fund for internal defence of the county, is most earnestly requested, and that the several Captains do deliver in their amounts to that day, as this committee are convinced of the necessity of taking into serious consideration the state of the said fund, and the expediency of continuing it by further subscriptions, so as to render it adequate to the keeping up the several Troop of Yeomanry Cavalry during the continuance of the war, according to the act in that case made and provided. That the thanks of this meeting be given to the Chairman.

Stowmarket June 16th 1796

At a General Meeting of subscriber   Philip Bowes Broke Esq in the Chair.

---

[46] A51–54, list of subscribers and the amount they paid. See Appendix 1, Introduction pp. xvii–xviii and footnote 43.

[47] Further general meetings were held and recorded on 2 July 1795, 27 August 1795, 22 October 1795, 14 January 1796 and 18 February 1796. Not included.

A59 It appearing to this committee, on inspecting the accounts of different Troops of Yeomanry Cavalry, that the balance in hand is insufficient to support them much longer, and that the expediency of continuing them should be taken into consideration by the county.

Resolved, That this Committee do adjourn to Saturday in the week of the ensuing assizes, to be there holden at the Angel Inn, Bury St. Edmunds.

William Pearson Secretary

Angel Inn Bury 16th July 1796

At a General Meeting of the Grand Juries and others, subscribers for strengthening the internal defence of the county of Suffolk, held here this day pursuant to adjournment.

John Clayton Esq High Sheriff in the Chair.

It appearing to this Committee, that by a letter received by the High Sheriff from the Right Honourable Lord Euston, Lord Lieutenant of this county, that the present balance of the Yeomanry Fund is inadequate to the maintaining and keeping up the several Corps of Yeomanry Cavalry in this county.

It is resolved, That the High Sheriff be and is, hereby requested to convene a General Meeting of the Committee to deliberate on the necessity and expediency of keeping up such corps by further subscription, on Thursday 4th day of August next, at Eleven o'clock at forenoon, to be holden at the White Hart Inn, in Stowmarket in this county. This resolution to be published in the Ipswich and Bury papers. That the thanks of this meeting be given to the High Sheriff for his polite attention to the Business of the day.

William Pearson Secretary

A60 Stowmarket 4th August 1796

At a General Meeting of the County of Suffolk, held here This day, to an Advertisement from the High Sheriff at the request of the Grand Juries assembled at the last Assizes.

John Clayton Esq High Sheriff in the Chair.

It is resolved, That it appears to this meeting that the Money raised by subscription, pursuant to resolutions made at Stowmarket, on the 3rd day of April 1794, has been wholly expended, in making an augmentation of seven men per company to the battalions of militia, and in raising and keeping up Five Troops of Yeomanry Cavalry; and further that some of the commanding officers are in advance.

That it is highly expedient to complete and keep up the said Five troops of Yeomanry Cavalry during the war pursuant to the resolution of the General Meeting held 17th day of April 1794.

That it appears to this meeting expedient to raise such further such sum by subscription, as shall be sufficient for the said purposes, and to pay the arrears.

That whenever the said five Troops of Yeomanry Cavalry are disbanded, the accounts shall be made up with all reasonable expedition, and whatever money raised by this subscription shall remain in hand, shall be returned to the subscribers in proportion to their several subscriptions.

That the following Bankers shall be impowered to receive subscriptions, namely Alexander and Co and Crickett and Co Ipswich, Brooke and Co Woodbridge,[48]

---

[48] Collett was a partner in this bank.

Spink and Co Oakes and Co Bury, Rede and Co Beccles, Badely and Co Halesworth, Kenn and Co Sudbury, Eaton and Co Newmarket.

It appears to this meeting of considerable importance, that the subscriptions should
be raised as speedy as possible, the subscribers are earnestly requested to pay their
several subscriptions to the said Bankers, on or before the 1st day of September
next, on which day the Bankers are hereby required to transmit a list of names to
the Secretary, in order for publication, and to pay to the Treasurer the several sums
they may have respectively received.

That Messr Spink and Cass and Crickett and Co be Treasurers to this subscription.

That the High Sheriff be requested to acquaint the Lord Lieutenant with the resolutions this day passed, and to return to him thanks for his liberal offer of £100 made
to this subscription contained in a letter from his Lordship to the High Sheriff, and
read at this meeting.

That every person who has or may subscribe to the county fund, be and is hereby
requested to attend at a general and open Committee to be holden at the White Hart
at A61 Stowmarket on Thursday the 8th day of September at Eleven o'Clock in the
forenoon.

That Mr. William Pearson (Under Sheriff) be appointed Secretary.

That these resolutions be published in the Ipswich and Bury papers.

That the thanks of this meeting be given to the High Sheriff for his attendance and
conduct in the chair.   William Pearson Secretary

Stowmarket 8th September 1796

At a General Meeting of the Subscribers, for strengthening the internal defence of
the County of Suffolk, held here this day, pursuant to adjournment.

John Clayton Esq High Sheriff in the Chair.

It appears to this Committee by accounts sent from several Bankers in Ipswich, Bury
and Woodbridge that the money subscribed amounts to £728 19s 6d and that from
the following towns viz Beccles, Halesworth, Sudbury and Newmarket no amount
has been sent in.

Resolved, That the Bankers already authorised, and also the Bankers at Bungay be
requested to receive subscriptions, until the 10th day of October next inclusive, when
they are to make up their accounts, and transmit them to the Secretary.

That this meeting be adjourned to Saturday, 15th day of October next, to be then
holden at the Angel Inn Bury at Twelve o'clock at noon where the attendance of all
those who have, or mean to subscribe, is earnestly requested, as the subscriptions
will be then closed.

That the thanks of this Meeting be given to the High Sheriff

William Pearson Secretary

Bury October 15th 1796

At a General Meeting of the Subscribers for strengthening the Internal Defence of
the County of Suffolk, held here This day pursuant to adjournment.

John Clayton Esq High Sheriff in the Chair.

Resolved, That it appears from such an examination of the accounts this day laid
before the Meeting as have been in their power to procure, that the balance remaining
in hand including the new subscriptions, amounts to £901 3s 6d is not more than
sufficient to discharge the arrears due, and to continue the Yeomanry Corps for a
quarter of a year.

That it is the opinion of this Committee, that untill the establishment receives a more adequate support, the above state of the subscription will not allow of the troops to be exercised oftener than once a month.

A62 That from this account of the funds subscribed, and their appropriation, it appears, that a General Meeting of the county should be called for the express purpose of taking the same into consideration, in order that the inhabitants of this county may be informed, either that this measure of arming the Yeomanry for its Internal Defence must be abandoned, at the very period when His Majesty has communicated to his Parliament the intention of the enemy to invade these kingdoms, or that some new and more efficient mode of support must be adopted. That the High Sheriff be requested to call a County Meeting for the above purpose to be held at the White Hart Stowmarket on 5th day of January next.

William Pearson Secretary

I do hereby convene a Meeting to be held, pursuant to the above Resolution, at which I earnestly request an early attendance, as the Chair will be taken at precisely at 12 o'clock.

John Clayton[49]

Stowmarket April 6th 1797

At an adjourned General Meeting of Subscribers for strengthening the internal defence of the County of Suffolk, held here This day pursuant to adjournment.

Richard Ray in the Chair.

Resolved, That it appears from an examination of such amounts this day laid before the Meeting as they have been able to procure, that the balance remaining in hand, of the General County Fund (including the new Subscription) amounts to £551 18s which is A63 not more than sufficient to discharge the Arrears due to the Yeomanry Corps, according to several statements delivered in by the respective Captains, up to this day; and a bill of £60 due to the Secretary.

That of the above balance of £551 18s, the sum of £401 18s appears to be in the hands of Messr Spink and Carss.

That the exhausted state of the General Fund makes it expedient that this Meeting should represent the same to the High Sheriff of this county, suggesting at the same time that it appears absolutely necessary to the existence of the Yeomanry Corps, that a County Meeting be held on as early a date as may be most convenient to the High Sheriff, to appoint, for the purpose of considering wether, at this crisis, the Yeomanry Corps should cease to be supported. That the thanks of the Meeting be given to the Chairman.

William Pearson Secretary

Stowmarket 20th April 1797

At a General Meeting of Subscribers for strengthening the Internal Defence of the County of Suffolk, held here this day, pursuant to an advertisement from the Sheriff.

Chaloner Arcedeckne Esq High Sheriff in the Chair.

An intimation having been given to this Meeting that the Government will shortly adopt some plan for the support of the several Yeomanry Corps.

---

[49] The County Meeting was postponed to 16 February and again to 6 April 1797.

Resolved, That this Meeting be adjourned to Thursday 8th day of June next to be here holden, at Twelve o'clock at noon, that the intention of the Government may be known on the subject.   Chaloner Arcedeckne High Sheriff
That the thanks of the Meeting be given to the High Sheriff.

William Pearson   Secretary

A64 Glevering Hall May 31st 1797[50]

The Captains commanding the Five Troops of Yeomanry Cavalry, having expressed a desire, that the Meeting which was to have been held at Stowmarket on Thursday 8th of June next, should be adjourned; I do hereby give notice, that such Meeting is accordingly adjourned to Thursday 13th day of July next there to be holden at Stowmarket at Twelve o'clock.[51]   Chaloner Arcedeckne High Sheriff

Glevering Hall August 8th 1797

I do hereby give notice that the Meeting of Subscribers for strengthening the Internal Defence of the County of Suffolk, which stands adjourned to Thursday the 17th August will be holden at Stowmarket on that day.
The Captains of the several Troops are requested to make up their accounts to the time, and produce them at the next Meeting.   Chaloner Arcedeckne High Sheriff

The Chair will take place precisely at Twelve oclock, and a Dinner will be prepared at two.
Memorandom   It do not appear that the meeting on 17 August was published in the County Papers.

August 17th 1797

It appears that at the meeting held at Stowmarket this day the Fund for defraying sundry Expenses of the Yeomanry Cavalry was declared to be exhausted and that no further subscription was entered into in consequence of a provision being likely to be made by the Government for the purpose.

In consequence of the County Subscription Fund being exhausted, a meeting of Non Commissioned Officers and Privates of the 2nd Troop of Loyal Suffolk Yeomanry Cavalry was held at the Crown Inn Woodbridge on Tuesday 7th November 1797, at which meeting an offer was made and unanimously agreed upon to continue their Services without any future pay.

A65 Suffolk Division of Woodbridge   May 14th 1794
Loyal Suffolk Yeomanry Cavalry 2nd Troop

We do hereby inrol ourselves to serve during the War in the 2nd Troop of Yeomanry Cavalry under the following Conditions.[52]

---

[50] Glevering Hall, just outside Wickham Market, was built between 1792 and 1794 for Chaloner Arcedeckne.
[51] It was further adjourned at the request of the Yeomanry to 17 August.
[52] This important document clearly sets out the basic conditions on which the Yeomanry were to operate throughout the war.

To have no levy Money.

To have no pay unless called out and embodied.

To find our own Horses and Cloathing.

Government to find Arms and Accoutrements as is usually Allowed to the Cavalry.

Government to allow pay for one Sergeant per Troop.

The Sergeant and his Horse to be Billeted at such places within the County as any Justice with the approbation of the Lord Lieutenant shall appoint.

The Horse and Cloathing for him to be provided at the expense of the Subscription.

To be Exercised only at such times and places as shall be fixed upon, with the approbation of the Lord Lieutenant.

To be liable to be embodied on appearance of Invasion of the County and to be called upon by order of His Majesty, or by the Lord Lieutenant or Sheriff of the County, for the suppression of Riots and Tumults within the County. One fourth to be liable to called out of the County by special direction of his Majesty in case of actual Invasion or of Invasion of any adjoining County or for the suppression of Riot and Tumult therein in Aid of any Corps which may be raised for the defence and security of the same, provided a mutual agreement shall have been entered into with the Corps so raised, in any adjoining County mutually to assist each other for the suppression of Riots and Tumults therein respectively. In either case, when and actually in Service, to receive pay as Dragoons and be liable to the provisions of the Mutiny Bill.

And as it is probable that such Persons (who for various reasons cannot serve themselves) may be desirous of rendering every assistance in their power towards the formation of these Troops and several Gentlemen may wish to furnish Men and Horses besides serving themselves it is resolved to accept Men and Substitutes under the following Resolutions, That they shall be men of good Character and that they shall have been accustomed to Riding; that they shall have a fixed Residence in the County, (of course Menial Servants must be deemed improper) that they shall not be Persons whose Situation make it at all probable that they should enlist in the Army or Navy, or Militia, and that they shall be approved by the Commanding Officer of the Troop in which they serve. These Men and Substitutes to be Equipped as those themselves and at the Expense of those persons in whose place they serve and by them furnished.

Every person acting as a Private to be allowed out of the Fund of the Subscription 2s per day for each day of exercise for the use of his Horse if required.

To Muster at Woodbridge on the Town Hall there on a Day to be appointed by the Commanding Officer of the Troop.

And further We do hereby pledge ourselves to attend in Person (or by our Substitutes duly enrolled) on the Days and at the Places to be approved by the Lord Lieutenant for Exercise within the Division.

A66 Copy of the Officers Commissions of 2nd Troop of Loyal Suffolk Yeomanry Cavalry by His Majesty George R (Seal)

George the Third by the Grace of God, King of Great Britain, France and Ireland Defender of the Faith etc. To our Trusty and Well beloved Philip Bowes Broke Esquire Greeting. We reposing especial Trust and Confidence in your Loyalty, Courage and good Conduct, do, by these Presents, constitute and appoint you to be Captain of a Suffolk Troop of Gentlemen and Yeomanry, but not to take Rank in Our Army except during the time of the said Corps being called into actual Service. You are therefore to take the said Troop into your Care and Charge, and duly to Exercise as well the Officers as Soldiers thereof in Arms, and to use your best Endeavours to keep them in good Order and Discipline. And We do hereby Command Them to obey You as their Captain, and you are to observe and follow such Orders and Directions from Time to Time, as you shall receive from Us or any other [of] your Superior Officers, according to the Rules and Discipline of War, in pursuance of the Trust hereby reposing in You.

Given at our Court of St James's the Ninth Day of May 1794 In the Thirty fourth Year of our Reign   By His Majesty's Command   Portland

Entered with Secretary of State for War M Lewis
Entered with the Commissary General Musters William Woodman
To Philip Bowes Broke Esq Captain of a Suffolk Troop of Gentlemen and Yeomanry[53]

A68 **Minutes of the days of Exercise and of sundry Occurrences on those days, also of various other matters relating to the 2nd Troop of Loyal Suffolk Yeomanry Cavalry from the commencement of their Institution**

The Non-commissioned Officers and Privates by a Resolution of the Committee of the County Subscription Fund (held at Stowmarket) are allowed Two Shillings per day per Man for the use of their Horse on days of Muster to be paid from the said fund.

In complyance with the above Resolution of the Committee, the non-commissioned Officers and Privates received pay for their attendance as under viz
From 7th October 1794 to 29th September 1797 Total 3179 days at 2s per day amount to £312 18s.[54]

At a meeting of the Committee 15th October 1796, it was resolved the Troops from that time should be allowed pay for one day in a Month only for exercise for the use of their Horse 2s per man and on 17th August 1797 it was Resolved by the Committee that the pay for the use of their Horses should Cease in consequence of the County Subscription for that purpose being exhausted.

Wednesday July 30th 1794
The first day of Muster of the Troop, at Head Quarters Woodbridge.[55] Being dismounted We adjourned to the Town Hall and having 56 members present Captain Broke in a very handsome Speech addressed us on the occasion of the meeting and of our Arming in defence of our King and Country. The Troops in return expressed

---

[53] Copies of commissions were also included for Francis Brooke Gentleman as lieutenant, Mileson Edgar as cornet and Dr Richard Frank, chaplain.

[54] This shows that Collett started writing the volume at least three years retrospectively and must have been drawing on a variety of sources to help him, possibly including his own memories, his notes, a private diary, evidence such as the muster book of the Troop and other material that he borrowed or safely stored.

[55] The headquarters of the Troop were in Woodbridge Town Hall, where they held their meetings. Also known as the Shire Hall, it stands on the Market Hill in the centre of Woodbridge. It was built by Thomas Seckford in 1575 as a hall for meetings of the magistrates in Quarter Session, hence its other name, Sessions Hall. The ground floor was open to serve as a corn market until it was filled in in the nineteenth century. See Plate 10.

their satisfaction on his being appointed Captain and of their readiness to go upon duty under his or their Officers Command at all times when called upon. The sundry non-commissioned Officers were nominated. A Pattern of a Uniform Jacket was produced by Captain Broke some alterations in same being proposed and adopted orders where given for the full Equipment of the Troop as early as conveniently it could be done. William Kell was appointed Trumpeter to the Troop. The business of the day being finished, Adjourned to Tuesday 26th August.

Tuesday August 26th 1794 General Muster

The Troop met at Bromeswell at 10 o'clock in the Morning being their first Muster on Horseback present 57 volunteers. Resolved to exercise in three divisions as under On Tuesday September 9th at Bromeswell, Thursday 11th Martlesham, Friday 12th Marlesford Common Tuesday September 16th Bromeswell, Thursday 18th Levington, Tuesday 23rd Bromeswell, Thursday September 25th Levington, Friday 26th Marlesford, Tuesday 30th Martlesham.[56]

A69 The Troop continued to meet at Bromeswell, Martlesham and Levington as agreed upon sundry days of Muster at such times as are noted in the Muster Roll, from the 26th August 1794 to the 13th January 1795.[57]
The first time the Troop met in uniform was on 2nd December 1794.
Corporal Joseph Scott from H.R.H Prince of Wales Regiment 10th Light Dragoons joined the Troop being recommended to Captain Broke by the Right Honourable Lord Euston and Lieutenant Colonel Cartwright to be attached to the Troop as a drill Sergeant. He was sent on tryal under a Furlough of 61 days. On 11 March 1795 he went to London and waited on Lord Euston and Colonel Cartwright to settle his discharge from the 10th Light Dragoons which discharge was granted on condition of his supplying the Regiment with two recruits in the place of himself. Having procured his discharge he returned to Captain Broke on Saturday 13th March at which time he signed the Muster Roll and was appointed Drill Sergeant to the Troop.[58] Sergeant Joseph Scott having joined the Troop and being appointed to drill Sergeant, a Barn was hired of Mr Jonathan Denny at Woodbridge and fitted out for the purpose of a riding house for the practice of the Men and Horses in the Evolution of Wheeling, forming etc etc in which during the Winter we were almost in constant practice and was very useful.

Tuesday March 10th 1795 General Muster

The Troop met at Head Quarters Woodbridge on Parade[59] in the Market Place at 11 o'Clock marched thence to Bromeswell and was Exercised in the sundry Evolutions by Sergeant Scott being his first time of Exercising the Troop.

---

[56] Divisions enabled a smaller group who lived near each other to practise more conveniently and more regularly.

[57] This summary is further evidence that Collett was writing a considerable time afterwards. Later, he was assiduous in writing very detailed accounts.

[58] The government, by paying for a sergeant for each Troop, recognised the need for some professional training if the volunteers, although good horsemen, were to be transformed into a disciplined, well-trained unit capable of working with the regular army if necessary.

[59] The members assembled and paraded for general musters on the Market Hill before moving off for exercises to fields where there was enough space for a sizeable number of cavalry to manoeuvre to practise their evolutions (movements).

Prior to Sergeant Scott's joining the Troop (on our General Muster days) Sergeant Mellish from the First Dragoon Guards used to assist Captain Broke in teaching the Troop the various Evolutions etc, etc, etc.

The First Return of the Troop was this day sent to the Secretary of War and Adjutant General by order of Lord Euston Lord Lieutenant of the County.

April 3rd 1795 Good Friday
Notice having been received by Express, late last Night sent for the purpose of preparing relays of Horses etc that Her Royal Highness the Princess of Wales[60] was arrived at Yarmouth and in consequence of the badness of the Weather, intending landing this Morning. Orders were sent to the Troop to Muster at ten o'clock on the Market Place Woodbridge, Mounted and fully Equipped A70 for the purpose of escorting Her Royal Highness through this Division. Carriages and Horses having been prepared and waiting in readiness for Her conveyance upon the Road from Yarmouth to London.[61] Every preparation was made upon the Road for Her accommodation and the Garrisons at Ipswich, Colchester and Chelmsford etc under Arms waiting in expectation of her arrival. In the Morning it was very thick Fog about 9 or 10 o'clock the fog being dispersed it was afterwards a very fine day.

We were under Arms all day until 8 o'clock in the Evening when on the arrival of the Mail Coach from Yarmouth advice was received that in consequence of the day proving so very fine and the wind fair with a fresh Breeze, Her Royal Highness sailed from Yarmouth in the forenoon for Greenwich, to the great disappointment of every person from Yarmouth to London who assembled in very great numbers upon the road with the expectation of seeing her pass.

Number of Volunteers present was 51. 8 absent not having notice in time and one Ill.

March 31st 1795 Hired a Field of Mr Jonathan Denny for the Troop to Exercise in till Christmas next.[62]

April 28th 1795 The Troop agreed to meet in three divisions to practice the Pistol Motions and Firings etc at Wickham Thursday 30th April, Woodbridge 1st May and Levington 2nd May.

Memorandum No particular occurrences are noted in the muster rolls on the day of meeting or at other times from the above dates until the second day of June when the Standard was consecrated.

(Circular)   **Woodbridge   May 23rd 1795**
Sir
I am desired by the Commanding Officer of the Second Troop of Loyal Suffolk Yeomanry to inform you, that the Troop is required to meet at General Muster at Woodbridge on Tuesday, 2nd June next, at 10 o'clock in the Morning, in order

---

60 Caroline of Brunswick married her cousin George, Prince of Wales in March 1795 and scandal accompanied the marriage throughout.

61 The road between Yarmouth and Ipswich, which passed through Woodbridge, had been turnpiked as recently as 1785 (D. Dymond and E. Martin, eds, *An Historical Atlas of Suffolk* (Ipswich, 1999), pp. 126–7). This allowed the fast service of mail coaches to London.

62 It was a requirement that the place of their meetings was recorded at a time when the government feared that unauthorised meetings might lead to protest and ferment unrest.

to march to Church here, and there remain under Arms during the Ceremony of consecrating the Royal Standard.[63] You are particularly entreated to appear with an exact neatness and propriety in all your appointments of Uniform, Arms, Horse and Furniture; in cases when the Boots or Breeches knees are not of sufficient length for the Boot Strap behind, to be fastened to a button in the Ham, the mode most military (and which the Captain beg leave first to recommend), it is hoped that if the Boot Garters are used, that they will consist of as small a piece of Leather as possible, be fixed below the Knee and of the same white as the Breeches.[64] After Divine service, the Troop will go through the Evolutions in the Field, and on their return, are requested to Dine at 3 o'clock with the Officers in the Crown Inn in this Town.

I am, Sir, your most humble servant   Cornelius Collett Quarter Master[65]

A71 Thursday June 2nd 1795

General Muster and Consecration of the Royal Standard

The Troop met and mustered on the Parade in the Market Place, Woodbridge at the time appointed and from the Parade they marched to the Abbey in the following order to take up the Standard which was deposited there, being the Residence of Francis Brooke Lieutenant in the Troop.[66]

Order of March[67]

The Guard covered, on each side at certain distances along the Line of the Troop from Front to Rear. Being arranged as above, with Swords drawn the Troop marched by slow time to the Abbey where the Royal Standard being lodged the Commanding Officer Captain Broke, received the same according to the usual form of delivering from a Window, the Music playing at the same time God Save The King. The Captain on receiving the Standard delivered it into the Hands of the Chaplain (the Reverend Dr. Frank) who bears it into the Church (marching on the Right of the Captain) and passing up the Centre Aisle to the Altar, there forming, he bends the Staff down towards the Communion Table in Order that the Sergeant of the Guard may uncase the Standard, which being done the Chaplain then slowly raised the same and delivered it to the Sergeant who placed it in the Centre of the Rails, with three Files on his Right and three on his Left forming a Standard Guard. The Chaplain then retired to habit himself and the A72 Captain took his place where he stood, the Lieutenant and the Cornet in Front of the Captain and Guard, the Troops where ranged on each side the Middle Aisle of the Church. On entering the Church the Officers and Guards Saluted and taking off their Helmets carried their Sabres in that position during the time of Service in the Church. The Files returned Sabres on entering the Church, and also taking off their Helmets remained standing during the Service, with the remainder of the Guard and Quarter Master in the Rear at the lower end of the Aisle. After the Sermon the Chaplain returned to the Altar, the Lieutenant and Cornet advanced two Steps, and facing inwards there remained during the Consecration. On the Chaplain approaching the Standard, the Sergeant of the Guard assisted in bowing at the same time towards the Altar, during the time

---

63 This took place in the large medieval parish church of St Mary's, almost adjoining the market square, where Collett was one of the churchwardens.

64 This was the first time the Troop would appear at an official occasion, and Captain Broke was concerned to ensure they appeared at their best.

65 Collett was appointed quartermaster on the Troop's formation in 1794.

66 Francis Brooke, lieutenant of the 2nd Troop, lived at The Abbey, Woodbridge, next to the parish church. Built on the site of the Augustinian Priory, it was once the Manor House of Woodbridge and much altered by Thomas Seckford.

67 Collett included a basic plan, omitted here.

Plate 11. Print of St Mary's parish church, where the Troop's royal standard was consecrated and where the new set of eight bells was celebrated. Next to it was The Abbey, the former manor house of Woodbridge, built on part of the site of the Augustinian Priory and home of Francis Brooke, the Troop's first Lieutenant, with some of his fields used by the Troop. The roof of the Market Hall can be seen in the background. © SROI, Fitch Collection HD 480/4, f. 98, no. 36. Photograph by Mike Durrant

of prayer of Consecration the Chaplin extended his Hand over the Standard after the form of Benediction. After the Consecration he delivered the Standard to the Captain who then delivered it to the Cornet, the Troops at the same instant drawing Swords. The Captain on delivering the Standard to the Cornet addressed him in an elegant speech on the occasion.[68] <the ceremony of Consecration being finished the Troops marched from the Church to the Abbey and the Horses being in the Meadow in readiness, they Mounted and marched to the field hired of Mr. Denny for our use on days of Exercise.>

A most excellent Sermon was preached by the Reverend Dr Frank (Chaplin of the Troop) and although the Church was in every part as full as it could possibly be, such was the good order and attention observed by the Congregation that every word from the Pulpit etc was most distinctly heard.

The Standard when placed on the Altar, the Guard over the same with the Officers in the Chancel and the Troops on each side of the middle Aisle with the Quarter Master and the remainder of the Guard at the lower end of the Church, together with the numerous Congregation, presented to the View of each Spectator a most pleasing sight and to their feelings an Object truly grand and awfull.

---

[68] Collett appears to have lost his concentration at this point, a very unusual occurrence, because the next three or four lines refer to the end of the service.

There being two Troops of the first Dragoon Guards under the Command of Captain Elliot Quartered in the Town, they where ordered on duty upon the occasion (dismounted) and were Stationed on each side of the Street and up the Church Yard forming a passage and clearing the way A73 as we advanced with the Standard on our approach to and return from the Church, the Officers Saluting as we passed. Being received in the Field a piece of Pasture land in occupation of Mr Denny belonging to Mr Robert Cooper, the Troop was Exercised in the various Evolutions in practice at the time. There being a small Grove at one end of the Field through which the Troops passed the firing on their approach and retreat from the same had a very pleasing effect. The day was very fine and the Troop performed the various Evolutions much to the satisfaction of the Spectators who were very numerous, in a general opinion there was not less than five Thousand people in the field.[69]

On our return the Standard was deposited at the Abbey and the Troop discharged from Duty.

The Members of the Troop, the Officers of the 1st Dragoon Guards Quartered here, (by invitation) with several Gentleman of the Neighbourhood dined together at the Crown Inn and the remainder of the day was spent in a pleasant and sociable meeting much to the satisfaction of all present.

The number present on duty was 61, one in the field Ill and one not able to attend being ill.

No memoranda appear on the Muster Roll of occurrences in the Troop from 2nd June prior to the 3rd July.[70]

July 3rd 1795

About three weeks since the Labourers etc of Hollesley, Alderton and that neighbourhood assembled and went to sundry Farmers Houses demanding a reduction in the price of Corn and Provisions. On their arrival at Dr Franks his being in Yorkshire and not expected to return soon, they then went away to Mr John Whimper who addressed them in a very proper manner on the occasion without any attempts (excepting by threats) to commit depredations. They determined on the Doctors return to wait on him and demand a reduction in the price of Corn etc etc, and fixed on this day for that purpose. Dr Frank returning prior to the time; directed inquiry to be made by every channel likely to gain information of their intentions. It was generally considered they would at the time assemble in a very large body from various parts of the Country. In consequence of such information summons's A74 were issued by order of the Magistrates for the Troop to assemble at an early hour this Morning on the Parade at Woodbridge completely equipped, armed, and prepared for actual service. The Troop being assembled each man received Eighteen rounds of ball cartridge and at 6 o'clock marched from the parade to Bromeswell in readiness to receive further orders from the Magistrates. At Bromeswell we had a field day, after which we advanced by Skirmishing parties towards Sutton and Hollesley and being met by Dr Frank he informed us the expected Riot was in his opinion prevented by the prudent measures which had been taken for the purpose, and in consequence of the same our further services on this day was not required.

---

[69] One of the major services the Yeomanry provided at this time of great uncertainty in the country was to act as a reassuring boost to the morale of the local population.

[70] Collett was obviously using memoranda added to the muster roll to prompt his memory of events since he was writing his account retrospectively.

Having received this information, we returned to Woodbridge about one o'clock and where dismissed from any further duty on this day.

NB On the Parade in the Morning a very considerable number of the lower class of people assembled who it was observed appeared much agitated on seeing the Ball Cartridges delivered out.

General Muster November 27th 1795

In consequence of the non attendance of many of the Members of the Troop on days of Muster the following Resolutions were this day unanimously entered into by the members present and information of the same sent to all the absentees.[71]

Resolved, That in future, every person who may be prevented attending the Weekly Exercise, General Muster, or any other Meeting of the Troop, do send to the Captain or Commanding Officer in the Field, a Note stating the reason for his absence, or in case, from the suddenness of the occurrence he should not have Time to write, that he should request some one of the Troop to deliver Verbally the Cause assigned for such Absence. That Sickness, Lameness, the Death of a Relative or Friend and all causes which from their Nature and Consequences are so urgent and affecting the Concerns of the Individual as to require immediate attendance, be considered as reasonable and honourable Causes for Non-attendance, and that the Charger being Lame or Ill be considered in the same light,

That the Muster Roll be called immediately after the Troop is told off;[72]

That every person joining after the Troop is told off, and everyone who was absent on the preceding day of Exercise, or other Meeting, and did not send in Writing, or otherwise, an Excuse for his absence, be formed into a Detachment to be Drilled by the Sergeant Major, in the Field, in the practice of such Evolutions and Manual Exercise, as, in consequence of A75 Absence, he may have omitted to practise regularly with the Troop;

The Credit and good Order which must evidently and materially suffer without such Instructions being taken, before he falls into his station in the Ranks provided the occasion of his not joining sooner, on the omitting to send an Excuse as above, be considered as not coming within the express Meaning of the Resolution No 2 respecting urgent affairs;

That all Reasons assigned for Absence be communicated to the Captain or Commanding Officer in the Field and by him read, if committed in writing, or repeated as verbal only, at the Head of the Troop;

That the Weekly Exercise, be continued to be on the Friday at the usual Hour.

Woodbridge   December 21st 1795

Sir,   I am desired by the Commanding Officer of the Second Troop of Loyal Suffolk Yeomanry to inform you that the Troop is required to meet at General Muster, at Woodbridge, on Thursday 31st instant, precisely at 11 o'clock in the Morning mounted and dressed as usual for Exercise.[73]

Cornelius Collett Quarter Master

---

71 This is the first of many attempts to try and sort out the problem of non-attendance, which continued throughout the war and indeed beyond.

72 A military term when each member would call out his number in sequence to determine the total present.

73 Such reminders of meetings continued throughout the three volumes, individually at first, and later making use of the local newspapers. These were recorded by Collett but have been omitted here to

(In Orders)   **Nacton   December 19ᵗʰ 1795**

The Captain was much pleased with the performance of the Troop in the Evolutions and Manouvres which he saw Yesterday, and likewise the general report made by Cornet Edgar respecting their improvement in Silence and Attention to Dressings in the Ranks. The Captain having lately seen Three other Troops of Yeomanry Cavalry of the County at exercise, feels he cannot with so much satisfaction to himself or consonant with the Credit of the Troop discharge the duty he owes to that high Station which he has the Honor to hold, as by communicating to them his Opinions, that they have a superiority over every other, in Neatness, Appointments, Steadiness and the Practice of Evolutions. In imparting this Observation, he derives a perculiar gratification and pleasure, to be surpassed only by the Zeal of the Troop, which has bought them to the present respectable State, and by those laudable Exertions in which they have persevered, and will not cease to observe, until they have attained that exemplary Silence and attention to Dressings in the Ranks, which will give them the First Station as Yeomanry Cavalry, in Military Order and Perfection.[74]

Philip B Broke Captain

A76 **Monday January 18ᵗʰ 1796**

Information having been last Evening sent to Edmund Jenny Esq one of His Majesty's Justices of the Peace[75] at Hasketon, by Mr Robert Rainbird, Governor of the House of Industry at Melton[76] that he had just received a Letter intimating to him it was the intention of a number of People of the lower Class in the Neighbourhood, to assemble the next morning for the purpose of attacking and Destroying the said House. Mr Jenny called on Mr Rainbird to inquire further particulars and being confirmed in the opinion of their design, sent the information to Captain Broke at Nacton who communicated the same to me about 2 o'clock this morning requesting I would wait on Mr Jenny at 6 o'clock when Mr Jenny considering from the information he had received there was every reason to expect a Riot and that it would be proper to be prepared, ordered out the Troop. I accordingly issued orders for their immediate assembly at Woodbridge and by eleven o'clock they arrived at the Crown Inn.

Many gentlemen on their march to join the Troop having passed on the Road many people Armed with Pick Axes etc on their way to the House Captain Broke with a Division of the Troop marched to Melton, leaving the remainder under my Command waiting further orders. On their arrival a Committee of the Directors and Guardians was sitting at the House and in consequence of many People having assembled in

---

avoid continuous repetition.

[74] This is an interesting example of the sort of psychology likely to be effective with members who had chosen to join the cavalry, some of whom he would have known well.

[75] Justices of the Peace were the main administrators of local government in the eighteenth century, undertaking the legal and administrative duties in the county and acting as the link between the parishes, the Lord Lieutenant and central government.

[76] The House of Industry at Melton was built in 1765, when the parishes of the hundreds of Loes and Wilford were incorporated. Such huge workhouses were established, largely in the eastern part of Suffolk, to replace individual parish poor houses, with the aim of saving money and providing more efficient poor relief. For a contemporary view of the Melton house at this period, see A. Young, *General View of the Agriculture of the County of Suffolk* [1813] (Newton Abbot, 1969), pp. 241–2. See also J. Shaw, ed., *The Loes and Wilford Poor Law Incorporation 1765–1826*, Suffolk Records Society, Volume 62, 2019.

various places in small Numbers, orders were given by the Magistrates for those Troops to search the Public Houses and to disperse all suspicious persons, they accordingly searched the Neighbourhood for several Miles round and such Persons who they received information had been assembled being alarmed at the appearance of the Troops dispersed and returned to their respective houses. Captain Broke and his party after the above Duty marched back to Woodbridge about 7 o'clock in the Evening and no further alarm taking place, discharged the Troop from any further Duty on this day.[77]

There cannot remain the least doubt that by prudent steps taken it was the means of preventing a most serious Riot taking place.

Memorandum Lieutenant Brooke was ill at Bath and Cornet Edgar confined with Gout.[78]

Margaret Street Cavendish Square February 7th 1796

Sir

Having received His Majesty's Commands (in pursuance of the Provision of an Act passed in the fourth Session of the present Parliament, for encouraging and disciplining such Corps or Companies of Men as shall voluntarily enrol themselves for the Defence of their Counties, Towns, or Coasts, or for the general Defence of the Kingdom during the present War)[79] to order the Officers, Non-commissioned Officers, and A77 Privates of the Volunteer Corps within the County of Suffolk, to be aiding and assisting in the quelling of any Riots or Tumults which may take place within the same, if called upon by the Civil Magistrate for that purpose; I must beg of you to circulate this Order throughout the different Troops of Yeomanry and Companies of Volunteer of whatever description within the County.

  I have the Honour to be Sir Your very Obedient and most Humble Servant
                     Euston

To Henry Collett Esq Clerk of the Peace[80]

Sir

In obedience to the Commands of the Lord Lieutenant, I transmit you a Copy of his Lordship's Letter to the Clerk of the Peace, and am Sir, Your most Obedient Servant
          T Notcutt Deputy Clerk of the Peace.[81]

To P B Broke Esq Nacton

April 6th 1796

Hired a Field of Mr Andrew Cockle at Woodbridge and agreed to give him Twenty Pounds for the use of the same from this time to 10th of October next.

---

77 Collett's account of what potentially could have been a serious incident is typical of his detached style throughout the text. He is concerned to give only a straightforward and factual account of events.

78 Collett was involved as next in line of seniority, but this gives a small insight into members' ordinary lives outside the yeomanry. Mileson Edgar was to suffer badly with gout throughout his time in the Yeomanry.

79 See the Act of 17 April 1794.

80 One of the people helping the Lord Lieutenant was the clerk of the peace, whom he nominated.

81 This is an illustration of how important the Lord Lieutenant was in providing the direct link with central government at a time, early in the war, when it was operating with a very minimal bureaucracy. It also shows the trickle-down method of dissemination of information and orders.

May 13th 1796

The Troop met at the usual time and place and marched to the Field hired as above for Exercise, it was a very Cold day, on our march had a heavy shower of Hail and Rain. After being in the Field about half an Hour another storm of Rain and about half past one o'clock a violent storm of Hail obliged the Troops to quit the field as the Horses could not be made to stand to face the storm.[82]

June 4th 1796 General Muster

The Troop met at the usual time the morning proving extremely Wet were prevented doing duty in the Field. It clearing up about 3 o'clock, they assembled in the Market Place and Fired a Feu de joye in Honor of his Majesty's Birth Day. At 4 o'clock we dined at the Crown Inn, and with us by invitation, several Gentlemen of the Neighbourhood and the Officers of the Queens Boys and East Kent Militia being at the time Quartered in the Town on account of the General Election for the County. We had a very pleasant meeting and concluded the day with Loyalty and the most harmonious Festivity.

June 10th 1796 General Muster

A charge of ill behaviour having been made against Trumpeter William Kell he was this day suspended on account of the same.[83]

A78 June 24th 1796

By an order of Captain Broke addressed to Lieutenant Brooke a Court was summoned to inquire with the Conduct of Trumpeter William Kell on the Charges exhibited against him the 4th Instant which Court being composed of Lieutenant Brooke, Quarter Master Collett, Sergeant Philip Gross, Corporal J Stow Baldry, John Couperthwaite and John Page. They met for the purpose of making the needful enquires and having examined Witnesses and hearing Kells defence, where of the opinion he ought to be put on Trial for same and reported their Opinion to Captain Broke who directed a Jury to be chosen in the following manner for that purpose viz In the Field after the duty of the day, the Troops formed in a Circle and Tickets in number to the Troops present (exclusive of those who sit on the Enquiry) being made out in the number to thirteen comprising the Number to sit on the Court Martial marked on as many Tickets they were put in a bag and handed round, when each person drew a Ticket on the bag being handed to him by rotation and those who drew the Numbers composed the Court Martial viz John Brand – President, John Whimper, William Pearson, Thomas Chandler, Samuel Gross, Stebing Gross, Richard Manthrop, Thomas Kimball, Robert London, Robert Moore, Henry Luffe, Tollemache Cole and Robert Clarke.

The Charges against Kell were made by John Slack Sergeant Major of the Queens Boys who deposed that Kell had grossly insulted him on the 4th June instant by abusive and indecent Language, drawing his Sword upon him and other unsoldier-like behaviour.

---

[82] Weather was a continual feature of Collett's reports, both because of the fact they were mounted troops and because of the distance and length of time spent travelling to and from Woodbridge on those same horses. They were not professional troops with nearby stables and replacement horses. Some members of the Yeomanry Cavalry might only keep one horse, which therefore had to be taken care of.

[83] Trumpeters together with sergeants were paid from government funds.

The Charge against Kell was read to the Jury by Lieutenant Brooke and Joseph Scott Sergeant Major of the Troop being called in support of same and fully confirmed by him it was not in the power of Kell to confute them although he pleaded not guilty. The Jury accordingly found him Guilty of drawing his Sword against the said John Slack etc etc and where of the opinion he should be discharged from any further Service in the Troop, which opinion was by Lieutenant Brooke delivered to Captain Broke and on the 28th instant was confirmed by him in the following order:

June 28th 1796 Dismission

I do hereby approve of the above Sentence of the Court Martial held on Friday the 24th instant and do, in conformity thereto, dismiss the said William Kell from being Trumpeter to the Second Troop of Loyal Suffolk Yeomanry, He receiving his pay up to the present Instant, and delivering up all his Cloaths, Arms, Equipment and Horse.[84]

Signed P B Broke Captain

A79 Thursday June 30th 1796

Captain Broke's order on 28th instant for Kells being dismissed the Troop was by the Captain's order read to Kell at Woodbridge by Lieutenant Brooke this day in the presence of Cornelius Collett Quarter Master and Kell was dismissed accordingly. At the same time Spencer Leek of Melton was appointed Trumpeter vice Kell.

July 22nd 1796

William Kell having delivered up his Horse with all its equipment, His cloathing, Arms and Accoutrements, with Trumpet and Bugle, they where this day given to Spencer Leek he being appointed Trumpeter to the Troop.[85]

Woodbridge   October 26th 1796

Sir

I am desired by the Commanding Officer of the Second Troop of Loyal Suffolk Yeomanry to inform you that the Troop is requested to meet at General Muster at Woodbridge on Friday 4th November next precisely at 11 o'clock in the Morning, mounted and dressed as usual for Exercise. Your attendance is particularly requested on that Day on Special Business; and it is therefore hoped by the Captain that you will do him the favour in case of your Charger being sick or lame,[86] to endeavour to attend on foot or otherwise. He trusts that nothing but positive Illness will deprive him of your presence.[87]

Cornelius Collett Quarter Master

Friday November 4th 1796 General Muster

Captain Broke having summoned the Troop to meet this day, a full attendance of members in consequence took place, and all those who were not in the field sent

---

[84] The Yeomanry could impose its own discipline, and this is an interesting example of the way it chose to implement it, involving the whole Troop.

[85] Kell was obviously in no hurry to concur.

[86] This was the only acceptable excuse for non-attendance other than illness.

[87] The language of the orders reflects the particular social make-up of the Yeomanry, emphasising that although willing to volunteer and serve as soldiers, its members remained essentially a group of gentlemen and prosperous farmers, many of whom knew each other well. This formed part of the attraction of the force.

satisfactory reasons for their not being present. The Special Business on which Captain Broke summoned the Troop in his most handsome manner communicated to them by information that Government had reason to expect the French (with whom We are now at War) where meditating and fully intend an Invasion of this Country. It was in consequence of such information his wish to be informed how far the Troop would volunteer their service in case such an event taking place.

In reply to Captain Broke the Troop unanimously volunteered their Services to Act, in any of the Counties of Essex, Suffolk and Norfolk in any way Government should please to command their Services. And the Captain was at the same time requested to communicate this Offer to the Lord Lieutenant of the County and request of him to lay the same before His Majestys Ministers.

The above resolution having been communicated as requested, the following answer was received to same by Captain Broke on the 18th December 1796.

Sir   **Margaret Street   November 5th 1796**
The very Spirited Resolution of the Second Troop of Loyal Suffolk Yeomanry Cavalry was laid before His Majesty, by the Secretary of State, and I have received through him the King's Commands, to take the early Opportunity of assuring all the Members of that respectable Troop, that his Majesty entertains a just sense of this mark of their Loyalty to him, and of their love for the Constitution of their Country. I have the honour to be Sir with much truth and respect
                Your very obedient, and most humble Servant   Euston[88]
To P Broke Esq Nacton

Captain Broke this day informed the Troop that in consequence of the County Subscription fund being nearly exhausted the Committee held at Bury 15th October last had Resolved to allow the pay of two shillings for the use of the Horse from that time for one day in a Month only. It was then resolved by the Troop to meet at General Muster one day in the Month and to assemble on such other days without the consideration of Pay as the Captain may judge proper to order them on duty. It was also this day unanimously agreed in hopes of assuring a more general attendance on every future day of Muster that from this day every member of the Troop who was absent from duty on any future Muster day (unless satisfactory reason was given to the Commanding Officer on that or the following day of muster for his having been absent) should forfeit the Sum of Two Shillings and Sixpence for non-attendance and that the money arising from such Forfeits should be applied to the Fund of the Troop in aid of Expenses of Cloathing etc etc.[89]

Monday November 7th 1796
In consequence of the Death of Mr Robert Moore of Bucklesham who departed this Life on the 2nd Instant aged 43 years, the Troop assembled on Bucklesham Common to attend his Funeral.[90] On the arrival of the Corps etc upon the Heath the Troop being previously formed the Procession took place in the following order Viz Twelve Carbineers in Front with Carbines reversed, under the direction of A81

---

88 It is interesting how personal the process seems to have been.
89 This is yet another attempt to solve the same problem of non-attendance at general musters.
90 This is a good example of a funeral with full military honours.

Sergeant Major Scott followed by the Horse of the deceased properly equipped and led by two Servants in Black Cloaks, next some friends of the deceased on Horseback, then the Hearse with the Body, next the Family in Mourning Cloaks followed by the Troop in double files with Sabres drawn and blades reversed, the Quarter Master in front and the Commissioned Officers viz Captain, Lieutenant and Cornet in the Rear, the Cornet carrying the Standard inclosed in a Case covered with Black Crape, the Helmet and Arms of the deceased placed on the top of the Hearse, reversed. We began our March at 11 o'clock and as we approached Ipswich the General of the Garrison met us with a Guard of 12 men mounted belonging to the Dragoons Quartered there, who preceded the procession through the Town and returned when we had passed it about a Mile. On our arrival at the Market Place and Barracks in St Matthews Parish the Troops of the Garrison being under Arms on the occasion, Saluted as we passed. The Streets and Houses were lined with Spectators, the Drums beating the Dead march, with the solemn sound of the Trumpet, Tolling of Bells and Slow Movement of the Procession, offered to View and Feelings of the Spectators a Scene most strikingly awfull and grand. Having passed Ipswich we arrived at Ashbocking at 4 o'clock, dismounted and the Corps being taken out of the Hearse proceeded to the Church. The service in the Church being ended the Carbineers formed on each side of the Grave the Troops on their Left with sabres reversed (points downwards) the burial service being finished, the Carbineers fired three volleys two in the air and one pointed to the Grave which was performed particularly well. The day being fine, a crowd of people collected at the Church to view the Ceremony of a Military Funeral, the conducting of which gave great satisfaction.

NB It was the first funeral in the Troop and was also the first death since the Troop was Instituted.

Adjutant General's Office   1st December 1796

The following Rules and Regulations for the Sword Exercise, are, by His Majesty's Command to be observed and practised by the Cavalry Corps in general in His Majesty's Service.[91]

By the command of Field Marshall His Royal Highness the Duke of York[92]

William Fawcett Adjutant General

A82 Rules and Regulations for the Sword Exercise being by the Command of His Royal Highness the Duke of York Published with Prints exhibiting the various Cuts and Positions on Horseback and on Foot in a Volume of 90 pages the same was purchased by the Members of the Troop for their use and Government having fixed on Newmarket being a Central situation for the Eastern Division sent proper persons there with orders to teach the Sword Exercise. Orders were at the same time Issued by the Lord Lieutenant of the County for the Sergeants of the sundry Troops of Yeomanry Cavalry who receive pay to assemble at Newmarket for the purpose of being taught under the above directions in complyance to which order Sergeant Major Scott sett off for Newmarket this day and remained there about a Month; on

---

[91] Such orders were obviously very necessary if the Yeomanry were required to work with the regular forces if the French landed.

[92] Frederick, Duke of York, was George III's second son. In February 1795 he became commander-in-chief of the British army and the volunteer forces.

his return the Troop were instructed by him at all times of General Muster and in Squads and at sundry meetings for that purpose in the intermediate time.
December 12ᵗʰ 1796

A Letter of which the following is a Copy was by order of Captain Broke delivered to each Member of the Troop
Sir
The late appearance of the French Fleet off Ireland,[93] provided to make a Descent on some part of that Country, manifestly exhibits a probability that the hostile Views of the natural and inveterate Enemy, against some part of the united Kingdoms, are founded on a plan of Invasion, regularly laid and determined upon by the Councils of France. How soon they may visit the Coasts of England, or that of this County is yet uncertain; but, from what has passed, Prudence and Self Defence require that the Troop do hold themselves in readiness on any Emergence, to assemble with the utmost Dispatch, completely armed and equipped for actual Service, on Summons thereof. I have therefore to request that you will be careful to have your Arms, Accoutrements and Furniture, Sword Knot, great Coats, Straps, and others, where defective, repaired or resupplied, a good Flint in Pistol, and a spare one in pocket. In order that the above may be in a state of Military Exactness, capable of bearing the nicest Inspection, and that you may be furnished with the necessary Bags, and Huzzar Cloaks, which will be made up if possible by that time, the next muster is postponed to 20ᵗʰ instant.
Feeling it incumbent on me, I beg leave further to observe, that in pursuance of certain Acts of Parliament, lately passed, containing Privileges and Exemptions to Yeomanry Corps, I am strictly enjoined to return those only as Effective, who punctually attend the Days of Exercise; except where prevented by Illness, or lameness of Charger or very urgent Business. Trusting to your Zeal and Alacrity to attribute the freedom of this Address to the same motives which urges you, to maintain so honourably the Credit of the Troop.
I remain with much Esteem, Sir, Your most obliged Friend and Captain,

Philip B Broke

Nacton   January 7ᵗʰ 1797[94]

A84 Friday January 20ᵗʰ 1797 General Muster
The Troop met this day in complyance with a summons in Captain Broke's letter of 7ᵗʰ Instant and where Exercised in the usual Evolutions. Sergeant Major Scott being returned from Newmarket, he this day began to teach each Troop in the use of the Broad Sword as practised in the Austrian army (in complyance with his Majesty's Command on 1ˢᵗ December last). Orders where given by Captain Broke for him to attend the Troops in Subdivision Meetings at times which were appointed for same. Saddle Bags were delivered to the Troops on duty this day also Huzzar Cloaks.[95]
The next meeting ordered on February 1797 next.

---

[93] The French had attempted to land at Bantry Bay but failed because of extreme bad weather. See p. xxxiii.
[94] It is interesting how soon the news reached them.
[95] The government at last seemed to be becoming more serious about properly equipping the volunteer forces.

Friday February 3rd 1797 General Muster
The Troop met this day and being dismounted marched into Mr F Brooke's meadow and practised the use of the Sword Exercise on foot, at the same time a Sergeant of the Oxford Blues from Ipswich with Sergeant Major Scott performed the Six Divisions on Horseback, also the attack and defence in speed etc; much to the satisfaction of the Spectators being the first time of their having seen anything of the kind.

Friday March 3rd 1797 The Troop Met at the usual time and place and practised the Sword Exercise on Horseback being their first meeting for that purpose at General Muster. Their performance gave general satisfaction to their Officers and spectators present.

Sir   **Woodbridge   April 8th 1797**
I am desired by the Commanding Officer of the Second Troop Loyal Suffolk Yeomanry Cavalry to inform you that the Troop is required to meet at General Muster at Woodbridge on Friday 28th Instant precisely at 11 o'clock in the Morning, mounted and dressed and Equipped with Cloak Pantaloons and Saddle bags.
  (Circular)   Cornelius Collett Quarter Master

Friday April 2nd 1797
The Troop met at 11 o'Clock Equipped (being the first time) with Cloaks, Overalls and Saddle Bags. Company practised the usual Evolutions and Sword Exercise. Many respectable Spectators in the Field who were much pleased with Sword Exercise etc.

                                     Whitehall   June 1st 1797
My Lord
The king having thought fit, with Advice from his Privy Council, to issue the within Proclamation for suppressing the treasonable and rebellions Proceedings therein set forth; for apprehending and bring to Justice the Persons concerned in them, their Aiders and Abettors. I have the honor to signify to your Lordship His Majesty's Commands, that you should immediately communicate the same to the Officers commanding the Corps of Yeomanry Cavalry and Volunteer Infantry within the County of Suffolk with special Instructions to them, that they and their respectable Corps shall be aiding and assisting to the Civil Magistrates, in apprehending and securing all persons concerned in the same rebellious Proceedings, their Aiders and Abettors and to attend to the Requisitions which shall be made to them by the Magistrates for that purpose.[96]
    I am, my Lord, Your Lordship's most obedient Humble Servant
                                          Portland[97]
To Lord Lieutenant of the County of Suffolk

---

[96] A84–87, 'A Proclamation for Suppressing of the Mutinous and Treasonable Proceedings of the Crews of certain of our Ships at the Nore' has been omitted because it refers only to seamen and mariners. It concerns the two naval mutinies of 1797, at Spithead (16 April to 15 May) and at the Nore (12 May to 13 June), which were largely about the need for better living conditions and more pay, although the government feared revolution and it shocked the country, coming so soon after the French attempted invasions.

[97] The Duke of Portland was the Home Secretary.

Sir   By command of the Lord Lieutenant, I transmit to you a Copy of his Majesty's Proclamation, and the Secretary of State's Letter to the Lord Lieutenant,
                    I am Sir Your most obedient Servant   Philip B Broke
Nacton 13th June 1797
The Letters of which the above are Copies and Proclamation was delivered to each member of the Troop.

Friday June 2nd 1797
The Troop met at the usual time and place Marched to the Field and practising the usual Evolutions and Sword Exercise. A very fine day and dusty. Captain Broke gave orders for more frequent Musters to prepare for being Reviewed which he expected soon to receive orders for, from the General of the Eastern District.[98]
The 4th June His Majesty's Birthday being on a Sunday the Troop was ordered to meet on Monday 5th Instant and such Gentlemen as were not otherwise engaged requested to dine at the Crown Inn agreeable to our Annual Custom on His Majesty's Birthday.

Monday June 5th 1797
The Troop met on Parade about 11 o'clock marched from there to the Field hired of Mr Cockle Practised the usual Evolutions and Sword Exercise afterwards fired a feu de joye in Honor of His Majesty's Birth Day. Dined at the Crown Inn spent the day very pleasant and agreeable to all the party.

June 17th 1797
I Received notice from Captain Broke the Troop was to be Reviewed at Woodbridge on Thursday next 22nd Instant.[99] Orders were immediately Issued for a previous meeting on Wednesday at one o'clock and on Thursday morning at 8 o'clock for the Review with particular Instructions for all the Horses to be trimmed, their Equipments put in the best order, Bridles new Fronted etc etc Swords, Pistols, Cloathing etc etc to be as neat as possible.[100] The Troop met and was Inspected on Wednesday when every matter was arranged for the Review next morning.

Thursday June 22nd 1797 Review
At 9 o'clock in the morning the Troop met on Parade in the Market Hill Woodbridge and being first Inspected by Captain Broke and Officers, about 10 oClock marched to the Field A88 and everything being properly arranged, about 11 o'Clock, the arrival of General Garth with his Aid de camp Major Pringle and with them Colonel Stavely of the Oxford Blues was announced.
The General appeared in the front of the Line the Officers at their Posts saluting, the Troops in open Order with swords Carried, he passed the Ranks in front and Rear and Inspected both men and horses, after which he Reviewed the Troop in various Evolutions, Sword Exercise and Firing etc etc as also of the neatness of the Equip-

---

[98] The Yeomanry would come under the general's command should it be embodied in case of invasion, and he would obviously need to have some idea of its capabilities.
[99] This is the first time the Troop was to be officially reviewed, and by the army. In an atmosphere of increased fear of invasion, it shows concern, really for the first time, about the effectiveness of the Yeomanry and its capability of co-operating with the professional forces if needed.
[100] As it was their first official review, they were very concerned that everything was well-organised.

ments and good appearance of the Horses. He was pleased to express himself in the most respectful Terms.

Previous to the Review, Captain Broke under the direction of (his son-in-law)[101] Colonel L Gower had fixed in the Corner of the Field two Tents in which tables were set and upon them a handsome Cold Collation to which after the Review the General and his Friends with Commissioned Officers of the Troop being invited they sat down in one of the Tents and partook of the same. The non-commissioned Officers and Privates in the other Tent by which arrangement it was made particularly convenient and very pleasant to all the Party. The day being very fine the Spectators were very numerous and respectable, the whole was conducted much to the satisfaction of all present.

Field Report of his Majestys Second Troop of Loyal Suffolk Yeomanry
Commanded by Philip B Broke Esq Captain   Woodbridge June 22nd 1797

Present fit for duty: Captain 1, Lieutenant 1, Cornet 1, Sergeant 4, Corporal 3, Trumpeter 1, Private 55, [?] H 55
Sick and absent: 8   P B Broke Captain
A Field Return of which the above is a Copy was delivered to General Garth

---

Memorandum No particular occurrences at the Meetings of the Troop, or the intermediate time, from this Days Muster to 27th October.

Friday October 27th 1797 General Muster
The Troop met at Parade in the Market Place at the usual time and 12 o'clock fired a Feu de joie in Honor of the Grand Victory obtained by Admiral Duncan over the Dutch fleet off Camperdown on the 11th October 1797.[102] After which they marched into the Field and practised the sundry Evolutions and Sword Exercise as usual.

Captain Broke informed the Troop that at a General Meeting of Subscribers for strengthening the internal defence of the County of Suffolk held at Stowmarket the 6th day of April last, it was declared by the Chairman that the fund of the Subscribers being exhausted no further pay from that time could be allowed for the use of the Horse.[103] In consequence of this Information (with the approbation of Captain Broke) it was unanimously Resolved to call a General Meeting of the non-commissioned Officers and Privates of the Troop, and the Quarter Master was requested to Issue a Circular Letter for that purpose.

(Circular)   **Head Quarters Woodbridge   October 30th 1797**
Sir   It being highly necessary to take into immediate consideration, what measures may be proper to be pursued, in consequence of the County Fund for the Support of the Loyal Suffolk Yeomanry Cavalry being exhausted; and to consult on the expediency of continuing the said Troop, associated and united for the Services on which it was first instituted. You are particularly requested to attend a Meeting of the non-commissioned Officers and Privates of the 2nd Troop, intended to be

---

[101] Captain Broke, inexperienced in army customs, was fortunate to have a son-in-law who knew what would be expected.
[102] Some good news was needed to boost morale after a rather disastrous year and was duly celebrated in the traditional way.
[103] It was surprising that the subscription of 1794 lasted as long as it did.

holden for that purpose, at the Crown Inn, at Woodbridge, on Tuesday the 7th Day of November next at Eleven o'Clock in the Forenoon. If anything should happen to prevent your Personal Attendance, it is hoped that you will nominate some Friend to act for you.   By particular Desire,   Cornelius Collett Quarter Master

---

Thursday November 7th 1797

In complyance with the above Notice the Troop this day met at the Crown Inn Woodbridge. The Quarter Master being requested to take the Chair, the purpose of the meeting being explained, a Committee was appointed and a Declaration being by them proposed was agreed to and signed by the Members present.

A90 Declaration

Head Quarters Woodbridge November 7th 1797

Sensible of the Propriety as well as Necessity of continuing our respective Services in the honourable Corps to which we belong, We whose names are herein subscribed, do pledge ourselves that we will be ready to attend and obey the Orders of our worthy Officers as often and as long, as our Services may be found necessary, under the same Articles and Agreement as heretofore, but at our own Costs and Charges Individually. The Expenses that may arise in repair of Arms, a supply of such as may become unfit for Service, and Ammunition excepted. (As under a Vote of Credit passed last Sessions of Parliament, by the Legislative they are expected to be Issued by Government, to the Yeomanry Corps respectively.)

Resolved: That the above Declaration with the Signatures, be entered in a Book kept by the Quarter Master, and Copies thereof be transmitted to the Captain, Lieutenant, and Cornet, and every Non-Commissioned Officer and Private of the said Troop.[104]

A Copy of the above Declaration having been sent to the Captain, Lieutenant and Cornet, an Address in reply was Read at the head of the Troop when on Duty 24th November being a General Muster viz

We the undersigned desire to testify our most hearty concurrence with that part of the Declaration (made at General Muster of Non-Commissioned Officers and Privates of the Second Troop of Loyal Suffolk Yeomanry Cavalry held on 7th of this month November 1797) A91 respecting the bearing Individually, the Costs and Charges that may arise from continuing associated in Troop. A Declaration, as highly honourable to themselves as worthy of that noble Spirit which has hitherto animated, and, at this important Crisis, inspiring them with redoubled Vigour, as true British Yeoman, to Exertions of Energy in defence of their dearest Interests, of their King and Country.

We further are anxious to communicate to the Troop the high Sense we entertain of the Honor confirmed on us by the Sentiments of Approbation and Attachment, they have been pleased to express towards us. We beg leave thus to return our thanks, and assure the Troop that it will continue to be a prime object in our Minds; to preserve, on every Occassion, how truly we esteem an Opinion so gratifying to our feelings as Officers to so truly respectable a Corps, and flattering, as Neighbours and Friends.[105]

---

[104] The list of names has not been copied.

[105] This sums up how the Yeomanry operated both as soldiers and friends.

Philip B Broke Captain

Francis Brooke Lieutenant
Mileson Edgar Cornet

The Address being read to the Troop on Parade the 24th November 1797 their thanks for same was communicated to the Officers in a Resolution of which the following is a Copy.

November 24th 1797   Resolved, unanimously that the Officers be requested to accept the thanks of the Troop for the kind and polite manner in which they have this day signified their approbation of their Conduct.

Signed at the request of the Troop   J Brand

November 24th 1797 General Muster

The Troop being met had a Field day as usual with no particular occurrances.

The Muster for some time past not having been fully attended, it was this day proposed and agreed upon that a Committee should meet on the 28th December next (being the Day previous to the next General Muster) to consider the most effectual means to enforce and insure a punctual and exact attendance of every Individual of the Troop on Days of Exercise.

A92   Woodbridge December 13th 1797[107]

We, the undersigned Magistrates, acting in and for the Division of Woodbridge having seen with satisfaction the Benefit, which has arisen to the internal peace and good order of the Kingdom, from the Establishment of the Corps of Yeomanry, cannot, but with sentiments of the highest Gratitude reflect upon the Loyal and Spirited Resolutions lately entered into by the Officers and Privates of the Second Troop of Loyal Suffolk Yeomanry Cavalry (installed within our Division) "to continue their Services at their own Individual Cost and Charges." A Measure, which, whilst it reflects the highest Honour upon themselves demands the grateful Thanks of all their Neighbours. A Measure which, whilst it increases the safety of the Kingdom at large, affords a constant Protection to the Civil Power against all disturbances of the Peace, Order and Tranquility of the Country.

Activated by these Sentiments, We take the Liberty of Suggesting to our Friends and Neighbours, the Inhabitants of the Division of Woodbridge, whether (in an object of so great Importance as the keeping up this new and truly Constitutional Bulwark)[108] it be not reasonable, that We should all bear some share in the Expense attending it. And whether (when our Loyal Brethren are standing forth in Arms personally at their own Individual Cost and Charges) it would not be unreasonable to throw upon them the Burthen which could not have been foreseen, or future extra contingent Expenses which cannot be avoided.

---

[106] A91–92, *London Gazette Extraordinary*, Captain Sir Sidney Smith's account of 23 March 1799 and the siege at Acre. Collett copied long sections of the *London Gazette*, which was, and indeed is, one of the most important official journals of the British government. During the French wars it was used to print the despatches, or reports written by the commanding officers for the government immediately after a battle, which led to the term 'being gazetted'. The *Extraordinary* editions were produced for very important and major events.

[107] This is the second of two pages both numbered 92.

[108] The Yeomanry had been formed to fight the French and aid the civil powers when riot and tumult occurred. This summing up of them as a constitutional bulwark is interesting.

Confiding in the well-known Loyalty and frequent experienced Liberality of the Inhabitants of the Division of Woodbridge, We request them the favour of them to meet us at the Shire Hall in Woodbridge on Thursday, the Fourth day of January 1798 at Eleven o'Clock in the Forenoon when the Loss incurred by an unfortunate Bankruptcy, and a proper Estimate of the Future extra contingent Expenses, with the propriety of entering into a Subscription for defraying the same, will be submitted to their Consideration.

R Frank, E Jenney, J Higgs, J Revett, F Capper

A93   **Head Quarters   December 28th 1797**

We the undersigned having been appointed at a General Muster of the Second Troop of Loyal Suffolk Yeomanry Cavalry held the 24th Day of November last past, A Committee to consider the most effectual means to enforce and insure a punctual and exact attendance of every Individual of the Troop, on Days of Exercise; to recommend the following Resolutions for their Approbation.

Resolved, That all Forfeitures for Non-attendance prior to the Date hereof, be entirely given up and dispensed with.

Resolved, That Sickness, Lameness or the Death of a near Relation, be considered as the only sufficient excuse for absence; which shall be delivered in Writing to the Officer commanding the Troop, at the Time of calling over the Muster Roll.

Resolved, That on calling over the Muster Roll, every Volunteer not answering to his Name, shall forfeit the Sum of Five Shillings for every Non-attendance, to be paid to the Quarter Master, Cornelius Collett, who is hereby appointed Treasurer.[109]

Resolved, That the above Forfeitures shall be solely applied in Aid of any Subscription that may be hereafter entered into, for the Support of the Troop.

Resolved, That it is submitted to the Officers, whether the Parade would not be the best place of calling over the Muster Roll.

NB The general Monthly Muster will be the last Friday in every month.

J Brand, J M Theobald, W Kemp, Samuel Gross, Philip Gross, John Couperthwaite, Thomas Simpson

Memorandum The above Resolutions being Printed, a Copy was sent to each Member of the Troop.

Friday December 29th 1797 General Muster

The Troop met and had a Field Day as usual no particular occurrences. The above Resolutions of the Committee being Read, where on a show of Hands fully agreed upon by a large Majority.

A94 At a Meeting held at the Shire Hall, Woodbridge January 4th 1798 the following Resolutions were unanimously agreed to.

1st Resolved, That the Thanks of this Meeting be given to the Officers, non-commissioned Officers and Privates of the Second Troop of Loyal Suffolk Yeomanry for their general uniform loyal conduct and particularly for their late spirited Resolution to continue their Personal Services at their own Individual Costs and Charges.

2nd Resolved, That it appears to this Meeting that there are sundry other contingent Expenses necessary to be incurred, and to be now provided for, and future contingent Expenses will amount to rather more than £50 per Annum.

---

[109] An appropriate appointment given that Collett was a banker.

3rd That it is highly reasonable that the Inhabitants of this Division should in general contribute something towards supporting and keeping up this new and truly Constitutional Bulwark, inrolled within their Division.

4th That it appears to this Meeting, that a Debt to the amount of Two Hundred Fifty seven Pounds and Fifteen Shillings, has been unavoidably incurred by the Troop.

5th That it would be unjust and ungrateful to throw upon our Loyal Volunteer Brethren standing forth in Arms for our Defence, the Burthen of the above Debt.

6th That it appears to this Meeting, that there is no Fund, whereout the abovementioned contingent Expenses, or Debt can be provided for, but from the well-known Zeal, Loyalty and Liberality of the Inhabitants of the Division of Woodbridge.

7th That a Subscription be opened for the above laudable purposes and that the Justices be appointed a Committee for receiving the Subscriptions.

8th That the Chairman be requested to transmit a Copy of these Resolutions to P B Broke Esq, Captain of the Second Troop of Loyal Suffolk Yeomanry, and to desire him to communicate the same to his Troop.

9th That a copy of these Resolutions be sent to every Parish.

NB That the Justices will receive the Subscription at the Shire Hall on Wednesdays.[110]

A96 Woodbridge January 12th 1798

Sir

I am desired by the Commanding Officer of the Second Troop of Loyal Suffolk Yeomanry to

inform you, that the Troop is required to meet at Woodbridge, on Thursday next precisely at 9 o'clock in the Morning to attend the Corps of the late Mr John Page to the Ground, at Clapton, for the purpose of paying military Honours due to the Remains of a Brother Yeomanry Soldier of the Troop. Cornelius Collett Quarter Master

To   (sent to each Member of the Troop)

In consequence of the Death of Mr John Page which happened on Thursday Morning the 11th Instant, the Family having signified it was their wish he should be Buried with Military Honours, a Letter summoning the Troop to meet on the occasion (of which the above is a Copy) was sent to each member of the Troop by order of Captain Broke.

Thursday January 10th 1798

The Troop met at Woodbridge to attend the Funeral of Mr. John Page who died at Woodbridge on Thursday the 11th Instant.

About ten o'Clock the Hearse with the Corps and the Carriages in which where his Family and Friends (having been previously arranged) moved out of the Yard from his House into the Street when the Procession proceeded in the following order:

Sergeant Major Scott with 12 Carbineers

The Undertaker with Mr Pages Tenants on Horseback

Two Trumpeters

The Hearse with the Body

---

[110] A95, the list of subscribers included 44 individuals (including Earl of Yarmouth £5 5s. and £1 1s. from a stranger), together with a list of 52 parishes, ranging from £21 from Woodbridge and £16 8s. 6d. from Nacton, to Bawdsey and Cretingham's 10s. 6d. It is perhaps understandable that a very local appeal received considerable support although the one to extend the county subscription had failed.

The Horse properly Equipped led by two men in Black Cloaks
The Carriages with Family and Friends
The Troop
Major Judgson of the Royal Horse Artillery being at the time Quartered in Wood-bridge, in Compliment to the Troop and respect for the Deceased ordered his Troop to assemble on the Market Hill and as the Procession passed the Officers and Troop Saluted which added very much A97 to the Solemnity and Dignity of the Procession. The Scene Was very Aweful, the Spectators very numerous and fortunately the Day proved very fine.

After passing the Troop of Royal Horse Artillery which was formed on each side of the Road on the Market Hill the Procession proceeded to Clopton. On their arrival at the Church the Troops dismounted and marched on foot following the Corps into the Church, the Carbineers remaining a Guard at the Church Door. After the Service in the Church, the Troop formed round the Grave and the Burial Service being finished the Carbineers fired three vollies in the Air over the Corps, according to the Custom of Military Burials.

From a Notice sent to each Member of the Troop in consequence of his having subjected himself to a forfeit for non-attendance in conformity to the Resolution of the Committee 28th December 1797
Sir   Head Quarters Woodbridge (date)
I am directed by Captain Broke to inform you, that agreeable to the Resolutions passed at a General Muster of the Second Troop of Loyal Suffolk Yeomanry Cavalry on 29th December 1797 you have incurred the forfeit of Five Shillings, for not attending at the Monthly Muster held on [blank] and not complying with the Form of Exercise required by the above Resolutions to be observed by all absentees.
Cornelius Collett Quarter Master

February 11th 1798 I received a Form of which the following is a Copy to be sent any Member of the Troop in case he should hereafter at any time withdraw himself from the service of same.
Sir   Head Quarters Woodbridge (date)
You having (at your personal request or otherwise) withdrawn A98 on the [blank] day of [blank] from the Second Troop of Loyal Suffolk Yeomanry Cavalry, I am desired by Captain Broke to require that you will 'deliver up your Arms, Accoutre-ments and Cloathing which have been intrusted to your Custody' according to the Provisions inserted in 34 Geo 3rd Cap 31 Sic 3. You are further requested to send them to me, within fourteen days from the receipt of this Notice in clean and perfect order.
Cornelius Collett Quarter Master

Friday February 23rd 1798 General Muster
The Troop being assembled in the Field at the usual time, Captain Broke and Lieutenant Brooke being Ill, Cornet Edgar Commanded and Colonel Hogman (Brother-in-law to Cornet Edgar) Reviewed the Troop and was pleased to express his approbation of their Evolutions etc. At 2 o'Clock it began to rain which prevented our doing the Sword Exercise. It rained very hard during the remainder of the day etc.

(Circular) Sir   **March 26ᵗʰ 1798**
I am desired by the Commanding Officer of the Second Troop of Loyal Suffolk
Yeomanry Cavalry to inform you, that the Troop is required to meet at General
Muster at Woodbridge, on Friday next precisely at 11 o'Clock in the Morning,
mounted and dressed as usual for Exercise.
                              Cornelius Collett Quarter Master
Lieutenant Brooke requests your attendance at the above time and place on particular
Business.

Friday March 30ᵗʰ 1798
The Troop assembled at the time requested in the above Circular Letter and marched
from the Parade to the Field and Exercised in the usual Evolutions and Sword Exercise much to the satisfaction of the Spectators present.
After the Exercise etc of the day was finished the Troop formed in a Circle when
Lieutenant Brooke informed them he had received a Letter from the Lord Lieutenant
of the County inclosing one from Mr Dundas[111] which he was directed to communicate to the Gentlemen composing the Troop. He accordingly read the same of which
the following is a Copy.

A99 My Lord   **Parliament Street   12ᵗʰ March 1798**
In order to form a just idea of the manner in which the Force of the Kingdom ought
to be distributed for its general Security, it is very essential that the General Officers
commanding His Majesty's Troops in the Several Military Districts of this Kingdom
should be accurately informed of the Force they may be entitled to call upon in
case of emergency to Act against a Foreign Enemy. This Information can only be
procured by previously ascertaining whether those Corps, which have enrolled
themselves for local Service by the terms of their engagements are at present liable
to serve only within certain limited distances, would be willing to consent in the
event of actual Invasion or very imminent danger thereof, to extend their Service
generally to the limits of the Military District in which they are situated, and with
this view, it is his Majesty's pleasure that your Lordship should in the manner in
which should appear to you most eligible for the purpose endeavour to ascertain the
point, with respect to the Voluntary Corps, both Cavalry and Infantry, in the County
of Suffolk, and that you should report to me the result of the enquiry, in order that
I may communicate the same to His Royal Highness the Duke of York.
The necessity of collecting without delay the sense of the Volunteer Corps on this
point, is founded on considerations so obvious and urgent, with a view to the final
arrangement and completion of our System of Defence, that it would be superfluous
to dwell longer on the subject.[112] Fully sensible of the manner in which they would
to a Man decide should an Enemy actually land on our Coasts, His Majesty has the
utmost confidence, that they will not, at present hesitate, in some degree anticipate
their decision, with a view to enable His Majesty's Government more effectually to
provide against such emergency.
I think it right here to mention for your Lordship's information, and to be communicated to the Voluntary Corps, that the District in which the County of Suffolk is
situated comprehends also the counties of Lincoln, Norfolk, Essex, Hertfordshire,

---

[111] Henry Dundas was the first Secretary of State for War, appointed in 1794 in Pitt's government.
[112] The crises of 1797 finally induced the government to involve the Yeomanry in its defence plans.

Cambridge and Huntingdon, and is now placed under the command of General Sir William House.

It is likewise His Majesty's pleasure that your Lordship should report to me, for His information, not only to what amount, and in what degree the Voluntary Corps within the County of Suffolk are willing to extend their Services beyond the terms of their original agreement, in the manner here proposed; but also what amount of Force (as far as your Lordship, in concert with your Deputy Lieutenants, can form an opinion upon the Subject), it will in prudence be requisite to appropriate to local purposes within the said county, in the event of the general Force of the District being called upon to act more immediately upon the Coast or near to it, or on some other **A100** point on the coast situated within the same District as the County of Suffolk. Unless this Point is accurately ascertained it will be impossible for the Officer in Command of the Troops in the Eastern District to form any opinion of what is the real amount of his Force disposable for the general service of this District, and what he is to consider as necessary to be appropriated to more local purposes or to more limited objects.

In order to enable your Lordship to make a more accurate report on the Subject, I would suggest to you the propriety of holding communication with the General Officer in command of the Eastern District, who will receive orders from His Royal Highness the Duke of York to consult with you on the objects of this Letter, and I take this opportunity of suggesting to your Lordship, that it will be of great importance to the general Service and Security of the Kingdom, that your Lordship and your Deputy Lieutenants, should embrace every opportunity of communicating and acting in concert with the Commanding Officer of the Troops within the District, on the subject of the Civil and Military Duties committed to your respective Charges, as under the circumstances of the Crisis in which we are now placed,[113] they must on many occasions necessarily be blended together, and the effect of the frequent and full communications will certainly be a more efficient co-operation in all those measures, which in the present moment are essential to the Public Service and to the safety of the Kingdom.

I have the Honor to be, my Lord, Your Lordship's most humble Servant,

Henry Dundas

To the Lord Lieutenant of the County of Suffolk

Lieutenant Brooke having read the above Letter to the Troop and at the same time the Officers declared their Resolution of going out on any Service with the Troops which they might resolve to engage themselves to act upon, the Gentlemen as under immediately declared their resolution of subjecting themselves to be under the Command of the General of the Eastern District and to hold themselves in readiness (on the shortest notice) when called upon to march to any part of the Counties of Suffolk, Norfolk, Lincoln, Hertfordshire, Essex, Cambridgeshire and Huntingdon in case of actual Invasion or very imminent danger thereof.[114]

B214 The following [is a] copy of a Circular letter addressed to the Lord Lieutenants of all the maritime Counties of the Kingdom; also of a plan for driving livestock

---

[113] The country stood on its own until Pitt put together another coalition agreed later in 1798.

[114] A101, list of names not copied.

off such parts of the County as may become exposed to the inroads of the enemy in case of Invasion.[115]

Circular Letter addressed to the Lord Lieutenants of all the maritime counties of the kingdom

My Lord **Parliament Square 1798**

In conformity to the act of Parliament 1798 just past entitled "an act to enable His Majesty more effectively to provide for the defence and security of the realm, and for indemnifying persons who may suffer in their property by such measures as may be necessary for that purpose",[116] I feel myself called upon, in obedience to His Majesty's commands, to address your Lordship upon several points connected with the defence of the county; and to which from a conviction of their importance, I most anxiously request your Lordships particular attention. Having lately had frequent occasion to require your Lordship's assistance in the execution of plans and arrangements adopted, and acted upon by His Majesty's government, as conducive to the same object it would have been a satisfaction to me if I could have avoided giving you further trouble for the present, but further exertions being deemed necessary, I am convinced I should not do justice to your Lordships sentiments, and to the zeal of every description of person acting under you, if I hesitate a moment to explain the full extent of these exertions, and the suggestions which have occurred for carrying them into effect. Whatever confidence I place in the actual security of these Kingdoms, in consequence of the decided superiority of our Navy and of the amount of the land forces already embodied or now collecting, for the protection of the Country against the menaced invasion of the enemy I should not feel that I discharged my duty if any system of defence did not imbrace such further means of security as appear to be evidently within our reach.

In the practical application of this principle, I am convinced that your Lordship, and generally every person, must concur in opinion with me, that it is of much importance to extend as widely as possible, that feeling of confidence which will naturally result from men of every description being placed in a situation to take, in their respective stations, an active part in the defence of their country, especially if this can be accomplished without any material interruption to the various habitual occupations in which they are severally engaged.[117] In many great and populous towns of the kingdom the principle has already been acted upon in so far as a variety of volunteer corps and armed associations have been formed generally for the purpose of local defence and security. I shall therefore confine myself to suggest the propriety of encouraging **B215** the formation of any further corps on similar principles within any such towns in the county of [blank] It must however be considered as an essential condition within the establishment of any further corps of this description, that they should consist of none but known and respectable householders or persons who can

---

[115] This letter and the plan are two of the most important documents transcribed by Collett. Between them they represent the government's plan for defending the country when a French invasion took place, known as 'Driving the country', which involved the whole population in putting it into practice. This is the most precise and detailed exposition as to how it was to be achieved. Collett actually copied the two documents on B214, although he noted that they were related to the letter that precedes them here and they have therefore been moved for clarity.

[116] The Defence of the Realm Act.

[117] This statement by Dundas, Secretary of State for War, shows how far the government's attitude had changed.

bring at least two such householders to answer for their good behaviour. Corps of this description, if formed in sea ports, would, in case of any hostile attempt being made, be neccessary to strengthen the garrisons of such places, and in all populous towns engaged in pursuits of manufacture or trade, whether situate on the coast, or inland, their presence within such towns, in case of emergency when regular forces might be wanted elsewhere, might be useful to relieve them in the preservation of internal tranquility and the maintenance of a proper police. With a wish to give every possible encouragement to persons willing to come forward for these essential objects and from the consideration of the great inconvenience and loss to which such persons (engaged as they are in extensive concerns of business) might be exposed if they were liable to be called away from the necessary superintendence of their respective avocations, his Majesty has been pleased to authorize me to inform your Lordship, that any armed association, either of cavalry or infantry, formed of the description of persons above mentioned, and within such towns as I now advert to, will, if recommended by your Lordship, be accepted by His Majesty, although the offer of their services should be limited respectively to the town in which they are to be raised, and within a few miles thereof; that the officers of the said corps will receive commissions from the King; upon your Lordships recommendation, and, if required, arms will be supplied by Government, but every other expense of armed association of this description must be defrayed by themselves.

It is however no less essential to the general security of the kingdom to interest and engage in its defence the husbandmen and labourers, inhabitants of the country, who being more dispersed, and from the condition of life, less able to associate together upon the plans pursued in the towns, appear to require that the exertions they are certainly willing to make should be duly directed by the interposition of your Lordship's advice and authority, in concert with the gentlemen of property and influence in the country, and aided by the respectable farmers with whom they are immediately connected. If the very valuable classes of men to which I now refer, are not apprised of the duties for which they would be wanted, and if some previous arrangements are not made, and regulations established with respect to the distribution, application and discharge of those duties, in case of actual invasion, the approach of the enemy, would necessarily produce among them a general confusion and alarm, highly prejudicial to their own interests and to the general safety of the country;[118] whereas if the modes in which their assistance B216 may be made useful, can be explained to them at present, so that each man may be instructed, and, if necessary, trained beforehand in the exercise of the particular service to be assigned to him in case of emergency, the result will be confidence and union among themselves, and that Government will not only acquire a great accession of strength, but what is perhaps more important the means of appropriating with regularity, and directing with vigour that strength against an invading enemy.

The measures which I have reason to believe have already been taken in the county of [blank] for assertaining, to a certain extent, the number of persons between the ages of 15 and 60, not engaged in any military capacity will, I believe, afford some facility in carrying so far into execution the provisions of the Act, now transmitted,

---

[118] This displays a real understanding of the whole problem, especially the position of the inhabitants of parishes on deserted parts of the coastline such as that of Suffolk. If they were involved in the plan and given a job to do, a chaotic retreat of panicking civilians might be prevented.

which it is His Majesty's express command, should be punctually attended to (as far as they are applicable in the county of [blank]. I am aware of the difficulties which may occur in procuring these necessary details, but I am confident they may be overcome by your Lord's zeal and purseverance, aided (as I trust you will be) by the cordial co-operation of every well disposed person, who, in his public capacity, or by his private influence, can afford you, any assistance in this respect.

I enclose herewith a form of schedule No 1 in conformity to which this return should be taken in each parish and division of the County, and agreeably to which a general return of the totals for the whole county is to be transmitted to me for His Majesty's information.[119]

No 2 is another schedule requiring information on the other heading referred to in the Act above mentioned and which is to be procured and transmitted in the same manner. One point which it will be very material not to neglect, is to assertain the number of boats, barges and small craft on the canals, and rivers of the country. The use to be derived, in certain cases, from this species of assistance to the movements of our own forces, and the advantage it might afford to the enemy, if suffered to fall into their hands, are so obvious that I need not press further the importance of obtaining respecting it every information in your power. I have however abstained from including in the schedule, as it appears to be impossible, in most cases, to consider this description of property, as exclusively confined to any particular county; but at the same time, I have so far thought it right to call your Lordship's attention to the subject, in order that, as far as possible, it may be brought under general arrangements of precautions necessary at the present moment.

The Schedule No 3 is prepared with a view to assertain the various points under the respective heads therein stated, and to which it is of the utmost importance that returns should be made with all possible expedition, and the totals transmitted to Government in the same manner. In assertaining the number of persons, inhabitants of any of the principal towns of the county of [blank] who may be willing to serve in a military capacity, your Lordship will take care to state whether they come under the description, and are willing to comply with the conditions specified in a former part of this letter.

From what I have already stated, and by a reference to the schedule No 3, your Lordship will perceive that in the country the associations, if armed, will not be formed upon the same principles as in the towns and that it is intended to encourage other associations equally necessary, in case of invasion, and which can be formed by inhabitants of the country only. Each of the points requires some special explanation.

1st B217 it is intended that no volunteer should be admitted into armed associations to be formed in the county whose habitual occupation and place of residence is not within the division of the county to which association may extend; that those who may prefer service on horseback shall (if the troop of yeomanry already raised

---

[119] The Lord Lieutenant was, therefore, in this one sentence, required to undertake the organisation and oversight of the whole plan in his county, to collect the information and ensure that the parishes played their part, as well as collating the totals for the government and army.

within the county shall not be complete, or should their present establishment admit, without inconvenience, of any augmentation) be received into the nearest troop of the same in all cases where the arrangement may suit local purposes, and be found acceptable to the said troop, and to the parties; and in the other case they will be formed into separate and independent troops of not less than 40 or more than 80 men each, to be commanded by such officers as may be recommended by your Lordship, in a similar proportion to the Yeomanry Cavalry, and they will be entitled to the same allowances and assistance from government to procure clothing and appointments; namely at the rate of £3 for each person serving in the Corps, per annum for three years, subject to the same regulation, and to be issued in the same manner as to the yeomanry already established as specified in the letter from the Secretary at War to your Lordships of this day's date. All new troops, formed upon this principle, to engage to be trained at least once a week, and for not less than three hours at a time; and in the case of actual invasion, or the actual appearance of an enemy upon the coast, to serve within the limits of the military district to which they belong. With respect to armed associations of infantry it is proposed that they be formed into independent companies of not less than 60 men or more than 120 men in each company, to be armed in the same manner as the volunteer corps in the town; or should it be found impossible, from their number to furnish them all with muskets in the first instant, then a certain proportion should be provided with pikes; and they should be supplied with a uniform clothing or a fair allowance to provide themselves with the same at the public expense; that each company shall be commanded by a captain to be recommended by your Lordship, having a Lieutenant, an Ensign and a proper number of non-commissioned officers in proportion to the strength of the company under him; but your Lordship is not to recommend any person to such command as has not a residence, and an income in land to the amount of £50 within the county of [blank] or who does not rent land with the same, to the amount of £100 per annum, and if possible with the division thereof, in which the said company may be raised, except the sons of persons so qualified, or person having previously held some military commission although they may not hold land, either in possession or occupancy, to the amount above mentioned. Should your Lordship be acquainted with any person accustomed to military service (whether on the half pay list of the army or not) who may be disposed to accept either of the subaltern commissions such a person will be proposed for the same if approved of and recommended by your Lordship, and in case no proper person of this description should be known to your Lordship, government will endeavour, as far as possible, to provide one, together with one non-commissioned officer for each company, to train the men, and teach them the use of arms. These non-commissioned officers would receive constant pay from government; the subaltern officers if selected from the half pay list, would be allowed the full pay of his rank; and in each case he has heretofore been engaged in any military line which does not entitle him to half pay, he will, if approved of, be **B218** entitled to an allowance equivalent to the half pay of whatever commission he may hold in company so long as he shall continue to hold such commission. Each company of infantry to engage to be trained at least once a week, and for not less than three hours at a time, and in case of invasion, to serve within the limits of the military district to which such company may belong.

Considering the great importance incouraging associations of this description amongst the inhabitants of the country, the inconvenience to which they may be exposed from their scattered situations in assembling to be mustered and trained, as the difference between their situations in life and circumstances of the persons composing volunteer corps in towns, His Majesty is graciously pleased to authorise me to inform your Lordship that every man of the former will be entitled (should he think proper to claim it) to an allowance of one shilling per week, to be paid by Government to such as may appear upon the return, signed by the Commanding Officer, to have attended at the muster and training above mentioned. Should the companies formed in any particular division of the county be numerous, and different days of exercise be fixed upon by the said companies respectively smaller number of arms, in the first instance non-commissioned officers to train them, may be sufficient. I mention this circumstance with a view to their mutual accommodation in these points, in case the full number of either cannot be supplied immediately; but certainly, with respect to arms, no exertion will be spared to provide such a depot, at a safe place within the county, as may be sufficient to supply all demands should the enemy, in prosecution of their avowed designs against this country, succeed in escaping the vigilance of our superior navy, and the final issue of this great contest remain ultimately decided by the valour and spirit of our land forces, that issue will very much depend on the precautions which I have now stated being executed with punctuality, and in the strictest concert with the officers commanding his Majesty's forces in the several military districts to which these counties belong. It is this issue as a possible event with all the responsibility, and all the consequences it involves, that his Majesty's confidential servants were bound to look, when they submitted to his Majesty the plan I have now stated. The same prospects, the same considerations they trust, will rouse the energy and animate the exertions of every man to whom any share of their executions is now committed under his Majesty's express commands. The great and fundamental advantages of the previous arrangements, it is his Majesty's pleasure should be forthwith executed, is that, if properly attended to they will assign to every man the duty he should fulfil, and the post to which he should repair in the hour of emergency, guarding him and the country on the one hand against confusion and panic, and on the other against disaster incident to temerity and ill concerted operations.

In preparing for that emergency, I cannot too strongly recommend to every description of persons, to lay aside all untimely and misplaced jealousy respecting the military power with which every arrangement must be connected. Your Lordship in particular, and all persons acting under you, cannot be too strongly impressed with the necessity of an unreserved and habitual communication with those to whom the direction of that power is entrusted in the [blank] district; and I can assure your Lordship, that on that part, they have His Majesty's most positive order to be equally unreserved and frequent in their communications with your Lordship and your Deputy Lieutenants, and in all doubtful occurrences connected with the civil power, where time **B219** will admit of it, to recur to your, or their advice, and to neglect no means of cultivating and maintaining with you a perfect harmony and good understanding.[120] Should the emergency actually exist from that moment, of course, every description of armed force and every association formed with a view to annoy or impede the enemy, or to support and assist our armed forces, would come under the immediate orders of the military commander, and as far

---

[120] Disagreement between the two must already have been a major problem for Dundas to have to include such an appeal to try to mitigate the issue.

as consistent with their conditions of service, taking the station assigned to each respectively in his general arrangement for the defence of his district, continue to serve in it under such orders as may be issued by those whom, in such a moment, it will be their first duty, and their best interest to obey.

I have the honour to be etc etc   Henry Dundas

(The forms of the Schedules are enclosed herewith)[121]

The 1st Schedule is to specify the total of men from 15 to 60. The second schedule is to give an account of cattle, horses, waggons, carts, corn mills, ovens dead stock, flour or other Mills, malt etc and the number of boats, barges and small craft on the rivers. The third schedule, number of persons from 16 to 60 willing to serve on horseback or foot; how armed; such as will act as pioneers or labourers, with the impliments they can bring; or to act as servants with cattle, teams or guides.[122]

A plan for driving the livestock off such parts of the country as may become exposed to the inroads of the enemy in case of invasion etc.

If an enemy should land upon our shores, every possible exertion should be made immediately to deprive him of the means of subsistence. The navy will soon cut off his communication with the sea; the navy will confine him on shore in such a way as to make it impossible for him to draw any supplies from the adjacent country. In this situation he will be forced to lay down his arms, or to give battle on such disadvantageous terms as can leave no doubt of his being defeated. But if unforeseen and impossible circumstances should enable him to make some progress at first, a steady perseverance in the same system will increase his difficulties at every step; sooner or later he must inevitably pay the forfeit of his temerity. How much the accomplishment of this object will be facilitated by driving away the livestock, and consuming or in case of absolute necessity, destroying all other means of subsistence in those parts of the county which may be in imminent danger of falling into his possession, is too evident to need discussion. The only question is, how to effect this purpose with the greatest alacrity and order, and with the least possible injury to individuals. To this end a well digested plan is obviously indispensable. In clearing the country likely to be in this situation, the first principle is an indemnification from the community at large to the individuals for the value of all stock which may be removed in consequence of invasion, if not, restored to the respective owners; as also for whatever moveable property may be destroyed by our own arms, to prevent its falling into the hands of the enemy, provided the proprietor comes forward and enter into such consequences as may be proposed to preserve it, either by personal attendance at the time, or otherwise in some mode of service, at the moment of invasion. It must at the same time be very clearly understood that no indemnifycation B220 whatever can be allowed, for any property destroyed either by our own arms, or by the enemy if it should appear that no previous preparation or exertion had been made use to remove it, and that all property left in this state is to be destroyed, if necessary

---

[121] Collett in fact did not enclose them.

[122] Parishes were asked to collect all this information. Michael Stone has drawn attention to John Longe's brief mention of the parish meeting held to organise such details and the great patriotic speech he made to encourage people to volunteer (*Diary of John Longe*, p. 36, footnote 133 and HA/24/50/19/44(6) for a handwritten copy of the full speech).

to prevent its falling into the enemy's hands. Upon these grounds, the following preparatory arrangements are proposed for immediate consideration.

1st the inhabitants of every parish, hundred, or other division of the country, of convenient size, should forthwith agree amongst themselves upon proper places of rendezvous, at which their cattle, waggons, and carts may be collected, in case of an order to drive the country be received from the General commanding in the district or any competent person authorised by him to give such an order or in case of any signal he or they may have appointed for this purpose being made; proper march routes should be fixed upon for driving them away to certain places of security in the interior of the country, taking care to choose bye-roads for that purpose; that the great turnpike roads may remain entirely free for the marching of troops and artillery; and where it may be unavoidable to pass one or more of the great roads, it should be done in such manner that they may not be crossed, and occupied during the shortest space of time possible. If a column of troops, artillery, or army supplies, should happen to be moving on the great road at the place of crossing, the stock may easily be stopt in its progress until the military shall have passed the same; every arrangement for these purposes must be concerted with the General commanding the district, or submitted to his approbation.

To avoid loss, confusion, and delay in this operation, it will be necessary that the inhabitants of each parish or other division, should choose from amongst themselves a sufficient number of persons to drive and attend the cattle, under the direction of one or more leaders, to be chosen by the proprietors; which leaders should have authority and means given them by the proprietors, to provide the necessary subsistence for the cattle and persons attending upon them, on the road and at the places of security fixed upon and to determine the places for halting and refreshment during this march, and other arrangements of detail after their arrival. Such places as afford good water and plenty of pasture, should be preferred and pointed out by the civil authorities of the country for the depots, in concert with Generals commanding the forces in the district who is instructed to give every assistance and accommodation in his power for the protection and subsistence of the cattle, and of the persons attending the same.

It will further be advisable that it should be concerted with the General commanding in the district, that some proper person of the commissariat staff under him should attend at each place of depot with instructions to give receipts, if required, for all the live and dead stock that may be brought to the depot, or to enter the same upon a register to be opened for that purpose; but the persons who attend such stock should nevertheless remain in charge of the same, unless it shall be disposed of by being appropriated to the consumption of the army. It is also to be understood, that the proprietor of any cattle or other produce that may be removed in consequence of this arrangement, or such person or persons as shall be authorized by him in this respect, will have the power to send such part of the said cattle or produce as he or they shall think proper, to be disposed of at any market or place in the rear of the depot, on returning to the commissary his receipts, or noticing such disposal in the register above mentioned, as the case may be; provided always, that the commissary should have signified that he was in no danger of wanting such cattle or produce for the supply of the army. It should be recommended to the proprietors to mark their cattle, not only with the initials of their names but also to add some distinctive mark, common to the whole parish, that confusion may be avoided; if the stock of several parishes should come to form in one body.

2nd As it may be impossible for the inhabitants in case of alarm, immediately to move the more bulky articles of property, such as grain, hay and straw which nevertheless cannot be suffered to fall into the hands of the enemy, consistently with the essential object of depriving him of all means of subsistence it should be recommended to them to appoint several discreet trusty persons from among themselves, to remain in the parish as long as the same shall not actually be in the possession of the enemy, or entirely cut off from the army. Thus arrangement will not only facilitate the means of supplying our own army with what must otherwise be distroyed to prevent its falling into the hands of the enemy, but it will in many instances also diminish the chance of loss. Receipts will be given by the troops for all articles which may be taken for their use on the production of which receipts the proprietors will afterwards be entitled to payment, at fair and reasonable prices, according to regulations to be established for that purpose, if the persons so named would point out the places where supplies are deposited and take the receipts of the troops in trust for the different proprietors.

3rd Care should be taken by the inhabitants of such parishes as may be in imminent danger of falling into the hands of the enemy, that all mills and ovens be rendered useless to him, by carrying or destroying some essential part of the machinery of the former, which cannot easily be replaced, and by breaking the lathe. In both cases, that mode of disengagement is the most eligible, which, while it effectively answers the purpose, may afterwards be repaired at the smallest expense.

4th A corps of guides not exceeding [blank], on horseback and on foot, consisting of those who are best acquainted with the roads, lanes, footpaths, bridges, creeks, rivers, fording-places, and other communications in the several parts of the country should be selected in the maritime counties; and their names and places of abode be communicated to the General commanding in the district to which such counties respectively belong.

B221 **5th** The unarmed inhabitants will have an opportunity of rendering services equally necessary and important, by forming themselves into companies of pioneers, under the direction of leaders to be appointed by the civil authority of the county. A numerous body of pioneers is so essential to the movement of an army, and to the obstruction of the progress of the enemy that it is intended, in case of their being called into actual service, to make a competent daily allowance to all who may offer to come forward in the capacity of pioneers. In that case these pioneers should, if possible, come provided with tools of the following description, viz 6 pick axes, 6 spades, 6 shovels, 3 bill hooks, and 4 felling-axes, to 25 men. Nevertheless it is not meant to exclude any man who may not have it in his power to bring any of those tools; let him say what tool he can bring and if he cannot bring any, his service in some way will be acceptable notwithstanding; the duty of the pioneers will generally consist in repairing and opening such roads, bridges and communications, as may facilitate the movement of our own army and in breaking up or obstructing such as it may be necessary to render impossible to the enemy.

B222 The allowances proposed to be made to pioneers from the day on which they may be required to assemble until their service may be no longer wanted, are as follows: To every able bodied man 1s 6d per day To every leader of 25 men and upwards 2d per day for every man under his command. These leaders to be styled captains, their companies to consist of not less than 25 men nor more than 75 men To every 25 men of which a company may consist, is to be allowed one overseer, to be appointed by the Captain, and removeable at his pleasure, at the daily allowance of 3s from the day on which the pioneers may be ordered to assemble. The duty of the leaders or Captains will consist in receiving such orders as may be given from time to time by the authority of the General Officers commanding, for the service to be done by the pioneers and seeing them executed with punctuality and dispatch; in keeping correct lists of the pioneers under their command and seeing that they are consistently provided with proper tools; in maintaining order and regularity among them and in viewing and distributing the wages to be given to them, taking proper receipts, and rendering amounts of the money entrusted to them, according to forms to be prescribed. Each pioneer, leader and overseer, to be at liberty to draw one ration of bread, consisting of 1½ lb from the King's magazine, and paying for the same at the rate of five pence for every four rations. The leaders or captains to give credit for the amount in their accounts; and receipts for the bread drawn by their companies, to be deemed satisfactory proof of the delivery thereof.

6th To the end that the several objects treated of in this plan may be completely attained for the general defence of the country, it is necessary that the results of the providing of the inhabitants therein should be well digested, reduced in writing in a uniform manner, and made known to the General officer commanding the district where such proceedings may take place, that they may be enabled to avail themselves thereof, and adopt corresponding measure.

A Plan for an association of the nobility, gentry and yeomanry, residing in the several counties, to supply such number of waggons, carts and horses, in aid of the provisions made by the meeting act, as may be necessary for carrying on his Majesty's service; as also to contribute to the supply of his Majesty's forces with flour, wheat, oats, hay, straw and fuel, in case of an invasion.

The necessity of being prepared to repel an invasion in the present state of public affairs is too obvious to require discussion. The only question is, how all necessary arrangements at the least possible expense. The country abounds in supplies of all kinds to a degree which render the laying in of extensive magazines unnecessary, small depots for a few days consumption are sufficient, provided means can be found to bring forward the resources of the country at the shortest notice. Depots of this description have accordingly been formed at the different places pursuant to orders given by His Royal Highness Field Marshall the Duke of York. The means of transporting them, and of obtaining and transporting such further quantities as may be necessary in case of emergency remain to be divised; the establishment of a waggon train of sufficient force to supply an army, would entail a very heavy expense upon the public, and take away a very considerable number of horses and men from the ordinary pursuits of agriculture. Both may be avoided by means equally simple and certain. The spirits of the country will do it most effectually; nor need that spirit be wasted to the detriment of individuals, it need only be roused at the moment of actual danger when all is at stake, when all must give way to the primary object of self-preservation. Such of the nobility, gentry and yeomanry of the country as may approve of the measure, should be requested to subscribe a paper, expressing opposite their names the number of waggons and carts provided with tilts and the number of horses, drivers and conductors which they propose to furnish respectively, the waggons, carts etc subscribed for, or such part as may be required from time to time ought to march as soon as possible, and at the latest next morning after notice received for that effect.

The waggons, carts etc marching in conformity to such notice to continue at the disposal and under the orders of the King's officers as the service may require. The said waggons and carts to travel at the rate of five miles in every two hours; 25 miles when loaded and 30 when empty, in every 24 hours, one or more discreet and intelligent persons, besides the driver, should accompany each detachment of 10 waggons or carts, and upwards. These persons should be stiled waggon conductors and their duty should consist in superintending the driver upon the road. The Commissary General to pay to the persons, who may be appointed agreeable to this and the second article, for their trouble and expenses, at the following rates viz For every empty waggon procured, in consequence of notice given one shilling, for every empty cart, ninepence; for every sack of flour of 880 lb net, loaded agreeably to the 12th article 2d; for every sack of oats of 4 bushells loaded as above, 1d; for every ton of hay, straw or fuel loaded as above 20s, but no charge to be made for procuring the waggons or carts respectively, unless they go empty.

A plan for insuring a regular supply of bread to His Majesty's forces in case of invasion

The establishment of flour magazines and of a field bakery, of sufficient force to supply an army, would entail a very heavy expense upon the public, which can only be avoided by ascertaining under this head the resources of the country, and the means of bringing them forward, in case of emergency without previously making any expensive preparations. Returns have been procured of the bakers and ovens at most of the considerable plans in several counties, from which it appears, that they are capable, in an emergency of baking for 4 times, nay, many of them 6 times the number of inhabitants; and troops now in garrison; and that with the help of additional journeymen bakers, they can supply double that quantity. All other counties may, without risk of error, be supposed equally capable with those above alluded to. Grain and mills abound everywhere. The result is, that an army of 30,000 men may without difficulty, be supplied with bread in any situation, at 4 or 5 days notice, and even two or three times that number at the longer distance, provided such preparatory arrangements are concerted with the millers and bakers as will enable the country to do justice to itself.

A101 A Letter From the Lord Lieutenant of the County to the Clerk of the Peace was also read out by Lieutenant Brooke.
Sir   **Colchester Barracks March 19th 1798**
You will be so good as to request the Officer commanding Yeomanry and Volunteer Corps to acquaint me of the earliest Day that it may be convenient to them to have their Corps Inspected by a General Officer.
      I am Sir Your very humble servant Euston
To Henry Collett Esq Clerk of the Peace

In answer to the above, it was unanimously Resolved that the Lord Lieutenant should be informed the Troop would be prepared in readiness to be Inspected by a General Officer this day Month. The Troop was ordered to meet at General Muster on Friday 20th and Tuesday 24th April next to prepare for same.

Friday April 20th and Tuesday the 24th

The Troop met to practise the Sundry Evolutions, Sword Exercise and Firings etc, etc, previous to the Inspection on the 27th Instant at which time every member of the Troops received instructions to have their Horses, Arms, Equipment, Cloathing etc. in the neatest possible order.

A102 Friday April 27th 1798 General Muster

The Troop met on Parade on the Market Hill Woodbridge, marched from thence to a Field in the Occupation of Mr. Glanfield at Martlesham and was then Inspected by General Balfour who was pleased to express himself very much pleased at the Soldier like manner in which the Troop performed the various Evolutions and Sword Exercise etc. declaring they very much exceeded his expectations also of the Horses, Equipments and every appointment of the Troop. The General was accompanied by General Manners and many Officers from the Garrison at Ipswich and the day being very fine the Spectators where very numerous and of the first respectability.
The next General Muster was by Captain Brokes order appointed on 4 June.
In consequence of the Threatened Invasion by the French, Captain Broke received Instructions with leave to augment his Troop. The Gentlemen as under immediately signed the Muster Roll and afterwards many others which will more fully appear on the copy of the Muster Roll.
Henry Short, W Wallis Mason, Thomas Simpson Junior, John Wood, Philip Riches Junior, Philip Trusson, Moses Gabbatas, John Field, John Hunt, George Bates Junior, John Orford Sawer, John Shiming, Benjamin Barthrop, Robert Sexton, Jonathan Clarke Reverend, Hyam Pierce, William Barthrop, Thomas Walton, George Curtis, John Cockle

May 18th 1798

By order of Captain Broke a letter of which the following is a Copy was sent to each Member of the Troop who are provided with their full Equipments, and at same time each new Member was desired to appear on Parade on 4th of June next.
Sir   **Woodbridge May 18th 1798**
I am desired by the Commanding Officer of the Second Troop of Loyal Suffolk Yeomanry to inform you, that the Troop is required to meet at General Muster, at Woodbridge, on Monday the 4th of June next, at precisely Eleven o'Clock in the Morning, mounted and dressed in full Uniform with Cloaks, Saddle Bags and every other Equipment for immediate Actual Service.
Cornelius Collett Quarter Master

A103 Monday June 4th 1798 General Muster

The Troop met this day equipped in complyance with Captain Brokes orders 18th May. From Parade they marched to a Field belonging to Mr Manby at the back of Mrs Nauntons house. It being his Majesty's Birthday the Royal Horse Artillery (Quartered in the Town) under the command of Major Judgson joined us in the Field with four Guns, also the Woodbridge Volunteers Commanded by Captain

Jermyn (it being their first appearance under Arms in Uniform).[123] The whole being formed in Line a Feu de joye was fired in honor of the day. The Spectators were very numerous and respectable, the situation being on an eminence the forming and firing of the Troops had a very pleasing effect, and the whole proceeding was neatly and satisfactorily conducted under the command of Major Judgson much to the satisfaction of all present.

Captain Broke with the Officers of the Troop, the Non-commissioned Officers and Privates, with the Officers of the Royal Horse Artillery dined together at the Crown Inn, had a very pleasant, sociable and merry meeting much to the satisfaction of all present.

From the Field of Mr Manbys as above, the Troops marched to Lieutenant Brookes Meadow when the Officers inspected the Arms, Equipments, Clothing, Horses etc etc. Such equipments as were deficient was ordered to be completed immediately and directions given for every Article to be kept in complete order fit for actual Service on the shortest notice.

List of Equipments

Rug, Saddle with Double Skirt and brass Cantle, one Girth, Leather Sursingle, Breast Plate, Crupper, Stirrup Irons and Leathers, Pad for Saddle Bags, Holster Straps, Pistol Holster and Shoe Case, Skin Covers for Holsters, Collar with Leather Rain, Cloak Case and three straps to ditto, One pair Saddle Bags, Straps to ditto, One Bridle Compt and chain, one Pistol, Sabre with Carriages, a Curry Comb and Brush, Mare Comb and Spunge, one Horse Pick, one Screw Turn, one Horse one Nose Bag.

The Troop being increased and intended to be augmented to 80 Members and Captain Broke having leave from Government to add another Commissioned Officer to the Troop, John Brand Esq was proposed and unanimously elected. In consequence of such election Cornet Edgar was nominated second Lieutenant and Mr Brand Cornet vice Edgar, which being by Captain Broke reported to the Lord Lieutenant of the County, His Majesty was pleased to sign their Commissions accordingly.

It being further signified to the Troop that Government has allowed the Captain **A104** of Yeomanry Corps in aid of their Expenses to draw the amount of Three Pounds per Man per annum doubts arose in the minds of the Members present whether the acceptance of such an allowance would not subject them to be called upon on such service as would be very inconvenient and contrary to the spirit of their Services as volunteers. Captain Broke in answer replied that he had made enquiry respecting same of Marquis Cornwallis and Mr Dundas and received for answer that it would not subject the Troops to any other Service that what they had voluntarily engaged upon and Captain Broke further said it was the intention of Lord Brome and Captain Maynard to accept the same.[124] In consequence of such an assurance it was unanimously resolved Captain Broke should draw such part of the payment as he thought proper, to be applied to the use of the Troop.

---

[123] An example of the new volunteer infantry groups rapidly being formed in Suffolk and the country as a whole, supported by the government, in response to the invasion and other crises of the previous year.

[124] Lord Brome was captain of the 4th Bury Troop, while Captain Maynard commanded the 3rd Hoxne/ Hartismere Troop.

Sergeant Joseph Scott having had an offer of Service in the Provisional Cavalry much more to his Interest than his present situation as Sergeant to the Troop, the same was considered by the Members present, and it being thought a continuation of his services in consequence of the intended augmentation of the Troop was needful it was unanimously resolved he should be continued and receive the pay of Adjutant being Five Shillings per day, in addition to his present pay of Sergeant, as allowed by Government and that said pay should be defrayed by the Fund arising out of the allowances from Government of three pounds per man as above stated.

That the sense of the Meeting might be clearly ascertained, the following propositions where suggested by Captain Broke and the respective resolutions passed thereon.

1st Is it the sense of the Troop that Sergeant Scott should continue with the Troop. Resolved unanimously that he should continue.

2nd Is it the Sense of the Troop that he should from hence be considered as Adjutant and should receive the pay from the Troop in addition to his pay from Government. Such pay to be deducted from the Fund arising from the £3 per man per Annum allowed by Government.

Resolved unanimously Scott should be considered as Adjutant, and that the Troop would allow him the pay of same, the Captain to deduct said pay from the money advanced by Government for the use of the Troop and of their expenses.

3rd Is it the sense of the Troop that the three pounds allowed by Government should be drawn for, it being considered to inforce no further obligation than what is contained in the terms of the Inrolment and what the Troops have already agreed for. Resolved unanimously that Captain Broke should draw for what part he think proper of the Money offered to be paid to the Troop by Government.

A105 Sergeant Joseph Scott being called upon and informed of the Resolutions of the Troop Declared his wish and desire was to continue in the service of this Troop and that he considered himself much obliged for the appointment, and the addition of his pay.

Thursday June 14th 1798

In consequence of the arrival of an Express from Alborough to General Balfour at Head Quarters, Ipswich announcing a Fleet of Ships being off that place and not answering Signals from the shore, they were to be considered an Enemy.[125] Orders were accordingly issued for the Troops here and at Ipswich, Colchester, Harwich etc to hold themselves in readiness to March and orders where also sent to the Officers of Second Troop of Loyal Suffolk Yeomanry Cavalry to prepare for mustering the Troop on receit of further orders from General Balfour. About 11 oClock in the forenoon advice was received, that the fleet was from Hudson Bay and that it was owing to the haziness of the weather that signals from the Shore could not be properly distinguished by the shipping in the earlier part of the morning.

The following arrangement of the Second Troop of Loyal Suffolk Yeomanry Cavalry was appointed by General Balfour, in case of a further alarm he should have occasion to call them into actual Service in consequence of Invasion or a probability

---

[125] An indication of how nervous the country was of false alarms and sightings made in unexpected places, which happened all the time, and how quickly an extensive force was put on alert.

thereof, or on any duty he should think proper to Command them by reason of any hostile appearance or landing on the Coast etc.

A Division to meet on Trimley Heath Commanded by Captain Broke

A second division at Hatchly Barn Commanded by Lieutenant Brooke

A third division at Ipswich Commanded by Lieutenant Edgar

A Fourth division at Woodbridge Commanded by Lieutenant Brooke with Cornet Brand

Each member received instructions to which Post he was to Rendezvous on receiving orders to muster.

NB A supply of Ball Cartridge was sent from the Magazine to each of the Officers having the command of the Divisions.

A106 Tuesday September 11th 1798

The Ipswich Troop of Voluntary Yeomanry Cavalry commanded by Captain Maitland Barclay[126] where Reviewed by General Balfour, commanding Officer of the Eastern Division, and at the same time Inspected by Lord Chatham. Their numbers consisted of 34 Members (only) exclusive of the Commissioned Officers, they went through the Evolutions with much credit to the Troop and the approbation of the General etc – their Dress was very neat and handsome.

At the request of the General Lieutenant Edgar attended with 24 members of our Troop to keep the Ground.[127] After the review we went to Lieutenant Edgars and was most handsomely entertained with a cold collation provided on the occasion.[128]

There being also a Review of 3 Regiments of Infantry on Westerfield Green we went from Lieutenant Edgars to see the same. They consisted of about 2000 men and the day being fine, the Company genteel and numerous, the appearance was grand and very satisfactory to the spectators, each Regiment had a Band of Music.[129]

Friday September 28th 1798 General Muster

The morning being very wet in consequence but few members of the Troop attended we did not go into the Field. The Muster Roll was called over at the Crown Inn and those present were accordingly dismissed. Captain Broke, Lieutenant Brooke, Cornet Brand and myself met at Lieutenant Brookes and examined the Muster Rolls for adjusting the Forfeits for non-attendance, as appeared to be marked on the sundry days viz June 4 and 29th July 27th, August 31st and September 28th. The word Forfeit being wrote against the respective names who incurred forfeits, on those

---

[126] This is rather misleading because there was no Ipswich Troop that was a member of the Loyal Suffolk Yeomanry Cavalry, but there was a Troop of the Provisional Cavalry. This had been instituted by the government in 1796, in an attempt to supplement the cavalry forces by imposing on those with ten riding or carriage horses, the provision of a man and one horse to serve in the new force. John Longe, vicar of Coddenham, supplied his man and a horse, becoming a member himself once the bishop added his encouragement. He enrolled in the Ipswich Troop of Light Horse captained by Charles Maitland Barclay. See Stone, *Diary of John Longe*, p. li. In most areas men chose to join the yeomanry instead, hoping the government would not force the issue if there were already enough cavalry, and by 1800 the remaining Provisional Cavalry regiments were being disbanded. See Beckett, *Britain's Part-time Soldiers*, p. 77.

[127] Safety measures were obviously in place to ensure the crowds kept clear of the horses given the size and numbers involved.

[128] The Red House and its estate, the home of Lieutenant Mileson Edgar, lay on the edge of Ipswich in Westerfield. Cornelius Collett's uncle was lord of the manor at Westerfield so the two must have known each other outside the Yeomanry.

[129] Such a sizeable number of volunteers is further evidence of the rush to volunteer.

days of General Muster, by Captain Brokes order each Gentleman was informed of the same by Letter following.

Head Quarters Woodbridge September 29th 1798

Sir

I am directed by Captain Broke to acquaint you, that, agreeable to the Resolution passed at a General Muster of the Second Troop of Loyal Suffolk Yeomanry Cavalry on 29th December 1797 you have incurred the Forfeit of Five Shillings for not attending at the Monthly Muster held on [blank] and not complying with the Form of Exercise required by the above Resolution to be observed by Absentees. The Number of Forfeits and amount of same was noted in each letter.

Cornelius Collett Quarter Master

A107 Tuesday October 2nd 1798

Information being this morning received from Yarmouth of a Glorious Victory obtained over the French Fleet in the Mediterranean by the English fleet commanded by Admiral Nelson.[130] By order of Captain Broke a circular Letter of which the following is a Copy was sent to each Member of the Troop.

Sir   Head Quarters Woodbridge   October 2nd 1798

I am desired by the Commanding Officer of the Second Troop of Loyal Suffolk Yeomanry to inform you, the Troop is requested to meet on a Special Muster at Woodbridge to morrow, precisely at Four oClock in the afternoon, mounted and dressed as usual for Exercise, to celebrate by a feu du joye the glorious defeat of the French Fleet.

Cornelius Collett Quarter Master

Wednesday October 3rd 1798

The News being confirmed of the French Fleet and the Troop being met in complyance to Captain Brokes request, We paraded in the Market Place about 4 oClock in the afternoon with the Royal Horse Artillery and a Troop of the first Dragoon Guards who were quartered in the Town at the time, marched from Parade into a Field belonging to Captain Carthius and in the occupation of Mr Edward Field (Farmer). The Royal Horse Artillery were commanded by Major Judgson, the Dragoons by Captain Balcom, the Loyal Suffolk Yeomanry by Captain Broke in the field, the Sea Fencibles[131] commanded by Captain Baker of the Royal Navy joined the Troops. The Troops being formed in Line, the Dragoon Guards on the Right, the Yeomanry on the Left with three Guns of the Artillery on each Flank and the Sea Fencibles in the Rear, the Firing commenced by the Artillery Guns on the Right and passing through the Line finished with Artillery on the left Flank. The effect was very grand and afforded a most pleasing view to the numerous spectators. Three rounds being fired the Trumpeters sounded God Save the King and Rule Britannia, after which the Troops cheered three times and being joined by the Spectators, occasioned a strong and loud Echo through the Town and neighbouring Vales.

---

[130] Pressure at home had been eventually relieved when Bonaparte decided an invasion was not yet possible and ordered the French army to Egypt, en route for India. It was stranded there after Nelson's great victory at the Battle of the Nile, also known as Aboukir Bay, which destroyed the French fleet on 1–2 August 1798.

[131] Sea Fencibles were the sea-based equivalent of the volunteer cavalry and infantry corps, who instead of exemption from the militia ballot, were exempt from being press-ganged.

NB The Sea Fencibles kept the Ground which prevented the populace from being incommoded by the Horses or any accident occurring.

Major Judgson Commanded and on quitting the Ground, the Troops and Sea Fencibles passed by him in Review order (the Evening was very fine). [132]

A111 To P B Broke Esq Captain 2nd Troop of Loyal Suffolk Yeomanry Cavalry Nacton

Sir   **Ufford October 4th 1798**

I am commanded by Lieutenant General Balfour to acquaint you, that it is his intention to have a Field day on the Ground near Martlesham on Monday next. He wishes that the Troop of Yeomanry under your command should be present under my orders. I therefore have to request, that you would have the goodness to inform me as soon as possible, whether they will attend; and if they do, desire, that they may be assembled on the Market Place at Woodbridge on Monday morning next at half past 7 oClock with a proper proportion of Pistol ammunition for each man. When on your ground you shall receive further orders relative to your situation in the column of march to the ground on which you are to act.

I have the honor to be Sir your most Obedient, Humble Servant.

J Leverson Gower Lieutenant Colonel 63 Regiment

(Copy) To the 2nd Troop Loyal Suffolk Yeomanry Cavalry

Head Quarters Woodbridge October 5th 1798

Gentlemen

Being aware that I am not authorised to issue an order for mustering on the occasion expressed in the annexed Letter, I have thought it proper to submit it to your consideration; and in case of its being agreeable, or convenient, to any of you, to be present, it is requested that such Gentlemen will sign his name at the foot of the same Letter. [133]

The Troop is considered as a Body of French Cavalry fully accoutered and equiped. [134]

I have the honor to be, Gentlemen, Your obliged Friend and humble Servant

P B Broke

The Letter of which the above is a Copy being sent to the sundry Members of the Troop those who were at home signed the same. [135]

The Troop assembled on Monday morning October 8th 1798 on the Market Place Woodbridge at half past Seven oClock, and being joined by the Woodbridge Volunteers, commanded by Captain Jermyn, the Volunteers from Melton and Ufford and the 63 Regiment of foot commanded by Lieutenant Colonel L Gower, also the Volunteers from Eyke, Rendesham, Ash and Tunstall commanded by P J Thellesson Esq, The Royal Horse Artillery and a Troop of the Dragoon Guards Dismounted (then quartered at Woodbridge) the whole marched soon after 8 oClock to Martlesham River from the Sluice crossing the wall opposite the Wood, across the Turnpike Road, past the Bridge along this side of the River towards Bealings. The

---

[132] A108–111, *London Gazette Extraordinary*. Nelson's victory at the Battle of the Nile is omitted.

[133] The army formally had no power to order the Yeomanry or the other volunteer forces to take part: only when embodied and called out did they come under martial law.

[134] This was the first and only time Collett recorded a field day of this kind, a mock battle involving professional forces and volunteers.

[135] The list of the sixty names of those who attended is omitted.

Garrison from Ipswich consisting of a detachment of the Kings Dragoon Guards Mounted, the East Norfolk, East Essex and Oxfordshire Militia were posted on the opposite [side] of the River for the purpose of making an attack on the Troops on this side. The attack was begun on their Right from the Wood to the Bridge which they endeavoured to pass with two field pieces, in which they were opposed by the Yeomanry cavalry who charged the enemy on their endeavouring to pass the Bridge and obliged them to retreat. A very heavy firing of same time was kept up by each party and several attempts where made to cross the River in various parts, without effect. Our opponents after the first unsuccessfull attack proceeded towards Little Bealings, our party marched on in opposition to them on this side of the River for Great Bealings and passing the same A113 a general engagement commenced which was most spiritedly supported by each party until such time as the Ammunition was all expended.

General Balfour commanding the Eastern Division had the direction of the Evolutions. Lord Chatham (with his lady), General Manners with many General Officers were present and the Spectators were very genteel and numerous, the day was particularly fine and very hot. The ground upon which the troops acted being a most beautiful situation the view of the same was truly grand and every person expressed themselves most highly gratified. Fortunately no accident whatever occurred.

General Balfour, Lord Chatham, General Manners and other General Officers were pleased to express their approbation of every part of the service of the respective Troops on duty.

Friday October 26th 1798 General Muster

The Troop assembled at the usual time and place and marched into the field and practised the usual Evolutions and Sword Exercise a Feu de joie was fired in honor of the Victory obtained by Sir John Bolace Warren over the French fleet on the Western Coast of Ireland.[136]

A115 Circular

Sir   Nacton November 14th 1798

Permit me to request the favour of your attending at the next General Muster to be holden on Friday 30th Instant, completely accoutred as for marching on actual Service, the Horse Cloth folded square, to be strapped on the necessary Bags; the Cloak rolled up long, and fixed on the fore part of the Saddle; and that you will be on Parade at Woodbridge precisely at Eleven oClock in the forenoon of the same Day.

I am, Sir, Your most obliged Friend,   Philip P Broke Captain

Friday November 30th 1798 General Muster

In complyance with Captain Brokes Letter of the 14th Instant the Troop met on Parade at Woodbridge this Morning at eleven oClock equipped agreeable to the directions therein given. From Parade they marched to a field at the back of Mrs. Nauntons House and was inspected by the Captain and Officers. After which a

---

[136] On 12 October Sir John Borlace Warren defeated a French fleet, which was sailing to reinforce General Humbert and the earlier French invasion force in County Mayo, unaware of its surrender. The fleet of one ship of eighty guns, eight frigates, a schooner and a brig, had 5,000 French troops on board and a great quantity of arms and stores. If they had not been defeated at sea, they could, in four hours (one tide), have landed a great part of these forces in Donegal Bay, Ireland.

Committee of 13 Members was chosen for the purpose of hearing and determining appeals respecting the forfeits of which a particular had been previously sent to each member who was subject to pay the same. One Commissioned Officer, three non-commissioned Officers and nine Privates composed the committee which were chosen by ballot, all appeals were afterwards determined and the business respecting same being settled the Captain discharged the Troops and ordered the next General Muster on 28th December.

In consequence of severe frosts and a very heavy fall of snow, which was very deep and in consequence prevented the Troops exercising in the field, the following Circular Letter was sent to each Member of the Troop

Sir   **Woodbridge December 19th 1798**

I am desired by Captain Broke to inform you the General Muster on Friday the 28th Instant is postponed to Friday January 25th 1799 when Captain Broke hopes that every Gentleman will come prepared to discharge the respective Forfeits, according to the Decisions of the Committee, to meet precisely at Eleven OClock in the Morning mounted and dressed as usual, for Exercise.

Cornelius Collett Quarter Master

The meeting of the Troop in consequence of the weather being unfavourable, was by Circular Letter postponed to Friday 29th day of March 1799.

Friday March 29th 1799 General Muster The Troop being met marched into the Field and exercised in the usual Evolutions, Commanded by Lieutenant Edgar, the day was extremely cold and it continued Snowing the greater part of the time we were in the Field. The next meeting was ordered on the 12th April next.

Friday April 26th General Muster The Troop being assembled marched from parade to the Field for Exercise and practised the usual evolutions and sword exercise, the day was very cold with frequent storms of Hail etc. A General Muster was ordered on Friday 17th May.

Friday May 17th General Muster
The Troop met at the usual time and place marched into the Field and practised the sundry evolutions and sword exercise, the day being very cold Orders were given for a General Muster on 4th June at ten oClock in the forenoon to celebrate His Majesty's birthday, at the same time such forfeits as remained due were ordered to be paid and sundry arrears for equipment. Also ordered a general inspection of arms etc etc.

Tuesday June 4th 1799 General Muster
The Troop met at eleven oClock being prevented on earlier attendance in consequence of the morning being very wet. At ten oClock, it cleared up and the remainder of the day was particularly fine and pleasant.
There having been a new set of eight bells cast by Thomas Osbourne of Downham in Norfolk for the use of the Parish of Woodbridge which were Advertised to be opened on this day, an immense concourse of People assembled on the occasion from all parts of the Country and it being his Majesty's Birth Day the sundry Troops quartered in the Town with the Volunteers of the place and neighbourhood paraded together and then marched to a field in the occupation of Spencer Leek at the back of the half way houses going to Melton and being formed in the following order

a feu de joye with a Royal salute was fired in honor of the day. The Troops being posted on an imminence which commanded an extensive view, with the immense number of spectators in the Field, the Road and Meadows below presented a most pleasing prospect and altogether a very grand scene.

A118 Arrangement of the Troops in the Field under the Command of Major Judgson.

The Royal Horse Artillery with four Guns on the Right – Major Judson

A Troop of the 1st or King's Dragoon Guards Commanded by Lieutenant Bletson

The 2nd Troop of Loyal Suffolk Yeomanry Cavalry – Captain Broke

The Woodbridge Volunteers (Infantry) – Captain Jermyn

The Melton Volunteers (Infantry) – Captain Kett

The Sea Fencibles belonging to the Port of Woodbridge – Captain Baker Royal Navy

The firing commenced with a Royal salute by the Guns of the Royal Horse Artillery, then a feu de joye by the Line of Cavalry and Infantry – after three rounds the Officers Saluted the Troops at the same time presenting Arms and the Trumpets with the Band sounding God Save The King. After which three Cheers were given by the Troops and spectators – the whole being well conducted from the advantage of an elevated situation presented a most pleasant view much to the satisfaction of all present. The Fields, Turnpike Road and Meadow were crowded with Spectators. The new Bells at the Church being rung during the whole of the time the Troops in the Field considerably increased the [blank]

After being discharged from the above duty the Troop met at the Town Hall. Captain Broke informed the members present that he had obtained an order from Government to draw on the General Agent for the payment of three pounds for each member of the Troop to be applied for the repair of Arms, Equipment etc etc. In consideration of same the following propositions were made by Captain Broke and unanimously resolved upon.

That Captain Broke do return to Government a Certificate of the application of the three pounds per individual of the troop Viz one pound thereof to the advantage of an Adjutant and two pounds to the reparation and replacing of Arms etc etc.[137]

That the two pounds be funded under the inspection and control of a committee to be chosen out of the Troop (by ballot). (To this proposition Mr William Kemp only dissented).

That the Arms be inspected every three Months by the Officer present at the General Muster and the state of the same be reported to the Committee who are to determine if the repair required was occasioned by misapplication of the Arms or otherwise - if by fair use on duty only they will direct them to be repaired at the expense of the Fund, otherwise by each individual who have neglected the proper care of the same.

That in future if any Gentleman has a new Jacket it is required to be made to the pattern in the possession of Mr William Gross and if a new Helmet is ordered it is **A119** to be made to the pattern in the possession of Mr Thomas Shiming of Woodbridge.

That a Committee be balloted for or chosen to sit every three months to audit the accounts of the General Fund and that such Committee do consist of one Commissioned Officer, one Sergeant, one Corporal and six privates.

Adjourned to Friday 14th Instant, then to meet at the usual time and place.

---

[137] This would seem to be a very large percentage of their allowance to pay to keep Sergeant Major Joseph Scott with the Troop.

At four o'clock Major Judgson and his Officers with the Officer of Dragoons, several Gentlemen of the Town and neighbourhood met Captain Broke and the Officers of the 2nd Troop of Loyal Suffolk Yeomanry Cavalry and such Members as chose to attend belonging to the Troop, at Dinner at the Crown Inn. The Room was quite filled a very good dinner being provided for the occasion – also for Captain Jermyn and his Corps of Woodbridge Volunteers who dined in the Room under that which we were.

After dinner, the Kings health was drank with three times three (cheers), the respective health of the Royal family and a variety of constitutional Toasts with the health of our brave Heros by Land and Sea. A number of good songs were sung and the Day was spent with greatest harmony and pleasant conviviality.

The Band belonging to the Woodbridge Volunteers was playing the greater part of the time.

Funeral of Sergeant Crane

In consequence of the death of Sergeant Robert Crane of Wickham Market who was unfortunately killed by a fall from his horse on the pavement at Woodbridge early on Wednesday morning last, the Troop attended his Funeral at Wickham. We mustered on the Bowling Green dismounted marched from thence to the house of his Brother in Law Mr J Churchyard and from thence in Procession as usual on such occasions to the Church. The Service was read by the Reverend Mr Johnson (the Rector) and three rounds were fired over the Grave by the Carbineers - a very great number of Spectators assembled on the occasion.

Friday June 28th General Muster

The Troop assembled at the usual time and place marched from parade to the field of Exercise went through the Sundry Evolutions with firing and sword exercise.

Corporal Thomas Symonds was elected Sergeant vice Crane deceased.

Philip Dikes was elected Corporal vice Symonds promoted.

A120 Death of Lieutenant Francis Brooke

Francis Brooke Esq of Woodbridge one of His Majesty's Justices of the Peace for the County of Suffolk and Lieutenant of the 2nd Troop of Suffolk Loyal Yeomanry Cavalry died on Tuesday Evening the 2nd of July 1799 aged 60 years.[138] He was privately buried at Ufford on Wednesday Morning 10th July at 9 oClock he having left directions not to be buried with Military honors.

He was a very worthy and respectable man and his death was much lamented by all ranks of Society in the Town and Neighbourhood.

Monday 8th July 1799

An Express was sent this morning from the Signal Post at Bawdsey to General Balfour at Ipswich with information of an Enemy being on the Coast and on the Act of Landing Troops near Yarmouth.[139] In consequence of such information the Troops in Garrison at Ipswich were under arms, and an advanced guard of about 100 Dragoons commanded by Colonel Hawley arrived at Woodbridge about 5 oClock in

---

[138] Francis Brook had been lieutenant of the Troop since its inauguration, and the Troop often used his fields by his home at The Abbey.

[139] Such an occurrence was the constant fear of all maritime communities after the French attacks the year before, and false alarms were frequent.

the afternoon and with the Royal Horse Artillery Quartered here under the command of Major Judgson in about half an hour continued their march for the Coast. Immediately on the arrival of Colonel Hawley I waited on him to know his pleasure respecting the 2nd Loyal Suffolk Yeomanry Cavalry.[140] He requested I would order a detachment of 10 or 12 men to follow him with all possible dispatch. In about half an hour they set off under the command of Sergeant Major Scott and overtaking the advance guard near Wickham Market, the Colonel informed them he had met the Mail Coach from Yarmouth[141] and on inquiry was informed there was no reason for being alarmed as no information of the appearance was known of on that part of the Coast and that must have been a false alarm by some mistake at the signal Posts. The Colonel ordered the Troops to return and about 9 oClock they arrived at Woodbridge, when he was pleased to express his approbation (and thanks) for the active part they had taken in joining him so early on their march. The remainder of the yeomanry had orders to march early the following morning, and orders were issued for that purpose, which on return of the advance guard were of course contradicted. The Woodbridge Volunteers were under arms waiting the arrival of General Balfour.

Monday July 15th 1799

I agreed with Mr John Dawson of Woodbridge to have the use of his field for the Troop to exercise on paying him for the use of the same 10s 6d each day of exercise.

A121 Friday July 19th 1799 General Muster

The Troop assembled on Parade at the usual time and marched from same to the Field hired of Mr Dawson for the purpose of exercising upon. We went through the usual Evolutions, Sword Exercise and Firing. Orders were given out for a General Muster on Friday next 26th Instant at which time an inspection of arms was directed to be made also of Equipments, preparatory to a Review.

Friday July 26th General Muster

The Troop being met marched to the field hired of Mr Dawson and having exercised in the sundry evolutions, sword exercise and firing an Inspections was made of the Arms and Equipments and such as were damaged were ordered to be repaired at the expense of the Fund for that purpose. The Troop being augmented Cloak Cases being provided were delivered to such members as required the same also fronts for Bridles preparatory to the Review.
[142]

A122 Friday August 9th 1799

The Troop assembled at the time and place appointed and marched to the field hired of Mr Dawson. A very heavy shower of rain came on soon after we got to the field which continued for several hours the Troop was in consequence dismissed.

---

[140] Collett lived in Woodbridge while Captain Broke was at Nacton and Cornet Edgar on the edge of Ipswich, both several miles away.

[141] It is interesting to consider how news travelled. As well as the mail coach, which travelled along the turnpike road from London to Yarmouth, there were signal posts such as the one at Bawdsey. After 1808, Yarmouth, being an important port and a Royal Naval dockyard, was linked to London by the British version of the French semaphore system, which worked by using shutters rather than arms; it took an inland route.

[142] *London Gazette Extraordinary*, an account of the naval action of 19 June 1799 leading to the surrender of French frigates that survived the Battle of the Nile, is not included.

Captain Broke communicated to the Troop his information of the General having received a Letter for Foreign Service immediately and which included regular troops in Garrison at Ipswich etc etc. The Review intended to take place on Friday next was consequently abandoned – the Troops having orders to hold themselves in readiness to march at an hour's notice and the following morning Saturday August 10th at 5 oClock the Royal Horse Artillery who had been in quarters at Woodbridge from 15th September 1796, marched out of Town on their Route for embarking on Foreign service.

On account of the Harvest the next meeting of the Troop is postponed until further orders.
[143]

A132 (Circular)   **Head Quarters Woodbridge September 16th 1799**
Sir I beg the favour of you to attend (in plain Cloths) a meeting to be held at Woodbridge on Wednesday morning next the 18th Instant at 10 oClock on special business of the Troop.

P B Broke Captain

By order C Collett Quarter Master

Wednesday September 18th 1806 (1799) [144]
The members of the Troop being met in complyance with the above request, at the Crown Inn, Captain Broke informed them the purport of his requesting their attendance at this time was for the purpose of electing an Officer in the place of the late Lieutenant Brooke, deceased. An arrangement being previously made Captain Broke proposed the following names viz
Lieutenant Edgar, first Lieutenant vice Brooke deceased
Cornet Brand, 2nd Lieutenant vice Edgar promoted
J M Theobald, Cornet vice Brand promoted
The above named Gentlemen being proposed and the proposal seconded they where unanimously elected, Captain Broke informing the Lord Lieutenant of the County of the choice the same was approved by His Majesty who was pleased to sign their commissions accordingly.

Arrangement for the purpose of expediting the meeting of the Troop on an emergent occasion
Head Quarters Woodbridge September 18th 1799
Arrangement of the Second Troop of Loyal Suffolk Cavalry by Divisions, which the following Commissioned and non-commissioned Officers are requested to undertake respectively, in order to expedite Notices with the easiest and quickest dispatch.

Philip B Broke Captain

Division of Captain Brokes   John Sawer, William Rooke, James Bryant and John Porter
A133 2nd **Lieutenant Edgars Division**   William Pearson Sergeant, Joseph Walford Corporal, Francis Chisnell, George Curtis, William Mendham, William Hewitt, Robert Sexton, Jonathan Broke

---

[143] A123–131, *London Gazette Extraordinary.* The defeat of Bonaparte at Acre is omitted.
[144] Collett presumably added the correct date later.

3rd **Cornet Theobalds Division**   Lieutenant Brand, J Rodwell, William Cockrell, C.B. Church.

4th   **Quarter Master Colletts and Sergeant Major Gross' Division**   Trumpeter Leek, Henry Short, John Couperthwaite, William Whincopp, John Clarke, Philip Riches, Tollemache Cole, John Woods, William Kemp, Nathaniel Gross, Joseph Bulmer, Jonathan Churchyard.

5th **Sergeant Everitts Division** Charles Collett, William Abbot, Daniel Orpen, Thomas Chandler.

6th **Sergeant Symonds Division**: Thomas Mitchell, H J Luffe, Francis Hayle, Philip Trusson, Moses Gabbatas

7th **Corporal Baldrys Division**   Jonathan Whimper, Thurston Whimper, Samuel Gross, N Benington

8th **Corporal Harper's Division** Robert Clarke, Nathaniel Moor, Jonathan Chapman, Thomas Walton, Solomn Rivers, John Roberts, Hyam Pierce, John Cockle.

9th   **Corporal Dikes Division**   Benoni Barthrop, James Churchyard, William Barthrop, Nathaniel Bartrop, William Walton

10th **Thomas Simpson senior Division**   Thomas Simpson junior, Robert Manthrop, Isaac Churchyard, Stebing Gross, Benjamin Burthrop, George Bates, Jonathan Hunt, Jonathan Field, William W Mason, John Shiming.

A printed Card of the Names in each division was delivered to the Officers and commanding same. [145]

A136 **Friday October 4th 1799 General Muster**

The Troop being assembled at the usual time marched from Parade to the field for exercise. After which the commanding Officer explained to them the arrangement which had been drawn up and now requested to be particularly attended to for the more expeditiously assembling the Troop in the case of emergency or for actual service for which they were required to have everything in readiness.

Mr William Pearson and Mr Joseph Walford being proposed were unanimously elected and attached to Lieutenant Edgars division. Mr Pearson a Sergeant and Mr Walford Corporal.

A General Muster was ordered on Friday 25th Instant.

Friday October 25th 1799 General Muster

The Troop met on parade at the usual time and marched to the field for exercise. The day was stormy and unpleasant. The next general muster was ordered on 15th November. By order of Captain Broke returns of the Troop for the last 5 months were made out and sent to the War Office, the General of the Eastern District, the Lord Lieutenant of the County etc etc etc. [146]

Friday December 13th General Muster

The Troop assembled and exercised as usual. The next General Muster ordered on Friday in the last week in January 1800 and the Troops were ordered to have all their arms and equipment in proper order and readiness in case of being called upon at the shortest notice for actual service.

---

[145] A134–135, *London Gazette Extraordinary*. The capture of Seringapatam in India, April and May 1799, not included.

[146] The administration was obviously showing signs of improvement.

January 25th 1800 Circular Letters were sent to each member of the troop, postponing the meeting ordered on the 31st Instant, in consequence of the weather being unfavourable, until Friday 28th February and then to meet at the usual time and place.

Friday February 28th 1800 General Muster
The Troop being met at the time appointed, in consequence of a very hard frost, could not take the field, the muster Roll was called over at the Crown Inn by Lieutenant Edgar. After which in consideration of the number of absentees of late on days of General Muster, the following resolutions were unanimously agreed upon, ordered to be printed and sent to each member of the Troop by the Quarter Master.

(Circular) Sir **Head Quarters Woodbridge March 1st 1800**
I am desired by the commanding Officer to send you the following Resolution and you are particularly required to attend the Meeting on the 14th instant.
Cornelius Collett Quarter Master

A137 At the Monthly Muster of the Troop this Day, It being the unanimous opinion that some Measures should be taken to insure a better Attendance of the Day of Exercise, than has for a considerable length of time been given; it was moved by Mr John Couperthwaite, and seconded by Mr John Rodwell (without any dissenting voice) that a Meeting of the Troop should be held at the Crown Inn Woodbridge on Friday the 14th of March at Eleven oClock in the morning, to take the same into Consideration; and that the Quarter Master be requested to communicate the same by Letter to the Absentees.
Woodbridge February 28th 1800 Mileson Edgar 1st Lieutenant

Friday March 14th 1800
A Meeting of the Troop was held this day at the Crown Inn in complyance with the notice and the following Resolutions were unanimously resolved upon by the Numbers present and a printed copy of same was delivered to each member of the Troop.
Head quarters Woodbridge March 14th 1800
At a Meeting of the Second Troop of Loyal Suffolk Yeomanry held this day, for the Purpose of adopting some Measures for insuring a better Attendance on the Days of Exercise. Mr Couperthwaite in the Chair.
The following Resolutions were proposed and agreed to
1st That a Committee be appointed on the next Muster day to adjudge the Forfeits incurred by absence on the days of Exercise
2nd That (as it appears there are many Forfeits of considerable standing still discharged) every person shall in future be required to discharge his Forfeits, either on the Day of which the Committee determines upon them, or previous to the following Muster or in Failure thereof, be no longer considered as one of the Troop.
3rd That in future the Committee sit upon the Forfeits incurred by absence once in three months.
4th That henceforth every person absenting himself on days of Exercise, without an excuse which the Committee shall deem satisfactory, shall Forfeit for each time of Absence, according to the following Scale viz Five Shillings for the first Time, Seven Shillings for the second time, ten shillings and sixpence for the three time

and as often as he shall absent himself with the year, commencing the 28th instant, and ending the same Day 1801 (it being understood that the Troop will not exercise oftener than once in the Month) except on any particular occasion, as prior to a Review, or from such cause as shall be deemed good and sufficient in the judgement of the Majority of the Troop. Any orders however from the A138 Magistrates or Generals commanding in the District, must necessarily be attended to.

5th That every person pleading Sickness or Lameness as an excuse of absence, be required to produce a Certificate of the same, under the hand of a Surgeon or Apothecary.

6th That no person shall be deemed present when the Muster Roll is called, unless he appears in Uniform.

7th That the resolutions of 28th December 1797 (except the third) remain in full force.

8th That the Chairman do sign on behalf of the Meetings the foregoing Resolutions, and that the Quarter Master be requested to send a printed copy thereof to every member of the Troop.

John Couperthwaite

Friday March 28th 1800 General Muster

The Troop being met, marched into the field, the day being unfavourable for Exercise, the muster Roll being called over, they passed the commanding officer in Review order and then adjourned to the Crown Inn when a Committee was chosen by Lot (or Tickets) consisting of thirteen members to hear and determine appeals against Forfeits. The same being settled by the Committee an order was sent to each person who had incurred forfeits of the amount of same to be paid on or before the next General Muster or they will no longer be considered Members of the Troop agreeable to the Resolution at the last special meeting.

(Circular)

Head Quarters Woodbridge 28th March 1800

I am desired by the Commanding Officer to inform you, the next General Muster of the Troop will be held on Friday the 25th April next at the usual Time and Place, and by unanimous consent of the members present this day on duty, a Dinner will be provided at the Crown Inn; for the Expense of which, Thirty Pounds is ordered to be paid from the amount arising from Forfeits. I am also (by the Committee who were appointed agreeable to the Resolutions of the meeting on the 14th Instant to decide on the Forfeits) requested to advise, you have adjudged to you [blank] Forfeits, and that payment of same is required to be made on or before the next General Muster, or in future thereof, you will no longer be considered as one of the Troop.

Cornelius Collett Quarter Master

Friday April 25th 1800 General Muster

The Troop being met marched to the Field for exercise, after the business of the day, returned to Woodbridge and dined together at the Crown Inn (agreeable to notice of same in Circular Letter 28th March). We had a very pleasant agreeable meeting and much to the entertainment of all present.

A139 Wednesday June 4th 1800

The Troop met to fire a feu de joye in honour of his Majesty's Birthday. The morning was very wet, the weather proving fine about 12 oClock the Troop with the Royal Horse Artillery quartered in the town commanded by Captain Gilbert,[147] the Woodbridge Volunteers and Sea Fencibles, marched into a Field in the occupation of Spencer Leek on the hills at the back of the halfway house going to Melton, being formed, the Artillery fired a Royal Salute, our Troop a feu de joye, and the Volunteers three Vollies (in honor of the day) three cheers were given by the Troops and Company present, which were very numerous and from the situation of the ground the appearance had a very pleasing effect. After the cheers the Troops saluted, marched into the Town to the parade and were discharged from further duty on the day.

A Dinner being provided at the Crown, a party of 30 met and dined. We had a very jovial and pleasant meeting, many good songs were sung, parted company about eleven oClock much gratified by the variety of the day.

Friday June 27th 1800   General Muster

The Troop mustered at the usual time and place and marched to Sutton and exercised the usual evolutions and sword Exercise. Orders were given for the next General Muster on Friday 25th July at 10 oClock in the Forenoon when a Committee is to be chosen to hear and determine on the appeals against Forfeits. Each member who had incurred forfeits was informed of same and particularly requested to attend the above muster.

A circular letter of which the following is a Copy was sent to each member of the Troop who were considered not to have attended a proper number of Musters to enable them to claim the exemptions from sundry Taxes expressed in the Act of Parliament respecting Volunteer Service etc etc.

Sir   Red House July 20th 1800

Mr Manning the surveyor having applied to me as commanding officer of the Troop in the absence of Captain Broke, to sign a Certificate of all those who have a right to exemption from the duties on the Cavalry Horse and use of hair powder, also from being balloted for in the Militia, by having in the Language of the Act (since the date of their Enrolment duly attended at the Exercise of the Corps, unless prevented by Sickness or such other sufficient reason as hath been duly allowed by the Captain or by the commanding officer of the said Corps for the time being) I have deferred signing such a Certificate till after Thursday the 25th Instant, our next muster, in the hope that you will make a point of attending on that day and A140 of your being able to afford me such sufficient reasons for your frequent absence from the Exercise of the Troop as will enable me safely and conscientiously to return your Name in the Certificate, which at present I am free to confess, I am not.

I am much yours, Mileson Edgar

A letter of which the above is a copy was sent to 21 members of the Troop who by the Muster Roll it did not appear had attended the proper number of times (or given satisfactory reasons for their non-attendance) so as to enable them to claim the exemptions under the Act of Parliament – in which also the commanding Officer is required to make a just return or be subjected to a considerable fine in case of making an improper one.

---

[147] The Royal Horse Artillery had returned to town after leaving for foreign service in the previous year. The fact that it returned, and was to remain, shows the importance the government placed on defending this part of the coast.

Friday July 25ᵗʰ General Muster

The Troop being met on parade at the time appointed, the muster roll having been called over, the commanding officer dismissed them from duty on horseback and adjourned the meeting to the Crown Inn (or Town Hall) when the forfeits were settled by a Committee chosen for that purpose – on the same purpose as before conducted.

Lieutenant Edgar commanding Officer in the absence of Captain Broke (who has been some time in Bath for the benefit of his health) called over the names of those Gentlemen who had been written too, to attend on this day in consequence of their non-attendance on days of General Muster and those who could not give a satisfactory reason (as required by the Act of Parliament) were returned accordingly and in consequence could not claim the exemptions mentioned in the Act. A General Muster of the Troop was ordered on 24ᵗʰ August next.

Circular   **Nacton August 24ᵗʰ 1800**

Sir, In consequence of the present wet, and the urgent demand that must be occasioned thereby the Exertions necessary to secure, when fairer Weather succeeds, the Corn yet abroad, it appears to me proper not to obtrude on the Anxiety and Interests of the Community, the Interruption of a General Muster.[148]

I do therefore adjourn the Meeting, intended to be held on Friday the 29ᵗʰ instant for that purpose, to Friday 26ᵗʰ day of September next, subject however to an intermediate call, if the Services of the Public requires it.

Philip B Broke Captain Second Troop Loyal Suffolk Yeomanry Cavalry

Riot at Woodbridge

On Tuesday 16ᵗʰ September 1800 Provisions being at this time very dear and the weather being unfavourable for getting in the Harvest and the Corns being much damaged A141 there was reason to expect they would not be lower but probably much higher, the lower ranks of the community appeared to be much dissatisfied at same and much inclined to tumult on the occasion[149] and on this day as many persons from the neighbourhood were bringing provisions to the Town (agreeable to weekly custom) they were stopped by sundry persons in various parts of the parish (chiefly by women who assembled for the purpose) and the sundry articles demanded of them at certain fixed prices, which not readily being complied with, the baskets etc were arrested from them the contents taken out and sold at such prices as they thought proper to give. It consisted chiefly of butter and eggs - the butter was sold at 1s a pint and the eggs at 6d a dozen which money was immediately paid for them, and none was taken without being paid for. The proceedings being immediately reported in the neighbourhood many people on their way to the Town on hearing of the same returned home on which account there was only six persons that were compelled to sell and not being at the time a resident Magistrate in the Town nothing was done (except by persuasion) to prevent their proceeding on this day. They were watched in their various movements throughout the day by the Inhabitants and no injury was done to anyone except in the instances above

---

[148] Evidence of a very poor harvest and therefore of the prospect of high bread prices.

[149] In this entry Collett provides one of his more infrequent comments on the prevailing social problems of the period. He clearly understood the reasons for the discontent and protest but limited himself to a factual account.

76

Plate 12. Sketch of market day on Market Hill, Woodbridge, 1830. The Yeomanry did not muster on Wednesdays because those were market days. This was the location of the riot described by Collett. © SROI, Fitch Collection, HD480/4, f. 98, no. 61. Photograph by Mike Durrant

mentioned. The following day Wednesday being Market day, threats were given out and there was every reason to expect a very large assembly would meet in the morning for the purpose of attacking in the same way, every person bringing Provisions and demand of the Millers, Bakers and Butchers a reduction of prices or that they should sell at such a price as those assembled should think proper to fix upon. From the information collected there appeared no doubt of a very riotous assembly on Wednesday morning. Being myself the only Officer belonging to the Troop who had any information of this business I considered it advisable to wait on Edward Jenny Esq at Bredfield he being a Magistrate who resided nearest to Woodbridge and consult him on the propriety of the 2nd Troop of Yeomanry Cavalry being called upon to hold themselves in readiness on the occasion. We agreeing in opinion that it would be prudent to assemble the Troop for the purpose of being prepared in case of any riotous proceedings to assist the Civil Power in quelling the same. I immediately acquainted Captain Broke what had occurred and orders were immediately issued for the Troop to assemble at Woodbridge at 9 oClock on the following Morning at which time the Magistrates in the neighbourhood agreed to meet at the Town Hall, (being about 2 hours previous to the time of their holding their weekly meetings).

In complyance with the order given out yesterday the Troop met at the time appointed. Captain Broke having with Magistrates arranged the Plan, they were directed to take their respective stations in detachments as **A142** follows. About ten oClock the Troop marched into one of my Fields at the back of Mr Field's house where the detachment ordered under the command of Captain Broke remained, and the other detachment were under the command of Lieutenant Edgar marched to a Field at Melton belonging to Mr Richard Wood at the back of the Wind Mills were they remained waiting further orders from the Magistrates. A very great number of people of the lower class appeared in various parties on the Town but finding the Magistrates where prepared no riotous proceedings were entered into, and about 3 oClock in the afternoon information was received by a dispatch from the Magistrates that all was become peaceable that it was not considered needful to detain us any longer and we were accordingly discharged from Duty. On my return home as I was crossing the market place the Magistrates being then going from the Hall to Dinner inquired of me for Captain Broke who I informed was in consequence of their orders for discharging the Troop, gone home. They immediately informed me that since sending such orders (and they supposed in consequence of it) a very much greater assemblage of the people inclined to riot had taken place and that appearances bore a much more serious aspect and requested I would immediately recall Captain Broke and again muster the Troop. I accordingly followed Captain Broke and was successful in overtaking him and Lieutenant Edgar on Martlesham Hill and mustering again the majority of the Troop who immediately returned to the duty of the day.

The persons disposed to Riot were by this time very much increased in Number and many more it was expected would join them in the evening. They were extremely insulting full of invectives and threats of violence. The Magistrates being again met on the Town Hall we paraded in the Quay Lane, and afterwards marched across the Market Place passing through the mob for the purpose of showing we were in readiness in case of being called upon to resist their proceedings. We took our stations on the Roads approaching the Town waiting the further order of the Magistrates who were using every means to persuade the people to disperse. A very great number of the Inhabitants where sworn Special Constables, and from the increased violence, and outrage, they proceeded to take into custody a part of the rioters who appeared most active, and sent orders to the Troop to load with Ball Cartridges and march into the Town. The same being generally known, the means taken had the desired effect, and in the course of an hour, finding the Magistrates resolved to disperse them by means of the Yeomanry, and the constables in readiness to apprehend such as did not immediately disperse (after the Riot Act being read) they thought it advisable to withdraw themselves, and at 10 Oclock at night all was quiet, the Troops discharged from duty, and all the horrible consequences which would otherwise have A143 taken place, were done away and peace and good order re-established to the great comfort and satisfaction of all peaceable Inhabitants.

There can be no doubt had not such prompt measures been taken, but that the riotous proceedings would have been attended with most serious consequences.

Friday September 26th 1800 General Muster

The Troop being assembled at the appointed time and place, marched from Parade to a Field in the occupation of Mr Field and exercised in the usual evolutions and sword exercise. It was intimated by Captain Broke that he had expectations we should shortly be reviewed by the General of the district.

(Circular)   Sir   **Head Quarters Woodbridge October 10th 1800**

The General having signified his intentions of Reviewing our Troop in the first week in November next, I am desired by Captain Broke to inform you of it, and to request your attendance at the General Muster on the 31st Instant, Arms and Equipments of every kind are required to be in the nicest Order.

Cornelius Collett Quarter Master

(Circular) **Head Quarters Woodbridge October 20ᵗʰ 1800**
Sir Major General Lord Charles Fitzroy having signified his intentions of Reviewing our Troop on Thursday the 6ᵗʰ of November next, it is the particular wish of Captain Broke to have a full meeting, and that you will attend equipped, as on a General Muster Day. Every Equipment is required to be in Condition to pass the most minute Inspection. You are also requested to attend the General Muster on the 31ˢᵗ instant, when you will receive further Instructions respecting the Review.
Cornelius Collett Quarter Master

Friday October 31ˢᵗ 1800 General Muster
The Troop met agreeable to notice for that purpose on the 10ᵗʰ instant, also on the 3ʳᵈ of November and Exercised in all the Evolutions and Sword exercise preparatory to the Review an inspection of arms etc etc was also made by the Captain and particular instructions were given to have everything in the neatest order on 6ᵗʰ November being the day appointed for the Review.

A144 Thursday November 6ᵗʰ 1800 General Muster
At 10 oClock in the forenoon the Troop assembled on Rushmere Heath and from thence marched to Ipswich to a field in the occupation of Mr Fuller near to the Town where we met the Ipswich Troop of Yeomanry. It unfortunately began to Rain at the time of our arrival and continued to rain very hard for several hours and we all in consequence got very wet. General Lord Charles Fitzroy came into the Field and inspected the Troops very minutely and was pleased to express his approbation of their Soldier like appearance, but in consequence of the continued rain, he declined the Review and after the inspection we were immediately dispersed.

Friday February 27ᵗʰ 1801 General Muster
The Troop met at the usual time and place and marched from the Parade to the Field and exercised in the General Evolutions etc etc. The muster being very small a general meeting of the Troop was ordered to take into consideration the cause, and to adopt such means as would prevent the same in future.

(Circular) **Head Quarters Woodbridge 27ᵗʰ February 1801**
Sir I am desired by the Commanding Officer, to inform you, there will be a General Meeting of the Troop on Thursday the 12ᵗʰ of March next, at 11oClock in the morning, at the Crown Inn, on Special Business, where you are particularly requested to attend; at the same Time all Forfeits will be settled. As the Troop will not go onto the Field, you are not to appear in uniform.
Cornelius Collett Quarter Master

A145 Thursday March 12ᵗʰ 1801
A Meeting of the Troop was held this day by order of the Commanding Officer (see circular letter of 27ᵗʰ February) for the purpose of revising the former resolutions regarding forfeits and to settle those already incurred.
At a Meeting of the Troop held this 12ᵗʰ day of March 1801 the Resolutions respecting forfeits which were agreed upon the 14ᵗʰ March 1800 and to be continued for one year expiring on this day, the same was taken into consideration and unanimously confirmed as binding for one year more from the 28ᵗʰ instant to the 28ᵗʰ March 1802.

At this meeting it was moved, and unanimously resolved, that Lieutenant Edgar be requested to state to Captain Broke the wish of the Troop that he will forthwith report to the War Office, Mr Mitchells continued Absence on the days of Muster, which appears so replete with Insults to the Corps and Injury to the Institution as to deserve a serious Notice.

Friday April 24th 1801 General Muster
The Troop being assembled at the usual time, adjourned to the Crown Inn, a Committee was appointed for settling the Forfeits and the next General Muster was ordered on the 15th May and a notice of the same was sent to each Member of the Troop. After the Business of the Committee etc etc the Troop assembled in the Market Place and fired a Feu de joye in honour of the Victory at Copenhagen.[150] The Sea Fencibles also formed on the Parade with the Colours belonging to the Ships at the Wharf which had a pleasing additional effect.

Friday May 15th 1801 General Muster
The Troop met at the usual time and place. Being a very wet morning the muster was in consequence very small. At 12 oClock the Muster Roll was called over at the Crown Inn and those present were dismissed and excused from attending in the Field for Exercise. A general muster was ordered on the 4th of June, which being his Majesty's Birthday, it was unanimously agreed we should dine together at the Crown Inn.
[151]

A152 Thursday June 4th 1801 General Muster
The Troop assembled at the usual time and place and being joined by the Royal Horse Artillery Quartered in the Town and the Woodbridge Volunteers marched into the Field hired by the Artillery, when being formed in Line, a Royal Salute by the Artillery, a feu de joye by the Cavalry and three Vollies by the Volunteers, was fired in honour of his Majesty's Birth Day. The Troop afterwards marched to their field for Exercise and practised the sundry Evolutions as usual with Sword Exercise.

As under is a Copy of a letter from Lord Euston the Lord Lieutenant of the County in reply to Captain Broke's representation of the conduct of Mr Mitchell in absenting himself on days of General Muster of the Troop.
Sir   **Margaret Street May 13th 1801**
The Letter you sent to Colonel Calver inclosing a resolution of your Corps of Yeomanry on the subject of Mr. Mitchells absence from its Meetings for a considerable time past was transmitted from the Adjutant Generals office to that of the Secretary of State for the home department (where) upon a Communication which I have had with that Office in consequence of the Case being in some measure referred to me, I find the opinion I sometime ago took the liberty of giving upon the subject completely confirmed it being clearly understood by the Duke of Portland that the absence or misbehaviour of an individual not bearing His Majesty's Commission in a Corps of Yeomanry or Volunteers is a Case in which the Corps itself is perfectly competent to decide according to its own Regulations.

---

[150] The Battle of Copenhagen, 2 April 1801. The British Fleet was led by Rear Admiral Sir Hyde Parker of Melford Hall. The battle is best known as the occasion when Nelson, second in command, won a victory after ignoring orders to withdraw, using his blind eye as the excuse.
[151] A146–151, *London Gazette Extraordinary.* The Battle of Copenhagen is omitted.

I have the honour to be Sir, your most obedient and very humble servant

Euston

To P B Broke Esq, Nacton

The above Letter from the Lord Lieutenant being read, the opinion of the Troop taken thereon, it was Resolved (with one dissenting voice only Mr Henry Luff who declined giving any vote) that Mr Mitchell's name should be struck out of the Muster Roll, it was immediately done by Captain Broke and a letter of which the following is a Copy was by desire of the Troop sent to Mr Mitchell pre post advising him of their proceedings etc.

Sir   **Head Quarters Woodbridge June 4th 1801**

I am sorry to be under the painful necessity of transmitting to you a Resolution which the Troop when on duty this day came to (with one Dissenting Voice only) **A153** Viz, that in consequence of your constant Absence on the days of Exercise and even at a time when the Country has had occasion to call the Troop for its services it would be an insult to the Corps and an injury to the Establishment to suffer your name to remain any longer amongst those who hold themselves pledged to a full discharge of all they undertook at their Enrollment and therefore, requested the Commanding Officer to Erase your name from the Roll which was accordingly done.

Your humble Servant Cornelius Collett Quarter Master

After the business of the day was settled, the Troop adjourned to the Crown Inn and dined together and the remainder of the day and Evening was spent very agreeably in mirth and good humour.

A181 (Circular)   **Head Quarters Woodbridge July 19th 1801**

Sir   I am desired by Captain Broke to inform you the next General Muster of the Troop will be on Friday the 31st instant at the usual time and place, when you are required to appear fully equipped for actual service, and you are further required to hold yourself in readiness to march on the shortest notice, in case of being called upon for that purpose.[153]

Cornelius Collett Quarter Master

London July 23rd 1801

Sir   You will be so good as to Circulate Copies of the enclosed paper throughout the Volunteer Corps in Suffolk without delay.

I am, Sir, Your Obedient humble Servant   Euston

To Henry Collett Esq Clerk of the Peace

London July 23rd 1801

The Volunteer Corps in Suffolk are requested to be Readiness to assemble at the shortest Notice at their usual place of Rendezvous in the Event of actual Invasion.

Euston   Lord Lieutenant

The Lord Lieutenant and the General of the Division having signified to Captain Broke his wishes that he Captain Broke with the Troop would inspect the passes from the marshes etc between Butley Ferry and Woodbridge River by which the

---

[152] A153–180, *London Gazette Extraordinary.* Various reports about Egypt and Alexandria are omitted.
[153] Invasion fears were at their height that summer.

stocks of Cattle etc may be driven to the Interior of the Country in case of Invasion and report the same.[154] An arrangement for that purpose was accordingly made by Captain Broke and the following Circular Letter issued.

Head Quarters Woodbridge July 26th 1801

Sir   At the request of Captain Broke by desire of the Lord Lieutenant of the County, you are desired to meet the first division of the Troop at Woodbridge on Thursday morning next the 30th Instant precisely at 10 oClock fully equipped for Actual Service.

Cornelius Collett Quarter Master

July 30th 1801

The first Division of the Troop (commanded by Captain Broke) being met agreeable to the above notice, marched to inspect the passes leading from the Marshes to the Uplands from Butley River to Bawdsey Ferry.

Report of Captain Broke to the General of the Division   July 30th 1801

First division of Second Troop of Loyal Suffolk Yeomanry Cavalry

Assembled at the place of Rendezvous (Woodbridge) marched to Wilford Hills **A182** where there met by the Reverend Dr Franks. From thence proceeded across the heaths in Sutton, Shottisham and Hollesley to Boyton by the high Road and to Dock Marshes in Boyton near the Dock, in the occupation of Mr Robert Bennington lying in the Butley River, from thence by the Road to the Marshes in the occupation of Mr John Woolnough and in the way leading to his Hardway lying in the Butley River, then to Cardwell Hall Marshes in the occupation of Mr Woolnough. The communication from the uplands to the same is by a drift way at the west end of Cardwell Hall Buildings, then past Mr Jeptha Wallers House and Cottages to the Marshes in his occupation and those also occupied by Mr Barthrop.

NB The direct way to the above Marshes of Mr Waller and Mr Barthrop is from Woodbridge over Boyton Allens passing the West end of Mr Waller's Cottages.

From those Marshes by the Road, passed Mr Barthrop's House to the House of Mr Tokelove to the Marshes late The Reverend William Boltons in which are Bowmans Creek and Bowmans Sluice in Hollesley and called Oxley Marshes. Adjoining to which Marshes the Level is continued and is in the occupation of Mr Brady, Mr Virtue and Mr Pytches, the Communication to which from the uplands are through their respective Farm Yards.

Next to the Marshes of Mr Brady, Virtue and Pitches are those in the occupation of Mr Whimper in the parish of Alderton and are called Buckenhaw and also others lying in Bawdsey called Scotes Marshes. The Communication to these is out of the High Road leading from Hollesley to Alderton close to Cowsley Lane in which a Branch leads off on the Right to Scotts Marshes. Thence passing by Marshes in the occupation of Francis Ablitt the Communication to which is by the Wheelwright's Shop in Alderton Street, also by the Marshes in the occupation of the Reverend Dr Frank and Mr Thomas Pytches, the communication to which are through their

---

[154] This was Collett's first reference to the implementation of the government's defence plan of 'Driving the country' and its application in the field. This specific area was of major importance since it was the only one they were asked to survey in this way. Two years later its important status was further recognised when General Sir Eyre Coote was brought in to draw up a detailed plan for its defence. He described the area as of primary importance. See Plate IV.

respective farm yards and then to Bawdsey by the Marshes of Mr Robert Cutting, the communication to which is from Bawdsey Street down the first Lane, thence to East Lane in Bawdsey Street to the Land called East End on Hollesly Bay close to the Sea and Beach. From East End back to Bawdsey Street forward down the Road to Bawdsey Ferry past Mr William Pages and through the Farm Yard held by Mr Cavell to the Field in which the Bawdsey Signal House stands.

NB There is a View on the Right over the level of Marshes in Bawdsey as far as Bawdsey Fleet and over the same and the Marshes in Alderton and Ramsholt on the side of Woodbridge River. The communication to and from the marshes lying on Woodbridge River from Bawdsey are by Alderton Street except the Marshes called Scotts in Bawdsey which communicate with the Hollesly Road by Cowley Lane Drift.

NB From Dock Marsh (Boyton) straight to William Bennington's House across a small Dam to Capel.[155]

A183 Sir   **Head Quarters Woodbridge July 26th 1801**
At the request of Captain Broke by desire of the Lord Lieutenant of the [blank] you are desired to meet the Second Division of the Troop at Woodbridge on Friday Morning next the 31st instant at 10 oClock fully equipped for actual Service
To Lieutenant Edgar   Cornelius Collett Quarter Master

July 31st 1801
The second Division of the Troop (commanded by Lieutenant Edgar) being met agreeable to the above Notice marched to inspect the remaining approaches from the Marshes at Bawdsey and which were not reported yesterday and reported the state of the same as under.

Report of Lieutenant Edgar to the Troop and the General of the District   July 31st 1801
Assembled at the place of Rendezvous (Woodbridge) and marched over Wilford Hills to Shottisham, and from thence to Ramsholt Marshes, observing the drifts and passes from thence (next to those inspected yesterday by Captain Broke) in the occupation of Mr Baldry and Mr Lynn in Bawdsey also Mr Page and Mr Cavell, likewise those in Alderton in the occupation of Mr L Collett and Mr Thomas Ablett. The approach to those Marshes in Bawsdey occupied by Mr Cavel and Mr William Page is through Bawsdey and Alderton Street. But it appears practicable should Circumstances occur to make it desirable to remove the stock from a considerable part of Bawdsey Marshes through the Ramsholt Marshes, into the Road leading from thence to Shottisham at the back of Mr Baldrys House.

From the Ramsholt Marshes we marched to the Signal House in Bawdsey to Cowesley Lane and East Lane all of which having been reported by Captain Broke, no further observations thereon are needful.

Having inspected the passes agreeable to the orders of the Lord Lieutenant etc and prepared the Report of same the Troops on duty this day on our return after we left Alderton, were dismissed.

---

[155] This was a very comprehensive survey, linking the marshes where the animals grazed, with the routes and driftways leading to the uplands together with the owners who could be alerted if an emergency arose.

NB The weather was excessively Hot and the Roads uncommonly dusty.

Copy of a Circular Letter sent by order of the Lord Lieutenant, and at the request of Captain Broke delivered to the sundry Persons as under, viz
Mr William Page Bawdsey, Jonathan Whimper Alderton, Jonathan Bartrop Hollesley, Jonathan Woolnough Boyton, Thomas Ablett Butley and Jonathan Mabsom Shottisham who were at the same time requested to inform their respective Neighbours of the Contacts.

A184 Sir   **Nacton July 28ᵗʰ 1801**
In consequence of the great preparations which the Enemy is making on the opposite Coasts in order to invade the Country, I am directed by the Lord Lieutenant to give every Aid by the Troop of Yeomanry I have the honour to Command and in recommending in the most urgent manner to the owners of Horses and Cattle on the Marshes by the Sea side in the Hundred of Wilford to unite their exertions in removing with all possible dispatch such Horses and Cattle, that they may not be seized by the Invading Army. Anxious as I am on my part to give you every Satisfactory Explanation and every Protection consistent with the Public service, I trust the regard you have for the General Good, and the Estimation in which you hold your own property will inable me by the 31ˢᵗ instant to make such a Report to the Commander in Chief of the District as will prove your zeal and Alacrity to cut off all such resources from the enemy.[156]

    I am, Sir, Your most obedient and very humble servant   Philip B Broke

---

                                     Nacton 9ᵗʰ August 1801
Sir   The annexed sketch for Divisions of Routs, you will be so good as to hold in Readiness but not Issue till you hear further from General the Marquis Cornwallis, Balfour, Egaton or from me who remain etc etc   Philip B Broke
To Mr C Collett Woodbridge

On Sunday morning August 9ᵗʰ 1801 died Mr Daniel Orpen of Felixstowe Aged 54 years and being a Member of the Troop was Buried with Military Honors at Felixstowe on Wednesday evening about 6 oClock. He was a Man very much respected by all the members of the Troop, his neighbours and Acquaintances. Almost all the Neighbourhood attended his funeral and much regret his loss.

Captain Broke's Troop of Yeomanry
Residence of the Captain, Nacton near Ipswich
                              Rendezvous of the Corps Woodbridge

In case an Enemy should Effect a landing upon or near the Coast of Suffolk, Captain Broke's Troop of Yeomanry Cavalry will be appointed according to the following Route and Instructions approved by the General Commanding the Eastern District and the Lord Lieutenant of the County. This tract of Country extend from the Stour to Butley River.[157]

---

[156] By asking the owners on the marshes to remove their animals, the Yeomanry was in effect starting to implement the plan, although it is unclear whether such instructions were carried out.

[157] It is noteworthy that at this stage of the plan the Yeomanry was in charge of driving livestock inland, rather than helping with evacuation of the people.

Samford Hundred This District must be cleared on one side up the Orwell to Sproughton and on the other up the Stour to Higham Marsh and the Stock driven by Lavenham to Bury. At Lavenham the detachment of Captain Brokes Troop will be relieved by a Detachment of Lord Bromes Troop, and Captain Brokes Detachment will join its own Troop and repair to the Head Quarters of the Army.

The Roads leading from Cattawade Bridges to East Bergholt and from that Bridge by Tattingstone to Ipswich and the principal Roads from Ipswich to Stratford, from Ipswich to Hadleigh and from Hadleigh to Stratford must not be driven upon, except in the necessary Crossing, which must be done with the greatest expedition.

This Division will not halt till it has cleared the London road from Stratford.

A186 Colnies Hundred Comprises the Country between the River Orwell and Deben. This district must be cleared from Landguard Fort up the side of the Orwell to Bramford Bridge and up the side of the Deben to Wilford Bridge and the cattle driven to Needham and Stowmarket where the Detachment being relieved by one from Lord Bromes Troop, it will join the remainder of its own Troop and repair to the Head Quarters of the Army.

The Road from Ipswich through Walton to Landguard Fort and the Road from Ipswich to Claydon must not be driven along.

The several crossings of the great Road between Ipswich and Wilford Bridge, and Ipswich and Claydon must be executed as quick as possible and no halt made till those Roads are passed.

Wilford Hundred The District lying between the Coast near Bawdsey and extending up the Deben to Wilford Bridge on one side, and along the Coast on the other up Butley River to Stour Bridge will drive to Debenham where the Detachment will be relieved by one from Lord Bromes Troop. Captain Brokes Troop after joining the remainder of its own Troop will repair to the Head Quarters of the Army.

The two principal Roads over Wilford Bridge to the Woodbridge Road, must be carefully avoided and the crossing of the several great Roads from Woodbridge to Orford to Aldeburgh and to Saxmundham must be made as expediously as possible.

This Division will not halt before it has crossed the Road from Woodbridge to Framlingham.

(Signed)   Euston

Colchester July 13th 1801

Death of Captain Broke

Sunday August 23rd 1801

Captain Broke who had been with his Brother in Law Edward Jenny Esq of Hasketon about 14 days attending upon him in an Illness of which he died last Evening about 7 oClock, returned to Nacton this morning, Mrs and Miss Jenny with him, he appeared as well as usual, but unfortunately just as he had finished his Dinner was suddenly attacked with a Paralytic Stroke and in a short space of time was insensible and Died about 9 oClock the same Evening, to the inexpressible grief of all his Family, every [one] of his acquaintance and the Country at large. It may be truely said of him he was a Friend of all Mankind.

A187 **Monday August 24th 1801**

In consequence of the Death of Captain Broke, I waited on Lieutenant Edgar at his house and he having written to Captain Broke (of the Royal Navy)[158] eldest son of our late captain respecting his Father's Interment with Military Honours received from him an answer as follows

My Dear Sir   Nacton Tuesday Evening

Though there is nothing which we did not expect from your Friendship, but this mark of attention to the remains of my dear Father, is peculiarly gratifying to us, we feel well convinced that all the worthy members of the troop would cordially assent to your proposal, but my dear mother with myself wish to avoid anything that may appear like the ostentation of Parade or cause a protraction of so melancholy a ceremony, we feel with equal gratitude the weight of obligation but as you have been so kind and considerate in proposing this Friendly Offer before the Troop at large suggested the plan to you we will venture to decline the compliment intended without fear of chagrining them as a more fixed determination on their part would have embarrassed us, I intrust you to explain our sentiments upon this subject to any of the Gentlemen who may propose the same flattering attention and to express our grateful sense of their goodness.

I remain, my dear Sir, Yours sincerely P B W Broke

To Mileson Edgar Esq Red House, Ipswich

(Circular)   **Woodbridge August 26th 1801**

Sir   I am desired by the Commanding Officer of the 2nd Troop of Loyal Suffolk Yeomanry to inform you, that the Troop is required to meet at General Muster at Woodbridge, on Friday 11th September next, precisely at 11 oClock in the morning, mounted and dressed as usual for Exercise.

Cornelius Collett Quarter Master

The meeting on Friday next is proposed in consequence of the Melancholy and much to be lamented death of our beloved Captain (who is not to be buried with Military Honors). You are requested to have a Crape on your Arm at the next Muster in token of respect to his Memory.

Friday September 11th 1801 General Muster

The Troop assembled at the time ordered in the above circular Letter and marched from the Parade to a Field in the occupation of Mr E Field in Woodbridge. In consequence of the death of Captain Broke it became needful to appoint a Captain and the Nominating officers being with the Troop agreeable to Act of Parliament and an arrangement for that purpose being prepared the same was submitted to the consideration of Members present and it was by them unanimously agreed upon that the names of the Gentlemen hereunto annexed should be sent to the Lord Lieutenant of the County (Lord Euston) and by him forwarded to His Royal Highness the Commander-in chief or to the Secretary at War to be by either of them laid before His Majesty for his approbation and appointment.

Mileson Edgar 1st Lieutenant to be Captain vice Broke deceased

---

[158] His eldest son was a naval captain who became a national hero when on 1 June 1813 his ship, HMS *Shannon*, fought the battle with the American USS *Chesapeake*, his victory restoring national pride after a number of British naval defeats during the American War of 1812.

John Brand 2nd Lieutenant to be 1st Lieutenant vice Edgar
J M Theobald Cornet to be 2nd Lieutenant vice Brand
Cornelius Collett Quarter Master to be Cornet vice Theobald.
At the same time the following arrangement was made of non-commissioned officers
Philip Gross: Quarter Master, Thomas Simmonds: Sergeant Major,
William Pearson, William Harper, John Stowe Baldry, Sergeants,
Philip Dikes, Joseph Walford, James Bryant, J M Rodwell: Corporals.

It being Two oClock in the Afternoon before the above arrangements were completed
and sundry other occurrences, the Troop was not required to go through the sundry
Evolutions or Sword Exercise, marched back to the Parade, deposited the Standard
and dismissed.
¹⁵⁹

Mr Addington by a change in Administration having succeeded Mr Pitt in the office
of Chancellor of the Exchequer, it was by the present Ministry thought advisable to
endeavour to treat with the Government of France on Terms for Peace, and Nego-
ciations for that purpose having been carried on for some time past, the following
notice was by Lord Hawksbury sent to the Lord Mayor of London.

Downing Street Thursday October 1st 1801 at night

My Lord,
I have the greatest satisfaction in informing you that Preliminaries of Peace between
Great Britain and France have been signed this Evening by myself, on the part of
his Majesty, and by Mr Otto on the part of the French Government.
I request you Lordship will have the goodness to make this intelligence immediately
public in the City.

I have the Honour to be etc etc Hawkesbury

To the Right Honourable Lord Mayor
¹⁶⁰

A191 **Ipswich October 14th 1801**
Sir   You will be so good as to circulate through the Yeomanry and Volunteer
Corps in Suffolk, the following extract of a letter from Lord Hobart to me as Lord
Lieutenant of the County.

I am, Sir, your most Obedient Servant   Euston

To Henry Collett Esq Clerk of the Peace Westerfield

Downing Street October 10th 1801

His Majesty has directed me to say that it is impossible for him on this occasion not
to repeat, in the strongest terms, the deep and lasting sense which he entertains of
that steady Attachment to our established Constitution and that Loyalty, Spirit and
Perseverance which have been manifested by the several Corps of Yeomanry and
Volunteers in every part of the Kingdom. It is therefore His Majesty's Pleasure, that
your Lordship should forthwith communicate this Letter to the Commanding Officer
of each Corps of Yeomanry and Volunteers within the County of Suffolk; and
direct them to read the same to their respective Corps, when next assembled; and
to return them Thanks in his Majesty's name **A192** for a conduct which has contributed so essentially towards maintaining Public Security, and enabled his Majesty to

---

¹⁵⁹ Appointment of Officers from the *London Gazette Extraordinary* 6 October 1801, omitted.
¹⁶⁰ A189–191, *London Gazette Extraordinary*. Peace Preliminaries not included.

bring the contest in which he has been engaged to an honourable and advantageous Conclusion.

His Majesty at the same time commanded me to state, that, there is every reason to hope that a continuance of the same disposition which has produced the Signature and Ratification of Preliminaries of Peace will speedily lead to a Definitive Treaty, but, that, until that Period arrives, it is indispensably necessary, that there should be no Relaxation in the Preparations which have been made for the general Defence. I have it therefore in Command from his Majesty to express his firm Reliance, that the several Corps of Yeomanry and Volunteers will continue to hold themselves in readiness for immediate service, and to be regularly trained and exercised as often as their Circumstances will respectively admit.[161]

I have the honour to be, My Lord, Your Lordship's most Obedient humble servant

Hobart[162]

To the Lord Lieutenant of the County of Suffolk

Sir   (Circular)   **Woodbridge October 20th 1801**
I am desired by the Commanding Officer of the Second Troop of Loyal Suffolk Yeomanry to inform you, that the Troop is required to meet at General Muster at Woodbridge of Friday 30th instant precisely at eleven o'Clock in the morning, mounted and dressed as usual for Exercise. Philip Gross Quarter Master
You are particularly requested to attend the Captain having orders from Government to communicate.

Friday October 30th 1801
The Troop being assembled marched to one of my Fields. A Feu de joye was fired in honour of the ratification of Peace and for the joyful news of the Surrender of Alexandria.[163] Lord Hobart's Letter being read by Captain Edgar (see copy above) the Gentlemen present (with one dissenting voice only) requested their further services might be offered to his Majesty, it being their wish to continue the same in case his Majesty should be pleased to accept them.

A193 Sir   **Head Quarters Woodbridge October 31st 1801**
I am desired by the commanding officer of the Second Troop of Loyal Suffolk Yeomanry Cavalry to inform you, that the Troop is required to meet at the Crown Inn in Woodbridge on Wednesday next precisely at eleven oClock in the morning dressed in plain Cloths when you are particularly requested to attend as the Captain has matters of importance to impart to you which your absence on Friday prevented him doing.
(Circular)   Philip Gross Quarter Master

Head Quarters Woodbridge November 4th 1801
At a meeting of the Troop held this day in consequence of the above Letter, in order that Lord Hobart's Letter of the 10th October might be again read, the Muster on the 30th October having been so thinly attended.

---

[161] This is almost a recognition that the so-called peace will only be a truce.
[162] Lord Hobart was Secretary of State for War and the Colonies.
[163] The end of the siege and capture of Alexandria, occupied by the French, on 2 September 1801.

Resolved that the Captain be requested to make known to his Lordship through the Lord Lieutenant of the County the lively sense they feel of his Majesty's gracious approbation of their Conduct and further to assure him of their readiness to continue their services during the Peace if his Majesty shall think proper to accept them.

It was at this meeting suggested and unanimously approved, that if his Majesty should be pleased to accept the continued services of the Troop, that a new Muster Roll should be formed and signed and regulations agreed upon for forming a Society to meet on certain days in the year for Exercise as might be thought needful and to dine together once in each Quarter in order to maintain the Spirit of the Institution and the good understanding which has at all times existed in the Troop. Arrangements were made for the same but in consequence of the short duration of the Peace it was prevented being carried into Effect.

November 6th 1801

My Lord,   I have the greatest satisfaction in informing you of the results of my reading Lord Hobart's Letter to the Troop of Yeomanry Cavalry which I have the honour to command and I believe I cannot do it better than by giving your Lordship the Resolution that was come to on the occasion viz 'That the Captain be requested to make known to Lord Hobart through the Lord Lieutenant the lively sense the Troop feel of His Majesty's gracious approbation of their Conduct and further to assure his Lordship of their readiness to continue their Service during the Peace if his Majesty shall think proper to accept them'. Your Lordship will I hope not only excuse the liberty we A194 take in requesting you to make the above Communication to Lord Hobart but receive it, as a mark of that Personal and Official Respect, which I can assume you is our wish to pay. Whenever your Lordship is made acquainted with his Majesty's Pleasure respecting the Offer made by the Troop I will request the Favor of hearing as also of being permitted to subscribe myself with much Respect and Sincerity,

Yours Mileson Edgar

Salcey Forest November 12th 1801[164]

Dear Sir,   I lost no time in communicating the Resolutions of the Troop of Yeomanry which you command to the Secretary of State, whose answer shall be transmitted to you as soon as possible after it has reached me. I scarcely need add that I felt the most sincere satisfaction in becoming the Channel of an Offer so Creditable to the Corps for whom as a body as well as for certain individuals in it with whom I have the pleasure of being acquainted, I entertain the truest respect.

Believe me always my Dear Sir, Yours most faithfully and truely   Euston

Friday November 27th 1801 General Muster

The number of Gentlemen who assembled at the General Muster on this day being so very few who were mounted and equipped for Exercise, we did not march from the Parade. After waiting till past 12 oClock the Muster Roll was called over and those present dismissed.

---

[164] Salcey Forest is part of a former medieval hunting forest seven miles from Northampton.

(Circular)   **Red House December 3rd 1801**

It is with real and unfeigned concern that I feel it indispensably necessary to address a General Letter to the Troop on the subject of Non-attendance on the Days of Muster. Both my own Recollection and a Review of the Muster Rolls too fully apprise me that it has been a growing Evil for these two years past, but it has of late increased to such an alarming degree as to defeat every Object of the Troops Meeting, and indeed even to threaten its Existence, or at least to any good and useful purpose. On the last Muster Day I fear it will appear that not many more than twenty members attended, and of those several were dismounted, the Consequence of which was that as soon as the Muster Roll was called, the Troop dispersed, and Gentlemen experienced the Fatigue and in convenience of coming 12 or 14 Miles for the sole purpose of answering their Names and saving A195 their forfeit.[165] A Moments Reflection will I am sure satisfy every Member of the Troop that such a line of Conduct must in every point of view defeat the Object of the Institution subject those who are in the habit of giving constant and regular Attendance to useless Fatigue and Inconvenience, and involve the innocent with the guilty in the general Observation the World will make, that the Troop has lost all its Zeal for the cause it engaged in.

You will perhaps be better able to picture to yourself my Feelings than I can describe them, at seeing such a Muster on the 27th of last month after having by the Instruction of the Troop made an offer of its Services during the Peace and more over on being informed that there were Gentlemen from whom I had received such Instructions, at this time unwilling to sign the Paper that is intended as a Pledge of their Services. I will hope that my Information is incorrect, But under all the Circumstances which I have stated, I cannot but wish for a free and ingenuous Declaration of the Feelings of the Troop on the Service we are engaged in, and for that purpose do most earnestly entreat your Attendance at the next Muster which will be on the 18th instant instead, of the 25th. You cannot but recollect that the Language of the Secretary of states Letter was decisive as to no Relaxation in the Exercise of the Volunteer Corps, which I mention least it should be thought that I had vexatiously called out the Troop to Monthly Muster. Nothing I can assure you is further from my Wishes than to harass you or give you unnecessary Trouble, and nothing have more at Heart than the Credit of the Troop, and the Good and Welfare of the Cause it is employed in.

           I am with much Respect, Yours Mileson Edgar Captain[166]

Friday December 18th 1801 General Muster

At a Meeting of the Troop this day a Copy of the intended new Muster Roll (in case our offer of services during peace should be accepted and a plan for forming a Society or Clubb of the Troop, being read, many Gentlemen in addition to the former signatures, added their names and sundry persons who were desirous of becoming Members being proposed where Elected and also signed their Names with assurances of future constant attendance on days of General Muster.

A General Muster was ordered on the 26th March 1802 which on account of the Assizes was afterwards postponed to the 9th of April on which day it was agreed we should after the duty of the day Dine together at the Bull Inn Woodbridge.

---

[165] Edgar mentions the distance some men were willing to travel to musters, which is further evidence of their commitment.

[166] The tone and approach of the captain's letter clearly illustrates the change in leadership.

A196 Friday April 9th 1802 General Muster

The Troop being assembled on Parade on the Market Place Woodbridge at the time appointed, marched from thence to a field belonging to myself in Woodbridge and practised the usual Evolutions and Sword Exercise, after which information having been received of the arrival of the Definitive Treaty of Peace of which Public Notice was given from the Office of Lord Hobart a feu de joye was fired on the occasion. The Gentlemen present Dined at the Bull Inn, had a pleasant and convivial Meeting and everything was concluded with pleasure and to the satisfaction of all present.

Copy of an Act of Parliament to enable His Majesty to avail himself of the Offer of certain Yeomanry and Volunteer Corps to continue their services June 22 1802[167]

Whereas it is expedient to enable His Majesty to avail himself of the Offer of certain Yeomanry and Volunteer Corps to continue their Services, And whereas it would tend the continuation of such Corps of Yeomanry and Volunteers, if persons enrolling and serving therein were to be exempted from serving personally, or providing substitutes, for the Militia, under certain Regulations; be it therefore enacted by the Kings most Excellent Majesty, by and with the advice and consent of the Lords Spiritual and Temporal, and Commons in this present Parliament assembled, and by the Authority of the same:

That it shall be lawful for His Majesty to accept the Offer of Service of any Corps of Yeomanry or Volunteers already formed or that have served during the late War, and that may be willing to continue to serve, and also to accept the Offer of Service of any Corps of Yeomanry and Volunteers that may at any Time hereafter be formed, upon such terms and Conditions respectively, as His Majesty seem fit and proper.

2nd And be it further enacted, that every person inrolled or to be inrolled, and serving in any Corps of Yeomanry or Volunteers in Great Britain, with the approbation of his Majesty for that purpose, who shall have attended the Exercise of the Corps on a certain Number of Days of Muster and Exercise, and who shall be returned in the Muster Roll required by this Act, and certified to have attended the respective Number of Days therein mentioned, unless prevented in manner therein mentioned, shall be exempt from being liable to serve personally or to provide a Substitute in the Militia of Great Britain.

3rd Provided always, and be it further enacted, That no such Exemptions shall be claimed or allowed in the present or any future year respectively, unless Muster Rolls in the form of the Schedule of this Act annexed marked A shall within three months after the passing of the Act, for the present year, and on or before the 25th day of September for any future year, in which such Exemption may be claimed, be transmitted to the Lieutenant of the County, Riding or place within which such Corps of Yeomanry or Volunteers be continued or formed, or to some person duly authorised by him to receive the same, which Muster Rolls shall be by him sent to the Clerk of the General Meeting of the said County, Riding or place, on or before the first

---

[167] This Act has been moved from B20 to its chronological position for ease of reference. Forms mentioned in the text are omitted here.

day of October next following, who shall there upon transmit Extracts from therein containing the Names of the said persons in each sub divisions, to the Clerks of the Subdivision Meetings, who are hereby required forthwith to Enter such Exemptions in the Rolls of each Militia; And the Commanding Officer so transmitting the same shall annex thereto a Certificate in the form in the Schedule to this Act annexed marked (B) signed by himself, certifying that he has not, to the best of his Knowledge and Belief, inserted in the said Muster Roll the Name of any Person who has not attended, properly armed and equipped, at the Muster and Exercise of the Corps to which he shall belong, Five days in the least in the course of the Year preceding such Certificate, unless prevented by actual Sickness, such sickness to be certified by some Medical Practitioner to such Commanding Officer as aforesaid; and no person shall at any time be entitled to claim such Exemptions unless his Name shall be found on the last Muster Rolls which shall have been transmitted and certified pursuant to this Act.

4th And be it further enacted, That in the same Muster Rolls there shall be inserted the names of every Person inrolled in any such Corps as aforesaid, who shall since the date of the last Muster Roll, have notified to the Commanding Officer thereof his intention of discontinuing his service therein, or have been discharged from such Corps, on Account of non-attendance or otherwise; and that if any such Person, during the Period of his having been enrolled in such Corps, shall have been drawn for the Militia, and shall have been exempted from Service therein, on account of his Enrolment and Service in such Yeomanry and Volunteer Corps, he shall, on Resignation or Discharge as aforesaid, be liable to serve for the District for which he was drawn, in the same manner as if he had not been exempted; and if there shall be at that time no vacancy for the District for which he was drawn, he or his Substitute shall be accounted Supernumerary for the same, until such Vacancy shall arise.

5th And be it further Enacted, That no Person shall be entitled to claim such exemptions as aforesaid, by reason of his Enrolment and Service in any Corps of Yeomanry or Volunteers or by reason of being returned in any such Muster Rolls as aforesaid, unless the Commanding Officer thereof, shall at the time of transmitting the Muster Roll as aforesaid of such Corps in manner directed by this Act, certify at the foot thereof, that such Corps has been inspected at least Once in the space of the preceding Year, by some General or Field Officer of His Majesty's Regular Forces or if such Inspection shall not have taken place, that such Corps is ready and willing to be so Inspected at the usual place or places and times of meeting; Copies of which Certificates shall be certified by such Lieutenant to the Clerk of the General Meeting, and by him to the Subdivision Meetings, together with the Muster Roll.[168]

6th And be it further Enacted, That the Clerks of the General Meeting, of the several places in Great Britain shall once in every year transmit to one of His Majesty's Principal Secretaries of State, Abstracts in the form of the Schedule to the Act annexed marked (C) of the several Muster Rolls so sent to them respectively within the year which abstracts shall express the Names of the several Corps, number of Persons enrolled and serving therein, and the number in every such Corps exempt from serving in the Militia respectively.

---

[168] B26, B27 and B28, forms referred to in the above Act, are not included here.

92

7th And be it further Enacted That every person enrolled and serving in any Corps of Yeomanry and Voluntary Cavalry, after the passing of this Act, who shall be returned in any such Muster Roll as aforesaid, as having used any Horse, Mare, or Gelding for such Services during such days of Muster and Exercise aforesaid, shall be exempted from the payment of the Duties granted by and consolidated in an Act, passed in the forty second year of the Reign of His present Majesty, instituted an Act for granting to His Majesty certain additional Duties on Servants, Carriages, Horses, Mules and Dogs, and for consolidating the same with the present Duties therein, in respect of such Horses Mares, or Geldings; and also from the Duties granted by an Act, passed in the forty first year of the Reign of his present Majesty, instituted an Act for transferring the Receit and management of certain Duties on Certificates for wearing Hair Powder, or using Armorial Bearings, from the Commissioners of Stamps to the Commissioners for the affairs of Taxes; and also for making further Provisions in respect of the said Duties so transferred in respect of such persons using Hair Powder; and every person Enrolled and Serving in any Corps of Voluntary Infantry of the passing of this Act, who shall be returned in any such Muster Roll as aforesaid, shall be exempt from the Payment of the last mentioned Duty, in respect to such person, such Exemption to be returned and claimed in the manner in which Exemption are directed to be returned and claimed by the last mentioned Act respectively; provided always, that every claim of either of such last mentioned Exemptions, shall be proved under the Certificate under the Hands of the Officer Commanding the Corps in which such person shall have Enrolled, in the form of the Schedules to this Act, annexed, marked (D) which Certificate shall, between the fifth day of April and the fifth day of May in every year, be delivered to the Surveyor or Inspector of the District where such Corps shall be enrolled; and every Person claiming to be exempt from the said Duties, or either of them, shall be charged thereto, unless such Certificate as aforesaid shall have been delivered pursuant to the Provision of this Act; any Thing in any Act to the contrary thereof notwithstanding.

8th Provided always, and be it further enacted, That every Person who shall have been enrolled and shall have served in any such Yeomanry or Volunteer Corps which shall have been or shall be disbanded, so as to entitle such person to be exempted from the said last mentioned Duties on Horses or for using Hair Powder, by the law in force, at and immediately before the passing of this Act, for the Years commencing from the fifth day of April 1802, shall, in respect to such Services, have and claim the like Exemption from the said list mentioned Duties for the said Year, as if this Act had not been passed to be claimed and proved in like manner as is directed by the said Laws now in Force; Provided always that every Person who shall have provided between the fifth day of April 1801 and the fifth day of April 1802, any Horse, Mare, or Gelding, for any Person serving in any Corps of Yeomanry and Voluntary Cavalry, or who shall at his or her Expense furnished any Horse, Mare, or Gelding, shall be exempted from the said last mentioned Duty on Horses, for and in respect of any Horse, Mare, or Gelding so by him provided and furnished as aforesaid.

9th And be it further Enacted That no Toll shall be demanded or taken at any Turnpike Gate or Bar, for any Horse, Mare, or Gelding, furnished by or for any Persons belonging to any Corps of Yeomanry and Voluntary Cavalry; and rode by them in going or returning from the place appointed for and on days of Exercise; anything contained in any Act or Acts to the contrary notwithstanding; Provided always, that such persons shall be dressed in the Uniform of their respective Corps, and have their Arms, Furniture and Accoutrements, according to regulations provided for such Corps respectively, at the time of claiming such Exemption as aforesaid.

10th And be it further enacted, That every Corps of Yeomanry and Volunteers, which shall hereafter be continued or formed in any Counties or Towns in Great Britain with approbation of His Majesty, under Officers having Commissions from His Majesty, or from the Lieutenants of Counties, or others who may be specially authorised by His Majesty for that purpose, and who shall at any Time, on being called upon by special direction of His Majesty in case of actual Invasion, or appearance of Invasion, voluntarily march out of their respective Counties or Towns, or shall voluntarily assemble with the same to repel such Invasion, or who shall voluntarily march, on being called upon in pursuance of any order from His Majesty, or from the Lieutenant or Sheriff of the County, to Act within the County, or adjacent County, for the Suppression of Riots or Tumults, shall in such cases, be entitled to receive Pay, in such manner and at such Rates as the Officers and Soldiers of His Majesty's Regular Forces, and shall during the Time of their being continued in such Service and so receive pay as above, be subject to Military Discipline and be entitled to be quartered or billeted, as the Rest of His Majesty's Regular and Militia Troops: Provided always, that no Officer or Soldier of any Yeomanry or Volunteer Corps shall be liable to be tried or punished by any Court Martial at any Time, unless such Court Martial be composed of Officers serving in Yeomanry or Voluntary Corps formed as aforesaid, such Court Martial to be assembled by Warrant under His Majesty's Signed Manual, or by Warrant from some General or other Officer duly authorised to hold Court Martial.

11th And be it further enacted That it shall be lawful for Mayors, Bailiffs, Constables, Tything Men, Headboroughs, and other Magistrates and Officers of Cities, Towns, Parishes, Tything and places in England, and (in their default or absence) for any Justice of the Peace Inhabiting with or near any such City, Town, Parish, Tything, or place (but no other) and they or he are or is hereby required to quarter or billet the Sergeants, Corporals and Drummers of such Corps as aforesaid, and their Horses in Inns, Livery Stables, Alehouses, Victualling Houses, and all Houses of Persons selling Brandy, Strong Waters, Cyder, Wine, or Metheglin, by Retail, upon application made to any such Mayor, Bailiff, Constable, Tythingmen, Headborough or other Chief Magistrates or Officers, by His Majesty's Lieutenant, or by the Officers commanding the said Corps, and that it shall be lawfull in Scotland for all Justices of the Peace or Magistrates of Cities, Towns, and places, and they and each of them are and is hereby required to quarter and billet such Sergeants, Corporals or Drummers aforesaid, in the same way and manner as the Sergeant, Corporals and Drummers of His Majesty's Regular Forces are at present quartered and billeted in Scotland.

12th And be it further enacted, That every person who shall have received or shall hereafter receive Arms or Accoutrements or Cloathing from the Public Stores or at the Public Expense or at the Expense or charge of a Subscription for providing Articles and who upon quitting any such Corp, or being discharged therefrom, or upon disbanding any such Corps, shall refuse, or neglect, on being lawfully required, to deliver up any such Arms, Accoutrements or Cloathing, shall, on being convicted thereof before any Justice of the Peace, of the County within which such Corps or Company, shall have been formed, forfeit, and pay the Sum of Ten Pounds, to be levied by Distress and

Sale, of the Offenders Goods and Chattels by Warrant under the Hand and Seal of such Justice rendering the Overplus (if any) on demand, after deducting the Charges of such Distress and Sale, to the Person whose Goods and Chattels shall have been so Distressed and Sold, and for want of such sufficient Distress, such Justice is hereby required to commit such Offender to the Common Goal of the County, Riding, or Place, where the Offence shall have been committed, for any Time not exceeding two Months and the Monies arising by such Penalty shall be paid to the Treasurer of the County, Riding or Place, where such offence shall have been committed, to be applied as part of the Stock of such County, Riding or Place.

13th And be it further enacted, That all Commanding Officers of the said Corps, who shall be disabled in actual Service, shall be intitled to Half Pay, and all Non Commissioned Officers and Soldiers so disabled, to the benefit of Chelsea Hospital, and the Widows of Commissioned Officers killed in Service, to a Pension for Life.

14th And be it further enacted, That the Muster Rolls, Returns, and Certificates respectively, made up, returned, and certified, according to the several forms thereof (ABC and D) annexed to this Act, shall be deemed to be sufficient and valid for the purposes of the same; but that if from any variation of Circumstances or other Reason, those Forms should not be strictly adhered to, Instruments of a similar Import, shall nevertheless, be deemed sufficient for the purposes aforesaid.

Sir   **Cambridge July 5th 1802**

I have enclosed by this Post a Letter from the Secretary of State, which you will be so good as to communicate to the Officers commanding the five Troops of Suffolk Yeomanry requesting them to favour me with their answer, in order that I may report the same to the Secretary of State for his Majesty's Information, in case any of the said Corps should express a Desire of continuing their Services on the Terms and Conditions proposed.

                  I am, Sir, Your most Obedient humble Servant   Euston

Clerk of the Peace Suffolk[169]

(Circular)   **Downing Street July 2nd 1802**

My Lord, I have the Honor to transmit for your Lordships Information, a Copy of an Act passed by the Legislature, enabling His Majesty to avail himself of the Offer of certain Yeomanry and Volunteer Corps to continue their Services; and I have received His Majesty's Commands to direct your Lordship to signify to the said several Corps of Yeomanry and Volunteers within the County of Suffolk that His Majesty will be graciously pleased to accept the Services of such Corps as may be disposed to continue them, according to the Provisions of the above mentioned Act. Your Lordship will further communicate to the several Corps of Yeomanry and Voluntary Cavalry within the County of Suffolk that Directions will be given to the Secretary of War (upon the Application of the Commanding Officer of any Corps whose Services may be continued, to pay Two Pounds per Annum for each Man, for his Appointments and Clothing; and Sixty Pounds per Annum for each Troop consisting of not less than Forty Rank and File to be applied as the Commanding

---

[169] This is another example of the way the bureaucracy operated. It is interesting to surmise how a letter from Lord Euston to his clerk of the peace reached Collett's hands for him to copy.

Officer shall judge proper, to the Service of the Corps, and A197 to be in lieu of every other Charge of whatever Description, heretofore defrayed by Government. Your Lordship will be pleased to make me a Report, for His Majesty's information of the several Corps, who may express their Readiness to serve upon the Terms and Conditions communicated.

It is not His Majesty's Intention, at this Time, to avail himself of the offer of any Infantry Corps within the County of Suffolk.

I have the Honor to be, My Lord, your Lordship's most Obedient humble Servant

Hobart

To the Lord Lieutenant of Suffolk

Sir   **Red House July 4th 1802**

Having just procured the Act enabling His Majesty to avail himself of the Offers of Service from the Yeomanry and the Volunteer Corps, I lose as little time as possible in appointing a day for the Troop to meet, in order that it may be read over, and its provisions taken under consideration. For that purpose I have taken the liberty of fixing Tuesday the 13th Instant in the Hope that you will make a Point of attending, and but for the Ipswich Races would have Named a Day in this Week. The Exertions called for under the Act appear to me so small, and the Privileges and Advantages resulting from them so great, as to afford me the fullest Hopes and most sanguine Wishes, that you will continue your Service. With Respect to myself, I shall be most ready to inrol my Name, and most happy to find that I have so used the Command intrusted to me, as to induce those who have been already under it to continue their Post.

I remain, Sir, with the greatest Esteem and Respect, Yours,   Mileson Edgar

PS The Meeting will be held at the Crown Inn Woodbridge at Eleven o'Clock in the Forenoon, where a Dinner is ordered at Three; you will of course attend in plain Cloth's.

Tuesday July 13th 1802

His Majesty by an Act of Parliament dated 22nd June last being Authorised to accept the Offers of continued Service of the Yeomanry and Volunteer Corps (during Peace) and Lord Hobart one of His Majestys principal Secretaries of State having signified his wish (by circular Letter 2nd Instant) to be informed by whom such offers are from that time made; the Troop this day met at the Crown Inn Woodbridge at the request of Captain Edgar in order to enable him without loss of time to return an answer to his Lordship. Captain Edgar being called upon to take A198 the Chair, he immediately requested to be informed if it was the Wish of the Troop to continue their Services, and in reply every Gentleman present answered in the Affirmative. A Muster Roll was accordingly prepared and signed and certain Regulations agreed upon for the Conduct of the Troop and appointing certain Days of General Muster. It was also unanimously agreed that the Captain shall be at Liberty to admit such new Members of the Troop from this day as he shall think fit and approve without a Reference to the Troop for their Election. It was unanimously agreed that the Troop should be new Cloathed – the Jackets to be made according to a pattern procured for that purpose and to be Trimmed with Silver Lace etc etc.[170]

---

[170] Apart from the mention of silver lace it would appear that the new uniform was much like the old since Collett made no mention of any detailed discussion in the Troop or reference to the War Office

On a Question whether a Special Meeting should be called for the Purpose of determining whether a Distribution of the fund which had accumulated during the War should take Place, it was unanimously agreed that no future Meeting was required, but that the Fund should be applicable to the Service of the Troop.

By order signed Mileson Edgar Chairman

Copy of the Muster Roll

We whose names are here under enrolled having this day made an Offer of our Services to his Majesty during Peace do hereby pledge ourselves to a full and proper discharge thereof Viz, That we will at all times obey any Orders that may be issued from his Majesty, from the Lord Lieutenant, the High Sheriff, or from the Magistrates acting in and from the Woodbridge Division for the Suppression of any Riot or Tumultuous Meetings, with the greatest promptness and alacrity.

That whenever and as often as we shall receive Intimation of his Majesty's Wish and Pleasure that we should be received by a General or other Officer Appointed for that Purpose, we will cheerfully accede thereto.

That we will by a constant and regular attention on the Days of Exercise and whenever called out on Military Duty study to maintain the Character we are disposed to think we have borne during the War for Discipline and Soldier-like Conduct.

July 13th 1802[171]

A199 Lord Euston begs Mr Collett would communicate the enclosed Resolutions to the Commanding Officers of the various Corps of Yeomanry etc

To Henry Collett Esq Westerfield Clerk of the Peace

From Lord Elden to Lord Euston Lord Lieutenant of Suffolk

My Lord,   In Obedience to the Commands of the House of Lords that I should signify to His Majestys Lord Lieutenants of each County, Riding and Place in Gt. Britain the following Resolutions of that House, I have the honour to communicate the same to you.

DTE MARTIS & APRILIS 1802

Resolved Nimine Dessintiente, by the Lords Spiritual and Temporal in Parliament assembled, That the Thanks of this House be given to the Officers of the several Corps of Yeomanry and Voluntary Cavalry and Infantry, and of the Sea Fencibles, which have been formed in Great Britain and Ireland during the Course of the War, for the seasonable and Imminent Services they have rendered to their King and Country.

DTE MARTIS & APRILIS 1802

Resolved, Nimine Dissintiente, by the Lords Spiritual and Temporal in Parliament assembled, that this House doth highly approve of and acknowledge the Services of the Non-Commissioned Officers and Men of the several Corps of Yeomanry and Yeomanry Cavalry and Infantry, and of the Sea Fencibles which have been formed in Great Britain and Ireland during the Course of the War; and that the same be communicated to them by the Colonels and other Commanding Officers of the several Corps, who are desired to thank them for their meritorious Conduct.

It was the Intent of their Lordships Resolutions commanding me to transmit these Resolutions to His Majestys Lieutenants, that I should request that you would be

about acceptable colours or designs.

[171] Names not copied.

pleased to communicate these Testimonies of their Lordships Gratitude to the Colonels and other Commanding Officers of the several Corps of Yeomanry, and Volunteer Cavalry and Infantry, and Sea Fencibles within the County of Suffolk, for which you have the honor to be His Majesty's Lieutenant.

I am with great Respect, My Lord, Your most obedient and humble Servant,

Eldon

(The above was read to the Troop by Captain Edgar)

A200 Friday July 20th 1802 General Muster

The Troop being assembled at the usual time and place marched to one of my Fields and exercised as usual. Afterwards adjourned to the Crown Inn, fully resolved upon the Cloathing and Equipments required and directed the same to be procured and made up as soon as they could be obtained from the sundry Manufactorys.[172]

(Adjourned to 31st August)

Woodbridge August 16th 1802

Sir, At the request of Captain Edgar I inform you, that both on account of the Harvest and by reason of the impossibility of having the new Uniform and appointments ready by the 31st Instant the Muster of the Troop will not take place on that Day as was intending but on Tuesday the 5th October next.

I am Yours etc Cornelius Collett Cornet

Red House Ipswich September 21st 1802

Sir I am sorry to be under the necessity of making a further adjournment of the Meeting of the Troop, as I find the Cloathing and Appointments will not be ready by the 5th of next Month. The Troop will therefore meet at Woodbridge on Tuesday the 9th of November next, at 11 o'Clock in the Forenoon, Mounted, and Dressed in the New Uniform, and afterwards Dine together as agreed upon on the Meeting in July. My motive for not fixing an earlier day for the Adjournment is to have the benefit of a full Moon.[173]   I am Sir Yours etc etc   Mileson Edgar Captain

---

Sir   **Red House Ipswich October 20th 1802**

Although I trust it has not escaped your memory that the Troop is appointed to meet at Woodbridge of Tuesday 9th of November, I take the Liberty of addressing a few Lines to say, That as the Appointments are arrived, and the Cloathing compleated nothing can occur to prevent the meeting taking place, and I hope you will make a point of being at the Crown Inn at 11 oClock in the Forenoon, in order that the Helmets may be fitted, the Sabres and other appointments delivered out, and in short, all the Business finished before Dinner.

I am Yours, much, Mileson Edgar Captain

A201 Tuesday November 9th 1802

The Troop met this day in their new Uniform agreeable to notice issued for that purpose by order of Captain Edgar and for receiving new Equipments and sundry various appointments, which being prepared were fitted and delivered out this day, and for appointing Non-Commissioned Officers, and arrangement of all other requi-

---

[172] The new uniform was agreed and ordered very quickly.
[173] A full moon made it possible to travel at night.

site matters respecting the Troop, as are required under the new Act of Parliament enabling His Majesty to accept the services of Volunteer Troops of Yeomanry etc etc etc during the Peace.

After the sundry Appointments had been delivered out the Members of the Troop (all of whom were present) assembled at the Crown Inn, the arrangement agreed upon respecting the Officers was settled and various other small matters. In consequence of the time being employed in making the sundry arrangements until 2 oClock the Troop did not march into the Field for Exercise a Dinner being ordered at the Crown Inn at 3 oClock. We all dined together and spent the remainder of the Day very pleasant and agreeable in mirth and good humour. The next meeting was ordered on the 3 May 1803.

Sir   **Head Quarters Woodbridge April 27th 1803**
By the Captains desire, I send you a Card, of the Days of Exercise, as fixed at the Meeting of the 5th July last and at the same time express his request, that you will appear with a piece of crape upon your Arm at the first Muster, as a mark of respect to our late worthy First Lieutenant Mr John Brand.
                              I am Sir, yours William Pearson Quarter Master

Card: Days of Exercise of the Troop as settled at a Meeting held at the Crown Inn Woodbridge July 15th 1802
              1803
    1st day Tuesday May 3rd
    2 day   Tuesday May 17th
    3 day   Tuesday June 4th
    4 day   Tuesday June 21st
    5 day   Tuesday July 5th
    6 day   Tuesday July 19th
    7 day   Tuesday August 2nd

Unless the Commanding Officer should find it requisite to make an alteration, of which Notice will be given. Hours of Meeting each Day – Eleven oClock precisely. NB Attendance is required on the first Five Days, which (if given) will render a meeting on the remaining two unnecessary.

A202   **Death of Lieutenant Brand**   On the 10th February 1803 died in London on his return from Bath John Brand Esq first Lieutenant of the Troop in the 47 year of his Age. He was Buried at Hemingstone in Suffolk on the 18th February. It was his particular desire to be Buried in as private a manner as possible. In consequence the Troop did not attend his Funeral. He was a Man most deservedly respected by all ranks of People and highly esteemed by every Member of the Troop.
NB he was a Member of the Troop from its Institution 1794

Tuesday May 3rd 1803 General Muster   The Troop assembled at the usual time and place and marched from Parade to Martlesham, exercised in a plowed Field in the occupation of Mr Glanfield. As the day advanced the Wind rose very high and blowed a strong Gale and being a piece of ploughed Land in which we Exercised the Dust rose in such quantities and blowing so very hard the Horses could not be kept in the Ranks or could the Men see before them, in consequence of which we were obliged to quit the Field. On our return we were met by Sir Sidney Smith whose Ship the Antelope was laying in Hollesley Bay.[174] He came from thence purposely to see the Troop in which he was a great degree disappointed by the weather being unfavourable and preventing their Exercise. On information of Sir Sidney Smith's approach we formed on the Turnpike Road and received him in proper form. Alighting from his Carriage he inspected the Troop and was pleased to express his satisfaction with their Military appearance.

After depositing the Standard, we adjourned to the Crown Inn and Elected Officers in consequence of the death of Lieutenant Brand – the following Gentlemen being proposed were unanimously Elected and their names sent to the Lord Lieutenant and by him forwarded to the Secretary of State for the approbation of His Majesty, who was pleased to confirm the choice and grant commissions accordingly.

John Meadows Theobald   1st Lieutenant vice Brand
Cornelius Collett   2nd Lieutenant vice Theobald
John Couperthwaite   Cornet vice Collett

Tuesday May 17th 1803 General Muster
The Troop being met at the time appointed marched to Sutton and Exercised in the usual Evolutions and Practice of firing with Blank Cartridges, in a Field in the occupation of Mr Samuel Gross.

A203   **WAR WITH FRANCE**
Downing Street May 11th 1803
My Lord, I think it right to inform your lordship that Mr Lyall the Messenger is just arrived with Dispatches from Lord Whitworth by which it appears Lord Whitworth had necessary his passports and was on the point of leaving Paris when the Messenger came away on Thursday evening.

I have the honor to be, your Lordship's most Obedient humble Servant,
Hawkesbury

May 16th 1803
The Chancellor of the Exchequer entered the House a little before Five o'Clock and shortly afterwards brought down the following Message from His Majesty.
George R
His Majesty thinks it proper to acquaint the House of Commons that the discussions, which he announced to them in his Message of the 8th of March last, as then subsisting between his Majesty and the French Government have been terminated, that the conduct of the French Government, has obliged his Majesty to recall his Ambassador from Paris, and that the Ambassador from the French Republic has left London.

His Majesty has given directions for laying before the House of Commons, with as little delay as possible, copies of such papers as will afford the fullest Information to his Parliament at this important conjuncture.

It is a consolation to His Majesty to reflect, that no endeavours have been wanting on his part to preserve to his subjects the blessings of Peace, but, under the circumstances which have occurred to disappoint his just expectations, His Majesty relies

---

[174] Sir Sidney Smith was in command of the flotilla guarding Hollesley Bay. See Introduction, p. xxxviii, footnote 134.

with confidence on the zeal and public Spirit of his faithful commons, and on the exertions of his brave and loyal subjects, to support him in his determination to employ the power and resources of the Nation, in opposing the Spirit and ambition and incroachment, which at present actuates the Councils of France, in upholding the dignity of his Crown and in asserting and maintaining the rights and Interests of his People.   George R

A213 Saturday June 4th 1803 General Muster
The Troop being assembled marched to a Field in the occupation of Mr E Field being joined by a detachment of the 7th Light Dragoons (Quartered in the Town) Commanded by Lieutenant Duckenfield fired a feu de joye in honor of his Majesty's Birthday. Sir Sidney Smith honouring us with his company, we had afterwards a field day together (in his presence) who expressed himself highly gratified with our Military appearance and the manner in which we went through the exercises etc etc. He afterwards honoured the Troop with his company at Dinner at the Crown Inn and the day was concluded with that mirth and conviviality which the occasion and presence of so illustrious a character, were calculated to inspire.
Dr Frank (our Chaplin) with several other Gentlemen were of the party at dinner.

A Letter of which the following in a Copy was addressed to sundry Gentlemen who were Members of the Troop during the former War but declined their further services on the Definitive Treaty being signed between Great Britain and the French Government.

Dear Sir   **Red House May 25th 1803**
As I will remember that many (if not all) the Gentlemen who left the Troop at the conclusion of the War, expressed their Readiness to join it again whenever Circumstances occurred to make it necessary, I have taken the Liberty of addressing a Circular Letter on the subject. I think you will readily agree with me that if ever there was a time which more peculiarly called for the services of every Man able to bear Arms, it is the present. Indeed I am happy to say the Influence of such an Opinion is fully manifest by the Number of Recruits who have lately joined the Troop. You will I hope readily admit the Truth of the assertion, that it is impossible for you to render greater Service to your country, greater Credit to yourself or greater Satisfaction to me, than to return to a Post which you so respectably filled and which but for the Arrival of Peace I am sure you would not have quitted. I will entertain a strong hope that my address to you will have the desired Effect, and that we shall meet you at the Crown Inn Woodbridge at 3 oClock upon his Majesty's Birthday when you can sign the Muster Roll and be measured A214 for the new Uniform. You will confer a great favour by giving me an answer with as little delay as possible, and believing me at all times with much respect and esteem.
                                        Mileson Edgar

To Philip Gross Woodbridge, William Harper Levington, Joseph Walford Rushmere, Thomas Simpson Ufford, Thomas Simpson Junior Ufford, William Whincop Woodbridge, Samuel Gross Caple, Stebing Gross Eyke, William Cockrell Barham, Philip Trusson Bruiseyard, John Porter Levington, John Weiding Ramsholt, Robert Benington Boyton, John Clarke Woodbridge, Henry Luffe Benhall, John Chapman Kirton, John Cockle Trimley, Hyam Pierce Trimley, Benjamin Barthrop Blaxhall,

Philip Riches Woodbridge, John Wood Woodbridge, John Shiming Rendlesham, George Bates Eyke, John Hunt Chilisford, Robert Simpson Shrubland Hall.

These Gentlemen who joined the Troop their names will be found on the Muster Roll.

It being His Majesty's pleasure that for the general defence of the United Kingdom, a larger force should be raised, many of the above named Gentlemen formed the Voluntary Infantry Corps, which were very numerous, in consequence of the threatened invasion by the French, for which the greatest possible preparations was made on their Coast.[175]

Copy of a Letter from the Secretary at War acknowledging the statement of the Accompts of the Corps and Settlement of the same for the Year 1803[176]

War Office 20th June 1803

Sir

I have the honor to acquaint you that the Accompts of the Corps under your Command, for the Year 1803 have been finally settled at my Office, agreeably to the annexed Statement.

I have the Honor to be Sir Your most obedient humble servant

James Pulteney

Captain M Edgar 2nd Corps Yeomanry Cavalry Red House Ipswich

Statement referred to in the annexed Letter

2nd Corps Volunteer Cavalry when not upon permanent Duty

Accompt from 25th December 1802 to 24th December 1803

	Sums Allowed
Pay	:
Contingent Allowance	240
Clothing	280
Total Amount of sums allowed	528
Amount of Bills drawn upon the General Agent	528
The Sum Charged	528

Tuesday June 21st 1803 General Muster

The Troop met at the usual time and place, marched to Bromeswell and exercised in a Field in the occupation of Mr Walson.

It was unanimously agreed upon that the Troop should meet at General Muster every five weeks from this time to December next and in the Interval in Divisions for practice in consequence of the augmentation of the Troop which divisions for the convenience of the members of the Troop attending, were agreed to be held as under – viz

1st Division commanded by Captain Edgar at Westerfield Green

2nd Division commanded by Lieutenant Theobold at Barham Common

3rd Division commanded by Lieutenant Collett at Eyke, on Mr Bates Land

The divisions thus arranged attended two days in each week for Exercise.

---

[175] The county and the whole country flooded to join volunteer infantry troops. In Suffolk there were forty-two Troops.

[176] This letter has been moved from B211 for chronological relevance.

Memorandum

Government having arranged a plan for the future pay and cloathing etc etc of the Voluntary Yeomanry Cavalry, as follows is a Copy of the Regulations adopted, which was sent by the Lord Lieutenant to the Commanding Officers.

A215 Regulations, during War, for the cloathing, appointments and the allowances for contingent expenses of corps of Yeomanry and Voluntary Cavalry.

1st Every Officer, non-commissioned Officer and Private man to take the Oath of Allegiance and fidelity to his Majesty.

2nd Every troop to consist of not less than forty rank and file, which comprehend Corporals and Privates only.

3rd Three pounds per man for Effectives will be allowed annually for Cloathing and Appointments and issued for three years at once, if required, and the Sum of One Hundred and twenty pounds per Troop per Annum, at the disposal of the Commandant to be in lieu of the pay of sergeant and Trumpeters, and of every other Charge of whatsoever description, hitherto defrayed by Government.[177]

4th Constant pay, at the rate of 6s per diem, to be allowed to an adjutant to Corps of three Troops and upwards.

5th Sergeants receiving constant pay and all Trumpeters (or Buglemen) receiving pay either at daily rate or weekly rate, to be attested and made subject to military law, until they shall be regularly discharged by the Commandant.

6th If a Corps or any part thereof, shall be called upon in case of Riot or Disturbance, the change of constant pay to be made for such Services must be at the Rate specified below, being the pay of the regular Cavalry, and supported by a Certificate from His Majesty's Lieutenant or the Sheriff of the County.

Pay

Captain 14s 7d   Lieutenant 9s   Cornet 8s · Quarter Master 5s 6d   Adjutant 10s

Sergeant Major including 9d for his horse 3s 11d

Sergeant	ditto	2s 11d
Corporal	ditto	2s 4½d
Trumpeters	ditto	2s per diem

Tuesday July 26th 1803 General Muster

The Troop being Assembled its numbers being greatly increased it was considered a proper time to draw up a new Muster Roll the present one being an engagement during Peace only, we accordingly adjourned to the Town Hall, when a new Muster Roll was drawn up, and being read was and unanimously approved was ordered to Engrossed. We then formed on the parade and marched from thence to a field in the occupation of Mr E Field and exercised in the usual Evolutions and Sword Exercise after which we returned to Woodbridge A216 adjourned to the Town Hall and signed the Muster Roll.

It was unanimously agreed to meet every Tuesday fortnight from this day at General Muster and twice in each week in divisions as before appointed and the attendance on days of division meetings to be reported to the Captain at the General Muster.

---

[177] The sergeant and trumpeter had been paid by the government since the establishment of the Troops in 1794.

Muster Roll July 26ᵗʰ 1803

We whose names are hereunder enrolled do pledge ourselves to a full and proper Discharge of the several Services here in set forth as follows

That we will at all times obey any orders which may be issued from His Majesty, from the General commanding the District from the Lord Lieutenant, the high Sheriff or the Magistrates acting in, and for, the Division of Woodbridge for the suppression of any Riot or tumultuous Meetings with the greatest promptness and Alacrity.

That in case of actual Invasion or appearance of Invasion we will readily march to any part of the Military District to which we belong under such Orders as we shall receive from the General or Generals commanding within the same.

And Lastly, that we will cheerfully obey and execute all orders we may receive from our Superior Officers in the Troop whether Commissioned or non-commissioned and give a regular Attendance on the Days of Exercise unless prevented by serious Illness awaiting ourselves or Families, to be certified by the Medical man attending. NB Signed by 148 members

Tuesday August 9ᵗʰ 1803 General Muster

The Troop being met at the usual time and place marched to Martlesham and exercised in a field in the occupation of Mr Glanfield and exercised in the usual Evolutions and Sword Exercise. Our number being so much increased we formed in two Troops it being intended they should so continue providing it met the approbation of Government the present numbers being too large for one Troop.[178]

Tuesday August 16ᵗʰ 1803 General Muster   The Troop assembled marched to Sutton and exercised (as on the 9ᵗʰ in two Troops) in a Field in the occupation of Mr Nathaniel Gross.

It being intimated that we should be reviewed by His Royal Highness the Duke of York on the 22ⁿᵈ instant the Troop was ordered to Muster on Friday next the 19ᵗʰ instant for exercise and arranging the Troop for said Review.

A217 Friday August 19ᵗʰ 1803 General Muster   The Troop met at Sutton agreeable to Adjournment on 16ᵗʰ instant Captain Edgar having received official information of the intended visit of his Royal Highness the Duke of York being postponed until the 28ᵗʰ instant, and at the same time desiring him to muster the Troop on Sunday morning the 28ᵗʰ at 8 o'clock to attend at said review, orders were given out accordingly, after which the Troops went through their Exercises as usual and a General Muster ordered on Thursday next.

From Sutton the Troops marched to Woodbridge and adjourning to the Town Hall when each Member of the Troop took the Oath of Allegiance and fidelity to His Majesty which was administered by the Reverend Frank Chaplin to the Troop.

Thursday 25ᵗʰ August 1803   The Troop met agreeable to adjournment of the last meeting when all the Arms and Equipments were inspected preparatory to the Review on the 28ᵗʰ at which time everything was directed to be in the neatest order possible.

---

[178] The Woodbridge Troop/Corps was always the largest in the Suffolk Yeomanry, although the 4th Bury Troop, for a few years, expanded to become a Corps.

The necessary arrangement being made the Troop was ordered to assemble on Sunday morning next at half past six o'Clock at Rushmere or Kesgrave and to march from thence to the ground on which the Review is to take place precisely by eight o'clock.

A220 Memorandum

The occurrences of the Troop with other matters relating thereto from 25th August 1803 are entered in Letter Book B which was in consequence of my not having obtained the particulars to enable me to make the preceding entries in this Book Letter A transcribed prior to the entries here.

Having had occasion to copy the Gazette accounts of sundry naval engagements etc etc in the remaining part of this Book I have continued to insert Copies of such further Naval Victories etc as have been distinguishable in the history of the War from the year 1793.

[End of Volume A]

VOLUME B

Copy of an Act of Parliament for authorising the billeting of such Troops of Yeomanry and Volunteer Cavalry as may be desirous of assembling for the Purpose of being trained together, in Great Britain and Ireland; and for subjecting to Military Discipline, during the War, such Sergeants serving in any Volunteer or Yeomanry Corps of Cavalry or Infantry as receive constant pay, and all Trumpeters, Drummers or Bugle Men serving therein, and receiving pay at daily or Weekly Rate; and for the further regulating of such Yeomanry and Volunteer Corps.[1]
August 11ᵗʰ 1803   43 Geo 3rd Cap 1

Whereas an Act passed in the Forty-second year of the Reign of his present Majesty, instituted, an Act to enable His Majesty to avail Himself of the Officers of certain Yeomanry and Volunteer Corps to continue their Services; and whereas it is expedient to regulate the Returns and Musters of Corps, and thereby to make provision in relation to such Corps that no persons enrolled therein shall be entitled to or have any Exemptions from being balloted to serve in an additional Military Force raised or to be raised for the Defence of the United Kingdom, unless they shall appear to be and are returned under this Act as effective and fit to serve;

And whereas many Corps and Troops of Yeomanry Cavalry in Great Britain whose offers of service have been accepted by His Majesty, or which may hereafter be formed in pursuance of the said Act, are or may be desirous of assembling together at such convenient places and for such Time as may be fixed under the Authority of the said Act, for the purpose of more effectively training and disciplining themselves, and for that purpose it may be necessary to provide quarters and to billet such of the said Volunteers as may not find it convenient to return to their own houses after each days exercise: and whereas it is also expedient to make Regulations separating Sergeant, Corporals, Trumpeters and Drummers, serving in or with such Corps in Great Britain and Ireland; may it therefore please your Majesty that it may be enacted; and be it enacted by the King's most Excellent Majesty, by and with advice and consent of the Lords Spiritual and Temporal and Commons, in this present Parliament assembled, and by the authorities of the same;

That the several and respective officers commanding such Corps respectively shall, on or before the first day of September succeeding the passing of the Act, and on or before the first Day of January, the first Day of May, and the First Day of September, in each and every succeeding year, during the Continuance of the War, make Returns to the Clerk of the General Meeting of Lieutenancy, according to the form in the Schedule to the Act annexed, marked (A) for the use of the respective Lieutenant of their respective counties, and certifying the same to be true, in the Form contained in the Schedule to this Act annexed marked (B); every such Commanding Officer shall distinguish in all such returns of all such persons as have joined their respec-

---

[1]   This was to allow members of Troops to spend a period of time exercising together away from their homes and civilian lives. They were thus subject to martial law and paid as regular soldiers.

tive Corps since the last Returns and which of such persons respectively shall have entered themselves as effective members thereof, and the names of all persons who shall continue effective members of such Corps respectively, **B2** and also the names of all such persons as shall by reason of Defaults in not attending the Exercise of any such Corps, have become non-effective members thereof, and shall also make to the Secretary of State, the Adjutant General of the Forces, and the General of the District, when any such shall be appointed, accurate Returns of their respective Corps, specifying the numbers of effective and non-effective men in their Corps at the time of making such Returns; and as such last-mentioned Returns shall be made as near as may be, according to the Nature of the Corps, in the Form in which Military Returns are usually made on the first of every month.[2]

2nd Provided always, and be it further enacted, That no person shall be deemed, construed or taken as an effective Member of such Corps, or shall be returned as such by any Commanding Officer, or entitled to any exemption from being balloted or inrolled to serve in any additional Forces, raised or said to be raised under an Act passed in this or any subsequent session of Parliament, for enabling His Majesty more effectively to raise additional Military Force for the better Defence and Security of the United Kingdom, and for more vigorous prosecution of the War, or to supply any vacancies in such additional Forces as aforesaid unless such Persons shall have duly entered properly armed, accoutred and equipped, at the Muster or Exercise of the Corps to which he belongs, if Cavalry Twelve Days, if Infantry Twenty four days at least, between the First Day of January and the last day of December in each year,[3] unless prevented by actual Sickness, (such Sickness to be certified by some medical practitioner to the Commanding Officer of the Corps), and who shall not be returned according to the Form in the Schedule to this Act annexed, by the Commanding Officer of the Corps, as having so attended Musters and Exercise as aforesaid, and as being, from his attendance and Exercise in such Corps, effective and fit for service Provided always that every person, shall from the Date of such Muster Roll and Return, be exempted from being balloted or enrolled to serve in any additional force raised or said to be raised under any Act or Acts on this or any subsequent Session of Parliament, or to supply any vacancy therein and shall remain exempted until he shall be struck out of the Muster roll of his Corps for non-attendance or Default.

3rd Provided always, and be it further enacted, That nothing in this Act contained shall extend or be construed to extend to alter or repeal any of the Provisions of two Acts, passed in the last Session of Parliament, to enable His Majesty to avail Himself of the Offers of certain Yeomanry and Volunteer Corps to continue their Services, and to accept and continue the Services of certain Troops or companies of Yeomanry in Ireland (except so far as the same are hereby expressly varied or altered).

4th And it be further enacted; That whenever the Men enrolled, or the Majority of them, in any such Troop or Troops of Volunteer Cavalry, shall, through their Captain

---

[2]   There was an attempt, at least at a basic level, to establish a more efficient system by providing simple forms, which were copied by Collett, but are omitted here.

[3]   This refutes accusations that the Volunteer Troops were largely untrained.

or Commanding Officer, signify in writing to the Lieutenant of the County, Riding, Thedwastry, City or Place where such Troops or Corps shall be raised, or in the case of vacancy, or in the absence of the Lieutenant, to the Deputy Lieutenant executing the Office of the Lieutenant, their Desire to assemble under the Command of their own Officers, at any place in particular, or at any **B3** convenient Place or Places either within the same County, Riding, Thedwastry, City, or Place, or without, for the Purpose of being trained and exercised, for any Space of Time not exceeding in the whole Ten Days, either successively or at Intervals within the space of Four Months; and either in separate Corps or Troops or together with any other Corps or Troops of Volunteer Yeomanry Cavalry, who shall also have signified their Desire of assembling in like Manner, or with any Regiment, Troop or Troops of His Majesty's Regular Forces of Cavalry or any Number of such Cavalry,[4] in case His Majesty shall think proper to give Directions to such of His Cavalry as aforesaid for that purpose, it shall be lawful for such Lieutenant or Deputy Lieutenant respectively in every year, in pursuance of the Desire of any Corps or Troops of Volunteer Cavalry, to be signified in manner aforesaid, to make an Order for assembling such Volunteer Cavalry, at such place or places as the said Lieutenant or Deputy Lieutenants as aforesaid, with the Concurrence of the General Officer having the Command of the District, and in case the Place appointed shall be in another County or Riding, then also with the Concurrence of the Lieutenant of such County or Riding or Deputy Lieutenant aforesaid shall think fit; and likewise to direct an Order to any Justice of the Peace of the County or Riding, Thedwastry, City or Place where such Volunteer Cavalry shall be appointed to assemble themselves for the Purpose aforesaid, in which Order shall be specified the place or places at which, and precise Time or Times during which such Volunteer Cavalry are to continue so assembled under the Authority of the Act; and the Justices of the Peace to whom such Order shall be directed shall issue his Receipt to the Constable, Headborough, or Officer of the Peace of the place where such Volunteer Corps or Troops are to be assembled, for quartering or billeting the Non-commissioned Officers, Trumpeters (or Bugle Men), and Privates, or such Volunteer Corps or Troops, upon such persons and in such Houses situated in the place or places specified in such order, as His Majesty's Regular Forces may by law be quartered and billeted upon; and that from and after the delivering of such order of the Lieutenant of any County or Riding, Thedwastry, City or Place, or Deputy Lieutenant acting as aforesaid, made with such consent and concurrence as aforesaid, to any Justice of the Peace of any County, Riding, Thedwastry, City or Place, where any such Corps or Troop of Volunteer Cavalry so assembled; it shall be lawful to quarter and billet the Non–commissioned Officers, Trumpeters (or Bugle Men), and private Men of any such Corps or Troop of Volunteer Cavalry, in all and every Houses situate in such place or places as aforesaid, in which, and upon all and every [the] person on whom any of His Majesty's Regular Forces may by law be Quartered and billeted; and that from and after the delivery of any such Order during the times appointed as aforesaid for such Training and Exercise, all and every [of] the Provisions, Rules, Penalties, Allowances, Matters and Things, provided and established by any Act or Acts now and hereafter to be in force for quartering and billeting His Majesty's Regular forces shall be used and put in practice for Quartering and billeting Corps or Troop of Volunteer Cavalry

---

4   Training together with other Troops was of great importance since only on one occasion had it met as a regiment. However, if the French landed, it would be as a regiment that it was expected to fight.

assembled under the Authority of this Act, as fully and effectively as if all and every [of] the said Powers, Provisions, Rules, Penalties, Allowances, Matters and Things, had been specially re-acted in the Body of this Act.

B4 5th And be it further enacted, That whenever the Lieutenant of any County, Riding, Thedwastry, City or Place, or Deputy Lieutenant as aforesaid shall have fixed the Day and Place of Exercise for any Corps or Troop of Volunteer Cavalry he or they shall, as soon as may be certify the same the Receiver General of such County, Riding, or place in England or if in Scotland to the Receiver General for Scotland, specifying the number of men and the number of Days appointed for exercising them, not exceeding in the whole Ten Days; and such Receiver General is hereby required, within fourteen days after the receipt of such Certificates, to issue and pay to the Officer having command of such Corps or Troops at the Rate of Two Shillings per day for each Volunteer who shall attend the place of Exercise, and one shilling and four pence per Day for each Horse, Mare or Gelding, belonging to such Corps or Troop, and used in Exercise.

6th And be it further enacted, That the Officers having Command of such Troop of Volunteer Cavalry shall make up an account of all monies received and paid by him on Account of such Exercise according to the following Form.[5] Which Account shall be signed by the Officer having Command of such Troop and such Officer shall, within Ten Days after the time such Exercise is finished, deliver such Account and pay the Balance, if any be due, to the Receiver General And such Account shall be as sufficient Vouchers in the passing of the Accounts of the said Receiver General by the proper Auditor of His Majesty's Court of Exchequer.[6]

8th And whereas great Inconvenience hath been found to arise to the Voluntary and Yeomanry Service in Great Britain and Ireland during War, from there being no authority to enforce Military Discipline amongst Sergeants, Trumpeters (or Bugle Men) or Drummers of the Voluntary and Yeomanry Corps receiving pay, or to prevent them from quitting such Corps and enlisting in His Majesty's or other Forces, without leave of their respective Commanders; and therefore enacted; That such of the Sergeants serving in any Voluntary or Yeomanry Corps of Cavalry or Infantry in Great Britain or Ireland as receive constant pay of their Rank therein, and all Trumpeters (or Bugle Men) and Drummers serving in any such Corps, and receive any pay therein either at Daily or Weekly Rate, shall, at all times during the continuance of the War, be subject to any Act which shall be in force for punishing Mutiny and Desertion, and for the better payment of the Army and their Quarters, and to the Articles of War established for the better Government of His Majesty's Forces, and shall be liable to be tried for any Crime committed against such Act or Articles of War, by a general Detachment or Regimental Court Martial according to the Nature and Degree of the offence, in like manner and under the Regulation as Sergeants, Trumpeters or Drummers of His Majesty's other forces may be tried; Provided that every such Court Martial shall be composed wholly of Officers of the Volunteer or Yeomanry Establishment; and that no punishment awarded by such

---

5   Forms not included here.
6   The 7th clause refers only to Ireland and has been omitted here.

Court Martial shall extend to Life and Limb, except when such Corps are called out in cases of Invasion or appearance of an Enemy in Force upon the Coast.

9th And be it further enacted, That in such cases of actual Invasion or appearance of an Enemy in force upon the Coast, whenever His Majesty shall order the Lord Lieutenant or Deputy Lieutenant acting in any county or Thedwastry, Riding, City or place in Great Britain, to draw out assemble and embody the Men enrolled under any Act of this Session of Parliament, or in which any Men so enrolled shall so assemble under any Provisional Order of His Majesty, on any such Invasion or appearance of an Enemy as aforesaid, all Corps of Yeomanry and Volunteers in Great Britain shall forthwith assemble in their respective Districts, and shall be liable to march according to their respective Drummers and Private Men in such Corps, shall from such Time, and until the Enemy shall be defeated and expelled, and all Rebellion and Insurrection then existing in the Realm shall be suppressed, be subject to any Act then in force for the punishment of Mutiny and Desertion, and for the better payment of the Army and their Quarters and to any articles of War made in pursuance thereof, and all persons not then joining their respective Corps, and assembling and marching therewith, shall be liable to be apprehended and punished as Deserters, according to the Provisions of any such Act aforesaid and of **B6** any Articles made in pursuance thereof.[7]

11th And be it further enacted, That such Corps of Voluntary and Yeomanry in Great Britain and Ireland shall, on so assembling a aforesaid, march under their respective Officers, but shall be put under such General Officers as His Majesty shall from Time to Time appoint for that Purpose, or shall be Commanding in the District.

12th And be it further inacted, That all Officers of Yeomanry and Volunteer Corps shall rank with the Officers of His Majesty's Regular and Militia Forces as the youngest of their respective Ranks.

13th And be it further enacted, That all money subscribed by or for the Use of any such Corps in Great Britain and Ireland, and all Arms, Stores, Ammunition, Drums, Fifes, or Musical Instruments, or other Articles, of whatever kind or sort the same may be, belonging to such Corps, not being the Property of any particular Individuals of such Corps, shall be and the same, are hereby declared to be vested in the Commanding Officer of the Corps; and shall be for the purposes of Indictment, Action or Suit, Criminal or Civil, in Law or Equity, be deemed to be the property of the Commanding Officer of the Corps, and shall and may be laid so to be in any Indictment, or may be sued for and recovered as such, or may be stated to be such in an Action relating thereto; and no Indictment, Suit action or Prosecution shall be discontinued or abated by Death or Removal of any such Commanding Officer but the same may be proceeded in by the succeeding Commanding Officer or the Commanding Officer for the Time being, any Law, Custom or Usage to the contrary notwithstanding.

B7 14th And be it further enacted, That where any persons enrolled in any such Corps in Great Britain and Ireland shall have neglected or refused, on Demand made

---

[7] Another purely Irish act.

for that purpose, to pay any sum or sums of money subscribed or required by the Rules and Regulations of such Corps to be subscribed to him towards any expenses of the Corps to which he belongs or to pay any Fines or Penalties incurring under any of the Rules and Regulations thereof, then and in such case it shall be lawfull for any Justice of the Peace residing in or near to the place where such Corps shall be, an Application made for that purpose and proof thereof by any Commanding Officer or Treasurer, or Two of the Committee or Secretary of any such Corps, to cause the same, together with Double the amount whereof or as a Penalty or Forfeiture to be levied by Distress or Sale of the Defaulters Goods, Chattels, by Warrant under his Hand and Seal, rendering the Overplus, if any, on Demand after Deducting the Charges of such Distress and Sale, to the Persons whose Goods and Chattels have been so distrained and sold; and the Sums so levied shall go to the general Stock of such Corps, to be applied in the general Expenses thereof in like Manner as any Subscription or sums of money received by or for such Corps may be applied or where there shall be no such subscription or stock of such Corps, then to such purposes relating to such Corps as the Commanding Officer thereof may think fit.

15th And be it further enacted, That this Act shall continue and be in force during the continuance of the War and until six months after the Ratification of a Definitive Treaty of Peace with France.

16th And be it further enacted That the Act may be altered, varied or repeated by any other Act or Acts in this Session of Parliament.[8]

B10 The following Letter Circular has been transmitted to the several Lords Lieutenant of the Counties, by the Speaker of the House of Commons.

House of Commons August 10th 1803

My Lord,

By command of the House of Commons I have the honour of Transmitting to you their unanimous Vote of Thanks to the several Volunteer and Yeomanry Corps of the United Kingdom, for the promptitude and zeal with which at a crisis the most momentous to their country they have associated for its defence; accompanied with an Order, that a return be prepared, to be laid before the House in the next session of Parliament, of all Volunteer and Yeomanry Corps whose services shall have been then accepted by His Majesty, describing each Corps in order that such Return may be entered on the Journals of the House and the patriotic example of such voluntary exertions transmitted to Posterity, in communicating this Resolution and Order, I have the great satisfaction at the same time, in bearing testimony to the Confidence with which the House is impressed, and that the same spirit and exemplary zeal will be exerted throughout the present contest, until, with blessing of Providence, it shall be brought to a glorious issue.

I have the Honor to be, etc   Charles Abbott, Speaker[9]

Copy of the Note of Thanks of the House of Commons to the Volunteer Corps of the Kingdom dated August 10th 1803

Resolved, Nomine, Contradicente

---

8   B8–B9, more copies of blank forms omitted.
9   The instructions to carry this out have not been included.

That the Thanks of this House be given to the several Volunteer and Yeomanry Corps of the United Kingdom, for the Promptitude and Zeal with which, at a Crisis the most momentous to their Country, they have associated for its Defence.

Ordered Nomini Contradicente

That a return be prepared, to be laid before this House in the next Session of Parliament, of all Volunteer and Yeomanry Corps whose Services shall have been then accepted by his Majesty; describing the Corps; in order that such Return may be entered on the Journals of this House. And the Patriotic Example of such Voluntary Exertions transmitted to Posterity.

Ordered That Mr Speaker do signify the said Resolution and Order, by Letter, to His Majesty's Lieutenant, of each County, Riding, and Place, in Great Britain, and to His Excellency the Lord Lieutenant of Ireland.   J Ley [?]Cl D Dom Com

---

B11   **Ipswich August 28ᵗʰ 1803**

Sir   You will be so good as to circulate the thanks of the House of Commons contained in the accompanying papers throughout the Corps of Volunteer Cavalry and Infantry in the County of Suffolk with as much Expedition as possible. I need scarcely add that it gives me great satisfaction to be the Channel of communicating so distinguished a mark of the approbation of their Countrymen to Corps who have so recently required a fresh title to it, by laying aside, as they have done, every consideration of Personal Convenience for the sake of appearing before His Royal Highness the Commander in Chief during his Military Tour in the Eastern District. It would have been highly gratifying to me to have been present on each Day, on which the Volunteers assembled at Ipswich and at Bromeswell[10] but Military Duty which I could not neglect, in another Quarter, prevented my Attendance until the 28ᵗʰ Instant and perhaps I cannot take a more fit opportunity of explaining the Cause of my absence on the two former Days than by desiring you to send Copies of this Letter with the Note of Thanks to each Corps.[11]

I am, Sir, Your most Obedient Humble Servant   Euston

Abraham Jenkin Esq Clerk of the Peace

To the Volunteers of Suffolk

In order that the following testimony of His Royal Highness the Commander in Chief's approbation of the zeal and loyalty of the Volunteer Corps of Cavalry and Infantry, in Suffolk, should be recorded in the most public manner, the Lord Lieutenant of the County has directed copies of it to be inserted in each of the County Newspapers, accompanied with every sentiment of respect from himself, which words can convey towards those who compose the Volunteer force of Suffolk.

Camp at Torrington September 1st 1803   Euston Lieutenant of Suffolk

Lieutenant General Sir James Craig has received the Commander in Chief's direction to request, that the Lord Lieutenants of Essex and Suffolk, will signify to the numerous and respectable Corps of Yeomanry, Volunteers and Sea Fencibles, which His Royal Highness has had an opportunity of reviewing, during his tour of those

---

10 A large number of regular forces were stationed at the army camp at Bromeswell.

11 Lord Euston was in command of the West Suffolk Militia stationed at Torrington in Devon. He had obviously missed the two earlier Review days for the Volunteer Infantry Troops.

Counties, the very great satisfaction he has derived from observing the general spirit and zeal with which they have at this important crisis come forward, and enrolled themselves for the defence of the country.

The energy which has marked their conduct on this occasion, affords the best security for the continuation of the invaluable blessings we have so long enjoyed; and is at the same time most honourable testimony of their attachment to the King, and of their determination to preserve entire the Religion, the Independence and unrivalled Constitution which we received from our ancestors.

Signed J H Craig Lieutenant General Commanding Eastern District

Colchester 31st August 1803

Review		**Sunday August 28th 1803**

Orders having been received from Lord Euston Lord Lieutenant of the County by sundry Officers commanding Corps of Yeomanry Cavalry in the County of Suffolk to assemble on Rushmere Heath at 8 oClock on Sunday Morning the 28th August 1803 prepared to be Reviewed by His Royal Highness The Duke of York Commander in Chief. The following Troops where formed on the Ground appointed for the purpose in the Parish of Rushmere viz[12]

1st Troop Commanded by	Captain Lord Rous	80
2nd Troop	Captain Edgar	150
3rd Troop	Captain Maynard	67
4th Troop	Captain Fowke	120
5th Troop	Captain Sparrow	62
6th Troop	Captain Gooch	80
7th Troop	Captain Moore	80
		639

All arrangements being made about half past 8 oClock His Royal Highness accompanied by His Royal Highness the Duke of Cambridge, Sir James Craig commander of the Eastern District, Lord Euston the Lord Lieutenant of the County Lord Paget Colonel Stewart and all the Officers of the 7th and 8th Light Dragoons in their full Uniforms appeared on the Ground. On his approach His Royal Highness was saluted by the Line after which he passed it in Review Order, the Troops afterwards passed His Royal Highness by single files and formed in the Line of Parade when His Royal Highness left the Field. The Officers of the sundry Troops being ordered to assemble in the Centre of the Line Lord Euston addressed them by order of His Royal Highness with his thanks etc etc for their Appearance.

The day being very fine the number of Spectators consisting of all Ranks of People was innumerable, the effect and appearance of so many Volunteers in Defence of their King and Country it was a Scene inexpressably grand and highly gratifying to every Spectator.

B13 By reason of the increased strength of the Troops the number of which now amounting to 150 Members, it was thought advisable to apply for leave to form the same into three Troops. In consequence of such application Captain Edgar received a Letter of which the following is a copy from Lord Euston the Lord Lieutenant of the County.

---

[12] 28 August 1803 was one of the only times all the Troops of the Loyal Suffolk Yeomanry Cavalry met together as one force.

Sir   I have great satisfaction in acquainting you that His Majesty has been graciously pleased to accept of the Offer made by you of forming your Corps of Yeomanry Cavalry into three Troops of 40 each and that he has been pleased to allow you the rank of Major.

I have the honor to be Dear Sir Your most faithfull and Obedient Servant

Euston

Camp at Torrington September 8ᵗʰ 1803
To M Edgar Esq Red House Ipswich

September 13ᵗʰ 1803 General Muster
The Troops assembled at the usual time and place and marched to a field in the occupation of Mr Andrew Cockle in Woodbridge and being formed in a square, the above Letter was read by Major Edgar to the Troop, and an arrangement for the appointment of Officers being previously made, was also read, and each Gentlemen being separately nominated where unanimously approved without a single dissenting voice.[13]

The above arrangement being completed we formed in three Troops and after a few Evolutions dispersed

B14 The Commanding Officers having arranged their respective Troops as follows same are names of the members of each Troop etc

Mileson Edgar Major Commandant   The Reverend Dr Frank Chaplin

1st Troop
J M Theobald Captain
William Pearson Lieutenant
J M Rodwell Cornet
James Bryant Quarter Master
Spencer Leek Senior Trumpeter
Nathaniel Collins Farrier
Robert Sexton Sergeant Major
C R Church Sergeant
Isaac Churchyard Sergeant
Buckle Allen Corporal
Thomas Edwards Corporal
Richard Grimwade Corporal
James Last, Edward Field, Titus Browning, Robert Bedwell, John Fryatt, George Skipper, Edward Watkins, James Garnham, George Harsum, Joseph Rye, Edward Adams, Lionel Dove, Benjamin Cook, Joseph Bulmer, Joseph Rivers, James Morgan, John Garnham, George Ashford, James Orman, Thomas Ouira, Jeremiah Cooper, Robert Welham, William Wilson, George Ranson, Ambrose Raynham, William Cockrell,   Robert Keeble, John Clover, George Ward,   Edward Jay, Peter Veasey,   John Edwards, Robert Rutland, Henry Farrer, John Mayhew, John Last, Willian Wilson, William Slade, George Vincent Claydon, George Morgan Bramford, John Edwards Bramford, William Cole Ash Bocking, John Dawson Ash Bocking

---

13   The names not included since they were repeated below.

2nd Troop
Cornelius Collett Captain
J Stow Baldry Lieutenant
Philip Dikes Cornet
Thurston Whimper Quarter Master
Thomas Symonds Trumpeter
Francis Hayle Sergeant Major
Nathaniel Gross Sergeant
Benoni Kemp Sergeant
George Bates Corporal
John Hunt Corporal
Thomas Simpson Corporal

Jonathan Churchyard, William Barthrop, Tollemache Cole, Thomas Denny, William Bunnett, John Smith, Samuel Denny, James Grout, Nathaniel Bunn, Daniel Fuller, William Skeet, Samuel Cooper, Robert Ablett, William Laurence, John Paine, John Easter, John Button, George Kier, John Thredkell, Daniel M'Cluer, John Aldous, William Orford, Thomas Miller, William Elvis, George Loft, Jonathan Kier, Nathaniel K Chandler, William Neeve, James Neeve, William Lungley, James Page, George Miles, James Churchyard, William Smith, James Newson, John Hayward, Richard Rope, John Thorton vice J Grout, Philip Pierce vice Laurence, Joseph Chapman Blaxhall, John Welham Martlesham

3rd Troop
John Couperthwaite Captain
G H Errington Lieutenant
John Brooke Cornet
Charles Collett Quarter Master
Spencer Leek Junior Trumpeter
William Hewitt Sergeant Major
John Field Sergeant
John Sawer Sergeant
George Curtis Corporal
William Cook Corporal
John Chapman Corporal

Nathaniel Moore, John Knight, Joseph Harris, Thomas Wake, Joseph Roe, John Porter, Daniel Orpen, John Ranson, Richard Hyam, James Fisher, Henry Waller, Jonathan Wasp, John Thorton, Robert Blomfield, William Shearman, Thomas Catlin, John Rivet, Richard Crowley, James Masters, Thomas Shave, Jeremiah Laws, Postle Jackson, William Klopser, John Cook, Philip Freeman, William Everett, John Ablett, J Seakamp, James Rivers, Cornelius Collett,[14] William Goldsmith, William Cobbold, William Salmon, Samuel Adams, Thomas Bolton, John Bird, Robert London, John Barnes, Robert Weeding vice Freeman, John Bryant

---

B16 Friday September 23rd 1803
At the request of Major Edgar, Captains Theobald, Couperthwaite and myself attended at his House for the purpose of arranging a plan for Mustering the sundry

---

[14] Collett was a common local name.

Troops as quick as possible if called upon for actual Service on occasion of Invasion or Internal Commotion etc etc.

Orderly Men appointed for the purpose of carrying dispatches, as under is a Copy of the arrangement of the Second Troop under the Command of Captain Collett.

Members resident in Woodbridge subject to be appointed Orderly

Spencer Leek Senior, Spencer Leek Junior, Nathaniel Collins, Samuel Denny, Tollemache Cole, James Grout, William Skeet, David M'Cluer, William Elvis, George Loft, Daniel Fuller, George Miles.

1st S Leek Senior dispatched To: Jonathan Churchyard – Melton, Isaac Churchyard – Ufford, George Bates – Eyke, Robert Ablett – Butley, Thomas Miller – Boyton

2nd Spencer Leek Junior To: James Churchyard – Rendlesham, Jonathan Keer – Wantisden, John Hunt – Chilesford

3rd Nathaniel Collins To: Nathaniel Gross – Sutton, John Easter – Sutton, John Paine – Sutton, William Laurence – Shottisham, J S Baldry – Ramsholt, Thurston Whimper – Alderton

4th D M'Cluer To: Samuel Cooper – Bredfield, Benjamin Cooper – Dallingho, William Bunnett – Dallingho, James Page – Charsfield, John Thredskell – Charsfield

5th George Loft To: Thomas Simpson – Ufford, Nathaniel Chandler – Pettistree, Philip Dikes – Pettistree, Nathaniel Bun – Wickham, William Neeve – Pettistree, James Neeve – Pettistre

G Loft also deliver dispatch To: N Chandler and N Bunn

6th N Chandler deliver To Benoni Kemp – Parham, William Barthrop – Parham, George Keer – Parham

7th Nathaniel Bun deliver To: John Buttom – Marlesford, William Orford – Marlesford, James Aldhous – Marlesford, James Newson – Glemham, Thomas Denny – Sweffling

Bun also deliver a dispatch to Newson and Denny

8th J Newson deliver To J Simmonds – Saxmundham, John Smith – Saxmundham, William Lungley – Saxmundham, F Hayle – Leiston

J Simmonds to forward the dispatch to F Hayle

9th Thomas Denny deliver To: John Hayward – Cransford, Richard Rope – Cransford, William Smith – Swefling

Memorandums

On the delivery of a Letter by an Orderly Man, providing the person to whom it is addressed is from home it is to be sent to him by some of his family with all possible dispatch.

On delivery of a dispatch the person to whom it is addressed is from home the orderly Man must go forward with it to the next Man on the rout, who is then to become orderly and forward the Letter as addressed.

The Orderly Man is requested to go out in plain Cloths and if possible not to ride his Troop Horse.[15]

---

[15] This suggests that a special horse was kept for Yeomanry use by those who could afford to keep more than one. It also highlights the fear of panic spreading if such a crisis arose.

Eight miles an hour is the time and distance of an Orderly Man to March, and the same is to be observed in joining the Troop in going from his own Home to the place appointed for assembling the Troop.
NB The place appointed for the 2nd Troop to assemble is at Woodbridge.[16]

B19 Regulations during War, for Cloathing Appointments, and the Allowances for the Contingent Expenses, of Yeomanry and Voluntary Cavalry

Every officer, non-commissioned officer and private man to take the oath of allegiance and fidelity to His Majesty. Every Troop to consist of not less than forty rank and file, which comprehends Corporals and Privates only. Three pounds per man for effectives will be allowed annually for clothing and appointments, and issued for three years at once if required, and the sum of one Hundred pounds and twenty pounds per Troop per annum, at the disposal of the Commandant, to be in lieu of the pay of sergeants and Trumpeters, and of every charge of whatsoever description heretofore defrayed by Government. Constant pay at the rate of six shillings per diem to be allowed for an Adjutant, to corps of three troops and upwards. Sergeants receiving constant pay, and all Trumpeters (or buglemen) receive pay whether at daily or weekly rate, to be attested and made subject to military law until they shall be regularly discharged by the Commandants. If a corps, or any part thereof, shall be called upon in cases of riot or disturbance, the change of constant pay to be made for such services must be at the rate following, being the pay of the regular cavalry, and supported by a certificate from his Majesty's Lieutenant, or Sheriff of the County.
Per diem
Captain 14s 7d   Lieutenant 9s   Cornet 8s
Quarter Master 5s 6d   Adjutants 10s
Sergeant Major including 9d for a horse 3s 11d
Sergeant including 9d for a horse 2s 11d   Corporals including 9d for a horse 2s 4½d
Trumpeters including 9d for a horse 2s 4d   Privates including 9d for a horse 2s

Such Troops as have received reduced cloathing allowance of Two Pounds per man for the years 1802 and 1803 may appear on the application of the Commandants, receive the difference between that allowance and the augmented rate as above specified.
The above Resolutions or Regulations are taken from an Act of Parliament June 22nd 1802 intitled an Act to enable His Majesty to avail himself of the Officers of certain Yeomanry and Voluntary Corps.[17]
[18]

B29 Copy of Sir James Craigs Memorandum for Officers Commanding Volunteer Corps
It is to be taken for granted that every Corps has its particular place of Assembly from whence it will proceed in order to the general Alarm Post to which it belongs.[19]
It is to be understood that on the event of the Enemy approaching any place, so as to show an evident intention of making an attempt on the Shores of the Harbour or

---

[16] This well-organised plan would allow a fast emergency turnout of the Troop.
[17] The full Act is under 22 June 1802.
[18] B20–25, copy of Act of Parliament moved to A196 for chronological relevance. B26–28, Collett's copies of forms mentioned in the Act, are omitted here.
[19] Their Headquarters, the Shire Hall at Woodbridge, was the Troop's place of assembly.

Coast near it the Volunteers of that place, as also those immediately contiguous to it, will not proceed to the Alarm Post or Place of Assembly to which they belong but will remain at hand to make every opposition to the Enemy that their number will admit of, and at all events to watch his motions, and to be continually harassing and annoying his motions, to check and impede his progress in any endeavour he may make to penetrate into the Country.

Instant notice must be sent to all the nearest Alarm Posts, from whence it is to be forwarded to others so as to draw the forces of the Country, to the Point attacked as speedily as possible. In cases where the attack does not threaten any part of the Coast of Suffolk the several Corps will wait for further orders at their respective Alarm Posts. It is taken for granted that every Corps has its particular place of Assembly, from whence it will proceed, in order, to the general alarm post to which it belongs.

September 28ᵗʰ 1803   Euston Lieutenant of Suffolk

Whearstead Lodge September 30ᵗʰ 1803

Sir   I have received a letter from the Lord Lieutenant informing me of the several Rendezvous that the Lieutenant General Sir James Craig purposes the Volunteer Corps within my Division to assemble at, on the Event of the Enemy being off the Coast, which I am ordered to Communicate to you. The Corps under your Command is to assemble at Woodbridge. I also inclose a Copy of a Memorandum received with the above letter.

           I am Sir Your most Obedient Humble Servant   R Harland

Major Edgar   Red House Ipswich

B30 Trumpeters

Copy of an Agreement between Major Edgar, Captains Theobald, Collett and Couperthwaite and the Trumpeters of the 2nd Troop (or Corps) of Loyal Suffolk Yeomanry Cavalry respecting their future pay.

Major Edgar and the 2nd Corps of Loyal Suffolk Yeomanry Cavalry agrees to give Trumpeter Leek Senior, Trumpeter Symonds and Trumpeter Leek Junior Fourteen Shillings per week each during the War, if they Conduct themselves to his satisfaction, to be Cloathed, armed and appointed at the Expense of the Corps. They on their Parts respectively engaging to attend on all Field Days, unless prevented by Sickness, properly mounted and keeping their Horses at their own Expense, and to go out with any Letters or Orders to Members of the Corps, when required, without any Remuneration for the same.

The pay to Trumpeter Leek Senior to commence the 12 day of August last, to Trumpeter Symonds the 16 day of August last and to Trumpeter Leek Junior the 13 day of September last. Lastly it is understood that when the Corps is on Actual Service, the Weekly Pay of Fourteen shillings from the Fund of the Corps shall not be claimed or expected.[20]

                                        Signed Mileson Edgar Major

Done at Head Quarters	Spencer Leek	
Woodbridge	Thomas Symonds	Trumpeters
October 4ᵗʰ 1803	Spencer Leek Junior	

---

[20] They would then be paid by the government as regular troops.

B31 Memorandums
Tuesday September 20th 1803 General Muster
The Troop met at Woodbridge at 9 oClock in the Morning on the Parade in the Market Place, marched from thence to a field in the Occupation of Mrs Stollery Hasketon, and were Exercised in three Troops in the usual Evolutions. Mr Middleditch a Quarter Master in the Light Dragoons Commanded by [blank] attended in the Field for the first time it being the intention of Major Edgar to appoint him Adjutant to the three Troops.

Tuesday September 27th 1803 General Muster
The Troops met at the time and place as above, and from thence marched to a Field in the occupation of Mrs Stollery Harketon and where Exercised in the usual Evolutions. A party of thirty being ten Men from each Troop went through the Sword Exercise that number being appointed to do the sword exercise at the time of the Troops being Reviewed by a General Officer in conformity to the Act of Parliament.
The Major with the Captains having arranged a plan, for mustering the Troops as early as possible on the shortest notice (His Royal Highness the Duke of York having expressed his wish to be informed the time in which we could assemble the Troop in case of emergency on the shortest notice) the Members of the Troop where informed of the plan and that on some future day an experiment would be made without the previous knowledge of any but the Major. Adjourned to Tuesday October 4th.
NB Mr Middleditch attended this day being his second meeting with the Troops.

Tuesday October 4th 1803 General Muster
The Corps (or three Troops) met at Woodbridge at the time appointed. At the time of meeting it rained very hard and continued to be very stormy that we could not march into the Field - no particular occurrence on this day except being disappointed in the field Exercise.

Monday October 10th 1803
The Major wishing to try the experiment of mustering the Corps on the shortest notice in case of being called upon for actual service in conformity to a plan for that purpose. This morning early issued orders to the Captains to assemble their respective **B32** Troops immediately at Head Quarters Woodbridge, the place of rendezvous appointed by the General of the District, no prior information of the time of issuing such orders had been given to anyone.
Orderly Men where dispatched with Letters and all Members of the Troop mustered in the Market Place in Six Hours from the time that the Major sent off his first Orderly Man from his own House, excepting nine Yeomanry who were confined by illness or absent from Home viz Dr Frank Chaplin who was not applied to, Lieutenant Pearson 1st Troop very Ill, of the 2nd Troop Sergeant Major Hayle, S Elvis, D M'Cluer from home and George Keir very Ill, 3rd Troop Daniel Orpen and Thomas Shave from home, William Goldsmith Ill Total 9
After parading on the Market Place and the Muster Roll called over the Troops dispersed having received orders to assemble on Tuesday 18th Instant at the hour of 11oClock forenoon.

Tuesday October 25th 1803 General Muster

The Troops met at the usual time and place and exercised in a field of Mr Nathaniel Gross as above no particular occurrence, except that Mr James Grant requested to resign in consequence of having got an appointment to a place in the service of the Barack Master in the Baracks at Woodbridge which required his constant and daily attendance in the Accounting House etc. Major Edgar accepting his resignation Mr [blank] of [blank] was elected in his place.

Tuesday November 1st 1803 General Muster

The Troops met at General Muster at Kesgrave at 11 oClock in the forenoon and exercised in a field in the occupation of Mr Cotton. Major Edgar informed the Troops on Thursday 3rd Instant Lord Paget intended to Review them and we where desired to meet on Thursday morning fully and properly Equipped for said Review at half past Ten oClock at Kesgrave.

B33   **War Office September 28th 1803**

Regulations for the Establishments, Allowances etc of Corps of Yeomanry Cavalry, accepted subsequently to the 3rd August 1803

A Troop to consist of not less than Forty, nor more than One Hundred Rank and File. To each Troop: one Captain, one Lieutenant, one Cornet and one Quarter Master. If 70 Rank and Files and upwards: 1 Captain, 2 Lieutenants, 1 Cornet, 1 Quarter Master.

A Squadron to consist of two Troops.

A Corps from 3 to 4 Troops both inclusive, may have 1 Major and 1 Captain to each Troop.

A Regiment to consist of from 5 to 12 Troops both inclusive.

A Regiment from 5 to 7 Troops, both inclusive may have 1 Lieutenant Colonel, 1 Major.

A Regiment from 8 to 12 Troops both inclusive may have 1 Lieutenant Colonel, Commandant, 1 Lieutenant Colonel, 1 Major.

1 Sergeant, 1 Corporal to every 20 privates

Staff

An Adjutant, Surgeon, and Sergeant Major, may be allowed on the Establishment of the Corps of not less than Three Troops, but neither of the said Staff Officers, nor any other Commissioned Warrant Officers, will have any pay, or Allowances whatever, except in the following Cases Viz

If a Corps or part thereof shall be called upon in Cases of Riot or Disturbance the Charge of constant pay may be made for such Services at the Rate specified in the Margin, being the pay of the Regular Cavalry; the same being supported by a Certificate from His Majesty's Lieutenant or Sheriff of the County. In Case of Invasion, the Corps is to be paid at the Rates aforesaid, and to be disciplined in all Respects as the Regular Cavalry.

The only instance in which pay will be allowed by Government for an Individual of the Corps when not so called out, are those of an Adjutant and Sergeant Major, for whom pay will be granted at the Rate specific in the margin, if authorised by his Majesty's Secretary of State in consequence of a particular application from the Lord Lieutenant of the County, founded upon the necessity of the case.

But this Indulgence cannot be allowed under any Circumstances, unless the Corps to which the Adjutant may belong, shall consist of not less than B34 Three Hundred Effective Rank and File, and he shall have served at least Five years as a Commissioned Officer in the Regular embodied Militia, Fencibles, or East India Company's Service; and unless the Corps to which the Sergeant Major may belong shall consist of not less than 120 Effective Rank and File, and he shall have served at least three years in some of His Majesty's Forces.[21]

The sum of £120 per Troop per Annum will be issued half yearly at the Disposal of the Commandant; in lieu of pay for Sergeants and Trumpeters, and of all the Expenses whatever, commencing from the date of the Acceptance of the Corps.

Sergeants receiving constant pay, and all Trumpeters (or Bugle Men) receiving Pay either at a Daily or Weekly Rate to be attested and made subject to Military Law until they shall be regularly discharged by the Commandant, as prescribed by Statute 43 Geo 3 C126

An Application must be made to the Secretary at War, by the Commandant of the Regiment or Corps of Yeomanry Cavalry when duly accepted, for the Allowance granted to such Regiments or Corps; and upon his sanction to the Claim, the amount thereof may be drawn for upon the General Agent for Volunteer Corps, in Bills at thirty days Sight.

Every Officer, non-commissioned Officer and Private Man, to take the Oath of Allegiance and Fidelity to His Majesty, his Heirs and Successors.

All proposals for Raising or Augmenting Yeomanry Corps, or for any alteration in the Title of the Corps, or names or Dates of Commissions of the Officers must be transmitted through the Lord Lieutenant of the County, in order to the Amendment being submitted to his Majesty.

An application for Arms and Accoutrements should be made through the Lord Lieutenant of the County directly to the Board of Ordnance; and all applications for Ammunition for Exercise and Practice should be made through the Inspecting Field Officer of Yeomanry and Volunteers to the Board of Ordnance Annually.[22] Ammunition for Service should be drawn through the Medium of the Inspecting Field Officer from the Depot, under the order of the General Officer of the District.

The Arms etc furnished by the Board of Ordnance to Corps of Yeomanry Cavalry, are as follows viz Pistols, Sabres with Scabards, Belts for Ditto, for the Compliment.

All Effective Members of Volunteer Yeomanry Cavalry accepted by His Majesty are entitled to the Exemptions from Ballot allowed by 42 Geo 3 Cap 66 and 43 Geo 3 Cop 121 provided that such persons are regularly returned on the Muster Rolls to be sent into the Lord Lieutenant or Clerk of the General Meetings of his County, at the Times, in the Manner, certified upon Honour by the Commandant, the Form prescribed by these Acts B35 and Schedules thereto annexed. The Monthly Returns should be transmitted to the Inspecting Field Officer appointed to supervise the District in which the Corps is situated, and to the Secretary of State for the Home Department.

October 1803

The following was communicated to Major Edgar by the Inspector for the Division. In the event of Invasion a Cavalry Non-commissioned Officer or Private, is directed to carry in his Saddle Bags only One Shirt, One pair of Stockings, one pair of Shoes, Razor etc and Combs Brushes and what is necessary for the care of his Horse.

---

[21] There are entries in the margin giving the wages to be paid per day if called out on actual duty, which is a repetition of those listed earlier.

[22] This is the first mention of inspecting field officers.

Advertisement (Copy) Suffolk Volunteer Corps
In future all applications relating to the Rules and Details of Service, and to Military Supplies of every kind, except for Arms and Accoutrements, are to be made by the Commandant of the different Yeomanry and Volunteer Corps and Companies, to the Commanding General in the Eastern District through Colonel M'Leroth, who is appointed Inspecting Field Officer for the County of Suffolk;[23] and every Regulation established for the Musters and Returns of the several Corps and Companies is to be strictly and punctually complied with in all respect. All Periodical Muster Rolls and Monthly Returns required by Act of Parliament will continue to be sent in as heretofore.

Euston Lieutenant of Suffolk

Camp at Torrington October 16ᵗʰ 1803
NB Colonel M'Leroth's station is at Bury

Sir   Being appointed by his Majesty an Inspecting Field Officer of Yeomanry and Volunteers I am directed by Lieutenant General Sir James Craig to acquaint you that all returns and applications are to be made to me. I shall soon go round and Visit the whole Volunteer Force of the County.
I have the honour to be Your most Obedient Servant

H M'Leroth Lieutenant Colonel Inspector

Major Edgar Red House Ipswich

B36–37 Return of Volunteer Corps in the County of Suffolk with their Places of General Assembly in the Eastern District[24]

Hundred	Corps	Commanding Officer	Numbers		Place of Assembly
			Cavalry	Infantry	
Lothingland	Lowestoft Volunteers	Arnold Captain		100	Blythburgh
	Gorleston Volunteers	Bell Captain		100	
	Southwold Volunteers	May Captain		120	
	Wrentham Volunteers	Gooch Captain		115	
	Halesworth Volunteers	Reeve Captain		120	
	Blyford Volunteers	Drosser Captain		92	

---

[23] The government was at last taking responsibility for ensuring an efficient military administration of Volunteer Troops at local level. The appointment of inspecting field officers relieved some of the pressure on the Lord Lieutenant, particularly since he was with the West Suffolk Militia in Devon.

[24] Collett's chart of the high number of people across the county who had volunteered to defend their county clearly illustrates the patriotism of the population but also its fear of invasion.

| Hundred | Corps | Commanding Officer | Numbers | | Place of Assembly |
			Cavalry	Infantry	
Blything	Yoxford and Darsham Volunteers	Davy Captain		88	
	Sibton and Peasenhall Volunteers	Jermyn Captain		85	
	Wangford and Henham Volunteers	Reeve Captain		90	
	Dunwich	Robinson Captain		83	
	Huntingfield Volunteers	Philpot Captain		123	
	Leiston and Theberton Volunteers	Josselyn Captain		75	
	Westhall, Brampton and Stoven	Baldry Captain		70	
Wangford	Beccles Volunteers	Smith Captain		120	
	Bungay Volunteers	Foster Major		180	Total 1561
Blything	Yoxford Yeomanry Cavalry	Lord Rous Captain	80		Yoxford
	Halesworth Yeomanry Cavalry	Vanneck Captain	60		
Hoxne	Hoxne Hundred Yeomanry Cavalry	Maynard Captain	67		
Wangford	Beccles Yeomanry Cavalry	Sparrow Captain	62		
	Southelmham Yeomanry Cavalry	Adair Captain	60		Total 329
Liberty of Ipswich	Ipswich Volunteers	Neale Captain		306	Woodbridge
	Blaxhall, Iken and Tunstall	Syer Captain		213	
Plomesgate	Alborough	Wynter Captain		66	
	Saxmundham	Freeman Captain		80	
Wilford	Hollesley Bay	Page Major		348	

Hundred	Corps	Commanding Officer	Numbers		Place of Assembly
			Cavalry	Infantry	
	Melton	Stammers Captain		114	
Hoxne	Kelsale and Carlton	Rabbet Captain		201	
	Hoxne Hundred	Clerk Captain		70	
Loes	Framlingham Volunteers	Shafto Major		201	
	Woodbridge Volunteers	Purcel Captain		156	
	Woodbridge Yeomanry Cavalry	Edgar Major	147		
	Rendlesham Volunteers	Crisp Captain		100	
Bosmere and Claydon	Bosmere and Claydon Volunteers	Middleton Captain		255	
Colnies	Colnies	Brooke Captain	Total 147	330	Total 2440
Thedwastry	Bury Cavalry	Fowkes Captain	120		Ipswich
Cosford	Hadleigh Cavalry	Gooch Captain	80		
Baberg	Baberg Cavalry	Moore Captain	80 Total 280		
Cosford	Hadleigh Volunteers	Leek Captain		160	Hadleigh
	Sudbury Volunteers	M'Lean Captain		120	
Babergh	Stoke by Nayland Volunteers			60	
	Bures Volunteers	Sidney Captain		70	
	Lavenham	Burch Captain		67	
Risbridge	Haverhill	Jackson Captain		100	
	Clare	Matthews Captain		67	Total 644
Thedwastry	Bury Volunteers	Oakes Captain		102	Stow Market
	Bury Volunteers	Benjafield Captain		100	
	Fornham and Bury	Powell Captain		80	
Hartsmere	Hartsmere Rangers	Fren Captain		200	
	Eye Volunteers	Wayth Captain		100	
Blackbourne	Saxham Volunteers	Mills Captain		65	

Hundred	Corps	Commanding Officer	Numbers		Place of Assembly
			Cavalry	Infantry	
	Ixworth Volunteers	Cartwright Captain		90	
	Hopton Volunteers	Webber Captain		100	
Stow	Stow Hundred Volunteers	Tyrell Captain		105	
Thedwastry	Thedwastry Volunteers	Bunbury Captain		80	
Lackford	Mildenhall Volunteers			100	
	Lakenheath and Wangford Volunteers	Eagle Captain		100	
					Total 1222
Total			756	5867	

It is taken for granted that every Corps has its particular place of Assembly, from whence it will proceed, in order, to the general alarm post to which it belongs.

It is to be understood, that in the event of the enemy appearing off any place so as to show an evident intention of making an attempt upon the shores of the harbour, or coast near it, the Volunteers of that place as also those under immediately contiguous to it, will not proceed to the Alarm Post, or Place of Assembly to which they belong. Should any body of troops be at hand they will immediately join them and post themselves under the orders of the officer who commands them, but should there be no troops at hand they will of themselves make every opposition to the enemy that their number will admit of, and at all events his motions, and by continually harassing and annoying him, check and impede his progress to any endeavour he may make to penetrate into the Country. Instant notice must be sent to all the nearest Alarm Posts, from whence it is to be forwarded to others, so as to furnish the means of drawing the force of the country to the point attacked as speedily as may be expedient.

The nearest body of troops has in every case instructions to proceed with all expedition to the threatened point, so that in such event the Volunteers may be certain of a speedy support. In cases where the attack does not threaten any part of the contiguous coast, the several Corps will wait for future orders at their respective alarm posts.

B38 The Instructions (Copied as under) to Officers Commanding Volunteer Corps etc where received from Lieutenant Colonel M'Leroth stationed at Bury October 28th 1803[25]

The several alarm posts to which the Volunteer Corps of the Eastern District are to repair, upon the firing of the beacons and displaying of the appointed Signals, being fixed on,[26] it becomes necessary to lay before them the equipment with which it will be expedient that on such an event they should be provided, in order that without further delay, and under every circumstance of comfort and convenience that the nature of the service in which they are engaged will admit of, they may proceed to the duties that the exigency of the moment require of them.

It will easily be felt, that the peculiar nature of the service, in which the army in general, and the volunteer part of it with them, is likely to be engaged, will imperiously call for the lightest state of equipments in every individual belonging to it. No Privations will be esteemed a hardship, no murmur will even be heard, nor will any difficulty for a moment cause the slightest hesitation amongst Troops actuated by such motives as those under which we are called to defend everything that is dear to us.

It is however certain that the inconveniences that must arise to individuals, many of them little accustomed to the situation in which they will on this occasion find themselves placed, may be much diminished by previous arrangement and being generally looked up to and provided for.

A Shirt, a pair of Shoes and Stockings, with brushes and the necessary apparatus for cleaning himself, is all that a volunteer should think of carrying as necessaries and they should be done up in as small a compass as possible. Every Volunteer should have a good blanket or great coat, and will be provided with a canteen for water and a haversack for carrying his necessaries and bread. To these the horsemen must add what is necessary for his horse.

To the officers of Infantry one horse will be allowed for each, including the staff, and an extra for each field officer. In the Cavalry, three for each field officer, two for each captain, and one for each subaltern including Staff, together with one to carry the portmanteaus of the Officer of each Troop. A small portmanteau will contain the baggage of each Officer of Infantry, and will be carried on his horse behind him.

It will be found highly beneficial that an arrangement for messing be immediately affected; every mess to consist of six men, and to be provided with a proper camp kettle, while every man should have and constantly carry with him a knife and a spoon. One light two wheel cart will be permitted to be attached to each troop or company. On this will be carried the camp kettles, a bill hook for every 6 men, which should be previously provided, and any other conveniency for the general comfort of the Troop or company, particularly as regarding their messing, which may be thought proper, and which does not tend to overload a carriage **B39** intended

---

[25] This is one of the most important documents copied by Collett and was the nearest to a detailed plan that it was possible to devise, given the uncertainty about the form any landing might take. The instructions are clearly written for volunteers and have a good psychological understanding of how they will feel and what they should do. They are sensible in their expectations, aiming to create reassurance and prevent panic. The instructions about the evacuation of the old, sick and infirm, women and children are particularly noteworthy.

[26] Goodwin's Diary, July 1803: 'Our Steeples are fitted up with high poles for red flags to be hoisted when the French come, and with Tar barrels to be fired as signals of the Enemy. Hail folly and absurdity.'

to be always at hand, with troops whose movements will at times be rapid, and where marches will frequently be long. No other carriage can be admitted, all such together with all baggage and spare horses, will be stopped. And not suffered to proceed within a day's march of where the enemy may be expected to be met with. These several objects ought all to be immediately provided and arranged, and the Troops and companies should frequently parade and march in this style of equipment, so as to become habituated to the circumstances; by which, delay in the moment in which they may be called on will be guarded against, and a certainty of proper provision for service will be obtained.

General Officers, who will be appointed to review and inspect the several corps of cavalry and infantry will be particularly inspected to examine into their state of preparation in this respect.

No deduction is expected to be made from the effective strength of voluntary troops or companies for servants or batmen; these are easily procured without diminishing the force of the troop. No women or children can be allowed to accompany the volunteers.

With respect to bread, provisions and forage, the voluntary force will be on the same footing as the regulars and militia.

Care will be taken to insure a constant supply of ammunition, beyond what the Volunteer carries.

In the first hurry of assembling and moving the several bodies of troops, as may be necessary on the landing of the enemy, it may be impossible to prescribe positive routes, or to prevent crossing, crowding and interference with each other. Such will, however, occasion little difficulty if the commanding officers exert themselves to preserve order, and immediately to take such steps and enter into such arrangements as may be necessary. The troops under such unavoidable circumstances of interference or crowding, will satisfy themselves with the slightest accommodation, but they must recollect that even the full display of such a disposition will not produce its effect, unless everything be conducted with order and regularity, and with the strictest subordination to the directions of their officers.

On the routs where the troops are to march, sufficient bread may be, it is imagined, always to be procured in the great towns, on the shortest notice, and persons should be sent forward for the purpose but should that not be the case, the commanding officer must make the best arrangements that circumstances will allow of. Individuals must not be permitted to provide for themselves by which great disorder might ensue; in all cases a rigorous discipline must be enforced.

If there is no commissary attending the Corps, and it is indispensably necessary that provisions of straw, forage, or bread be procured on the spot, the commanding officer must provide one or more intelligent officers to act as commissaries for the time, who will go forward with proper assistance, call upon the magistrates in the neighbourhood, and represent the necessity of the case to them, that they may be induced to take such measures, and give such orders, as will, with the attention to the preservation of property, and without interference with discipline of the troops, immediately produce the necessary supplies, for all which the commanding officer of each troop will give full and distinct receipts, in writing, specifying in words, the quantity of each article received **B39** the number of persons and horses thereby provided for and for what time, which receipts are also to be signed by the commissary or officer acting as such. Registers of receipts so granted, will be kept by the commanding officers, as necessary cheques if called upon, and the receipts themselves will afterwards collected and displayed by the commissary general.

The volunteers of the Eastern District will always bear in mind the extent of the district, and the consequent probability of the necessity of their marching, immediately upon them assembling, in the event of the alarm, out of their own County and to a considerable distance. They will therefore feel the expediency of their coming to the place of assembly of their Corps, perfectly prepared for their proceeding, wherever their services may be requisite, and for this purpose it is essential, that every man bring with him three days bread which is 4½ lbs and each horseman at least two days forage for his horse.

From the moment of assembling, the utmost discipline will be expected, and strict subordination will take place; implicit obedience will be looked for, and order and regularity will be established. It is by these alone, that the spirit and zeal which animate every true volunteer in his country's cause, can be carried to the accomplishment of the object for which they have been displayed. It is these alone that can conduct courage to victory; and unless directed upon these principles individual bravery will frequently lead to unnecessary loss of lives.

It is impossible to foresee exactly the species of services, on which the volunteers may be employed as it must depend very much upon the conduct which the enemy shall pursue; they will be prepared for everything that can be required of them, whether it be to adopt the solid evolutions of the close column, to pierce the enemy's line with the bayonet, or to skirmish in the loose order of light troops. Every occasion that can present itself by using the bayonet will be eagerly and spiritly seized on; it is the weapon of true courage, and most peculiarly fitted for the nervous arm a Briton, especially when chastising the insolence of a vain boasting enemy, who in dispite of the numerous instances to the contrary, has dared to assert that we cannot cope with him single handed.

The instructions for exercise and movement, recommended by His Royal Highness the Commander in Chief are directed upon principles adopted to the movements of light troops and are particularly fitted for those of a composition, similar to that of the volunteers. If carefully attended to and practised they will enable them to pursue that system with every advantage; and it is that kind of warfare, in which they are most likely to be engaged.

The Enemy must never be lost sight of. Should it be possible to collect a body of sufficient strength to attack him the moment he is landed or still more while in the act of disembarking, such a circumstance will be highly desirable. It is to him, always a period of weakness and disorder; but at any rate, the nearest troops are instructed to advance immediately upon him and the volunteers will feel of what importance their expeditious assembly must be, by which we may be enabled to collect in that force, that will be requisite to attack the enemy; but if such force cannot immediately be collected, and we are compelled **B41** to fall back as he advances, it must be done only by slow degrees. A disposition will be immediately made for gaining his flanks and rear; he must be passed on all sides; the light troops of whatever description they may be, volunteers, militia, regulars, all will be conscious of keeping him constantly in view, of continually harassing and annoying him; an unintermitting fire must be poured upon him upon every part of his columns; his flanking parties must be destroyed or driven in; no rest must be allowed him at night and no party or detachment will be suffered to stir from his main body without being instantly attacked and destroyed.

To effect these services, coolness and strict attention to the orders of their officers are the circumstances that will be chiefly requisite. It is pointed out in the instructions, that men are to cover themselves with trees, stones, hedges and whatever may present itself, this is never to be omitted. It is absolutely necessary to impress on the minds of the men, that the doing so, is no indication of fear, in which light, a British soldier is too apt to consider it; on the contrary it is a demonstration of that cool resolution which always accompanies true bravery and inables a man to possess his perfect recollection in the midst of danger. Under the cover here pointed out, the light infantry man may wait, with coolness and deliberation, doing execution on his enemy with safety to himself till the very near approach of superior numbers oblige him to retire; this is his business, he is never to be ashamed to do it, however precipitously it may be requisite for him to change his situation; that every precipitation is a proof that he has maintained his station to the last, and that he has thereby acquitted himself as a good soldier.[27] The enemy having no cavalry cannot pursue him, while the protection of his own will very soon ensure his safety – at three or four hundred yards he may always stop and rally, and of course will do so; from thence he may advance and gain such an advantageous station, from which he may recommence to deal destruction to the enemy.

In general it is to be a rule, that companies are never to disperse or separate, but in such manner that the detached parts can fall back upon the main body; Regular corps will, in every possible case, be appointed to support and protect them, and as already been observed the enemy can have no cavalry to pursue them, it is obvious, that while they act with coolness and exact subordination to command they never can be in danger. In truth circumstanced as we shall be, with respect to the enemy, under the particular consideration of the impossibility of his having no cavalry or artillery, of any consequence with him, the conduct here pointed out, may be pursued with scarcely any hazard to the individual engaged in it. But however divested of danger it may be, it is not to be concealed, that it will not be equally free from fatigue. On the contrary, the activity of light troops, especially in a strong county, such as this, cannot be executed without very considerable fatigue. To this, the volunteer must particularly look up, and he must embrace the resolution of encountering it with firmness, and spirit and perseverance. The companies will relieve each other in every practicable case, and whatever **B42** may be the exertions required by the exigency of the moment, or whatever may be the privations that those exertions may call for, it will be the case of the commander that they shall be equally shared by all, and that every comfort and conveniency, that is within our reach be allowed to those by whom they have been undergone, while it is their tour of resting from them. The business of driving the country, has been systematically arranged under the direction of the lieutenancy, and ought not to require the interference of military aid to effect it. Indeed, as the atrocity with which the enemy has conducted himself in every part in which he has carried his arms rioting in unrestrained pillage, massacre, and every outrage that can disgrace the name of a soldier, is pretty generally known. It is reasonable to suppose, that everyone will be anxious to remove his family and effects from the line of his operations If however, tardiness should appear, if terror and panic among the old, the infirm, the women and children, should operate so far, as to induce them to neglect the only means of safety to them, in a timely removal, it may become necessary to compel them to it; and if any part of the volunteer force should be employed in this service, they must be deaf to every representation,

---

27 These are very important and reassuring instructions for volunteers and display a real understanding of their position.

and steeling themselves against the apparent call of humanity, they must obey their orders with the most rigid inflexibility.

The pioneers of the several parishes will assemble on the first alarm, and should be equally with the volunteers, prepared to move wherever their services may be required, those within six miles of a part where the enemy land, or off which he may appear, with the evident intention of landing, must repair immediately to the nearest body of troops. The captains and lieutenants must march them in order and without noise or confusion, to any convenient spot off the great road and about a quarter of a mile in the rear, where they will make this sit down and wait till they are called for. The pioneers at a greater distance will remain in their respective parishes, but always prepared to move on the shortest notice. It is essential that they should be provided with a good blanket, which should be previously prepared with a leather sling or a cord, so that the man may know how to roll it up and sling it across his shoulder for carriage; every man should likewise endeavour to procure a canteen for water, or strong bottle to be slung instead of it, and a knife. When it is recollected, that it is extremely probable that the presence of the pioneers may be required for some days, and that it may be necessary that they should accompany the army in the movements that it may make, the experience of their being properly provided will be felt.

The guides will in like manner assemble, and those of every hundred should immediately join whatever body of Troops may be in their hundred; where there no troops in the hundred they should be kept together, ready to move when called for and a very careful guide, **B43** well mounted, should be sent to the nearest body of troops, where he should announce himself to any of the quarter master general's department who may be there, or if there are none, to the major of Brigade. Another careful guide or two from each hundred, on horseback should be sent also to the head quarters of the army wherever it may be.

H M Gordon Lieutenant Colonel Assistant Adjutant General
H M'Leroth Lieutenant Colonel Inspector

1803 October 25th
Copy of a Printed Card this day delivered to the sundry Members of the Troop

Second Corps Suffolk Yeomanry Cavalry
When ordered out in Marching Order, every Non-commissioned Officer or Private is to carry in his Saddle Bags as under:
one Shirt, one pair of Stockings, one pair of Shoes, Razor, Comb, Brushes, Curry Comb and Brush, Mane Comb with Sponge, Horse Picker and Nose Bag, Stable waistcoat and Cap.

B44 Review Thursday November 3rd 1803
The Corps mustered at Kesgrave agreeable to Orders received in the first Instant for the purpose of being Reviewed by Major General Lord Paget. About 12 oClock his Lordship appeared in the Field accompanied by a Number of Officers of the 7th 9th and 18th Light Dragoons and many others from Ipswich and Woodbridge also a number of Gentlemen of the Neighbourhood, Captains of Volunteer Corps or Troops of Cavalry etc etc. His Lordship was received by the Troops in Line in the customary form and having inspected them they afterwards passed his Lordship and performed the various Evolutions required with exactness, spirit, and action, so satisfactory to his Lordship that he was pleased to express the same in terms most gratifying to the Troops and which was also repeated by every Officer present.

Copy of a letter by order of Major Edgar sent the Members of the 2nd Troop

Sir   **Woodbridge November 11ᵗʰ 1803**

I this morning received orders from Major Edgar desiring me to inform every Gentleman of the Troop that they will be inspected with the Corps on Tuesday next at Woodbridge at 11 oClock by Lieutenant Colonel M'Leroth. It is requested that the Arms and Equipment are all in the best condition – and further I am desired to say that no excuse will be accepted for non-attendance but Illness attested by a Medical Practioner.

I am, Sir, Your Most Obedient Servant   Cornelius Collett Captain

Pantaloons or overalls are not to be worn on parade.

B45 Tuesday November 5ᵗʰ 1803 General Muster

The Company was this day Inspected by Lieutenant Colonel M'Leroth Inspecting Officer of the East District in a Field in the occupation of Mrs Stollery opposite Farlingay Hall[28] who was pleased to express himself much satisfied with the spirited manner in which we went through the various Evolutions and also to say he should be proud in making his report of us to the Commander of the District.

Tollemache Cole (of Woodbridge) having desired Mr George Loft to inform Major Edgar he should no longer continue his services in the Troop under my Command without any reason assigned for same.[29] The Major consulted Lieutenant Colonel M'Leroth wether it was in his power to accept his resignation. The Colonel in reply said most certainly he should not, but that in consequence of his non-attendance and other misconduct, his name should be erased from off the Muster Roll as he considered him unworthy of being a member of the Corps and that the Major had a power of doing so. The Colonel further publicly declared he was in his opinion in consequence of such Conduct a greater Enemy to his King and Country than any Man who might come from the French shores to invade this Kingdom. Major Edgar in consequence of the Colonel's reply took the opinion of the Corps wether or not Mr Cole's name should be struck off the Roll and on a show of hands it was unanimously agreed it should be struck off which was immediately done by the Major in the presence of the Colonel and a considerable number of very respectable Spectators. It was further desired by the Colonel M'Leroth that the proceedings should be publicised in the Ipswich Newspaper on Saturday next.

Head Quarters Woodbridge November 15ᵗʰ 1803

Sir,   In consequence of your Name being struck off the Muster Roll of the Corps I am ordered by Major Edgar to request of you to deliver up and send to the depot here in good condition, all the Arms and Equipment belonging to the Corps in your possession.

Your humble Servant Cornelius Collett Captain

To Mr Tollemache Cole Woodbridge

---

28 Farlingay Hall lands belonged to Collett.
29 Tollemache Cole had joined the Yeomanry on its formation in 1794. See Collett's Register (Plate 13).

B46   Copy from the Ipswich Journal November 19th 1803

Tuesday the 2nd Corps of Suffolk Yeomanry Cavalry commanded by Major Edgar was reviewed by Lieutenant Colonel M'Leroth the Inspecting Field Officer of this district. The different evolutions were performed in a manner much to the satisfaction of that Officer who expressed himself in the highest terms of commendation; saying that he most warmly concurred in the opinion given by Lord Paget at his late review of the corps which he should not fail to communicate to Major General Sir James Craig. In the presence and with the approbation of Lieutenant Colonel M'Leroth Major Edgar struck off the roll the name of one of the privates of the corps, for repeated neglect of his duty as a soldier.

Copy of an Advertisement in the Ipswich Journal November 19th 1803

2nd Corps of Suffolk Yeomanry Cavalry

A Mr Tolemache Cole of Woodbridge has in too many instances neglected his duty, as a private in this Corps, to make his continuance in it, either desirable or proper, I have this day, in the presence, and with the approbation of Lieutenant Colonel M'Leroth, the Inspecting Field Officer of the district, struck his name off the Roll, conceiving that there cannot be a greater enemy to his country than a Volunteer bearing arms, more with a view of obtaining personal exemption, than of rendering personal service.

Mileson Edgar Major

Woodbridge November 15th 1803

From the London Gazette November 15th 1803

2 Suffolk [Corps] of Gentlemen and Yeomanry Cavalry

Mileson Edgar Esq to be Major

John Meadows Theobald, Cornelius Collett, J. Couperthwaite Esq to be Captain.

William Pearson, John Stow Baldry, George Henry Errington to be Lieutenants.

John Meadow Rodwell, Philip Dikes, John Brooke Gentlemen to be Cornets.

The arrangements for the forming the Corps into three Troops was made in September last and their offer of services accepted by his Majesty.[30]

B47 Tuesday November 22nd 1803 General Muster

It being a day of almost continual rain the Muster was in consequence expected to be small. The Major having a slight attack of gout was obliged to decline his attendance. Captain Theobald being present read the Major's Letter to the Troop assembled amounting to 84 and adjourned the meeting to Tuesday 29th Instant at the usual time and place.

November 23rd 1803

In consequence of Mr T Coles name being struck off the Muster Roll of the Corps, an Advertisement of which the following is a Copy was this day put in the Bury News Paper.

To Major Edgar 2nd Troop Loyal Suffolk Yeomanry Cavalry

---

[30] The correspondence of both Lord Euston and Mileson Edgar sometimes contains the originals of those copied by Collett in his volumes. See a copy of Lord Euston's Letter Book, SROI P454, p. 13.

The advertisement inserted by you This Day in the Ipswich Journal, strongly urges the expediency of my thus addressing you in order that the public may have the opportunity judging how much you wish to feed your arrogance and ostentation at the expense of my character, which by artifice and insinuation you have attempted to vilify, but which I venture confidently to assert stands as irreproachable and upon as unshaken a basis, as his to whom this is addressed.

In consequence of the several impertinent declarations having been made by you, in the field of exercise on the 15th instant, that I never was a good Soldier, and that you looked upon me as an Enemy to this country etc, I who have served in the Corps upwards of seven years, with Credit and Reputation, under my late brave worthy Commander, do hereby call upon you to answer me publicly the following Questions, Did you not pressingly solicit my continuance in the Troop, after the late War, when an almost general discontent prevailed respecting how the money then in stock, belonging to the Troop, should be applied? Did you not, very recently after your ungentlemanly treatment to me in the Field which I resented by my non-attendance, send for me to Captain Colletts and acknowledge you had conducted yourself too warmly, and request that what had passed should be consigned to oblivion? and, upon the very next muster day, did you not violate the good faith between us, by haranguing the Corps, upon the subject above alluded to? Under these and similar circumstances, as I did not choose to be commanded by a man whom I could not respect, I sent in my Resignation when you said with your usual self importance, I will not accept the Resignation but will strike his name off the Roll and I now look upon him as a greater Enemy to this Country than any Frenchman who lands here with an hostile intention; and I will take care he shall be drawn for the Militia. I defy you and all the World to impeach my Loyalty to the King and attachment to his Government, and he who dares to make a declaration to the contrary is a Lyer and the truth is not in him.   Tollemache Cole

Woodbridge November 19th 1803

B48 November 29th 1803 General Muster

The Corps being met at the usual time, prior to the Major's arrival assembled at the Market Hall in Consequence of the Advertisement of Mr Cole published in the Bury Paper, when Captain Theobald having addressed the Gentlemen present a Resolution of which the following is a Copy having been read and approved, it was unanimously agreed the same should be published in the Ipswich and Bury Papers.

Head Quarters Woodbridge November 29th 1803

We the Members of the 2nd Corps of Loyal Suffolk Yeomanry assembled this day at General Muster feel ourselves called upon Explicitly to declare that the late Expulsion of a member of our Corps on Account of repeated instances of neglect of duty, took place with the Concurrence of us all, which we expressed by a Unanimous Vote, and that therefore this measure can by no means be deemed the individual Act of our Commander, but the blame or merit of it must be shared by the whole body. We are led to state this in Consequence some reflections that have been made, with a total disregard to the rules of decorum upon our Major's conduct on this Occasion, and though Misrepresentation and illiberal abuse, might be justly consigned to silent Contempt. We are desirous of Stigmatizing this unwarranted attack on our Commander by our unanimous and decided reprobation; and we embrace, with pleasure the opportunity now afforded us, of Expressing the warm Sense we Entertain of his unremitted Exertions for the Welfare and improvement of the Corps, and for his zealous attention to the duties of his Station, which entitle him to any Cordial

Acknowledgement, and we wish him to be assured, that he stands much too high in our estimation to be injured by malicious Calumny. We request the Senior Captain to subscribe the above in the name of the Corps and that he will have the same inserted in the Ipswich and Bury Paper.
Jonathan Theobald Captain of 1st Troop.[31]

B49 On the Major's arrival he was informed of the resolution of the Corps, and having read and approved the same he addressed them in a speech which did him the greatest Credit. He fully confuted every charge of Mr Coles against him, but also pointed out the impropriety of his answering such an infamous advertisement through the means of a public Newspaper. The language of the same being considered by every person of respectability a sufficent answer to itself. He particularly requested if there any friends of Mr Coles present who wished him any respect to justify him or who could in any way contradict what had now been said of him or who might have assisted him in drawing up the advertisement or any other matter respecting the business he would step forward and declare his sentiments. No one doing it the business of the meeting concluded and it being a very wet day, members present where ordered to disperse and providing the weather be fine to meet again on Tuesday next at the usual time and place.

NB Mr Elvis and Mr Kemp not holding up their hand in approbation of the Resolution for or against it, where asked by Captain Theobald if they had any objection to which they replied they had none, either to the resolution or its publication as directed, but that they did not wish to hold up their hands for or against Mr Cole.

In answer to the above resolution of the Corps the following reply from Mr Cole was inserted in the Bury Paper.
To the Printer of the Bury Post
Mr Jackson, the printer of the Ipswich Journal having refused to insert my address to Major Edgar I again in consequence of an Advertisement in the same paper today, resort, through the medium of your impartial and intelligent publication, to suggest a few remarks.
Whatever the language used by the Major, in reference to my being an Enemy to this Country etc or the Facts as stated in my address to him, savours most of "malicious calumny." I appeal to the public; such an unjustifiable charge at all times is awfully serious, and more particularly at the present crisis, as it is calculated to take from me, what must to an individual be his greatest happiness, my reputation and character, and brand me with the name, which of all others I most abhor, that of an Enemy to my country.
I am charged with misrepresentation; if so, why did not the Major reply to me in the way I called upon him, and specify particulars? I however retort the misrepresentation, that the expulsion, as it is hautily termed, after my resignation, was not by an unanimous vote of the Corps, as there were several gentlemen who composed a minority, not only in that instance, but at the General Muster on Tuesday last, the 29th Ult and how Captain Theobald reconciles his having signed the advertisement by the concurrence of all, I am at a loss to conjecture, as he knows it was not unanimously agreed that it should be published.

Woodbridge December 3rd 1803   Tollemache Cole

---

[31] This was signed by 105 members.

B50 Memorandum of the steps required to be taken in regard to the recommendation and appointment of a Paymaster to a Volunteer Corps called out into actual Service.[32]

The Colonel or Commandant is to recommend one of the Subalterns of the Corps to be Pay Master, transmitting at the same time the Names, Residences, and situations in Life, of the Pay Masters intended Sureties; accompanied by a Reference on the part of each proposed surety to two respectable House Keepers, or other Persons of known Credit, whose Residence Profession or Occupation, is likewise to be specified.[33]

If after inquiry to the respectability of the proposed sureties, they are deemed eligible, in point of Character and Circumstance, Bonds will be made out at this Office, and forwarded to the Pay Master and the Sureties; which Bonds are to be executed, and returned, without delay, to the Secretary at War, who on receipt thereof, complete, will immediately transmit an instrument of appointment for the Pay Master, to the Colonel or Commandant, who is to sign, seal, and return the same to the War Office, from whence when registered, it will be again sent to the Colonel or Commandant, to be by him delivered to the Pay Master.

A Pay Master gives Bond for one Thousand pounds, the Sureties for five hundred pounds each.

In Corps of only one or two Troops or Companies the Pay Master is only required to give his Personal Security for five hundred pounds and to find two sureties in two hundred and fifty pounds each.

It is necessary that the Christian Name of the Person recommended to be Pay Master as well as those of his Sureties, should be stated at full length; and that in describing the respective places of Residence of the latter, the particular County, or City, wherein they are situated should be accurately specified; in order to prevent those mistakes which frequently arise from want of such proper descriptions being furnished by the Colonels or Commandants of Corps, and by the Persons recommended for Pay Masterships.

Circular   Sir   **War Office 22nd November 1803**

In order that in the event of the Corps under your Command, being called out into actual Service, no time may be lost in appointing a Pay Master thereto; I enclose herewith Memorandum, explaining the steps to be taken for that purpose; and am to request that you will now recommend an Officer for the above employment in the manner therein mentioned.

Upon receipt of your recommendation, the usual enquiries as to the responsibility of the sureties will be immediately made; so that when the Corps is called out, it will only remain to prepare the Bonds, and when they are executed, to make out the instrument of appointment

---

[32] The following letter should obviously have been included before the memorandum.

[33] This was a more secure way of funding the Troop if needed quickly, since the banks might fail if there was a crisis.

B51 The Officer recommended may however act as Pay Master, under your responsibility, from the time when the Corps may be placed on regular Pay; and may receive his allowance accordingly, provided he make up all his Accounts from that date.

Whenever the Pay Master is called upon to act, a Pay Master's Clerk may also be appointed from among the Non-commissioned Officers or Privates, of the Corps, who if a Sergeant, will continue to receive the pay of the Rank; or if a Corporal, or Private, will have his pay made up to that of a Sergeant.

The allowance to the Pay Master and the Clerk are of course only to continue while the Corps remains on regular Pay; but if the Corps should at any time cease to be employed, and should afterwards be again be called out, the Pay Master may resume his Functions, under the authority of his original Appointment.

Instructions etc for the information and guidance of the Pay Master, will be forwarded to you with little delay as possible.

I have the Honor to be Sir Your most obedient humble servant C Bragge

Major M Edgar Red House Ipswich   2nd Suffolk Gentlemen and Yeomanry Cavalry

The Pay of a Pay Master of a Corps of not less than three Troops or Companies, is Fifteen Shillings a Day, including that of his Regimental Commission.

In a Corps of Two Troops or Companies he receives an allowance £4 5s per Month and in a Corps of one Troop or Company £2 10s per month, in addition to his Regimental Pay. The Contingent Allowance for Portage and Stationary etc will be specified in the Instructions above alluded to.

Lieutenant William Pearson being by Major Edgar recommended for Payments to this Corps Edward Studd and Edward Hasell Esq of Ipswich where nominated his Sureties.

B52 Tuesday December 6th 1803 General Muster

The early part of the Morning there was a considerable quantity of Rain and Snow. Between 9 and 10 oClock it cleared up and the day appeared very fine, and between eleven and twelve the Members of the Corps to the Number of ninety assembled. We waited with expectation of the Major until near one oClock. In consequence of his not arriving and Captain Theobald being prevented attending which he noticed at the last meeting, I ordered the Troops to assemble on the Market Place. From thence we marched to Mr Cockle Field and having called the Muster Roll there being every appearance of a heavy fall of Snow I ordered them to disperse to meet again on Tuesday next if the Weather permitted. It was a very sharp Frost in the Evening which continued for several days. On Tuesday I received a Letter from Major Edgar requesting me to inform the Members of my Troop the meeting on Tuesday next was postponed in case the frost continued to that time. I accordingly sent the following Circular Letter to each Member.

Sir   Woodbridge December 10th 1803

I am directed by Major Edgar to inform you of the next meeting of the Corps is postponed until the first Tuesday after the weather break when you are required to meet at the usual time and place.

I am Sir Your most obedient Servant Cornelius Collett

Tuesday December 13th 1803 General Muster

A sudden change of weather taking place and the Frost being gone, Major Edgar, Captain Theobald, Lieutenant Pearson, Cornets Rodwell and Brooke, apprehending that many of the Troops would assemble appeared at the usual time, but having had a great fall of Rain, the Roads very bad, and the appearance of the day rather unfavourable, there was not a Meeting of the Troop not more than 3 or 4 who live near Woodbridge being present. There was of course no Muster.[34]

B53 Copy of a Letter from Lord Euston, Lieutenant of the County to Sir Robert Harland, Lieutenant of Division

Sir   Camp at Torrington October 25th 1803

The exposed situation of certain points upon the Coast of Suffolk have induced Government to consider of the means of collecting as large a force as possible for their protection without incurring the necessity of detaching from other points of no less importance;[35] with a view to this object, it would be desirable if it could be effected without serious inconvenience to Individuals; that this Duty should be taken for a short period only, and in rotation, by the Volunteer Corps; who would be put under permanent Pay for that purpose, and be marched to such points upon the Coast of Suffolk as stand most in need of being watched, and are at the same time capable of affording them Quarters.[36] If any of the Corps of Volunteers in the Division of the County of which you are the Lieutenant are disposed, by acceding to such a plan, to promote the Public Service, and to assist in a peculiar manner in the defence of their own Coast, I would wish to be made acquainted with their Intentions through their Commanding Officers; to all of whom you will be pleased to make this communication.

I have the honour to be, Sir, Your most obedient, Humble Servant,

Euston Lieutenant of County

To Sir Robert Harland, Lieutenant of Division

Tuesday December 20th 1803 General Muster

It being a very rainy Morning prevented the greater part of the Corps attending, about 54 assembled at 1 oClock at the Crown Inn, when the Major read the Letter from the Lord Lieutenant. The Gentlemen present immediately volunteered their Services and a notice was sent to each of the absentees to meet the Major and Officers on Friday morning at 11 oClock at the Crown Inn, it being the wish of the Lord Lieutenant to have as early an answer as possible.

Friday December 23rd The absentees on Tuesday being this day met, those Gentlemen who volunteered their services subscribed their Names to a list of which the following is a Copy.[37]

---

[34] Other than the turnpike roads, maintained by turnpike trusts with the money from tolls, most roads were maintained by the parishes and were of very poor quality.

[35] In 1794 one of the original intentions of the subscribers' committee for the internal defence of the county was to have a volunteer force to man the coastal batteries, and perhaps not surprisingly no volunteers were prepared to do it on a long-term basis. However, members of the Yeomanry were willing to watch the most vulnerable parts on a rota system, given the nature of the threat.

[36] In view of the area's considered importance, the need was a critical one.

[37] B54, 20 December 1803. The list of the members of the Corps who volunteered their service on the coast has been omitted, but the total numbers who volunteered were: Captain Theobald's Troop 47; Captain Collett's Troop 48; and Captain Couperthwaite's Troop 41. This is a very considerable number given the hardship this would have involved and the disruption to normal life, a clear illustration of the fear that the danger of invasion generated and their commitment to duty and their country.

B55 Copy of a Letter from P T Thellusson Esq Lieutenant of Division to Major Edgar

Dear Sir,

I was duly favoured with your letter of Monday last, I have lost no time in communicating its contents to Lord Euston. I now have the pleasure of transmitting to you the Copy of a letter which I have received from him and which I beg you will read to your Corps at its first Meeting.

I have the honor to be Dear Sir, Your faithful humble Servant,

P T Thellusson

Rendlesham 29ᵗʰ December 1803

Lord Euston's Letter to P T Thellusson

Sir

You will be pleased to make known to the Commanding Officers of the several Corps of Cavalry and Infantry in your division of the County of Suffolk, which have offered to be placed for a limited time and in rotation upon permanent duty, that the zeal which they have displayed at this Important Crisis, has been highly approved of by His Majesty and would have been immediately accepted, if Circumstances had made it expedient, at this Season to have called upon Troops whose domestic concerns or Engagements in Business would have been considerably interrupted by any Service at a distance from their Houses. **B56** Cases however may occur, short of actual Invasion, in which for the protection of the Coast of Suffolk, His Majesty may think it advisable to avail himself of the Spirited offers which he has received from the several Corps alluded to, and it may be deemed expedient in a Season better calculated than the depth of Winter, for the advancement of Troops in the knowledge and practice of Field Movements and Duties, to assemble them for such time as may suit their convenience, at such stations as may afford means sufficiently extensive to receive several Troops or Companies at the same time. With a View however in the meantime, to Service against the Enemy, which every Corps may be called upon to perform when perhaps they least expect it, I am persuaded their own good Sense and Public Spirit will have pointed out to them, the necessity of a constant application to the duties of a Soldier as their ordinary avocations will admit of: and I feel a Confidence of the strongest kind, that every consideration, not only of private Convenience but all Personal objects whatever, will continue to give way to that which may be thought most expedient for the Public Service, during the present arduous Contest, which, as it has roused us, at the outset to Exertions hitherto unknown, will require our utmost circumspection and Perseverance to bring it to an honourable and successful termination.

I have the honor to be, Sir, Your most obedient, Humble Servant,

Euston Lieutenant of Suffolk

Tuesday January 3ʳᵈ 1804 General Muster

The Corps being met at the usual time and place marched into a field in the occupation of Mr Cockle, after calling the Muster Roll, Major Edgar read the Letters from Lord Euston and Mr Thellusson. The Major also addressed the Troops on the propriety of establishing Laws and Regulations for the future Government of the Corps and appointing a Committee to conduct the same, and moved for the opinion of those present: the question being put, on a show of hands, a very great Majority were in favour of the motion. It was then proposed that the Committee should consist of thirteen, viz: the Major, two Commissioned Officers, with two non Commissioned Officers or Privates elected from each Troop; which motion was also carried by a considerable Majority, proceeding to an Election, a return was made of the Gentlemen, as under to be a standing Committee, with orders to meet at the Crown Inn Woodbridge on Wednesday the 11th Instant to frame such Laws and Regulations as they may think proper, after which we went through sundry Evolutions, and adjourned to Tuesday the 17th Instant then to meet precisely at 11 o'clock and in future to march alternately to Martlesham or Sutton for the purpose of Exercise; as no field can be had at or near Woodbridge that is large enough for the purpose. It was also agreed we should from this time meet at General Muster once a fortnight at the usual time and place until further orders.

First Meeting of the Committee at the Crown Inn Woodbridge

Second Corps of Loyal Suffolk Yeomanry Cavalry January 3rd 1804
At a General Muster of the Corps this day, the following Resolutions were moved by Major Edgar, seconded by Captain Theobald and carried by a large majority.
1st That a Committee consisting of thirteen viz seven commissioned Officers, and six non commissioned Officers or Privates be formed for the purpose of making from time to time such rules and regulations for the Corps as shall appear to them necessary.
2nd That two of the commissioned Officers, and two of the non-commissioned officers or privates be taken from each Troop.
3rd That every rule and regulation that is proposed and seconded shall be approved by nine of the Committee, and then shall become binding on every member of the Corps.
The following Gentlemen were then Elected to form the Committee: Major Edgar
1st Troop Captain Theobald Lieutenant Pearson Sergeant Major Sexton William Cockrell
2nd Troop Captain Collett Lieutenant Baldry Quarter Master Whimper Corporal Bates
3rd Troop Captain Couperthwaite Lieutenant Errington Corporal Cook Thomas Shave
The Committee then agreed to hold their first meeting at the Crown Inn Woodbridge on Wednesday, the 11th Instant at Eleven o'clock in the forenoon.

Woodbridge Crown Inn January 11th 1804

Major Edgar in the Chair.[38] At a meeting of the Committee this day, the following resolutions were moved and approved:
1st That Lieutenant Pearson be requested to act as Secretary to the Committee.
2nd That no Law or Regulation for the Corps shall be proposed unless every member of the Committee is present.
3rd That whenever serious indisposition awaits any member of the Committee or his family (and it is taken for granted that nothing else is to prevent his attendance whenever the Committee meets) he is to give timely notice of it to every member, unless it should be so sudden as to render it impracticable.

---

[38] The first real attempt to formalise their rules and regulations.

4th That the minutes of every meeting be entered in a book to be procured for that purpose, together with the rules and regulations which may from time to time be made for the Corps.

5th That the book be signed at every meeting by all the members of the Committee, and remain in the care and custody of the secretary.

6th That whenever by death, or leaving the Corps, a vacancy is made in the Committee, it shall immediately be filled by a member elected from the same Troop to which the person belonged who made the vacancy.

7th That all the rules and regulations made for the Corps shall be printed, and a Copy delivered to every member.

B59 8th That it shall at any time be lawful for the Committee to repeal, alter or amend any of the above resolutions, or any of the rules or regulations which they shall make for the Corps.

9th That the Committee may adjourn to any time and place they shall agree upon, or may adjourn *sine die,* subject to the call of any three, and that whenever a meeting that has been appointed to be held does not take place in consequence of the indisposition of any member, the Committee shall be looked upon as adjourned *sine die.* Adjourned to Thursday 19th Instant then to meet at the King's Head Inn, Ipswich, at 12 oClock at noon.

Signed by all the members of the Committee.

Copy of a Letter from Lieutenant Colonel McLeroth Inspector of the District to Major Edgar

Sir   Bury 12th January 1804

As the most exact report of the state of the Yeomanry and Volunteers is now required by the Commander in Chief, specifying those that may be thought fit, as also, those that may be Judged in the minds of the Inspecting Field Officers, unfit to act with the Troop of the Line in Case of necessity; I am to apprize you, that a Strict State of Horses, Cloathing, Arms and Accoutrements must be made, therefore anything wanted, or exchange to be made in Officers, Men, Horses or appointments, I lose no time in acquainting you with the necessity of your being prepared. There are Sabres and Pistols to be received at Stowmarket and make up any deficiency or change any that are bad, therefore send a return of what you will want to me, and you shall have an order.

I have the Honor to be, Your most Obedient Servant, H. McLeroth
Major Edgar, Red House Ipswich

Tuesday 17th January 1804 General Muster (adjourned to the 31st Instant)
The Corps being assembled at the usual time and place, marched into the field in the occupation of Mr Cockle after calling the Muster Roll were exercised in the practice of new evolutions agreeable to the instructions issued by order of HRH the Duke of York Commander in Chief.

B60 Second meeting of the Committee King's Head Inn Ipswich January 19th 1804

A Meeting of the Committee was this day held pursuant to Adjournment.

At a General Muster of the Corps on Tuesday the 17th day of January instant Mr Thomas Shave having wished to decline continuing a Member of this Committee, Sergeant Major M. Hewitt was elected by the 3rd Troop to succeed him.

Captain Theobald in the Chair It is resolved:

1st That every person on being admitted a member of the Corps shall sign the Muster Roll and take the Oath of Allegiance.

2nd That every member shall sign a receipt for whatever appointments he is found with out of the Fund of the Corps, all of which he is to keep in good order and repair, at his own expense, and to yield them up on his quitting the Corps, (reasonable allowance being made for the length of time they have been in use), provided nevertheless that any injury done to them when at exercise, or on service, shall be repaired at the expense of the Corps if the same is reported on the day it happens, to the Commanding Officer, except it shall appear that either of them shall have been used at other times.

3rd That every member who shall not appear at Muster before the Corps march from the place of Parade, shall forfeit the sum of one shilling, and if not present to answer to his name at Roll Call, the sum of five shillings, unless prevented by Illness of himself or Family to be certified by a medical Man, or by the death of a near Relation.

4th That all forfeits shall be paid to the Secretary on the next muster day after they are incurred or the next time the member forfeiting shall appear at muster. The forfeits to be expended at the discretion of the Major.

Signed: I M Theobald, Chairman, George Errington, Robert Sexton, Mileson Edgar, William Pearson, William Hewitt vice Shaw, Cornelius Collett, I.S. Baldry, George Bates, John Couperthwaite, Thurston Whimper, William Cockrell, William Cook

---

B61 Dear Sir,   **Stoke by Nayland 18th January 1804**

I intend being at Ipswich on the 20th if there is anything you wish to report of your Corps let me know, orders are now strict about horses fit for service, should you have any that are not, I know you will say so, any Sabres, or Pistols the least out of order had better be changed at Stowmarket, as what are there not wanted in Suffolk, are to be sent for by the Ordnance.

I have the honor to be, Your most obedient Servant,

H. M'Leroth, Lieutenant Colonel Inspector

Major Edgar Loyal Yeomanry Cavalry Red House Ipswich

On the 3rd February 1804 Major Edgar in consequence of the above Letter and one on the 12th January from Lieutenant Colonel M'Leroth applied at Stowmarket for an exchange of some Pistols and Sabres, but being informed they could not receive any in return/or exchange for those issued, he sent the Colonels Letters and received the following letter in answer from Mr Aldrich

Sir   **Vicarage Stowmarket February 4th 1804**

I have as you requested showed the enclosed Letters from Colonel M'Leroth, to Mr Sawyer who says, the Colonel when last at Stowmarket desired him to exchange either Sabres or Pistols in any number you might think proper to send. In future therefore, he will without hesitation, follow your directions. Your Servant brings with him 138 Canteens 138 Haversacks and 27 Bill Hooks from me, which I have your Receipts, and from Sawyer 10 Pistols and 10 sabres.

I remain Sir Your etc etc William Aldrich

To Major Edgar Red House Ipswich

B62 Tuesday January 31st 1804 General Muster

The Corps marched from the Parade to a Field in the occupation of Mr Nathaniel Gross at Bromeswell and where exercised in various Evolutions etc etc.

The resolutions of the Committee respecting Forfeits etc being printed a copy was delivered to each member of the Corps, the forfeits to commence on the next Muster day, February 14th. The Major inspected the arms etc and upon their not being kept in proper condition gave directions for the Captains to inspect them and the Equipments of their respective Troops on each day of Muster from this time and report the same to him, in order that they may be kept in a proper state for service on the shortest notice.

Orders were also given by the Major that the Corps should march from the Parade on the Market Place Woodbridge precisely at the time the Chimes of the Town Clock strike the time of half past Eleven o'clock, under the command of the Senior Officer present when the forfeits of all absentees will commence.[39]

Wednesday February 1st 1804 In the House of Commons, Mr Secretary Yorke gave notice, that on this day sen'night he should move for leave to bring in a bill to consolidate, explain and amend the different Acts relating to Volunteer Corps.[40]

The following circular letter has been sent to the Lords Lieutenant of Counties
My Lord,   Whitehall January 23rd 1804
As in the event of any of the Volunteers in the County under Your Grace's charge being either placed on permanent pay and duty, or ordered out on actual service, they are to be subject to military discipline, and to all the provisions contained in any Act of Parliament, for the punishment of mutiny and desertion, by any articles of war made in pursuance thereof, in all cases whatever.[41] It appears to be expedient that your Grace should lose no time in directing the Commandants of the different Corps, in the case of their being so called out, to cause the Articles of War to be read to their Corps, as soon after their first assembling as may be practicable, and to repeat the same from time to time as opportunity may be given, in the manner practised in the Militia and Regular Forces.

I have the honor to be etc etc   C Yorke
To His Majesty's Lieutenant of the County of [blank]

B63 Tuesday February 15th 1804 General Muster

The Committee met prior to the Corps assembling, and in consideration of the motion of Mr Secretary Yorke in the House of Commons on the first Instant, resolved unanimously, that the forfeits agreed upon at their meeting the 19th January, which were to take place this day, be suspended until such time as the new Act of Parliament for Consolidating and Explaining the different Acts relating to Volunteers, be passed into a Law.

---

[39] There was a need for such precise instructions about timing because of the distance many members had to travel to reach Woodbridge.

[40] In August 1803 the responsibility for the volunteer forces passed from the War Office to Charles Yorke, the Home Secretary. He had inherited a staff of only fifteen to deal with a situation of administrative and organisational chaos. Many men had volunteered at different times and were serving under different regulations in the same unit. There was an obvious need to consolidate all the regulations into one Act. Beckett, *Britain's Part-time Soldiers*, pp. 100–1.

[41] The government's confidence in the volunteer forces would appear to be somewhat limited.

The Corps mustered in the Market Place at 12 oClock and marched into a Field in the Occupation of Mr Andrew Cockle and was exercised in the usual evolutions etc etc.

Mr John Thornton and Mr Samuel Denny of the 2nd Troop, sent in their Resignations by Letter to Major Edgar, as did also Mr Thomas Shave, I Seakamp and William Klopfer of the 3rd Troop.

Saturday February 18th 1804

Lieutenant Colonel Sharpe (Inspecting Field Officer)[42] having signified his intentions to Major Edgar of Inspecting the Corps on Tuesday the 28th Instant, Notice of same was immediately sent to the respective Members with orders to assemble at Woodbridge on Thursday next preparatory to the meeting of the 28th.

As Lieutenant Colonel Sharpe (the Inspecting Field Officer) has appointed Tuesday sennight the 28th instant, for the inspection of the Corps, Major Edgar much wishes for another Field Day before it takes place, and has therefore sent out Notices for a Meeting on Thursday next at Woodbridge at 11 oClock precisely, unless the day should be compleately wet, in which case it will be on Friday.

After the Inspection a longer adjournment than usual will take place.

Thursday February 23rd 1804

The Troops met in complyance with the order from Major Edgar as above and marched from the Parade to a field at Sutton in the occupation of Mr Coates and exercised in various evolutions preparatory to being inspected by Colonel Sharpe on Tuesday the 28th Instant.

William Laurence of the 2nd Troop and George Ranson of the 3rd Troop sent in their resignations to the Major.
[43]

B66 Circular   **Colchester 15th February 1804**

Sir   The Yeomanry Cavalry not having been included in the return sent with my Circular Letter of 28th January and Containing instructions for the Issue of the Camp Kettles to the several Corps of Volunteer Yeomanry I have the honor to state to you that additional Articles of Camp Equipage according to the annexed return have been forwarded to the depot at Ipswich and Stowmarket and that the same instructions hold good respecting them as were Contained in my Letter of the 28th January.

    I have the honor to be Sir Your most Obedient Humble Servant   [blank]

To Lieutenant Colonel Sharpe Inspecting Field Officer Ipswich

NB The Allotment to the Woodbridge Cavalry is four Tents and Twenty Camp Kettles.

Circular   **Ipswich 16th February 1804**

Sir,   I am directed to inform you that tents and Camp Kettles have been forwarded by Order of the Quarter Master General for the use of the Volunteers of Suffolk, and are lodged at the depot at Stowmarket and Ipswich: the Number of Articles Allowed the several Corps has been Calculated according to a late return of their strength in the proportion of one tent to 30 Men and one Camp Kettle to 6 men the Corps being taken rather under their Establishment.

---

[42] This is the first mention of Colonel Sharpe as the new Inspecting Field Officer of the Troop.

[43] B64–B65, the general muster roll of the 2nd Troop under the command of Captain Collett, is omitted.

Lieutenant General Sir James Craig is pleased to direct that the Tents may remain at the Depot ready for delivery at the shortest notice, but with respect to the Camp Kettles, he desires they may be issued, agreeable to the above proportion, in which Twenty Kettles are Allotted to your Corps and which you will receive on applying to Mr Robert Fulcher at Ipswich and giving a receipt for the same.[44]

I am directed to make the necessary Communication on this Subject with the Commanding Officers of Corps and take the Steps necessary for the execution of this Order as the most eligible means for which I would advise the Officers Commanding Corps in each Hundred to send one person for the whole number, who might bring them to the most Central Situation in the Hundred, then to be divided and deposited as each Commanding Officer may think most eligible taking Care they are in a place of security and as near as conveniently can be to the place of Assembly of the Corps. The Camp Kettles will be Conveyed in the cart allowed to attend each company for the purpose of conveying their Camp Necessaries, and which by a Letter from the Secretary of State to the Lord Lieutenant of the County is directed to be held Constantly marked and ready for that Service.

I have the honour to be Sir; Your Most Obedient, Humble Servant,

M Sharpe, Lieutenant Colonel

To Major Edgar etc etc

B67 Tuesday February 28th 1804 General Muster

The Corps Inspected by Colonel Sharpe

The Corps met this day agreeable to orders for the purpose of being inspected by Colonel Sharpe Inspecting Field Officer for the Eastern Division. From the Parade we marched to a field at Sutton occupied by Mr Coates at which place we arrived soon after 11 oClock, being formed in readiness, the Colonel was received and saluted by the Corps in Line at open order. After the Salute he passed the Line and inspected the Troops Front and Rear. We afterwards passed the reviewing Officer by Troops in a Walk, (saluting as we passed) and by half troops on a Gallop but did not Rank off. We went through various Evolutions by changing our front and forming in different direction on fresh ground, also from Line into Column and vice versa; we made sundry charges by single Troops and in Lines, retreated by threes about and by half Troops covered by the Skirmishers.[45]

The Colonel was pleased to express himself much satisfied at the appearance of the Men and Horses and the spirited manner in which they performed the various Evolutions, declaring at same time they much exceeded his expectations, and that as he should soon have the honour to see His Royal Highness, the Duke of York, Commander in Chief, he should make a point of reporting to him the high opinion in which he held the Corps.

The Hollesley Bay Volunteers, (Infantry), commanded by Major Page being by order assembled in the same field, was also inspected by the Colonel.

At the time of calling the Muster Roll, sundry Members having withdrawn from the Corps without any satisfactory reasons for same and having been equipped at the expense of a former established Fund of the Corps at the rate of twenty four pounds per man the Major addressed the Members present on the impropriety of resigna-

---

44 Detailed preparations had obviously reached a state of readiness.

45 This is the most detailed description Collett gives of cavalry evolutions as practised by the Troop at each muster, which were laid down centrally by the government.

tions at this critical moment[46] and proposed that in case anyone wished to withdraw himself he should on leaving the Corps pay for the prime cost of his jacket and return all other equipment with which he had been furnished (the Jacket not being considered useful to any person who might succeed him who resigned) this proposal being seconded, was not objected to by any member present.

The Major further addressed the Corps on the importance of their continued services, and wishing to know the determination of every member present, requested they would be very candid and declare themselves for or against the continuation of their services, and separately answering to the question as their respective names were called over. On the question, do you mean to continue your service? being separately asked (on calling their Names) everyone present answered in the affirmative and that they would not withdraw during the present War, which answer was received B68 with the greatest satisfaction by the Major and all the Commissioned Officers, of whom no question on their resignation was asked in consequence of their holding Commission from His Majesty or of the Trumpeters or Farriers they receiving constant pay.

When we marched from the Parade it snowed very hard but about the time we got to the field it cleared up and the remainder of the day was very fine but extremely cold.

Copy of a Return of the 2nd Corps of Loyal Suffolk Yeomanry Cavalry when inspected by Lieutenant Colonel Sharpe (Inspecting Field Officer of the Eastern District) February 28th 1804

Present

Major 1, Captains 3, Lieutenants 3, Cornets 3, Chaplain 1, Quarter Masters 2, Sergeants 8, Trumpeters 3, Rank and File 106   Total 136

Absent from Illness 7 (1 Quarter Master, 1 Sergeant, 5 Rank and File)

Absent from lameness of Horses 5 (Rank and File)

Total Strength of the Corps 142   Signed Mileson Edgar Major
[47]

B70 As under is the Account of Sundry Articles received from Government for the use of the 2nd Corps of Loyal Suffolk Yeomanry Cavalry Commanded by Major Edgar, such as are immediately required being delivered to the Troops the remainder are deposited in the Magazine at Head Quarters Woodbridge, the whole are to be accounted for at any time when called upon by the Board of Ordinance etc for the delivery of same to the Corps

1804 February 4th

138 Haversacks

138 Canteens with straps

27 Bill hooks

21 Camp kettles

10 Sabres with belts and sword knots

10 Pistols

71 Sabres, 71 Pistols, 12 Carbines (these received in the years 1795, 1798 and 1799), remain to be accounted for with the above.

---

[46] It is unclear why, at such a critical point in the crisis, anyone should have wanted to resign. No reasons were given.

[47] B69, a blank Copy of a Monthly Return, is omitted.

The Belts etc for Sabres and Carbines where bought and paid for from the Fund of the Troop.[48]

Memorandum

The Troop having been supplied with Sabres, Pistols and Carbines in the years 1795 1798 and 1799 the Commanding Officer have to account for same to Government when called upon.

A return was made to Lord Euston, Lord Lieutenant, of the County, in complyance with his request to Major Edgar 8th September 1803, of 71 Sabres, 71 Pistols and 12 Carbines with Bayonets to same.

No return was made of the Belts for Sabres and Carbines the same being paid for from the Fund of the Troop.

The additional number of Sabres with Belts etc. and Pistols, required for the Members who have since joined the Troop on its Augmentation, have been supplyed and paid for from the Fund of the Corps and Government not having been put to any expense for same they are in consequence the property of the Corps.
[49]

B72 Copy of a letter from the Secretary of State to the Lord Lieutenant

My Lord,   Whitehall 6th March 1804

It appearing that the Instructions and Discipline of such of the Corps of Yeomanry and Volunteers of the Maritime Counties of Great Britain, as have been placed on permanent pay and duty by His Majesty's Order, on the existing appearance of Invasion, have been upon the whole, essentially promoted by that measure, Should it appear to your Lordship, upon Communication with the Commandants of Corps within the County under your Lordship's Charge, that any of the Corps or detachments of Corps under their command, which are properly armed and equipped, are still disposed to avail themselves of His Majesty's invitation, I have it in command to signify to your Lordship that every facility will be afforded to such of them as shall express a desire to be placed on permanent pay and duty for any period not exceeding one Month or less than ten days.[50] With the view of enabling your Lordship the more easily to communicate to them the regulations by which they are to be governed in carrying this measure into effect, I have caused the same to be drawn up in the form of Instructions, and an adequate number of Copies for immediate use to be transmitted herewith, together with a proportion of blank returns.

I have the honor to be My Lord Your Lordships most obedient
humble Servant
(Signed)   C Yorke

His Majesty's Lieutenant of the County of Suffolk

Instructions to Volunteers who are to assemble on Permanent Pay and Duty
Whitehall 6th March 1804

Previous to the actual assembling of any Corps or a detachment of Volunteer Corps on permanent pay and duty, the proposal for their so assembling is to be made in the first instance by the Commandant of the Corps, through the Inspecting Field

---

[48] While the government from the beginning had provided the arms, additions had been purchased by the Troop themselves from their own fund.

[49] B71 is blank.

[50] This marks a very important point in the Yeomanry Cavalry's development because it gave the opportunity to practise together for an extended period and perhaps exercise with other Troops of the Suffolk Yeomanry.

Officer, to the Lord Lieutenant of the County transmitting a duplicate at the same time to the General commanding the District. These proposals are in such case to be accompanied by an exact return of the effective number and rank of the Volunteers who are to be assembled, and by a statement of the time and place proposed for their assembly, and of the period for which it is proposed that they should remain on duty, such period not to exceed one month or to be less than Ten Days.

If upon Communication between His Majesty's Lieutenant and the Commanding **B73** General, the proposal shall be approved of it is to be transmitted by the Lord Lieutenant, with as little delay as possible to the Secretary of State for the Home Department, in order that His Majesty's special directions may be given thereupon and signified by such Secretary of State to the Lord Lieutenant, before any Corps or detachment of Corps shall be actually placed on duty, and that the requisite authority may be given for the issue of their pay and allowance.[51]

During the period of any Volunteers being so assembled they are to be under the command of the General Commanding in the District or if in Garrison under the command of the Governor or Commandant thereof for the time being; and they are in all respects diligently to conform to the rules, regulations and Ordinances of His Majesty's military service.[52] And the Commanding Officer of the Corps or detachment is to follow such directions as shall be communicated to him through His Majesty's Secretary at War, with respect to the payment, subsistence and Economy of the men so assembled.

It is intended to advance to each Non-Commissioned Officer, Drummer and Private so called out, in proportion to the length of time for which they may agree to assemble, a sum not exceeding one guinea for the purpose of assisting in providing necessaries; and the Captains of Companies may draw for the same upon the Receiver General of the County, in the same manner as the Captains of the Militia Regiments are accustomed to do, and may also layout the same in the manner they may think the most advantageous for the Men, for whom it is, amongst other things particularly desirable that Great Coats should be provided where they are wanted. And such Captains or Commanding Officers shall on or before the 24th day of the month next ensuing that in which they shall have received such money as aforesaid account to such Volunteers how the said sum hath been applied and disposed of, and shall at the time of settling such account pay the remainder (if any) to the said Volunteers.

It is thought desirable to avoid as much as possible the calling out on permanent pay and duty any men having Families who are likely to become chargeable, And it is to be observed that the wives and families of the men so called out, are not entitled to any allowance, unless such men shall actually leave their Families and then only where such Families are unable to support themselves.[53]

The Commanding Officer is to cause the Articles of War to be read to his Corps as soon after its first assembling as may be practicable, and to repeat the same from time to time in the manner practised in the Regular and Militia Forces.[54]

---

[51] This is a good example of the hierarchy and command structure for volunteer units. The speed with which the arrangements were organised and paid for is impressive.

[52] When on permanent duty they were subject to martial law and became part of the country's armed forces under the army's command, and were therefore paid.

[53] The Act applied to volunteer infantry troops as well as to cavalry. It is a reflection of the economic problems of the period that such a clause needed to be inserted; that there were members of the volunteer infantry who found their families needing to claim help from the parish poor law.

[54] The blank form across the bottom of B74 and B75 is not included.

B74 Copy of a Letter from the Lord Lieutenant to Robert Harland Bart

By this night's post I have sent you a copy of the Secretary of State's Letter of the 6th instant, the object of which is to give Every facility and incouragement to such Yeomanry and Volunteer Corps as are disposed to be placed on permanent pay and duty, and I have to request that you would circulate the same without delay throughout the Commandants of Yeomanry and Volunteer Corps in the division of the County of which you have been appointed the Lieutenant, acquainting them that, in the event of their Corps being disposed in order to advance themselves in military discipline, to be placed upon permanent duty, they are desired to signify their intention to the Inspecting Field Officer and to fill up such returns as that of which I have inclosed a form, with the number and rank of the Volunteers to be assembled. Which return, together with the propositions made by the different Corps, will be transmitted to me by the Inspecting Field Officer, in order that I may lay them before the Secretary of State, for His Majesty's approbation.

I have the honor to be Sir, your most obedient humble Servant

(signed) Euston

Sir Robert Harland.

PS The papers you will receive by this Post are numbered 1, 2, 3. As the object of the measure is to give Corps an opportunity of becoming more perfect in military discipline, the place of their assembling will probably be at no great distance from their homes than is necessary to effect this desirable purpose.

April 3rd 1804

In consequence of the expected death of Major Edgar's Mother of which he received an account this Morning and from which circumstance he is prevented attending on Tuesday next the meeting of the Corps on that day is postponed to Tuesday the 24th instant.

NB Mrs Edgar died on Sunday 8th April in London, aged 72 years

---

Tuesday April 24th 1804   General Muster

This being a General Muster about 60 members in the vicinity of Woodbridge met about 12 oClock the day being so extremely cold and wet prevented others from attending. Those present attended on the Market Hall, when the Major informed them of the intention of Colonel Sharpe to inspect the Corps on Friday next also that a proposal would be then made for the Corps going out on permanent duty, notice of which was sent to all the absent members with orders to attend on Friday.

Copy of a Letter from Lord Euston to Sir Robert Harland Bart

Margaret Street March 26th 1804

It is some days since I had the honour of enclosing to you and the other Lieu-tenants of Divisions in Suffolk, the Secretary of State's letter of the 6th Instant, accompanied by Instructions of the same date to Volunteers who may be disposed to undertake permanent Duty, and a form of return to be filled up by the Commandants of Corps, and I have little doubt but that the same zeal which was displayed when a similar proposal was made to the Volunteers before Christmas will again show itself, the object being one of the highest importance, nothing less than an endeavour on our part to avail ourselves, by every means within our reach of the short time the Enemy may allow us for improvement in that Art in which we may be destined to encounter him.

From the official reports which I have received of the Volunteers in Suffolk, I am persuaded that many of the Corps are as forward in discipline as any of the same description in the Kingdom, but I acknowledge it has long been a subject of regret to me that at the outset, the Corps were not put upon an establishment more calculated for Service; that is that they were not formed into Corps of 300 men instead of Independent Companies, as they are for the most part, at present, of from 80 to 100 men. In the event of actual Service, such a measure must of necessity be adopted, when the command of a Corps of 3 or 4 Companies will devolve upon the Senior Officer belonging to their Company, be he whom he may; amongst regular Troops the Senior Officer will in most cases be the Officer of most experience; in the Militia, the Senior Officer would have had sufficient training to be, to a certain degree, qualified; but in the Volunteer Service, when several Independent Companies accidentally meet at the same rendezvous, it must be quite a matter of chance upon whom the command may devolve, the rendezvous of Companies having been originally determined upon, not with reference to the dates of commissions or experience of Commandants of Companies, but from the local situations of the Corps themselves.

No one who considers this object can have a different opinion upon it, and I am glad to find that where it has occurred to Commandants of Corps to turn their thoughts to it, the utility of the adoption of such a measure has been so clear as to lead them still further to think of the means of effecting it; which perhaps in all Cases does not at first view appear so practicable as a calm discussion, upon mature consideration, will in general render it.

B77 In the Risbridge Hundred, the Companies have been consolidated, and form one respectable Corps of 300 men and upwards; in the hundred of Blything, a Corps of 850 men has been formed; in that of Babergh, a Corps of 2 or 3 hundred,[55] which give them the greater advantage arising from the appointments of Adjutants or Sergeant Majors, or both of these useful assistants. If upon consideration and communication with the Inspector of Hundreds and Commandants of Volunteers Corps, the same arrangement should appear practicable in the division under your Lieutenancy, I am persuaded that you will take such measures as appear to your judgement best calculated for giving effect to it, the measure being one strongly recommended by Government, and which has been already adopted in one or two of the most exposed Counties on the Coast.

I have the honour to be, Sir, Your most obedient humble Servant

(signed)   Euston Lieutenant of Suffolk

Instructions to be observed by the Volunteers, if suddenly ordered to march and assemble on any named point

Horse Guards, March 1804

Being provided with Horses and Carriages, as pointed out in the Secretary of States Letter of the 16 January, the Corps will leave every Incumbrance whatever behind them. No Women are to move with the Corps on any Account. They will march as much as possible together in the Brigades or Corps into which they are formed, agreeable to the particular Routes and orders that have been forwarded from the Head Quarters of their District, to be acted upon after the Certainty of the Enemy's appearance on the Coast.

---

[55] This refers to infantry volunteer corps and is an example of their very large membership.

In the first hurry of assembling the Troops, on the landing of an Enemy, it may be impossible, in all cases, to prescribe positive Routes, and to prevent crossing, crowding and interference in the March of so many Bodies moving from distant places, and tending to the same point. The Prudence and Arrangement of the Commanding Officers must therefore, as far as possible, provide against these unavoidable difficulties.

When the Troops march in Corps, and encamp, they are more easily provided for; but when they are cantoned and pressed forward, they must be satisfied with the most crowded and slightest Accommodation, and a rigorous Discipline must prevent them from requiring more than the Country and Circumstances can allow.

On the Routes where Troops are to march, sufficient Bread and Oats may **B78** certainly be provided by the Army Bakers and Purveyors of Oats in the Market Towns on a short Notice; should not this be the case, Commanding Officers must themselves make the best general Arrangements on this Head that Circumstances will permit, and not allow Individuals to trespass or commit Outrages; and it is again earnestly recommended to the Corps, both Cavalry and Infantry, also to the Proprietors of Waggons which are employed for conveying Troops, to leave their Homes with not less than three days Bread and Forage.

As soon as the Corps collect in sufficient Bodies and the Troops canton or encamp, the Commissariat, (to whom every necessary assistance must be given), will provide for them. If there is no Commissiary, and that the Pressure is such that Provision of Straw, Forage, Bread or Fuel must be provided from the Country, the Commanding Officer will appoint one or more intelligent Officers[56] to act as Commissaries for the Time being, who will go forward with proper assistance, and call, in the first Instance, upon the Commissiarat Contractor, of which there has been one appointed in each Market Town, to furnish the Supplies required; but in situations where there is no such Contractor, or that he is unable to provide for the Demand, the officer is to address the Magistrate or Magistrates of the Neighbourhood, and representing the Necessity of the case, induce them to take such Measures, and give such Orders, as will, with due Attention to the Preservation of Property, and without Interference with the Discipline of the Troops, immediately produce the necessary Supplies; for all which, distinct Requisitions in Writing, signed by the Commissiary (or Officer acting as such) must be presented, specifying the Number of Persons and Horses, the Quality and Rates of Rations, the number of Rations and for what Time. Upon receiving the Supplies, proper Receipts, signed by the Quarter Master or other Person must also be given according to the accompanying Forms.[57]

When Troops encamp they will chose the Commons, where there are such, otherwise they must encamp on such Grass fields as are most convenient for their March, and to which they can do the least Damage, and if unavoidable Damage in such case is done, the Commanding Officer of the encamping Corps will grant a Certificate of the Nature and Amount.[58]

B80 Copy   Circular   **Colchester 2nd April 1804**

Sir

Circumstances requiring that some arrangement for the assembling of the Volunteer force of the Country throughout the Kingdom should take place with a view to

---

[56] The implications of the adjective are interesting.
[57] Examples of forms are omitted.
[58] B79, a blank form.

its being brought into activity in support of the Military Operations in which His Majesty's forces may be engaged. I am Commanded by Lieutenant General Sir James Craig to call your attention to such Regulations and Instructions as His Royal Highness, the Commander in Chief has directed him to Issue, with respect to those of the Eastern district, in order to the Carrying the Measure into execution.

You are directed to observe that upon the General Signal of alarm being given, the Corps under your Inspection are immediately to assemble and commence their March to the place of General Assembly appointed for them.

The Commanding Officer upon the March is to be instructed that he must at all times appraise the General or Officer Commanding at any Station of General Assembly, or other upon which the Troops are moving, of the time they may be expected to arrive at such Stations, by detaching an Officer for that purpose.

Commanding Officers, where there is a deficiency of Arms, will direct those belonging to the Non-Effectives, or such as may remain for the police, to be made over to the Men of their own Corps who March.

Measures will be taken for supplying the Men who may still remain deficient before they are brought into actual Service, but none are, on account of want of Arms, to remain behind.

Quartering and supplying Carts on the March must sometimes be discretionary, it will however be the duty of the Inspecting Field Officer, or in his absence, the Commanding Officer of the Corps, to make such arrangements as will tend least to the inconvenience of the Inhabitants.

I am directed by the Lieutenant General to Transmit you the Inclosed Marching Instructions transmitted to him by H,R,H the Commander in Chief, copies of which are to be generally Circulated by you to the Corps under your Inspection.

With respect to the Cantonments which in the event of the Force under your Inspection being required to assemble at any particular Station, it would be expedient to occupy; further Instructions will be Issued to you on that head, and although the mode of quartering to be pointed out hereafter would only be resorted to in the Event of Alarm, it should be generally understood that in such Case, every Private Consideration must Yield to public Service.

B81 I am further to observe to you that the Carriages attached to the different Corps are to be Parked in situations that may be hereafter pointed out by the Lieutenant General and that they are to be Conducted to the Park on their Arrival, that the Horses are to be tied to the Carriages to which they belong, and the Drivers to remain with them. The Waggon Park will be guarded by Picquets of Cavalry, and none suffered to depart without an Order from the General Staff. Of the Waggons and Carts provided in pursuance of the Secretary of State's letter dated 16 January the Carts only are to be permanently attached to the Corps. The Waggons for Carrying Men ordered in support of a point attacked, will continue with them until the Corps Comes into the Vicinity of the Enemy, or longer as may be by the General or other Officer commanding, Judged Expedient. In some Circumstances the nature of the Communications may be such that greater inconveniences may arrive to the Service (by encumbering the Roads) than can be Compensated by the Benefit, looked too in the more speedy arrival of the Troops, in which case, of course, such measures will not be adopted.

Should the Situation of the Country require the Volunteer force under your Inspection to be called out, Lieutenant General Sir James Craig desires that the foregoing Instructions may be a guidance for your conduct in every case in which Circumstances of a particular emergency do not require a deviation from them, and you will take Care to make such Communication to the Officers Commanding the several Corps of your Inspection (besides furnishing them with a Copy of the accompanying regulations) as may insure their perfectly comprehending what in such Event they will have to do.

I have the honor to be, Sir, Your most obedient humble servant
(signed) F. Birch Assistant Quarter Master General
Lieutenant Colonel Sharpe, Inspecting Field Officer

B82 Copy   Circular

Whitehall 12th April 1804

In explanation of my Circular Letter of the 5 ult, I think it necessary to appraise your Lordship that it is not intended to place any Corps of Volunteers upon permanent duty, for the purpose of Training and Exercise, in the Town to which it may belong, unless it be a Garrison Town, and the Corps shall undertake, and be permitted by the General commanding the District, or by the Commandant of the Garrison, to assist in performing the Duty thereof; or unless, from special Circumstances, it should be deemed particularly desirable by the Commanding General of the District.

There will however, be no objections to allowing Ten Days additional Pay at the rate of one shilling per man per Day, to each Non-Commissioned officer, Drummer and Private, of such Corps of Volunteer Infantry, accepted subsequent to 3 August 1803 (if recommended for this purpose by your Lordship) as may be willing to perform so many additional Days Exercise in the course of the two ensuing Months, without leaving their homes; but in this case, they will not be entitled to the Allowance for the purpose of Necessaries, which is to be made exclusively to Volunteers who shall march for the purpose of training or Exercise out of the Towns to which they belong, or assemble within them for the purpose of doing the Garrison duty thereof; or under the special Circumstances before adverted to.

I have further to add, that it is not proposed to call upon any of the Corps of Infantry serving upon the June allowances, to be exercised, on the whole, a greater Number than 85 days in the Year, but in the event of their Assembling upon permanent Duty for any time not exceeding that Period, it is intended that the Number of Days, during which they shall be so assembled shall be accounted as part of the 85 days Exercise, which, by the Terms of their Institution, they are bound to perform. And upon their so assembling upon permanent duty, it is to be understood that these Corps are to be entitled to the like Bounty in aid of Necessaries as other Volunteers.

But it is not meant that any Artillery should be placed on permanent Duty, except in cases where they can have the advantage of being trained with some Party or Detachment of the Royal Artillery, or at least of being under the direction or Instruction of Officers or Non-commissioned Officers of the Royal Artillery.

I have the Honor to be, my Lord, Your Lordship's most obedient humble servant
C Yorke
To Lord Euston

From Lord Euston to P J Thelusson Esq
Circular   **Margaret Street April 16th 1804**

It being considered as extremely important that His Majesty's Government should, without Delay, be correctly informed of the Manner in which the Volunteers throughout Great Britain have actually been supplied with Arms, Accoutrements and other Articles necessary to Military Equipment, and of the Extent to which the Supply has been carried, I am directed by Mr Yorke to desire, that you will forthwith fill up correctly and distinctly in every Particular, the Duplicate Blank Returns which I have the Honour to enclose; and that you will transmit one Copy thereof, when so filled up, through the Lord Lieutenant, to this Office, and the other directly to the Board of Ordnance.

      I am, Sir, your most obedient humble servant   R Pole Carew

To the Commanding Officer of the Suffolk Gentlemen and Yeomanry 2nd Corps

---

April 28th 1804

Copy of an Account of the Arms etc with which the Corps have been supplied at the Expense of Government from the Institution of their Volunteer Service in 1794 to the present time, also of those Bought by the Corps at their own expense and for which no allowance has been claimed.

A Copy of this Account was also delivered to Major Edgar to be by him forwarded to Lord Euston Lord Lieutenant of the County, in conformity to the instructions as above.

B84   **County of Suffolk**

Return of the Suffolk Volunteer Cavalry under the command of Major M. Edgar 1804

[Appendix 4]

I do hereby certify that the above is a correct return of the Effective strength of the Corps under my Command and of the Number of Arms, Accoutrements etc in its possession.

(Signed) Mileson Edgar Major

Memorandum

On examining the Accounts and Letters from Learmonth and Beazley, I find the Belts etc for Sabres and Carbines in 1794 and 1795 where paid for from the fund of the Troop.

B85 (Copy)   **Colchester April 22nd 1804**

Sir   I have the honor to inform you that the Camp Equipages for the Horses of the Yeomanry Cavalry in the County of Suffolk has been deposited at the Depots in Ipswich and Stowmarket. The different Troops under your inspection are to be supplied from the Depots herein specified (viz)

1st	Loyal Suffolk Yeomanry Cavalry	
2nd (or Woodbridge)	Ditto	From Ipswich
5th (or Beccles)	Ditto	
3rd (or Hoxne)	Ditto	
8th (or Heveningham)	Ditto	From Stowmarket
9th (or Southelmham)	Ditto	

The different Articles are to be delivered in the following proportion, viz,

Cornsacks	one per horse
Water Decks	one per horse
Nose Bags	one per horse

Setts Forage Cords	Half a sett per Horse
Water Buckets	four for 30 horses
Tilling Axxes	1 per Troop
Picket Ropes	One or 18 Horses being half proportion
Picket Poles	6 to each Rope
Picket Mallett	One per Troop

I am however Commanded by Lieutenant General Sir James Craig to acquaint you that none of these articles are to be delivered out untill further Orders.

I have the honor to be Sir Your most Obedient Humble Servant

(Signed) J Birch Lieutenant Colonel and Quarter Master General E D

To Lieutenant Colonel Sharpe Inspecting Field Officer East Suffolk District Ipswich

---

B86 Inspection Friday April 27ᵗʰ 1804 General Muster

The Corps met at 11 oClock and marched into a field in the occupation of Mr A Cockle in Woodbridge, when Lieutenant Colonel Sharpe, Inspecting Field Officer of this District, inspected the Corps in the customary mode, after which we exercised in various Evolutions as usual.

Major Edgar informed the Corps it was the wish of the Lord Lieutenant to be informed if they were inclined to go out on permanent duty for a space of time not exceeding one month or less than ten days. The Question being put and seconded, every Member present expressed their wish to go out, and requested the Major to inform the Lord Lieutenant of same and in conformity to instructions for that purpose, fixed on Bury and Yarmouth as places calculated for the accommodation of the Corps and Monday 14ᵗʰ May for the time of Marching.

Major Edgar having signified to the Lord Lieutenant the wishes of the Corps to go out on permanent duty for the time specified as above, received in answer from Lord Euston (Copied as under)

Sir   **Margaret Street May 7ᵗʰ 1804**

His Majesty has approved of the 2nd Corps of Suffolk Yeomanry Cavalry assembling at Bury on 14ᵗʰ Instant for permanent duty unless it should be as convenient to Major Edgar and his Corps to assemble for the same purpose at Stowmarket, on which subject you will be pleased to communicate with Major Edgar; and in the event of Stowmarket being fixed upon I will beg the favour of you to send me a single line in order that I may communicate the alteration to the Secretary of State.

I have the honour to be Sir, Your most obedient humble servant,

Euston Lieutenant of Suffolk

Lieutenant Colonel Sharp Inspecting Field Officer Ipswich

In consequence of the above letter being sent by Colonel Sharpe to Major Edgar, he fixed on Bury for the assembling of the Corps and received a Rout etc, of which the following are Copies,[59] with order for the Corps to March on Monday next May 14ᵗʰ 1804.[60]

---

[59] Not included.

[60] The whole enterprise was very well-organised, accommodation for men and horses being provided in a short time.

B87 (Copy)   **Ipswich 30ᵗʰ April 1804**

I am directed by Sir James Craig to transmit to him as early as possible a return of the Arms in the possession of the Yeomanry Corps in the District under my Super-intendance. I have therefore to request you will send back the inclosed Return filled up and signed, specifying whether the Carbines are Muskets or Carbine Bore in the Column of Remarks.

I am, Sir, your most obedient humble servant,

               M Sharpe Lieutenant Colonel Inspector General Suffolk

Major Edgar, Ipswich

Swords Carbines Pistols
166   12   201

Remarks

The carbines are Carbine Bore. We have purchased 140 Sabres and 120 Pistols of the Arms herewith returned.   (signed) M Edgar Major May 4ᵗʰ 1804

You are hereby directed to cause the 2nd or Woodbridge Corps of Loyal Suffolk Yeomanry Cavalry to March and be quartered at Bury St. Edmunds till the expira-tion of their time of permanent duty then to return by this route to their respective Quarters.

Wherein the Civil Magistrates, and all others concerned, are, by the Authority above shown, required to be assisting, as is therein directed.

Given at Head Quarters Colchester May 8ᵗʰ 1804

               J H Craig Lieutenant General Commanding Eastern District

To Major Edgar or Officer Commanding, 2nd Troop or Woodbridge, Yeomanry Cavalry

---

B88 It is His Majesty's pleasure that you cause the Troops stationed in the District under your Command, to march from Time to Time as Occasion shall require, by such Routes and in such Divisions as you may judge expedient, to such Place or Places within the said District as shall be thought necessary, where they are to be quartered and remain till further Orders.

Wherein the Civil Magistrates and all others concerned are to be assisting in providing Quarters, impressing Carriages, and otherwise, as there shall be occasion.

Given at the War Office, this 24 day of May 1803 by His Majesty's Command

               (signed) C Yorke

Lieutenant General Sir James Craig, KB etc or Officer Commanding Eastern District

---

A Copy of the Strength of the Corps as offered to go on Duty for 16 days

Major 1, Captains 3, Lieutenants 3, Cornets 3, Paymaster 1, Quarter Masters 3, Sergeant Major 1, Sergeants 8, Corporals 9, Trumpeters 3, Privates 106

Total 141

Place to march to Bury (or if occupied) Yarmouth

Period of commencing Duty   May 14ᵗʰ

Period for remaining on Duty   16 days

NB Offer delivered to Lieutenant Colonel Sharp April 28ᵗʰ 1804

               Signed Mileson Edgar

B89 Thursday May 10ᵗʰ 1804 General Muster

The Corps met at the usual time and place and marched to Mr Andrew Cockle's field, was exercised in sundry Evolutions on Horseback as usual, also in sundry foot Evolutions preparatory to our Marching on permanent duty on Monday next, the Major having received the route for that purpose. The Corps was ordered to assemble at Needham Market on Monday morning next precisely at 9 oClock, and to march from thence to Bury St. Edmunds.
[61]

Monday May 14ᵗʰ 1804

In compliance with the orders of General Sir James Craig, the Corps this day assembled at Needham Market at 9 oClock in the morning and marched from thence to Bury St. Edmunds on permanent duty for 16 days including the days of march out and home.

The Babergh Troop commanded by Captain Moore[62] also marched at the same time to Bury and were Brigaded with us during the time of our stay there, the whole under the command of Major Edgar.

The Brigade was practised daily in the various evolutions, Mounted and Dismounted, and the Sword Exercise. The Articles of War was read to the Brigade by the Major in compliance to orders for that purpose.

The Troops received much benefit in the practice of the Evolutions in consequence of being Brigaded, every member most cheerfully complying with the duty of a Soldier in the Field, and in Quarters everything was conducted in a manner that gave entire satisfaction to each of us, and was highly creditable to us as Volunteers, of which the most honourable mention was made by the Inhabitants of Bury and the numerous Spectators who assembled at sundry times to see the Brigade in the field.[63]

Captain Moore's Troop on the last Field Day, expressed their wish to meet us for the purpose of exercising together if possible once a month, which not appearing altogether practicable in consequence of the distance of situation from each other, it was thought proper to leave it to the consideration of the Officers to fix such time and appoint places for meeting as frequently in the course of a year as circumstances will permit.

On our return home Tuesday 29ᵗʰ May, we were met by Lieutenant Colonel Sharpe Inspecting Field Officer near Stowmarket, who inspected the Corps on their March and was pleased to express himself much satisfied with the appearance of the Corps and the manner in which the Baggage etc was placed on the horses etc.

B91 Monday June 4ᵗʰ 1804 General Muster

It being His Majesty's birthday, the Corps met at the usual time and place and marched into a field in the occupation of Mr Andrew Cockle at Woodbridge, exercised in sundry Evolutions and fired a Feu-de-Joye in honour of the day, and dispersed.

Circular (Copy)   Sir

Having just received the Volunteer Act lately passed, I am desirous of making known the Powers and Provisions thereof to the Corps, without delay, and there-

---

[61]   B90, a list of members of the Corps who attended at Bury on permanent duty, May 1804, is omitted.

[62]   Captain Moore of Kentwell Hall, Long Melford.

[63]   Collett's account of the first permanent duty is rather subdued and lacking in detail.

fore request you will make it a point of meeting me at the Town Hall, Woodbridge, in plain Cloth's, on Monday July 2nd at Eleven oClock in the Forenoon, for that purpose, and the consideration of other important Business.

I am, with much respect, Yours etc   Mileson Edgar

Red House June 22nd 1804

A printed Copy of the above Letter was sent to each Member of the Corps

---

Monday July 2nd 1804

The Corps met at the Town Hall Woodbridge in complyance with Major Edgar's Circular Letter (as above). The Major, having taken the Chair, read the Volunteer Act lately passed, a proposal was then made that we should inroll ourselves under Articles of a certain allowance to the Fund of the Corps towards defraying the Expenses incurred in Clothing and Equipments in case any Member withdrew himself, Or that we should Ingage in a continuance of our services during the War. The opinion of the Company was taken by a show of hands, when it appeared by a very great Majority in favour of Ingaging our services during a continuance of the War.

The Major was then requested to draw a form for a new Muster Roll. The same being done was read and approved and immediately Engrossed and Signed by the Members present.

B92 Copy of the Muster Roll of the 2nd Corps of Loyal Suffolk Yeomanry Cavalry

July 2nd 1804

We whose Names are hereunto subscribed, having this day heard the Volunteer Act lately passed, read to us, and conceiving that much spirit and good would be rendered to the Noble Cause we are engaged in, were we to make a tender of our services during the War, seize eagerly this opportunity of declaring that we are animated with the same feelings now, that first induced us to take up arms, and that we will not lay them down so long as our Country has an Enemy, and use the ability of using them, unless we remove to such distance (for Instance 20 miles) as will not enable us to discharge properly the duties of a Soldier in this Corps.

And we do hereby pledge ourselves to a full and proper discharge of the several services herein set forth as follows.

That we will at all times obey any orders which may be issued from His Majesty, from the General commanding in the District, from the Lord Lieutenant, the High Sheriff or the Magistrates acting in and for the Division of Woodbridge, for the suppression of any riot or tumultuous meetings, with the greatest promptness and alacrity

That in cases of actual invasion or appearance of invasion, we will readily march to any part of the Military District to which we belong, under such orders as we shall receive from the General or Generals commanding within the same

And lastly, that we will cheerfully obey and execute all orders we may receive from our superior Officers in the Corps, whether commissioned or non-commissioned and give a regular attendance on the days of Exercise, unless prevented by some serious illness awaiting ourselves or families, to be certified by the medical man attending.

Sundry Members objecting to engage their Service during the war – a Resolution respecting them is entered on Page 122.[64]

---

[64] Collett, B122. There follow the signatures of practically the whole Corps. Omitted.

B93 Copy of an Act of Parliament to consolidate and amend the Provisions of the several Acts relating to Corps of Yeomanry and Volunteers in Great Britain; and to make future Regulations relating thereto. 44 Geo 3.Cap 54.[65]

B118   **Invasion**   (Copy Circular)   **Whitehall August 20th 1804**

My Lord

I have received His Majesty's Commands to communicate to your Lordship the enclosed particulars of an Arrangement to be adopted in the several Counties of Great Britain, in the event of the Invasion of the Country in force by the Enemy; His Majesty relies on your zeal and exertions in giving effect, within the County committed to your charge, to these Regulations, which in the supposed crisis may become indispensible for the purpose of preventing the confusion which in the first moment of alarm, might otherwise arise, and of the utmost importance with a view to the operations of His Majesty's Army, to the protection of the property of individuals, and to the internal peace and tranquillity of the Country.

I request that your Lordship would inform me, with as little delay as possible, of the names of the Magistrates to whom you would propose to entrust the different divisions within the County of [blank] and that you would communicate to them the heads of the proposed Arrangements, and concert with them as to the most effectual means of carrying them into complete execution.

It is essential that the Magistrates who are thus employed, should, if possible, be persons not holding Commissions as Volunteer Officers, nor liable on any other account to be removed from the County in which they reside.

His Majesty has the fullest reliance that, in the event of the Enemy's succeeding in making good a landing on the Coast of this Kingdom, the loyalty and public spirit of all classes of his subjects will induce them to submit to every sacrifice, and to concur in every exertion which the safety of the Country may render necessary; and that they will be impressed with the conviction, that the peace and good order of those districts which shall not be attacked by the Enemy will contribute most effectually to assist the exertions of his Forces in those parts of the Country which may become the theatre of the War, and of enabling him thereby to bring the contest in which we may be engaged to a speedy and glorious termination.

I have only to add that directions will be given to the General, or other Officers commanding the District in which the County of [blank] is included, to communicate with your Lordship on the subject of these Regulations, and to afford you every assistance in carrying them, if necessary, into execution.

                    I have the honor to be etc   Hawksbury

To the Lords Lieutenant of Counties in Great Britain

Regulations for the preservation of good Order to be adopted in case of actual Invasion, in each County in Great Britain   **August 12th 1804**

The Magistrates of each Division of the County, remaining at home, to sit Daily at a place to be appointed in each Division for that purpose.

---

[65] B93–B117: Collett copied the twenty-five pages of this Volunteer Consolidation Act with its 61 clauses including his own index of four pages. The Act was of major importance to the Yeomanry, remaining in place until 1901, but it was one that consolidated the numerous Acts previously passed and has been omitted here. See Beckett, *Britain's Part-time Soldiers*, p. 101.

To procure the trustworthy housekeepers and others to enrol themselves to serve as Special Constables under their orders, where the same has not been already done pursuant to the Secretary of State's Circular letter of the 8th November last.

To be attended at the place appointed for each Division, by an Officer of the Volunteer Force, if any should remain in that Division, and by the Chief or Superintendant of the Special Constables enrolled for that Division. Such Volunteer Officer and Chief of the Special Constables, to receive and execute the Orders of the Magistrates, in preventing and quelling disturbances, in taking up and conveying offenders to Prison, in supplying Escorts **B119** for all Military purposes required by the General or other Officer left in the command of the District, and in furnishing a Guard for the County Gaol or other Prisons if wanted.

If, contrary to expectation, any impediments should occur in the regular supply of the different markets, every assistance to be afforded to the persons who are accustomed, or who offer to supply them, and escorts to be granted in cases where it may be necessary for the secure passage and conveyance of cattle and provisions.

The Constables within each Division, assisted by patrols of Volunteers, if requisite, to see that all public houses within the same are orderly and regularly conducted, and, if thought necessary by the Magistrates, to be shut up at such hours as they may direct; and to bring all unknown persons who cannot give a satisfactory account of themselves, before the Magistrates.

A certain portion of Constables and Volunteers in rotation, to go such different rounds in the night as shall from time to time be prescribed by the Magistrates of the Division, to whom they are to make their report each morning.

The Magistrates of each Division to report daily to the Lieutenant of the County, or Deputy Lieutenant within the Division appointed to receive the same.

The Lieutenant or Deputy Lieutenants so appointed to report all matters of importance immediately to the Secretary of State, for the Home Department, and to the General or Officer left in command of the District, or to the Officer who shall be appointed by him within the County to receive the same, to whom they are to apply in case of wanting further military aid.

Upon the subject of these services expected of the Volunteer Corps, a Circular Letter has been written, by order of the Duke of York, to the several General Officers commanding Districts, which contains the following important instructions:[66]

The provision that the Government has thought proper to make for the superintendence and various arrangements relating to these Corps will suggest to you the importance which is attached to their services, and His Royal Highness desires that you will strongly impress on the General Officers as well as the other Staff Officers who are at this time, or may be hereafter attached to them, that it will in a very great degree depend on their individual exertions to ensure that the expectations of the Country, on this material point, are not disappointed. With this View it will be essentially necessary that each General Officer or other Officer to whom a command of Volunteers is entrusted, shall reside in a situation central and conven-

---

[66] The relationship between the volunteer forces and the regular army in the event of an actual invasion could have been a pivotal factor in the success of the defence plan. The Duke of York, in charge of the army, was concerned to try and pre-empt any problems. Once the volunteer forces were called out and embodied they became subject to military discipline. If commanded by some regular army officers, their strengths might be ignored, given the low opinion held by some who had never seen them in action. As far as the Woodbridge Troop was concerned, when army officers attended inspections or reviews, Collett often reported that their performance far exceeded expectations.

ient to the Corps under his orders, and make himself immediately acquainted with every particular relating to them, with the nature and extent of the service for which they are respectively engaged, with their effective strength, with the Characters, and the extent of military information of the Commanders, with the state of the Corps with regard to their internal economy, their horses, arms, ammunition and every species of military equipment, and, above all, with the degree of forwardness they have attained in their discipline and field movements, and whether they are or are not competent to act with the troops of the line, of which he can only become a competent judge by frequent inspections, and by taking as many opportunities as possible of seeing them under arms.

It will also be incumbent on the General Officer, or others, commanding Brigades, in concert with the Commanding Officers of Corps, to fix the routes by which, in case of being called out, each Corps is to arrive at the general place of rendezvous of the Brigade, and to assure by every previous precaution and preparation, that no obstacle shall occur to prevent the regularity and certainty of their movements at that critical moment; for which purpose it is highly material for him to ascertain that the arrangements for providing carts for the camp kettles, and **B120** Waggons for the conveyance of the men, are carried into effect, in pursuance of the instructions of His Majesty's Secretary of State.

The Commander in Chief is aware that the duties hereby enjoined to the General Officers employed with the Volunteer Force, cannot be discharged with advantage to the Country without the utmost zeal and unremitted personal exertion on their part. In his expectation on this head, His Royal Highness is persuaded that he shall not be disappointed, but it is moreover equally essential these Officers should continually bear in mind that the Corps under their command are composed of men unused to a military life, over whom they have not any direct control till placed on permanent duty, but who have voluntarily enrolled themselves for the generous purpose of sharing with the Regular Troops in the labours, difficulties and honours which are presented to those who are engaged in the defence of their Country, by the arduous contest in which we are at this time engaged.

It is to be presumed that they will feel the force of these considerations, and will conduct their Command, on every occasion with all the urbanity, mildness and indulgence which is consistent with Military discipline, without compromising or impeding the important primary object of rendering the Corps effective and fit for actual service.[67] To ensure the efficiency of the Corps, it is necessary that the Commanders of Brigades should constantly attend the inspections ordered by Act of Parliament, and require a strict account of all absentees. With respect to their discipline, it is the Commander in Chief's expectation, that they will offer their attendance to such Commanding Officers of Corps, (not placed upon permanent duty), as are desirous of receiving the advantage of their instructions.

B121 General Muster July 9th 1804 Monday

The Corps met at Barham for the purpose of a days exercise with Captain Moors Troop. The morning was rather unfavourable and at the time of assembling, about 10 oClock, it rained excessive hard and continuing so to do for the remainder of

---

[67] It is interesting that the Duke of York highlighted the points, as is the fact that he realised they needed to be made at all.

the day We were disappointed in our intended Exercise and obliged to return home, postponing the meeting to Monday 23rd Instant.

July 16th 1804 Major Edgar sent me information of his having received a Letter from Major General Money advising his being appointed to the Command of the Yeomanry Cavalry in Suffolk and Norfolk and expressing his wish to see us out.[68] By Major Edgars desire I sent a Circular Letter to the Corps informing them of same, viz

Sir,   Woodbridge July 17th 1804

I have just received an order from Major Edgar to inform you that Major General Money has signified his intention of Inspecting our Corps with Captain Moors Troop on Monday next at Barham at 11 oClock. Major Edgar hopes that every Gentleman will make a point of attending.

　　　　　　　　I am Sir Your most Humble Servant   Cornelius Collett

To Mr, [Blank]

Monday July 23rd 1804 General Muster

The Corps met at 10 oClock at Barham and being joined by Captain Moors Troop about 11 oClock marched into a field in the occupation of Mr Rodwell and was inspected by Major General Money. The day being very fine the Brigade made a handsome appearance and Major General Money with the Officers who attended him were pleased to express themselves much satisfied with our Evolutions etc etc. A very great number of Gentlemen and Ladies honoured us with their Company in the Field. Many hundreds of spectators where present and every thing was conducted very much to their satisfaction.

Tuesday September 25th 1804 General Muster

The Corps met at the usual time and place, marched from the Parade to Martlesham and Exercised in a field in the occupation of Mr Glanfield. The day was very fine. Major Edgar proposed we should meet once a week in the Autumn and adjourn for the Winter Months, which being **B122** seconded by Captain Theobald, was unanimously agreed to and the next meeting ordered on Tuesday October 2nd.

In consideration of the great expense we had been at in Clothing and Equipments for the Corps etc and the uncertainty of retaining the Numbers in the respective Troops there having been several Instances of Members withdrawing soon after they had been equipped, it had been proposed that a new Muster Roll should be drawn up engaging their Services during the War, for which purpose a Meeting was held on the 2nd July last and that such Members who did not engage their services during the War should, on quitting the Corps, pay the Cost of their Jacketts the sum of £5 15s 6d. Several Members objecting to sign the new Muster Roll it was this day proposed by Corporal Bates and seconded by Corporal Hunt, that an Article of Agreement should be drawn up obligating the payment above stated and on a show of hands it was unanimously agreed to and such Members present who did not intend to sign the new Muster Roll on their names being called declared their readiness to sign the agreement to pay for their Jacketts £5 15s 6d each on quitting the Corps;

---

[68] The army at last appointed a commanding officer for the various volunteer troops in Suffolk and Norfolk.

at same time considered themselves Members of the Corps under the Muster Roll dated July 26th 1803.

Ordered that the above Obligation be entered on the back of the New Muster Roll in readiness for signatures at the next meeting of the Corps.

Copy

We whose names are hereunto subscribed not wishing to sign the Muster Roll bearing Date July 2nd 1804 but at the same time considering ourselves to all Intents and Purposes as Members of the Corps under the Muster Roll of July 26 1803 and having no Intention whatever of quitting, do hereby agree to pay the Fund of the Corps the Sum of five pounds fifteen shillings and sixpence in case We withdraw our Services during the War, agreeable to a Motion made September 25 1804 (being a day of General Muster) by Corporal Bates and seconded by Corporal Hunt and approved by all present.

Samuel Elvis James Last Joseph Bulmer John Threadhall John Ablett

September 25th 1804

The Non-Commissioned Officers and Privates of the Corps having sent to Major Edgar a Sabre of the Value of Fifty Guineas, it was this day shown to the Corps by the Major, who in a most handsome speech, acknowledged his obligations for the same.[69]

Copy of the Inscription Engraved on the Hilt of the Sabre

Presented to Major Edgar by the Non-Commissioned Officers and Privates of the 2nd L.S.Y Cavalry as a small Testimony of their Gratitude and Esteem for his Exertions, for their Interest and Comforts and for his Skill in bringing them to a proper State of Discipline.

B123 Volunteer Record to be Inrolled in the Archives of the Tower of London

To the Officers and Privates of the [blank] Volunteer Cavalry in the County of Suffolk.

Gentlemen,

The unparalleled Unanimity and exemplary spirit of the Volunteers of the United Kingdom, who, in the Hour of Danger, inrolled themselves in Defence of their Country, when threatened with Invasion by the French Nation, and who with Loyalty to the best of Monarchs, and under the Will of Divine Providence, are determined to sacrifice all private Interest to the important Duties of the just and honourable cause in which they are nobly engaged, ought in some manner to be publicly recorded, that Posterity may, with equal Zeal, preserve everything that is dear to them, and repel with Vigour any Enemy that may have the audacity to attempt to assail their Shores. Impressed with the Idea that a Record containing the Names, Places of abode, and Associations of all Officers and Privates being deposited in the Archives of the Tower of London, would be a National Momento of the admirable Spirit of His Majesty's Loyal Subjects, and meet with the approbation of every Volunteer, I took the liberty of submitting a Plan to the Consideration of His Royal Highness, the Commander in Chief, who has been graciously pleased to approve and patronise the same, as has also Major General Calvert, Adjutant General of His Majesty's Forces.

---

[69] This shows the very real appreciation and respect the Troop felt for its major, Mileson Edgar.

I have not the least Doubt but that every Gentleman will immediately and cheerfully pay into the hands of a Sergeant of his Company, the trifling Subscription that appears in the undermentioned Ratio, for the purpose of defraying the great Expenses that have, and will daily arise, in the undertaking and of re-imbursing their Commandant the money by him advanced on their respective Accounts.

I am, Gentlemen, your most obedient humble Servant

Thomas Pierce

Examiners Office, Rolls Yard, Chancery Lane and Penton Place, Walworth, Surrey 30th July 1804

Horse Guards July 14th 1804

In reply to your Letter of Yesterday's Date requesting the Commander in Chiefs approbation of your Plan, I have to acquaint you, That having submitted the same to His Royal Highness, he has desired me to say, That the Plan you have projected for recording in the Annals of our History, the Names of the Officers and Privates of the Volunteers of the United Kingdom, who have nobly come forward and enrolled themselves for its defence at this important Crisis, meets with the entire Approbation of the Commander in Chief. And His Royal Highness further Commands me to say, That whenever you shall have completed your Plan, he will receive and submit the same to the King, in order that His Majesty's Permission for its being deposited in the Archives of the Tower of London may be obtained.

I have the honour to be Sir Your most obedient humble Servant

W H Clinton

To Thomas Pierce Esq

Examiner's Office Roll's Yard Chancery Lane Commander in Chiefs Office

---

B124 Major General Calvert presents his Compliments to Mr Pierce, and assures him, in answer to his Letter of the 25th that he shall feel sincere pleasure in rendering every assistance in his power to any Undertaking calculated, as that proposed appears to be, to record and transmit to posterity, the noble Exertions now making in Defence of the Country.

Horse Guards 27 June 1804

Mr Pierce Examiners Office Rolls Yard Chancery Lane Adjutant Generals Department

---

Ratio of Subscriptions

Commanding Officers of each Corps whether Colonel, Lieutenant Colonel, Major or Captain   7s

Every Field Officer except the Commandants   5s

Captains of Companies   3s

Subalterns   2s

Staff Officers   1s 6d

Sergeants and Corporals   1s

Privates   6d

Sir

I beg leave to inform you that His Royal Highness the Commander in Chief has approved and patronized a plan, projected by me, for recording the names etc of the Officers and Privates of the Volunteers of the United Kingdom, and for transmitting to Posterity the Unanimity and exemplary Spirit of His Majesty's loyal Subjects, when the Kingdom was threatened with Invasion by the French Nation.

His Royal Highness has also been graciously pleased to undertake that, as soon as I have completed the Record, he will receive and submit the same to the King, and obtain His Royal permission for the same being deposited in the Archives of the Tower of London, and I likewise inform you, that such plan has met with the Approbation and Support of Major General Calvert, Adjutant General of His Majesty's Forces.

On the other side I have taken the liberty of sending you a Copy of a Letter I have had the Honour to receive from Colonel Clinton, Secretary to the Commander in Chief and of a note from Major General Calvert.

For the purpose of accelerating the Completion of the Undertaking, I beg the Favour of your Assistance in procuring me a correct List of the Names, Places of Abode, Professions, Trades and Callings of the several Officers and Privates comprising the Troops under your Command, and that you will be pleased to sign such List as an Authority for its Insertion on the Record.

Hereunder I furnish you with the Amount of the trifling Sum each Officer and Private is to contribute towards defraying the great and daily Expenses that will necessarily arise, and I beg you to have the Goodness to pay the Gross Sum that will, on Calculation, be payable for your Troops; and I am to inform you that your Sergeants are to collect for their respective Companies, the Individual Subscription of each Officer and Private, for your immediate Reimbursement, this being the plan maturely considered and adopted, for the purpose of speedily laying the Record before His Majesty.

I have the Honour to be, Sir, With due Respect, Your most obedient, humble Servant,

Thomas Pierce

Examiners Office, Chancery Lane, London and Panton Place, Walsworth, Surrey
September 1ˢᵗ 1804

B125 Copy of the Names, Places of Abode etc of the Members of the Corps of Loyal Suffolk Yeomanry Cavalry commanded by Major Edgar, sent to Mr Thomas Pierce for the purpose of being inserted on the Record, and deposited in the Archives of the Tower of London.[70]

2nd CORPS OF LOYAL SUFOLK YEOMANRY CAVALRY
Mileson Edgar Esq, Major, Red House, Ipswich.

1st TROOP

Captain	John Meadows Theobald	Claydon	Farmer
Lieutenant	William Pearson	Ipswich	Attorney
Cornet	John Meadows Rodwell	Barham	Farmer
Qtr Mstr	James Bryant	Nacton	Farmer
Trumpeter	Spencer Leek	Woodbridge	Basket Maker
Farrier	Nathaniel Collins	Woodbridge	Shoeing Smith
Sgt Major	Robert Sexton	Nettlestead	Farmer
Sergeant	C.R.Church	Otley	Farmer
Sergeant	Isaac Churchyard	Ufford	Farmer
Corporal	Buckle Allen	Henley	Shop Keeper

---

70 This is an important document since for the first time Collett records both members' place of residence, showing how far they had to travel to Woodbridge, and their professions.

Corporal	Thomas Edwards	Ash Bocking	Farmer
Corporal	Richard Grimwade	Naughton	Farmer
	James Last	Otley	Farmer
	Titus Browning	Gt. Blakenham	Farmer
	Robert Bedwell	Henley	Farmer
	Jeremiah Cooper	Claydon	Farmer
	William Welton	Ash Bocking	Jobber
	William Cockrell	Claydon	Farmer
	John Clover	Creting	Farmer
	Edward Jay	Badley	Miller
	Robert Rutland	Claydon	Farmer
	John Mayhew	Gosbeck	Farmer
	William Wilson	Tanington	Farmer
	George Vincent	Needham	Farrier
	John Edwards	Bramford	Farmer
	John Dawson	Ash Bocking	Farmer
	John Fryett	Ipswich	Inn Keeper
	George Skipper	Lt. Blakenham	Farmer
	Edward Watkins	Henley	Farmer
	James Garnham	Hemingstone	Farmer
	George Harsum	Otley	Farmer
	Joseph Rye	Gosbeck	Farmer
	Edward Adams	Brandeston	Farmer
	Lionel Dove	Cretingham	Farmer
	Benjamin Cook	Holton	Farmer
	Joseph Bulmer	Cretingham	Farmer
	Joseph Rivers	Nettlestead	Farmer
	James Morgan	Flowton	Farmer
	George Ashford	Cretingham	Farmer
	James Orman	Bramford	Farmer
	Robert Welham	Ash Bocking	Farmer
	Ambrose Raynham	Gt. Blakenham	Farmer
	Richard Keeble	Creting	Farmer
	George Ward	Needham	Farmer
	John Edwards	Gosbeck	Farmer
	Henry Farrer	Cretingham	Farmer
	John Last	Otley	Farmer
	William Slade	Stonham	Shop Keeper
	George Morgan	Bramford	Farmer
	William Cole	Ash Bocking	Farrier
	William Goldsmith	Brandeston	Farmer

2nd TROOP

Captain	Cornelius Collett	Woodbridge	Banker
Lieutenant	John Stow Baldry	Ramsholt	Farmer
Cornet	Philip Dikes	Wickham Market	Farmer
Qtr Mstr	Thurston Whimper	Alderton	Farmer
Trumpeter	Thomas Symonds	Saxmundham	Surgeon
Sgt Major	Francis Hayle	Leiston	Farmer
Sergeant	Nathaniel Gross	Sutton	Farmer

Sergeant	Benoni Kemp	Parham	Farmer
Corporal	George Bates	Eyke	Farmer
Corporal	John Hunt	Chilesford	Farmer
Corporal	Thomas Simpson, Junr.	Ufford	Farmer
	Jonathen Churchyard	Melton	Butcher
	William Barthrop	Parham	Farmer
	Thomas Denny	Swefling	Maltster
	William Bunnett	Dalingho	Farmer
	Nathaniel Bunn	Wickham Market	Miller
	Daniel Fuller	Woodbridge	Corn Merchant
	Samuel Cooper	Bredfield	Miller
	Robert Ablett	Butley	Farmer
	Benjamin Cooper	Dalingho	Farmer
	John Paine	Sutton	Farmer
	John Easter	Sutton	Horse Farrier
	John Button	Marlesford	Farmer
B126	George Keer	Parham	Farmer
	John Thredkell	Charsfield	Farmer
	David M'Cluer	Woodbridge	Merchant
	James Aldous	Marlesford	Farmer
	Jonathen Keer	Wantisden	Farmer
	William Neeve	Pettistree	Farmer
	James Neeve	Pettistree	Farmer
	George Miles	Woodbridge	Brickmaker
	William Smith	Swefling	Farmer
	John Hayward	Cransford	Horse Farrier
	Richard Hyam	Martlesham	Farmer
	Joseph Chapman	Blaxhall	Farmer
	William Orford	Marlesford	Farmer
	Thomas Miller	Boyton	Farmer
	Samuel Elvis	Woodbridge	Merchant
	George Loft	Woodbridge	Inn Keeper
	Nathaniel Keeble Chandler	Pettistree	Farmer
	William Lungley	Samundham	Licquor Merchant
	James Page	Charsfield	Farmer
	James Churchyard	Rendlesham	Farmer
	James Newson	Glemham	Farmer
	Richard Rope	Cransford	Farmer
	Philip Pierce	Ufford	Farmer
	John Welham	Martlesham	Farmer

3rd TROOP

Captain	John Couperthwaite	Woodbridge	Brewer
Lieutenant	George Errington	Westerfield	Esquire
Cornet	John Brooke	Caple	Farmer
Qtr Mstr	Charles Collett	Walton	Farmer
Trumpeter	Spencer Leek Junr.	Woodbridge	Miller
Sgt Major	William Hewitt	Wherstead	Farmer
Sergeant	John Field	Trimley	Farmer
Sergeant	John Sawer	Ipswich	Farmer

Corporal	George Curtis	Rushmere	Farmer
Corporal	William Whimper Cook	Rushmere	Farmer
Corporal	John Chapman	Kirton	Farmer
	John Knights	Whitton	Farmer
	James Fisher	Wherstead	Farmer
	Jonathen Wasp	Ipswich	Farmer
	John Rivett	Ipswich	Carpenter
	James Masters	Ipswich	Army Tailor
	Postle Jackson	Ipswich	Printer
	John Ablett	Clopton	Farmer
	Cornelius Collett	Walton	Farmer
	Samuel Adams	Hemley	Farmer
	John Bird	Witnesham	Farmer
	John Garnham	Offton	Farmer
	Nathaniel Moore	Bucklesham	Farmer
	Joseph Harris	Grundisburgh	Farmer
	Thomas Wake	Grundisburgh	Farmer
	John Porter	Grundisburgh	Farmer
	Joseph Roe	Tudenham	Farmer
	Daniel Orpen	Felixstow	Farmer
	Robert Blomfield	Hemley	Farmer
	Thomas Catlin	Playford	Farmer
	John Cook	Rushmere	Farmer
	William Everett	Falkenham	Farmer
	Robert London	Hasketon	Farmer
	William Salmon	Foxhall	Farmer
	John Ranson	Ipswich	Glass seller etc
	Henry Waller	Ipswich	Farmer
	William Shearman	Witnisham	Farmer
	Richard Crawley	Ipswich	Wine Merchant
	Jeremiah Laws	Ipswich	Maltster
	Robert Weeden	Trimley	Farmer
	James Rivers	Trimley	Farmer
	William Cobbold	Ipswich	Brewer
	Thomas Bolton	Akenham	Farmer
	John Baines	Witnesham	Cooper
	John Bryant	Ipswich	Maltster and Merchant

B127 Tuesday October 16th 1804

The Corps met at the usual time and place, marched from the Parade to a Field at Woodbridge belonging to Mr Robert Cooper, and Exercised in sundry evolutions etc. Major Edgar having received notice from Colonel Sharpe Inspecting Field Officer of the district that he should Review the Corps with the Baberg Troop Commanded by Captain Moore and the Hadleigh Troop by Captain Gooch (together) at Barham on Tuesday the 23rd Instant Orders were accordingly given by Major Edgar for the Corps to assemble on Tuesday next at Barham precisely at 11 oClock and to appear in their overalls with other Equipment in Field order.

Tuesday October 23rd 1804 General Muster and Inspection

The Corps assembled at Barham at 11 oClock and with the Baberg and Hadleigh Troops where Inspected by Colonel Sharpe Inspecting Field Officer of the District who was pleased to express himself highly gratified at the Soldier-like manner in which the Brigade performed the various Evolutions etc, declaring he considered them equal to most Troops of the Line and that he should be proud of the Command to take the Field with them against the Enemy should they at any time Invade this Country.

After the Inspection, Captains Moore and Gooch signified to Major Edgar it was the wish of themselves and their Troops to be united with us in one Corps. The proposal was immediately accepted by us and in answer Major Edgar informed Captains Moore and Gooch we felt ourselves highly honoured by their offer and that from this time we considered ourselves Consolidated under the command on Major Edgar who was required to notify the same to the Lord Lieutenant for His Majesty's approval.[71]

NB Captain Moore Commands the Babergh and Captain Gooch the Cosford Hundred Troops

---

Tuesday November 6th 1804 General Muster

The Corps met at the usual time and place, marched from parade to a field belonging to Mr Robert Cooper and exercised in various evolutions etc. Major Edgar gave notice the Corps being Consolidated with the Baberg and Cosford Hundred Troops, We are now become a Regiment and that the Inspecting Field Officer has orders from the Commander in Chief to Review the Troops every two months. The next General Muster would be in December at Barham. The Act of Parliament requiring 12 days muster per annum, it was proposed and unanimously agreed upon by all present, in consequence of the very great distance of residence from the place of General Muster We should meet the days prior to the Review at Barham and attend at a Muster on each day, making **B128** together six meetings and 12 days Muster as required by the Act, and the same being considered would be much more convenient to the Members in general. Major Edgar was requested to inform Captains Moore and Gooch of this our Resolution in hopes of their adopting the Plan which would enable us to exercise together on every occasion of General Muster.

December 6th 1804

By desire of Major Edgar orders were sent to each Member of the Corps to attend at General Muster at Barham on Thursday and Friday the 20th and 21st instant. It being a hard frost, and deep snow on 20th and 21st December, the time of Musters was postponed till further orders.

(Copy) Circular   **Red House January 28th 1805**
Sir

In consequence of Letters from General Money and Colonel Sharpe, informing me, that they propose inspecting the Corps on Thursday, February 14th and desiring me to secure a full Muster, as a particular Examination will take place of Arms, Appointments and Cloathing, as also of horses, I have thought it desirable to address

---

[71] The addition of the 6th and 7th Troops to the three Troops of the 2nd Woodbridge Corps would allow the formation of a Regiment of Suffolk Yeomanry Cavalry.

myself to every member of the Corps, rather than to the Captains of Troops, and to request you will make a point of Mustering on Wednesday February 13th and Thursday the 14th, at the Barham House of Industry, at Eleven oClock in the Forenoon, in Field day Order and with Overalls; the first day being for Drill and the latter for Inspection.

The Military character you have acquired, independent of the communication made in the first part of my Letter, affords me the best security for seeing your Arms, Appointments, Cloathing and Horses in good and soldier like order and condition.

I am with much respect Yours,   Mileson Edgar Major

February 9th 1805

Major Edgar having this day received a Letter from General Money to say that in consequence of Instructions from His Royal Highness, Duke of York Commander in Chief, there would be no Inspection untill the month of April. Information of same was immediately sent to each Member of the Corps and that the meeting on Wednesday was also postponed until further Orders.

B129 (Copy of a Circular Letter from Major Edgar to the Corps)

Sir,   Having Business of Consequence to communicate, which affects you and every Member of the Corps, I must request that you will make a point of meeting me on the Town Hall, at Woodbridge, on Tuesday the 12th Instant, at 12 oClock in the forenoon, in plain cloths.

I am Sir With much respect Yours   Mileson Edgar Major

Red House March 4th 1805

Norwich February 28th 1805

Sir   I have received Major General Moneys command to inform you that the arrangements for the next Inspection of the Troops of Yeomanry Cavalry in Suffolk are made out, and that it is the wish of the Major General to see the Troops under your Command at their usual Ground of Inspection on Wednesday the 3rd April next at 12 OClock, which arrangement the Major General hopes will be convenient to you and to the Gentlemen composing the Troops under your command.

I have the honor to be Sir Your most obedient humble Servant,

Henry Loftus, Major late 24 L D Brigade Major

Major Edgar, Red House, Ipswich

Tuesday April 2nd 1805

The Inspections having been postponed, orders are since received for the Corps to Assemble on the 2nd and 3rd Instant. They accordingly this day met at Barham and were inspected by Colonel Sharpe (Inspecting Field Officer), who was pleased to express himself much gratified by the masterly manner in which they performed the various Evolutions etc. etc.

The Cosford Hundred Troop Commanded by Captain Gooch having withdrawn themselves from the Union with us as resolved upon at a meeting together on 30th October 1804 are not now considered as belonging to the Corps.[72] The Union with our Corps and the Babergh Troop Commanded by Captain Moore being fully

---

[72] This ended the hopes of forming a regiment in the immediate future.

arranged a return of same was made to the Lord Lieutenant of the County, and we being now Consolidated, the returns are made to the War Office of one Corps consisting of 4 Troops Commanded by Major Edgar

Wednesday April 3rd 1805

The Corps met at Barham and where Inspected by General Money who in the highest terms of respect was pleased to express his satisfaction of the manner in which they performed the sundry evolutions etc etc.
[73]

Copy of Major Edgar's Letter to Lord Euston accompanied by a Memorial to be presented to Lord Hawkesbury[74] dated December 10th 1804[75]

The Memorial of Major Edgar commanding the Second Corps of Yeomanry Cavalry in Suffolk Is meant to show that through an anxious desire of increasing the Volunteer Force of the County of Suffolk, and thereby forwarding the public Service, he did in the Year 1803, and previous to the 3rd day of August in that Year, increase the Troop of Cavalry under his Command from 48 to 122 Private Men, but that not having made the necessary Application to the Secretary of State for an Increase in his Establishment to the amount of the Number of Men of which his Troop did actually consist, he is likely to be deprived of the Pecuniary Aid allowed by Government in consequence of an Omission on his part, of mere Form.[76] At the same Time that he is able to prove by the Testimony of many respectable Officers who inspected and actually reported upon the strength of his Corps, that the Number of Men for which he has requested the regular Allowance were not only Bona Fide inrolled, but effective in the field. It is meant to show that it is not in Consequence of any dissent from the general Principle by which the Office he addresses has been guided in its View of your Memorialist's Case, that he has ventured to lay it before your Lordship in this new shape, but from a sense of what is due to those on whom the Expense incurred in the Equipment of so many well appointed Cavalry must ultimately fall, unless there should be some Remission on the Part of Government, in favor of the unwary, of a Determination evidently formed to check abuse and prevent fraud.

Copy of Major Edgars letter to Lord Euston December 10th 1804

After keeping the Memorial which I submitted to your Lordship thus long unemployed you will perhaps be a little surprised at finding it now called into use, and I do assure you had it not been for the very flattering application I have had made to me by Captains Moors and Gooches Troops to accept them as part of my Corps. I should not, I believe have renewed a Business which has already given your Lordship so much Trouble, and been attended with so little success.[77] The two Troops

---

[73] B130–B131, a copy of the general muster roll of Collett's 2nd Troop is omitted, together with the muster rolls of the other Troops kept by their commanding officers.

[74] Lord Hawkesbury was Home Secretary.

[75] Collett kept together this group of letters concerning the non-payment of the allowance for the extra men for whom Edgar failed to fill in the requisite forms, which resulted in them being slightly out of chronological sequence.

[76] In view of the disorganised state of the central bureaucracy this would seem to be a really harsh decision especially when the country vitally needed such recruits at this juncture. It shows an attempt to tighten up the bureaucracy of the volunteer forces.

[77] A copy of Lord Euston's letter on Edgar's behalf can be found in his Letter Book, SROI, P454.

above mentioned are very desirous to a man of joining my Corps, and of course I cannot be less so of receiving them. The total strength of Captain Moors Troop is 62, that of Captain Goochs 61, that of my own 149 total 272, the five Troops Act remarkably well together and have on every Inspection highly pleased Major General Money and Colonel Sharpe. But if we are to become one Corps, or to be Regimented I hope the Secretary of State will see the necessity of allowing me the Cloathing Money for the 74 men I have received nothing for, or fresh and serious difficulties will await me on any future Issue of Cloathing Money, as Moors and Goochs will receive a full allowance for their Troops and I shall receive an allowance for 48 men only out of the three remaining Troops whereas if Government were to persist in with holding from me the Cloathing Money of the 74 men and my Corps receives no Augmentation of other Troops, we shall in that Case apply the Cloathing Money when issued for 48 men in Aid of the Debt we at this time labour under, and continue to wear our old Cloaths.

Your Lordship being in possession of course of all the Letters which have given Statement of this Business, as coming either from your own pen or mine, can readily refer for any Particular you may wish to state to the Secretary of State, you will there find that out of 122 men raised and enrolled from the 3rd of August, but unfortunately prior also to the obtaining His Majesty's permission to form my Troop into a Corps of 3 Troops, I have been allowed to draw only for 48 men. Surely it will not be refused me. If it is, I really do not se how I can accept Moors and Goochs Troops from the Circumstances I have stated. I know your Lordship will exert yourself in the matter, and if it is thought necessary or desirable to make a reference to Colonel Sharpe, General Money or Sir James Craig, I am well assured the good appointments and the merits of the Corps will be admitted. If the 5 Troops are to be formed into one Corps or Regiment, which I really think cannot with propriety or advantage take place unless all the Troops which compose it have the same benefit from the Cloathing Money, I should hope that we shall be allowed an Adjutant, and in that case I would wish to recommend Lieutenant Ray of Captain Moors Troop as thoroughly well calculated for the situation, having been several years in the King's Dragoon Guards.

I am, my Dear Lord, Yours most sincerely   Mileson Edgar

B133 My dear Sir,

I lose no time in forwarding the result of my endeavours to give effect to your Memorial. I could have wished the decision had been of a different kind.

Yours most faithfully   Euston

January 25th 1805

My Lord   **Whitehall 28th January 1805**

I have had the honor of receiving your Lordships Letter of the 24th Instant inclosing the Memorial of Major Edgar; and have in Compliance with your Lordship's request, referred to the Correspondence which passed between Your Lordship and Mr Yorke last year on the subject of Major Edgars Claim; I am, however, sorry to say that after having given the Case the fullest consideration and with every disposition to show the most favourable attention to a request made in behalf of so deserving an Officer as Major Edgar is represented to be, it is wholly impossible for me to authorize the payment of the June allowances to more than one Troop under Major Edgars command, the rest having been accepted subsequent to the 3rd of August 1803.

I shall regret extremely any Expense which may fall upon Major Edgar in consequence of an omission which he then considered only as a matter of form, but I do not think myself competent to depart from a Rule which has been now so long acted upon and so invariably adhered to, as that which makes the date of His Majesty's acceptance the ground of Distinction with regard to the Allowances of Volunteer Corps.

> I have the honour to be my Lord Your Lordship's most Obedient
> humble Servant
> Hawksbury[78]

The Earl of Euston

B134 Town Hall Woodbridge   March 12th 1805

At a Meeting of the 2nd Corps of Loyal Suffolk Yeomanry Cavalry held here this Day in consequence of a Circular Letter for that purpose, Major Edgar having submitted the present State of the Fund, it appears that the sum of £1085 is due to him and other officers of the Corps, and the further Sum of £191 18s 4d to tradesmen, the Trumpeters and Farrier; making together a Total of £1276 18s 4d[79]

1st Resolved unanimously, That Quarter Master Collett, Corporal Bates and William Cobbold be a Committee for Examining the Accounts of the Corps.

2nd Resolved unanimously, That all the money which shall be issued by Government for the Service of the Corps whether on the Head of Cloathing or Contingent Money, shall from this time be strictly applied towards a Liquidation of the above debt.

3rd Resolved unanimously, That every member of the Corps is from this Time to keep his Cloathing and Appointments of every kind in good and proper order and repair at his own Individual Expense.

4th Resolved unanimously, That two Books be forthwith prepared for the purpose of receiving Subscriptions from the Members of the Corps, one to be left with Major Edgar and the other with Captain Collett, and that the Resolutions of the Day be entered therein.

5th Resolved Unanimously, That the Thanks of the Meeting be given to Major Edgar for his Conduct in the Business.

It being proposed that a Subscription should immediately take place, the following sums were subscribed.[80]

B136 Copy of a Circular Letter from Lord Hawkesbury to His Majesty's Lieutenants of Counties in England and Wales

My Lord   **Whitehall, 5th April 1805**

The obvious and important Improvement which the State and Discipline of the Volunteers have already experienced from the Measure of placing them for a limited Time, on permanent Pay and Duty, has determined His Majesty to give effect to the Disposition which has already been manifested by many Corps of Volunteers to renew their Offers of going out on Permanent Duty, under Regulations similar to those which were established and acted upon during the last year.

---

[78] He was Home Secretary in Pitt's second government and later became Lord Liverpool.

[79] This is a very large amount to be paid, on top of the debt that would inevitably accumulate in the future for the sizeable number of the extra men, since there was no question of asking them to resign.

[80] The list has been omitted but named forty-six people who raised £368 15s.

With regard to those Regulations, I am desirous of directing your Attention particularly to the previous Steps to be taken before the Proposal of any Corps to assemble on permanent Pay and Duty is transmitted to me; in order that the Concurrence of the General of the District to the proposal may be signified to me, at the same time with an exact Return of the Effective Numbers and Rank of the Volunteers who are to be assembled, and accompanied by a statement of the Time and Place of their Assembling, and of the Period for which it is intended that they shall remain on Duty.

For the Purpose of giving every due Encouragement to this Description of Service, it is the Intention of His Majesty's Government to propose to Parliament to authorise them to advance to the Non-commissioned Officers, Trumpeters, Drummers and Privates, a Sum not exceeding One Guinea for Twenty one Days, and in that proportion for any shorter Period; to be drawn for by the Captains of Companies, upon the Receiver General of the County to which the Corps may belong. I have the honour to be My Lord

        Your Lordship's most obedient humble Servant,   Hawksbury

To His Majesty's Lieutenant of the County of [blank]

Circular   **Great George Street April 2nd 1805**

Sir

Having been directed to transmit to you the enclosed Circular Letter upon the subject of the optional Renewal of the Service of permanent Duty, I am induced to submit the following general Observations to your attention.

As the Secretary at War will be guided in the Issue of the Pay and Allowances, and the Receiver General of the County authorised to pay the Marching Guinea for any Period of Duty not less than Twenty one Days (or the proportion thereof, at the Rate of One Shilling per Diem if for less than that number) by the Return transmitted through the Lord Lieutenant of the County to the Secretary of State, it will be highly desirable that the precise Number of each rank to be assembled should be specified therein; but in any case where the numbers exceed those contained in the original, it will be necessary that a Supplementary Return should be forwarded through the same Channel; The expediency of this Arrangement is equally **B137** applicable to duty that may have been performed during the Years 1803 and 1804.

In order that as little Delay as possible may be experienced in obtaining the Allowances for this Service, I have to request that as soon as His Majesty's Approbation of the Proposal to assemble shall have been signified to you by the Lord Lieutenant, you will transmit to me an Estimate of the Sums required, specifying the intended Appropriation thereof under the different Heads, when I shall most readily accept the bills in advance.

The accounts for Permanent Duty must be kept perfectly distinct from every other, to which I have to request your particular Attention, as much difficulty may otherwise arise in the final Settlement of them.

All Bills for this Service must be drawn by the Paymaster at the longest Period after Sight at which they can be negotiated at par, in no instance not less than three days, but where his Appointment has not been completed, by the Commandant.

The Regulations applicable to this Service, and Instructions for the Guidance of Paymasters, with the necessary Forms for the Accounts, are nearly completed at the War Office, and will very shortly be circulated.

The Pay and allowance to Yeomanry when placed on permanent Duty will be similar to those of the Regular Cavalry, but when called out by the Lord Lieutenant of the

County under the Act 44 Geo 3rd Cap 56 Sec 48, the Commandant will be guided in every Respect by my Circular Letter dated 5th July 1804.

I have the honour to be Sir Your most obedient humble Servant   George Hassell
To Major Edgar

Friday March 15th 1805

Quarter Master Charles Collett, Corporal Bates and William Cobbold the Committee appointed the 12th Instant for Examining the Accounts of the Corps (the same being kept by Major Edgar and Captain Collett) met at Major Edgars this day and having strictly examined every particular relating thereto and finding them perfectly correct acknowledged their approbation of same by their signatures. Signed Charles Collett George Bates William Cobbold

---

B138 Tuesday May 7th 1805 General Muster

The Corps met at 11 o'clock on Parade on the Market Place, Woodbridge, marched from there to Sutton and exercised in a field in the occupation of Mr Nathaniel Gross. Major Edgar being in London, the Corps was commanded by Captain Theobald.

Lord Hawkesburys Letter of 1st April respecting their Offer of Service for Permanent Pay and Duty for a limited Time, was read to the Corps (by Captain Theobald) and at same time he requested they would be prepared to return their answer to same to Major Edgar at General Muster on Tuesday next 14th Instant.

Tuesday May 14th General Muster

The Corps met at the usual time and place, marched from Parade to Melton and Exercised in a field belonging to Mr Jonathen Studd.

It being Major Edgars wish to be informed of the Sentiments of the Corps in answer to Lord Hobarts Letter of 1st April, which was read to them by Captain Theobald on the 7th Instant, On the Question for an offer of Service to go out on permanent Pay and Duty for a limited Time, it was the unanimous Resolution of the Corps present, on a show of hands, to decline making the Offer, upon the consideration of our Numbers being sufficiently large to admit of the Practice of any Evolutions required by a Regiment, and that by a full attendance on duty upon the 12 days required by Act of Parliament, (with the Inspections every two months in the course of the Year) We should receive equal Benefit and avoid the Expense attending permanent Duty etc. etc.[81]

Tuesday May 21st General Muster

The Corps being assembled at the usual time and place, marched from Parade to Kesgrave and Exercised in a Field in the occupation of Mr Cotton, having gone through the usual Evolutions, fired several rounds of Blank Cartridges for practice of the Men and Horses preparatory to the 4th of June.

Tuesday May 28th General Muster

T'he Corps being met marched to Sutton and Exercised in a Field occupied by Mr Nathaniel Gross and having gone through the general Evolutions practised on days

---

[81] Given the amount of debt caused by the government's decision not to pay the allowances arising out of the administrative oversight, the decision was foreseeable.

of Muster, fired 6 rounds of Blank Cartridges for the purpose of Practice of the Men and horses against the 4th of June.

A letter of which the following is a copy was sent at the request of Major Edgar by the Captains of Troops to such Members of the Corps who have not properly attended on days of Muster.

B139 Sir   **May 28th 1805**

By desire of Major Edgar I inform you that on the 1st August the next Return will be made of the Corps to the Lord Lieutenant, before which every member unless prevented by Illness, must have appeared at Exercise 12 times or be returned Non-effective.

The Corps have already met 6 times, [blank] of which you have been absent. I am directed to say that if your horse is lame or ill, and you attend in the field in uniform, it will be deemed a Muster. After this information, Major Edgar trusts you will not impute any blame to him for the consequences that must necessarily await your absence on the days of Muster for exercise.

                               I am Sir Yours respectfully [blank] Captain

To Mr [blank]

(Copy)

Sir, Hearing it is your intention of taking your Corps out tomorrow, I have sent you the Order of the Day.

I have the honour to be Dear Sir, Your obedient humble Servant

                               R Diggins Major of Brigade

To Major Edgar

Garrison Order (Copy)   **Ipswich 3rd June 1805**

The Garrison of Ipswich and Woodbridge (including Major Edgar's Corps of Yeomanry and the Loyal Ipswich Volunteers) will fire a feu de joie at 12 oClock tomorrow in honor of His Majesty's Birth Day.

They will assemble on Rushmere Heath at a quarter past eleven Oclock in Brigade Columns of half Squadrons and of Companies left in front at quarter distance.

That of the Cavalry in the Valley with its rear clear of the Road, on its Right the Column of Artillery with a front of 4 Guns; next that of Lieutenant General Lord Charles Fitzroys Brigade, and on the Right and near the Hedge, that of Brigadier General Gower's Brigade. From this situation, a Line will be taken up and further directions given.

                               B G (on Brigades Orders)

The Brigade will be in Review Order to morrow but the cloaks may be Lapped, 3 Rounds of Blank Cartridge per Man to be taken.   R Diggins Major of Brigade[82]

B140 His Majesty's Birthday June 4th 1805 General Muster

The Corps met at the time appointed by Major Edgar at Kesgrave in a field in the occupation of Mr Cotton, marched from thence to Rushmere Heath, the Troops from the Garrisons of Ipswich and Woodbridge being arrived the Line of Cavalry was

---

[82] The difference in approach between the orders of the regular army and requests of the Yeomanry Cavalry is clearly evidenced in this exchange.

175

immediately formed and being arranged marched out of the Valley and occupied their Station in the Line which was formed in the following order from right to left The Royal Horse Artillery with their field pieces, Royal Scots Greys, 21st Light Dragoons and 2nd Corps of Loyal Suffolk Yeomanry Cavalry, 7th Light Dragoons, North York Rifle Corps, East Middlesex, West Suffolk and North York Militia, Loyal Ipswich Volunteers, and Royal Berkshire Militia, the Royal Foot Artillery, with their field pieces, were placed about 20 yards in front of the line.[83]

At 12 oClock the firing commenced with a royal salute of 21 guns which was followed by a feu de joie from the whole line of cavalry and infantry, which was repeated three times, the music playing and the Officers saluting in the intervals between the firing, the effect of which was very grand, and executed much to the Credit of the troops on duty.

The line then broke into column, and in ordinary time and open order, passed the Royal Standard where Major General Lord Paget (who commanded the whole) took his station, officers saluting and the different bands playing. There were 33 pieces of cannon upon the ground, and not less than 7000 men under arms. The whole afforded a truly grand military spectacle; the excellent appearance of both cavalry and infantry excited the admiration of the spectators. The day being very fine the company of spectators was very numerous and of the first respectability. The line was considered to be about two miles in extent.[84]

There were only three troops of the 2nd corps of Loyal Suffolk Yeomanry Cavalry on duty viz Captains Theobalds, Colletts and Couperthwaites. The Baburgh Troop commanded by Captain Moore which compose a part of the Corps not being in the Field.

Thursday June 13th 1805 General Muster

The four Troops composing the 2nd Corps of Loyal Suffolk Yeomanry Cavalry commanded by Major Edgar met at Barham at 11 oClock, marched into a field in the occupation of Mr Browning and were Inspected by Lieutenant Colonel Sharpe Inspecting Field Officer, in the usual Evolutions etc etc. The day being very fine there were several Carriages in the field and a number of Spectators.

Tuesday July 16th 1805 General Muster

The Corps, 3 Troops, met at the usual time and place, marched to Kesgrave and Exercised in a field in the occupation of Mr Cotton. The number of days of meeting agreeable to Act of Parliament which entitle the Members of the Corps to claim an exemption from certain Taxes being this day expired and a return of the names of such persons being required to be made on the 1st day of August next by the Commanding Officer, many Gentlemen not having attended the proper Number of times to entitle them to the exemptions Major Edgar appointed certain days of meeting prior to the first day of August of those Members and very politely engaged

---

83 The high concentration of military forces in the area clearly highlights how vulnerable this part of the coast was considered to be, particularly the number of cavalry and artillery units who could react quickly to any landing. General Sir Eyre Coote's recommendations for the defence of the area had included the need for such forces because of the open nature of the land between Hollesley Bay and Woodbridge, much of which was heath and sheep walks.

84 This great show of strength was very good for the morale of the people, both military and civilian, who were suffering the strain of a third summer when an invasion was considered imminent.

to attend himself in order that he may make his return compleat without any being noted non-effective.[85]

Major Edgar informed the Corps present that General Money had postponed the meeting for Inspection in consequence of the wet season for getting up the Hay and the near approach of Harvest untill further orders.[86]

Crown Point Norfolk August 8th 1805

Sir   I send you a Copy of a Letter I have just received from Lieutenant General Sir James Pulteney

(Copy)   Head Quarters Colchester August 8th 1805

I am directed by Lieutenant General Sir James Pulteney to request that you would apprize the Volunteer Corps under your Orders of the possibility of their being speedily called upon for service, and that you would take an early opportunity of Inspecting each Corps in order to see that it is in readiness for taking the Field if necessary. It is in consequence of intelligence recently received by His Majesty's Ministers, and communicated to the Lieutenant General by His Royal Highness the Commander in Chief, that the above instructions are given.[87]

I have the honour to be, Sir, your most obedient humble servant
W M Armstrong Assistant Adjutant General
To Major General Money etc etc etc

As it is impossible for me to see all the Troops of Yeomanry and Volunteer **B142** Cavalry placed under my superintendance and command on the event of Invasion, as soon as I could wish, I have to request you will order your Troop out without loss of time, in Marching Order, informing me of the place and hour you intend being out, that they may be seen either by me, or the Inspecting Officer, and if we cannot be on the Ground, you will not fail I hope, to send me a correct return of your strength in the field, and the state of your Troop, and to apprize them of the possibility of their being called upon for service; also to inform me if you are complete in all your appointments.

I have the honour to be, Sir, Your most Obedient humble Servant,
J Money, Major General
To Major Edgar, Red House, Ipswich

Sunday August 11th 1805 In consequence of the above orders which were this morning received by Major Edgar, and by him communicated to the Captains of the four Troops, an order of which the following is a Copy was on Monday morning sent to each Member of the Corps.

---

85 This is more evidence of the problems of non-attendance. Exemption from the militia ballot was important to members but if they knew the extra meetings would be arranged there was less pressure to turn up at general musters.

86 The Yeomanry consisted largely of farmers and the hay crop was very important to them, providing winter feed for animals.

87 This was the most dangerous period of the year with the weather and tides set fair and Napoleon's invasion fleet complete and eager to sail.

Sir, The Major having received orders from General Money to call out the Troop immediately, you will not fail to be at the Barham House of Industry[88] on Tuesday Morning at 10 oClock in Marching Order and with Overalls.

I am, Sir, Your most humble Servant   c.c. or Captain

To Mr [Blank]   Sunday Evening August 11th 1805

Tuesday August 13th 1805

In complyance with the order issued by directions of Major Edgar yesterday under the signature of the Captain of each Troop, the Corps (4 Troops), met at Barham at the time appointed and in consideration of the short notice, no previous information whatever having in any way been received by anyone, the Muster was very fully attended, and it was only in consequence of sickness or being from home that any of the Members who were absent did not attend. Those present were fully equipped for immediate service. The Corps being formed in 3 Troops, marched from Barham House of Industry into a Field in the occupation of Mr Rodwell and exercised in the various Evolutions practised on days of General Muster. Having assembled in so short a time from the notice being received neither General Money or Colonel Sharpe, (Inspecting Officer) attended the Muster. The Return was accordingly sent to General Money by Major Edgar.

B143 Notice was given by Major Edgar to the respective Members of the Corps to hold themselves in readiness to march on Service on the shortest possible notice, in complyance with the Orders of His Royal Highness the Duke of York, Commander in Chief.

NB About 7 oClock in the morning we had a heavy shower of rain which lasted about half an hour. After that time it cleared up and the day was particularly fine and pleasant.

October 2nd 1805[89]   By order of Major Edgar, the following Circular Letter was sent to such Members of the Corps who were not personally informed of the Troop being ordered to meet for Inspection on Wednesday 16th instant.

By desire of Major Edgar I inform you that the Corps will be inspected on Wednesday the 16th Instant, at Barham, by Major General Money and Lieutenant Colonel Sharpe; he particularly requests you will make a point of attending and be at the House of Industry at half past 10 oClock precisely, in Review Order, and consequently without Overalls

I am Sir Your most Obedient Servant   Cornelius Collett Captain

---

Wednesday October 16th 1805 General Muster and Inspection

The Corps met at the time and place appointed in the above Circular Letter. Colonel Sharpe appeared in the Field and inspected the Horses, Equipments, Arms etc of same he was pleased to express his satisfaction. In consequence of it being the day on which His Royal Highness, the Duke of York, Commander in Chief, Reviewed

---

88 The House of Industry at Barham built in 1766 was for thirty-five parishes in the hundreds of Bosmere and Claydon. For a contemporary description, see Young, *General View of the Agriculture of the County of Suffolk* [1813], pp. 244–6.

89 Napoleon's army started melting away towards the end of August, but it may have taken some weeks for this to be definitely confirmed and therefore the Yeomanry must have been on full alert for the rest of August and September.

the Troops of the Garrisons of Ipswich and Woodbridge, Colonel Sharpe being obliged to attend, could not wait to Inspect the Corps in the Evolutions, and it being the wish of the General present to attend the Review, we were by Major Edgar, discharged from any further duty on this day, with orders to meet at Woodbridge on Tuesday the 12th of November at the usual time and place.

The early part of the day was favourable for the Review, and a greater assemblage of Company was never witnessed, The Troops amounting to about Eight Thousand **B144** Men, presented a most grand and military appearance, and their movements evinced the highest state of discipline.[90] The Troops on duty consisted of the Royal Horse Artillery, Royal North British Dragoons (Greys), the 7th and 21st Regiments of Light Dragoons, the Royal Berkshire, Shropshire, Royal East Middlesex, Hertford and West Suffolk Regiments of Militia. His Royal Highness was attended by the Earl of Chatham, General Sir James Pulteney, Lord Paget and many other Staff Officers. On his arrival on the heath, a discharge of 21 guns was fired by the Royal Foot Artillery, and the line formed under the Command of Lieutenant General Lord Charles Fitzroy and Brigadier General Robinson. About 12 oClock it began to rain and the latter part of the day was very stormy which was rather unfortunate for the Troops on duty and the numerous Spectators.[91]

Tuesday November 12th 1805 General Muster

The three Troops met at the time and place ordered in the above Circular Letter[92] and marched from Parade to a field at Martlesham in the occupation of Mr Frost and fired a feu de joie in honour of the late glorious Victories obtained by the British Fleet against the Combined Fleets of France and Spain.[93] Major Edgar being obligated to make a Return of the Corps by the 2nd December, in order that each member should have an opportunity of attending his proper number of times required by Act of Parliament, it was unanimously agreed such Gentlemen as had not attended the proper Number of times should meet on the following days: Friday 15th Tuesday 19th and Instant. No further particular occurrences upon this day.

Intelligence being received of Captain Sir Richard John Strachan's Victory a feu de joie was also fired in honour of same.
[94]

B152 Copy (Circular)   **Colchester November 11th 1805**
Sir,   His Royal Highness the Commander in Chief has been pleased to direct that all the Yeomanry and Volunteer Corps in this District should be Inspected this Month and in the most minute and particular manner. His Royal Highness therefore observes that superadded to the instructions conveyed in the Adjutant General's

---

[90] This is a very large number of Troops to be garrisoned in two towns just five miles apart. All were full-time troops, both regular and militia, with no volunteer corps taking part.

[91] The review was a magnificent display of power and patriotism.

[92] Omitted.

[93] Collett is referring to Nelson's victory at Trafalgar on 21 October, which ended Napoleon's hopes of invasion for the foreseeable future, although he had already, at the end of August, started removing his Army of England to fight the Austrians, which he successfully achieved with victories at Ulm and Austerlitz by Christmas. The war continued with little hope of a conclusion, since Great Britain commanded the sea, but Napoleon the land. It is rather difficult to understand why Collett wrote such a brief and restrained entry about such a major and all-important piece of news in view of the impact it must have had on the county.

[94] B145, *London Gazette Extraordinary*. Battle of Trafalgar, 21 October 1805, not included.

letter of the 7th January etc etc you will be pleased to specify in your inspection and report the Corps under your superintendance in the following classes, viz:
1st as fit to act with Troops of the Line
2nd as advancing in Discipline
3rd as deficient in Discipline
and you will be pleased further to state the number of these who appear under Arms, an account of the Deficiencies, and wether the absent are with leave, from sickness, without leave, or wanting to complete.

I have the honour to be etc etc M K Armstrong Assistant Adjutant General

To Lieutenant Colonel Sharpe, Dedham

Dedham, November 12th 1805

Dear Edgar,

Annexed is a Copy of a Letter I have this moment received from the Adjutant General, in complyance with which I shall inspect your Corps on Friday the 22nd at 12 oClock. I regret the shortness of the notice, but from the pressing nature of the order I have put it off as late as I possibly can.

Believe me, yours truly   M Sharpe

To Major Edgar Red House Ipswich

Dear Sir   **Crown Point November 14th 1805**

I have to return you many thanks for your polite attentions to me when on my Tour of Inspections, and I have to congratulate you on commanding one of the first Corps of Yeomanry in this Kingdom. I am no longer on the Staff, yet I am not without hopes, though they are but slender; there are Lieutenant Generals, as I understand, on the Staff with Major Generals' Appointments. The Marquis Townshend[95] as well as all the Gentlemen in the Yeomanry are very desirous I should be continued, but whether I am or am not, I beg you will consider me as your obliged and faithful servant.[96]

J Money Lieutenant General

To Major Edgar Red House Ipswich

Friday November 15th 1805 General Muster

The Corps met in complyance with their Adjournment on Tuesday last and marched to a field in Woodbridge in the occupation of Mr Frost and were exercised in the usual Evolutions etc. Letters from Colonel Sharpe and General Money of which the above are Copies were read to the Corps and an order for a General Muster on Tuesday next for Exercise and on Friday the 22nd for Inspection, was sent to all the Absentees of the Corps in a Circular Letter of which the following is a Copy

Sir,   **Woodbridge November 15th 1805**

I am desired by the Major to inform you that the Corps will meet at Woodbridge on Tuesday next for exercise and at Barham on Friday for Inspection, and it is his particular request, that you will attend on both days at 11 oClock, as he has received a Letter from Colonel Sharpe in the strongest terms, requiring a full Muster.

Cornelius Collett Captain

---

95 Despite being nearly eighty-three, he commanded the Western Regiment of Yeomanry Cavalry in Norfolk, having raised the famous Norfolk Rangers in 1782.
96 Major General Money had commanded the Yeomanry Cavalry in Suffolk and Norfolk since June 1804.

B154 Tuesday November 19ᵗʰ 1805 General Muster

The Troops met this day at General Muster and marched to Sutton and were exercised by Major Edgar preparatory to the inspection of the Corps by Lieutenant Colonel Sharpe on Tuesday next at Barham (in a field in the occupation of Mr Nathaniel Gross). The day was very fine and the Troops went through the sundry Evolutions with great correctness.

Friday November 22ⁿᵈ 1805 General Muster and Inspection

The Corps met this day at Barham and was inspected by Lieutenant Colonel Sharpe who was very particular in his inspection of Men, Horses, Arms and appointments, also of the Evolutions; on the whole of which he was pleased to express his perfect satisfaction and to say that he should report them to the Commander in Chief as fit to Act with Troops of the Line. NB The day was particularly fine and pleasant. [97]

B169 (Circular)

Sir   **Woodbridge February 10ᵗʰ 1806**

Major Edgar having yesterday received a Letter from Colonel Sharpe advising his intention of Inspecting the Corps on Monday next, at Barham, desires me to advise you of same. You are accordingly requested to attend at Barham on Monday morning the 17ᵗʰ Instant, precisely at 11 o'Clock, in Marching Order; it is needful you have the Baggage particularly well put on, and every equipment in the best order possible, and not to exceed the time appointed.

Your most humble Servant, Cornelius Collett Captain

PS. None of the Equipments are to be omitted

February 15ᵗʰ 1806

A meeting of the County being ordered by the Sheriff to be held at Stowmarket on Monday next for nominating a proper Person to Represent this County in Parliament in the place of Lord Brome,[98] who is called to the House of Peers in consequence of the much lamented Death of his father, (the late) Marquis Cornwallis, and at same time appointing the Election of a Representative on Thursday next the 19ᵗʰ Instant at Ipswich, the meetings of the Yeomanry Cavalry for Inspection by Colonel Sharpe, are postponed until further orders. For the information of Volunteers the following Advertisement was inserted in the Ipswich Journal of this day.

It having been represented to the Inspecting Field Officer that the intended Inspection of Loyal Suffolk Yeomanry would interfere with the Election, and that no attendance could be expected, the commanding Officer is hereby informed, that the Inspections will be deferred. Further notice will be given previous to its taking place.

(by order of Colonel Sharpe Inspecting Field Officer)

Ipswich 14ᵗʰ February 1806

---

[97] B154–B155 and B160–B168, *London Gazette Extraordinary*, Battle of Trafalgar; B156–B159, Muster Roll, 15 November 1805–7 November 1807. All omitted.

[98] Before the first Reform Act of 1832, the county was represented by only two members of parliament, while seven boroughs within Suffolk each had two representatives, namely Ipswich, Bury, Sudbury, Eye, Aldeburgh, Orford and Dunwich.

(Ipswich Journal) February 12th 1806
In consequence of the Nomination of a Representative for the County of Suffolk being fixed for Monday next, the 2nd Corps of Loyal Suffolk Yeomanry will not be Inspected till further notice.[99]

M Edgar Major

B170 Tuesday March 18th 1806 The Corps met at the place and time appointed, marched from Parade to Kesgrave at 12 oClock. The morning being very wet, could not muster sooner. Had a field day in the practice of the usual Evolutions. Captain Theobald Commanded in the absence of Major Edgar who was confined with the Gout.

Tuesday March 25th 1806 General Muster
The Corps being assembled at the usual time and place marched to Kesgrave and being met by Major Edgar who was recovering from a fit of the Gout, (in a field in the occupation of Mr Cotton, the same as we used on the 18th Instant), were exercised in the usual Evolutions preparatory to our meeting on Tuesday for Inspection. We fired a Feu de joie in Honor of the Victory gained by Sir T Duckworth etc etc over the French Fleet.[100]

B174 Tuesday April 1st 1806 General Muster and Inspection
In complyance with the orders received from Major Edgar, the Corps, four Troops, viz: Captain Moors, Theobalds, Colletts, and Couperthwaites, met at Barham at Eleven O'Clock and marched into a field belonging to [blank] and were inspected by Lieutenant Colonel Sharpe who was pleased to express himself highly satisfied with the Evolutions of the Corps and their soldierlike appearance, and further he said that having received particular orders to return a correct statement of the discipline etc etc, of the sundry Troops, under his inspection in this District, he felt great pleasure in saying that he should in his return to the Commander in Chief, His Royal Highness the Duke of York, report the Corps fit to serve with Troops of the Line.

Wednesday April 9th 1806
The three Troops, viz: Captain Theobald's Collett's and Couperthwaite's under the command of Major Edgar, met at Woodbridge and marched from thence to Kesgrave and exercised in a field in the occupation of Mr Cotton. In consequence of many of the Members of the Corps not having attended a sufficient number of times required by Act of Parliament, to enable them to claim an exemption from sundry taxes, that they might not be excluded the same, Major Edgar appointed three days for those Gentlemen to meet him at Kesgrave prior to his making his return to the War Office and Lord Lieutenant of the County as directed by said Act of Parliament. In consequence, such Members of the Corps who did not comply by their attending the extra meetings were from their neglect returned 'Insufficient' and excluded the benefit of the exemptions.

---

[99] For a contemporary account of an eighteenth-century election, see Scarfe, *A Frenchman's Year in Suffolk, 1784*, pp. 72–6.
[100] The French fleet, destroyed in the Caribbean, was their Atlantic Fleet, which had not been involved in the Battle of Trafalgar. B170–B173, *London Gazette Extraordinary*. Omitted.

Wednesday May 28th 1806

The Corps met at the time appointed and marched out of the Town but did not Exercise. The Muster Roll being called over, Major Edgar informed those Gentlemen who had not attended their proper number of times to claim the exemptions from sundry taxes, that he had been obligated to return them 'insufficient', and that in consequence they must expect to be called upon to pay the taxes (specified in Act of Parliament) which **B175** he much regretted not only for their having incurred the same but more particularly their being absent on days of Muster which was injurious to the discipline of the Corps and to those members who made it a point of duty to attend.

The four next days of meetings was fixed upon to be on the 10th 13th 16th and 20th of June and ordered to be inserted in the Ipswich Journal on Saturday 31 Instant.

It was also unanimously resolved that in future the Major or any one of the Captains who are on parade at the time appointed for the meeting of the Corps, should march with such Troops or part thereof as are assembled to the field of exercise, and as soon as the troops in the field are formed, the muster roll shall be called over and such members as do not at the time answer to their names shall be deemed absent. And it was particularly requested that strict attention should be paid to same for the purpose of insuring a more punctual attendance at the times appointed for the respective future meetings.

It being the wish of Major Edgar to know if it was the particular desire of the Corps to meet on the 4th June, (his Majesty's Birthday), it appeared to be the opinion of the majority of those present to discontinue the Annual meetings on that day from the impossibility of our dining together in one Room, and not having at this time a fund to support the same, the Expenses would be individually too great, and from various other considerations many inconveniences would probably occur which might not render the meeting altogether so pleasant as at the times we were only one Troop. A show of hands being required on the Question only seven appeared in favour of the meeting; in consequence it was resolved that no meeting of the Corps should take place on that day.[101]

Tuesday June 10th 1806 General Muster

The three Troops being met, marched from the parade about half past nine o' clock to Sutton and exercised in a field in the occupation of Mr Nathaniel Gross. The day was very warm and the roads dusty in the extreme. No particular occurrence. On the 28th May died Mr James Fisher of Wherstead aged [blank]. He was a member of Captain Couperthwaites Troop. The Corps did not attend his Funeral it not being the wish of his Friends to have him buried with Military Honours.

Monday June 16th 1806 General Muster

The three Troops met at Kesgrave about 10 oClock and exercised in a Field in the occupation of Mr I. Cotton. After the duty of the day, Major Edgar informed the Members that he should not require the attendance on Friday next of those who had missed the proper number of times required by Act of Parliament. Those who had

---

[101] The contrast between this decision and the great celebrations of the year before could not be greater. It reflects a loss of purpose and general lack of morale felt after the pressures of the previous years, together with the effects of the shortage of money because of the debt they were still having to pay off.

not so attended were particularly required to be present on Friday morning next at the place and time appointed.

A letter of which the following is a copy, having been received by Major Edgar from Colonel Sharpe, was by Major Edgar, read to the Troops, after which the Major was requested to return the General thanks of the Corps to Colonel Sharpe for his polite treatment at all times during his appointment to the Inspection of the Yeomanry, and particularly for his good opinion which he was pleased to express of the 2nd Corps, and handsome manner of taking leave of them.[102]

(Copy) Sir,   Dedham, June 13th 1806

His Majesty having been pleased to dispense with the further services of the Inspecting Field Officers, the only duty I have now to perform is to take my leave of the Loyal Suffolk Yeomanry. Having constantly avoided every semblance of flattery, I shall now confine myself to an offer of my very sincere thanks to the 2nd Corps of Yeomanry for the constant attention to their duty, and to my wishes during the time I had the honour of being employed with them. If any individuals may have felt themselves hurt by anything I may have said or done I trust it will now be forgot, and that their own good sense will convince them that the faithful discharge of duty, uninfluenced by any selfish feelings, has on all occasions been the principle of my conduct.

To the 2nd Corps however, I trust this appeal is unnecessary. Their zeal and willingness in discharge of their duty, their attention and respect to their Officers and eagerness to improve, have ever merited my **B177** approbation, and their progress often excited my astonishment.

Allow me to offer my most sincere good wishes to the corps, assuring them I shall always look back with pleasure and satisfaction to the time I have been employed with them.

          I remain Sir, Your very Obedient humble servant

                                        M Sharpe Lieutenant Colonel

To Major Edgar Red House Ipswich

Red House June 19th 1806

Dear Sharpe,

Your Letter of the 13th Instant, I read at the Head of the Corps on Monday last, when assembled for Exercise, and I am desired to express to you the concern they feel at finding you are no longer to hold the Situation you have uniformly filled with so much Credit to yourself, so much advantage to the Service and so much Satisfaction to every Individual engaged in it. At the same time I am to state the Gratification they feel in hearing their Conduct has merited your good opinion, which I know would have been the most powerful Stimulus to every exertion on their Part to secure a continuance of, as long as you were in any way connected in Service with them. I trust you will give me Credit for feeling no common degree of satisfaction in the Employment of my Pen on this Occasion, and a full Participation with my

---

[102] After the death of William Pitt in January 1806, a change of government under Lord Grenville brought Windham into the cabinet as Secretary of State for War and the Colonies. He was hostile to all volunteers, believing them to be too expensive. Persuasion by the Duke of York allowed the retention of a good number of volunteer corps but only after stringent cuts were imposed, which included the removal of inspecting field officers. See Beckett, *Britain's Part-time Soldiers*, pp. 107–8.

Brother Soldiers of every Sentiment of Regard and Respect for you. I have only to add that our days Exercise concluded with three Cheers of health and prosperity to you, instead of a General Salute and that I am Truly yours   Mileson Edgar
To Lieutenant Colonel Sharpe

(Circular)   Sir   **Great George Street 10ᵗʰ June 1806**
I am directed by the Secretary at War to acquaint you that it has been deemed expedient that the annual Allowance to Corps of Yeomanry and Volunteer Cavalry of £120 per Troop for contingent Expenses, should be discontinued, and that the sum of Two Pounds per annum will in future be issued in lieu thereof, for each Person (Commissioned Officers only excepted) who shall be certified at stated periods, to be then actually serving. The alteration is to take place from the 2ⁿᵈ instant.
This allowance to be issued Half yearly, viz £1 for each man, who shall be certified to be actually serving on the 24ᵗʰ Instant, and the like sum for each man who shall be certified to be so serving on the 24ᵗʰ December.
You will after the 24ᵗʰ June, and 24ᵗʰ December respectively, transmit to the Secretary at War a Return of the Persons actually serving in the 2nd Suffolk Corps, certified by yourself, and at the same Time make application by Letter for the Issue of the Allowances. In the Event of Directions to the contrary not being communicated to you in fifteen Days after having transmitted such claim to the War Office, a bill for the amount may be drawn on me at 30 days sight.
             I have the honour to be, Sir, Your most obedient humble Servant,
                                                              George Hassell

---

Circular,
Sir   **War Office July 12ᵗʰ 1806**
His Majesty's Secretary of State for the Home Department having communicated to me the several Alterations which it has been judged expedient to make, with respect to the allowances to be issued to Corps of Volunteer Cavalry, accepted subsequently to the 2ⁿᵈ August 1803, I have the honour to enclose a copy of the Regulations now in Force, and have to request that you will be pleased to govern yourself thereby.[103]
             I have the honour to be Sir, your most obedient humble Servant,
                                                              R Fitzpatrick
Officer Commanding 2nd Suffolk Volunteer Cavalry

                                     War Office July 12ᵗʰ 1806
Regulations to be observed with respect to the Pay and Allowance for Contingent Expenses in future to be granted to Corps of Volunteer and Yeomanry Cavalry accepted subsequently to the 3ʳᵈ of August 1803
Constant Pay will be allowed for an Adjutant (if properly qualified) to Corps consisting of not less than 300 Rank and File, at the Rate specified in the Margin, and for a Sergeant Major to a Corps under 300 Rank and File but consisting of not less than 3 Troops of 40 Rank and File at the Rate specified in the Margin.
Adjutants pay 6s a day. Allowance for the keep of a Horse 2s a day, Sergeant Major 3s 11d a day including 9d for a horse.
Allowance in lieu of pay for a Sergeant and Trumpeter, and for Contingent Expenses.

---

[103] Yet further cuts to allowances were imposed by Windham. See Beckett, *Britain's Part-time Soldiers*, pp. 107–8.

An allowance of £2 per annum will be granted to the Commanding Officer, for each effective Member of the Corps (Commissioned Officers excepted), out of which Fund he is to pay his Drill Sergeant and Trumpeter, and to defray all contingent Expenses. The Commanding Officer will also be allowed the actual Expense of the Stamps upon which the Bills are drawn upon the General Agent.

Where Corps are desirous of Exercising for a number of successive days, under the Provisions of the 46th section of the Volunteer Act, the Commandants thereof are to send a Return, in the Manner herein directed, to His Majesty's Lieutenant of the County, and may immediately, upon having received a notification from him that the Return has been transmitted to the Secretary at War, draw upon the General Agent for a sum, agreeably to the numbers therein contained, at the rate of 2s for each Volunteer and 1s 4d for each horse; and within ten days after such duty shall have been performed, the Commanding Officer is to make out and forward an Accompt to the Secretary at War, the Form of which he will be furnished with, and remit to the Bank of England the Balance, if any, which may remain in his Hands.

NB It is to be clearly understood that the Exercise above mentioned is to be in addition to the usual Drills, for which the men are not entitled to any pay, the above allowance of 2s and 1s 4d are only granted when the Corps are actually assembled and billeted for a certain number of successive days.

If a Corps or any part thereof, shall be called out in Cases of actual Invasion or the Appearance of an Enemy on the Coast, or for the Suppression of any Insurrection, Riot or Disturbance, or to escort **B179** Prisoners or Deserters,[104] Pay will be allowed at the Rates and in the Manner specified in the Memorandum of Allowances granted when upon permanent Duty. The Certificate of His Majesty's Lieutenant or Sheriff of the County for the first mentioned Services, and of the General of the District for the two last, will be required as a Voucher for the Duty having been necessarily performed, and with their sanction.

General Observations.

The Contingent Allowances will be issued Half yearly in advance: the Commandant is to apply for it by Letter addressed to the Secretary at War enclosing a certified Return of the Persons actually serving and unless he should hear to the contrary, within ten days after the Letter by usual course of the post has reached the War Office, he may draw on the General agent for same, by a Bill at 30 days Sight, taking care to advise him of such a draft. The pay of the Adjutant or Sergeant Major (if any) is to be applied for, and drawn in like manner.

The Bills for Sums due, on account of Exercise under the 46 Section of the Volunteer Act, or when called out as specified in the 5th Article of these Regulations, may be drawn at 3 days sight.

All Adjutants and Sergeant Majors in future to be appointed must be Qualified as follows viz

Adjutant. By four Years Service as a Commissioned Officer or Sergeant Major in the Regulars, Fencible Forces, embodied Militia or East India Company's Service.

Sergeant Major. By three Years service as a Non-Commissioned Officer or Private in ditto.

---

[104] This is the first time such an eventuality had been included.

To obtain pay for an Adjutant, Application should be made through his Majesty's Lieutenant of the County, to the Secretary of State for the Home Department, but for a Major, to the Secretary at War.

In case a Commandant shall have to remit any Balance to the Bank of England, he may pursue the following mode, viz Pay the Sum due into the Hands of a Banker in the County and instruct him to direct his Correspondent in London, to pay the amount in the name of the Corps, to the Account of the General Agent at the Bank; the Commandant will advise the General Agent of such Instructions having been given, particularly stating in the Letter the Sum as well as the year for which such Balance is applicable. Should any difficulty occur in complying with this Regulation, the sum overdrawn may be remitted directly to the General Agent.

Ammunition for Exercise and Practice is in future to be obtained through the medium of the General of the District.

In addition to the Returns of the Effectives to be transmitted to this Office on the 24th December and 24th June, of each Year, Three Returns are to be transmitted each year to his Majesty's Secretary of State for the Home Department. Viz, on the 1st April 1st August and of 1st December, as required by the 9th Section of 44 Geo 3rd Cap 54, and monthly returns are to be sent to the General Commanding in the Districts.[105]

The Allowance for Contingent Expences will not be issued for supernumeraries exceeding the Establishment.

All Bills must be advised by a Letter signed by the drawer and drawn upon Stamps required by Law.

If £2 and not exceeding £5 5s 0d – 1s, Above £5 5s 0d to £30 – 1s 6d, £30 to £50 – 2s,

£50 to £100 – 3s, £100 to £200 – 4s, £200 to £500 – 5s, £500 to £1000 – 7s 6d Above £1000 – 10s

B180 Cloathing Certificate
I do hereby certify upon my Word and Honor as an Officer and a Gentleman, that the undermentioned Number of Warrant Officers, Non Commissioned Officers, Trumpeters, and Privates, are actually serving in the Corps under my Command, and that they were enrolled and serving on or before the 24th day of July 1806 and I accordingly claim the allowance for providing Clothing and Appointments.[106]

Ipswich Journal October 4th 1806   Second Corps Loyal Suffolk Yeomanry
The Members of Captain Theobald's, Captain Collett's and Captain Couperthwaite's Troops are requested to assemble at Woodbridge on the 14th 21st and 28th days of this month and on the 4th, 11th and 18th days of next month, at Eleven o'clock in the forenoon precisely; in Field Day Order.
M Edgar Major, Red House, October 2nd 1806

The Act of Parliament requires the Members of the Corps to meet four days between the 1st of August and the 1st of December for the purpose of Exercise for reasons specified in the Act.

---

[105] Increasing bureaucracy in the absence of an adjutant was yet more work for a commanding officer who was a volunteer.
[106] The blank claim form is omitted.

Major Edgar in consideration of some of the Members being unavoidably prevented by Business attending on either of those days, has appointed six days of General Muster, during which time four days attendance must be given by each member, and by the Muster Roll the time of each attendance will appear, and such Members who have neglected to comply with the Act will in consequence be deprived of the benefit arising by the non-payment of sundry Taxes therein named and other Privileges.[107]

B181 Circular   Copy   **Whitehall 25ᵗʰ April 1807**

His Majesty being impressed with the most favourable opinion of the value and importance of the Volunteer Forces of the United Kingdom, of the good Order and Discipline of a considerable Proportion of them, and of the Zeal and Alacrity which they have all invariably manifested on every Occasion in which their Services have been required, is desirous of affording to them every Encouragement which a due consideration of the other branches of the Military Service and an Attention to Public Economy will permit.

He has therefore commanded me to acquaint you, for the Information of the different Volunteer Corps, within your [blank] that it is his Intention to propose to Parliament that the Pay and Allowances settled for the Yeomanry Cavalry and Volunteer Infantry and Artillery, by the regulations of July 1806 (which were intended at that time to be granted to those men only who had been enrolled antecedently to the 24ᵗʰ July 1806), should in future be extended to all Volunteers who may have been enrolled subsequent to that period, or who may be enrolled hereafter, provided the respective Establishments of Volunteer Corps are not thereby exceded.

His Majesty entertains the most sanguine Hopes that the Adoption of this Measure will have the Effect of preventing the gradual Decline of the Yeomanry and Volunteer Corps, and that it will furnish a strong Inducement to the Officers commanding those Corps to maintain them in a State of Efficiency and good Order.

As the Employment of Inspecting Field Officers in a due proportion appears to His Majesty's Government to be essentially necessary for preserving the Volunteer Force in a State of Efficiency, and for enabling His Majesty's Government from Time to Time to form an accurate Judgement of the Condition, Numbers and good order of the respective Corps, it is His Majesty's Intention to appoint without Delay, a certain number of Persons to execute the Duties of Inspecting Field Officers in the different Districts.[108]

There are many other Circumstances connected with the Volunteer Establishment upon which I have received reports from several Quarters, which are under the Consideration of His Majesty's Government, and upon which it may be necessary for me to make some further **B182** communication to you hereafter; but it has been deemed important that no time should be lost in communicating to you His Majesty's determination upon the above Points.

I have the honour to be, Your most obedient, humble Servant,

Hawkesbury

To His Majesty's Lieutenant of the County of [blank]
Sent from the War Office to Major Edgar Red House Ipswich

---

[107] Edgar was trying a more flexible approach to solve the problem of non-attendance.

[108] The number of volunteers had fallen by 13,000 in one year, and in March 1807 Windham was replaced by the able Hawksbury in a new government under the Duke of Portland. He realised the continuing need for inspection if standards were to be maintained and for allowances to be reinstated. Beckett, *Britain's Part-time Soldiers*, pp. 108–9.

On the 5th, 12th and 19th of May, the three Troops met on the Parade at Woodbridge at the times appointed and marched from thence to Sutton and Rushmere alternately and exercised in the usual Evolutions etc. No particular occurrences. In consequence of Inspecting Field Officers being again appointed by Government, Major Edgar requested the four Troops to meet together at Barham on 26th May.

Tuesday May 26th 1807

The four Troops met at Barham at the place and time appointed, marched into a field in the occupation of Mrs Rodwell Barham. Major Edgar, having a fit of the Gout, and not being able to mount his Charger, attended in his Curricle, from which he gave the word of Command.[109] The day was very fine, the Troops went through the sundry Evolutions and Sword Exercise much to their Credit and the Satisfaction of the Major, who was pleased to express himself highly gratified.

June 1807

Government having re-appointed Inspecting Field Officers to the Yeomanry and Volunteer Corps of Cavalry and Infantry throughout the Kingdom, whose Services had been dispensed with, and Colonel Sharpe being again appointed to the Eastern District, he in consequence of his appointment wrote to Major Edgar as follows. This letter being mislaid at the time, I have not yet had the opportunity of copying it. It appears to be lost.[110]

Tuesday June 23rd 1807 Inspection at Barham

The Corps met at Barham for the purpose of being Inspected by Lieutenant Colonel Sharpe Inspecting Field Officer[111] but from the short Notice and the Season for Hay-Making (every person being very busy who are in Farming Business),[112] the Muster was small, there being only a sufficient Number for forming two Troops.

An Inspection of the two Troops was made by Colonel Sharpe and there was present in the Field Colonel Virsion and other Officers of the 7th Light Dragoons who were pleased to express themselves highly gratified with the manner in which the Troops performed the various Evolutions which they said was greatly superior to their expectations. The Day was very fine.

B184 Tuesday August 13th 1807 General Muster and Inspection

The Weather being particularly favourable and the Farmers very fully engaged in their Harvest which from the dry Season commenced early, the Muster under those circumstances was particularly small, there being not more Members present than was sufficient to form one Troop. Colonel Sharpe on finding the Muster to consist of so small a proportion of its Members, said he was fearful it would be the Case from its interference with the Harvest, and that in making his return he should Report those Particulars; that he should not again direct a General Muster prior to October

---

[109] This creates a wonderful vision and demonstrates how important his leadership and personality were to the Corps.

[110] B183. Collett left a blank half page and added in pencil the comment about it being mislaid. It is an interesting example of his method of working.

[111] Lieutenant Colonel Sharpe had been reappointed to his old job as inspecting field officer.

[112] Given the high percentage of farmers in the Woodbridge Corps and the importance of the hay harvest to them, the low turnout was excusable.

next when he hoped to have the pleasure of meeting every Member of the Corps.[113] Colonel Sharpe inspected the Horses, Arms and Equipments. Being one Troop only, we were not required to go through any Evolutions.

The Act of Parliament requiring every person who serves in the Yeomanry Cavalry or Volunteer Infantry, should produce to the Constables of their respective Parishes, to be by them delivered to the Deputy Lieutenants, a Certificate from their Commanding Officer of their Effective Services for the purpose of their claiming exemption from serving in the Militia, in case they should be drawn for that purpose, a Certificate of which the following is a copy was delivered to each Member of the Corps entitled thereto.

I hereby certify that A   B   of the Parish of W   is an effective member of the 2nd Corps of Suffolk Yeomanry Cavalry under my Command, according to the Laws in Force for the Regulation of Yeomanry and Volunteers.   Mileson Edgar Major
Red House September 11th 1807
NB You will not fail to deliver this to the Constable of your Parish, between the 10th Instant and the 1st of next Month.[114]

B185 Tuesday October 27th General Muster and Inspection by Lieutenant Colonel Sharpe
The Corps met at Barham at the time appointed in a Field in the Occupation of Lieutenant Rodwell and was Inspected by Lieutenant Colonel Sharpe Inspecting Field Officer who was pleased to express himself in the most respectful terms of approbation of the movements and the sundry Evolutions in which the Troop were Exercised.
Mr Samuel Stearn of Debach, Mr John Cooper of Hoo and Mr Jonathan Rivers of Trimley having each expressed to Major Edgar their wish to join the Corps, they were by the Major proposed to become Members and each of them unanimously elected.
It being the General Opinion of the Officers that the two extra days of Muster for the purpose of giving the Members an opportunity of attending the 4 days required by the Act of Parliament, has in a very great degree prevented a full Muster of the Troops, and consequently was very prejudicial to the practice of the Evolutions, by dividing the Members and preventing a full Muster on the first four days of meetings, it was proposed to abolish those extra meetings in future, but on a show of hands it did not appear to give general satisfaction. It was then proposed that one extra day only should be allowed, for which, on the sense of the Troops (or Members present) being taken, by a show of hands there was a considerable Majority.[115] It was consequently fully agreed that in future there should be one Extra Muster day only in addition to the four days required by the Act of Parliament, prior to each day of the Return being made and at same time it was by the officers most strongly recommended each Member make a point of attending on the four first days appointed for **B186** the meetings, and thereby ensure full Musters, so very desirable for the practice of the Troops in the sundry Evolutions that cannot be done

---

[113] It is easy to understand why Sharpe was so liked.
[114] More workload was imposed on the already overworked and largely unpaid parish vestry system.
[115] It is an example of yeomanry democracy in action.

by small Numbers, and by which practice only we can retain and ensure the future Credit of the Corps which have at all times been most handsomely spoken of by the Inspecting Field Officers.[116]

This being the third meeting prior to the Return required to be made in December next, it was unanimously agreed the Troops should Muster at Woodbridge on the Tuesday in the three succeeding weeks from this day viz: November the 3rd, 10th and 17th for the purpose of completing their number of attendances required by the Act of Parliament.

Major Edgar having represented to Colonel Sharpe that from the very great distance of the residence of many of the Members of the Corps from Barham, it was impracticable for them to attend the inspections there during the Winter Season unless they were from home at least Two days, which was consequently attended with considerable expense and extra loss of time,[117] the Colonel in consideration of those circumstances agreed with Major Edgar to inspect Captain Theobald's, Captain Collett's and Captain Couperthwaite's Troops at Woodbridge in the months of February August and December, or rather to divide the Meetings for Inspections as follows viz: at Barham in the months of April, June, and October, at Woodbridge in February August and December, in each year until orders are received from the War Office to the contrary.

Tuesday November 3rd 1807 General Muster

The three Troops being met at the appointed time marched to Kesgrave and Exercised in a Field in the occupation of Mr Cotton the day was cold but very fine. The Troops Exercised in the accustomed Evolutions. Mr Ephraham Stannard of Woodbridge Hasketon wishing to become a Member of the Corps was nominated by Major Edgar and on a show of hands was unanimously Elected.

Yesterday (Monday) in the Morning, November 2nd 1807, Lewis the 18th (King of France)[118] landed with his Suite from the Swedish frigate Freya, at Yarmouth, under the title of Count de Lille, by which only he will be recognised during his stay in England. The Count came on shore in Admiral Douglas's barge in the most private manner. On his landing he was received by Admirals Douglas and Essington, Captain Curry of the flag Ship and Mr Brooks of the Alien Office, London. The party immediately assembled at the House of Admiral Douglas's Secretary, which stood contiguous to the spot. Here the Count had his first interview with Monsieur (the Count d'Artois).[119] The scene was truly interesting and affecting. The carriages of Admirals Douglas and Essington were shortly ready to Convey the Count and his suite to the house of Admiral Douglas to breakfast, where the illustrious guests received a hearty welcome and were treated with that true English hospitality, so congenial to the feelings and heart of a British Seaman. The party was joined at Breakfast by Admiral Russell, Sir S. Hood and several Captains. The Count seemed highly gratified at finding himself surrounded

---

[116] The new flexible system did not ensure a big enough attendance to practise the evolutions effectively, which had always been the problem.

[117] This highlights the distances some members were having to travel to attend general musters and the need, presumably, to stay overnight in the winter.

[118] He was the brother of the guillotined Louis XVI, whose young son Louis XVII died in prison. With Napoleon's downfall he was restored as King of France. In the meantime, he had just arrived in England and was staying at Gosford Hall, Essex, and later Hartwell Hall, Buckinghamshire.

[119] He was Louis's younger brother and became Charles X of France after his brother's death.

by so many brave men. **B187** To Admiral Douglas and his family he more than once expressed his gratitude for the attentions and hospitality shown to him. After Breakfast he took his leave and set off from Yarmouth in his own Carriage.[120] This day (Tuesday November 3rd 1807) about two o'clock, he passed through Woodbridge, and on my return from Exercise I had the satisfaction of seeing him upon the Road, and riding some considerable distance by the side of his Carriage, had the opportunity of viewing his person, the window of the Carriage on the side on which he sat being down (being in my Regimental dress and Equipments he was graciously pleased to notice me by his bodily Gesture as I retired from the side of the carriage).[121] He is a very stout man and his features strikingly represent the likenesses which I have seen in the Prints and Paintings of his brother, Lewis the 16th. He was accompanied by the Prince de Conde, Monsieur Duc d'Angouleme, Duc de Bourbon, Duc de Grammont and suite. He was on his way to the seat of the Marquis of Buckingham at Gosfield Park in Essex, at which place I understand he is to reside (at least for the present).

Tuesday November 10th 1807

This being the fifth day of Muster such Members as had attended the number of times (viz four) within the limited time required by Act of Parliament, did not attend, consequently the meeting consisted of such Members as had not attended the prior meetings and was proportionally less in Numbers. I understand about 70 attended. They marched from the Parade to a field in Hasketon and was exercised in the sundry evolutions practised by two Troops.

Tuesday November 17th 1807

This being the sixth meeting of the Troops such Members as had attended the four previous meetings as required by Act of Parliament did not now attend, consequently the meeting was small, only consisting of those who had to make up the Number of times required. The meeting being consequently small, there was not a sufficient Number to form one Troop, and Major Edgar being lame was prevented attending. Lieutenant Errington, the only commissioned Officer present, having taken down the names of those present, dismissed them, there not being a sufficient Number to practise any Evolutions. To prevent such thin meetings in future and insure full meetings on the general Muster Days, it was taken into consideration by the Members present on 27th October and determined that from this date there should in future be only one extra day of meeting and that for the benefit of such Members as had been prevented by unforseen circumstances not to be avoided, and not for the purpose of meeting those who absented under frivolous pretences.[122]

---

[120] No source is quoted by Collett for this description but it was presumably from newspaper reports.

[121] For Collett it must have been an unexpected and surprising experience.

[122] B188–B199, Collett's Troop muster roll. B200–B210, list of the names of all members who enrolled in the 2nd Troop/Corps, together with their first day of muster, place of residence, date and reason for leaving. Eleven extra pages have been stuck in, with the last entry being 3 July 1820. The text is omitted, but see Plate 13. B211, the letter, has been moved to its chronological position, 20 June 1803. B212–B213, copies of forms of return for pay and clothing certificate, are omitted.

A List of the Names of the sundry Persons, who enrolled thems

Names	Place of Abode	first day of Meeting	Time of quitting the Troop	
Philip B.K. Broke	Nacton	July 30th 1794	Died Aug.t 23 1801	
Francis Brooke	Woodbridge	do	ditto	Died July 2.d 1799
Milsson Edgar	Best House Ipswich	ditto	ditto	
John Boahd	Hemingston	ditto	ditto	Died Feb.y 10, 1803
John Page Junr	Woodbridge	ditto	ditto	Died Jany 11. 1798
Cornelius Collett	Woodbridge	ditto	ditto	Resigned Oct.r 1820 — Deafness & Infirmities of Age &c
Richard Manthrop	Ufford	ditto	ditto	September 11. 1801 removed into Essex
William Harper dun	Levington	ditto	ditto	July 13th 1802 resigned ill health
Tolemache Cole	Woodbridge	ditto	ditto	November 15. 1803 expelled
James Churchyard	Wickham Market	ditto	ditto	March 23. 1800 resigned ill health
Chas Thos Bisooun	Melson	ditto	ditto	July 10th 1795 resigned from ill health
John Cowperthwaite	Woodbridge	ditto	ditto	Resignd October 1820 Gout & Infirmity of Age
William Kemp	Pettistree	ditto	ditto	March 14th 1800 resigned
William Everett	Walton	ditto	ditto	Died May — 1800
Stephen Robinson	Wickham Market	ditto	ditto	October 27th 1797 resigned
Thomas Simpson	Ufford	ditto	ditto	September 11. 1801 resignd ill health
John Brooke	Capel St. Mary	ditto	ditto	November — 1804 resignd being remd
John Stow Baldry	Ramshold	ditto	ditto	Aug.t 13th 1808 resignd ill health
John Whimper	Alderton	ditto	ditto	June 4th 1800 resigned ill health
Thurston Whimper	Alderton	ditto	ditto	Died Nov.r 10, 1810 drowned at Alderton
Thurston Whimper	Woodbridge	was a Member of the Troop but died suddenly on the being frore to the first Meeter	
Thomas Mitchell	Saxmundham	July 30th 1794	June 4th 1801 expelled
Philip Gross	Woodbridge	ditto	ditto	July 13th 1802 resigned
Robert Crane	Wickham Market	ditto	ditto	Died June 5. 1799
William Whimper	Woodbridge	ditto	ditto	July 13th 1802 resignd
Isaac Churchyard	Ufford	ditto	ditto	
Philip Dikes	Pettistree	ditto	ditto	
Nathaniel Gross	Sutton	ditto	ditto	October 22, 1813 removed to
John Sewell	Bendlesham	ditto	ditto	April 28 1798 resigned ill health
Robert Benington	Ufford	ditto	ditto	July 13th 1802 resignd do P. Gross
Samuel Gross	Capel St. Andrew	ditto	ditto	ditto — ditto ditto do P. Gross
Stebbing Gross	Eyke	ditto	ditto	September 11. 1801 resigned being remd
Thomas Symonds	Saxmundham	ditto	ditto	October 2th 1804 ditto misconduct
William London	Trimley	ditto	ditto	May 19th 1797 resigned misconduct
Edward Collis	Trimley	ditto	ditto	December 30 1796 ditto ill health
James Clubbe	Carlesham	ditto	ditto	October 30th 1795 ditto being removed
Martin Harsant	Carlesham	ditto	ditto	February 17, 1797 ditto — ill health

Plate 13. The first page of the 2nd Troop's register of members, showing the first volunteers to join in 1794 and the dates and reasons for leaving. Names include those of Collett, Broke, Edgar and Tollemache Cole. Collett reserved the central pages of Volume B for registers and muster rolls when he started his book. © Suffolk and Norfolk Yeomanry Museum Trust. Photograph by Mike Durrant

B213 (Circular)

Sir   **War Office 10ᵗʰ November 1807**

I have the Honor to acquaint you that it has been deemed expedient to reduce the Number of Inspections of Volunteer Corps of Cavalry, Artillery and Infantry, to four annually, instead of six; and that such Inspections shall take place between the first day of March and the first day of November in each year.

The necessary Directions will be transmitted to the Inspecting Field Officers accordingly. I am to add, that this is not intended by this Regulation to make any Diminution in the Number of Days Exercise, for which Pay is allowed within the Year.

          I have the Honor to be Sir Your most obedient humble servant

                                         James Pulteney

To Major Edgar Commandant of the Suffolk Volunteer Cavalry

Sir   **Office of Ordnance 25ᵗʰ January 1808**

It appearing by a report from the Inspecting Field Officer in the Eastern District that there are, in the possession of the Woodbridge Volunteer Cavalry, under your Command, twenty five superfluous Swords and Pistols, with Belts and Knots, I have the Boards Commands to desire you will return that number of Arms into Store at Bury, consigned to the Ordnance Store Keeper at the Depot.

          I am, Sir, Your most obedient humble Servant,   R H Crew

To the Officer Commanding the Woodbridge Volunteer Cavalry Woodbridge Suffolk

Memorandum   The arms etc above alluded to belong to Captain Moor's Troop

---

Tuesday March 22ⁿᵈ 1808 General Muster

The Troops assembled at the time appointed and marched from Parade to Sutton and exercised in a Field in the occupation of Mr Cook. The day was very dry and fine and the Troops went through the sundry Evolutions with an exactness highly creditable, with which the Major was much gratified.

Three vacancies being announced by the resignation of three Members of the Corps in consequence of their removing to a distance too far to allow of their attending on days of Muster,[123] the three following were proposed and unanimously elected Members of the Corps viz Mr Samuel King of Ipswich, Robert Finch Waldringfield and Walter Godbould, Woodbridge.

Tuesday March 29ᵗʰ 1808 General Muster

The Troops being assembled at the time appointed, marched from parade to Kesgrave and exercised in a field in the occupation of Mr Cotton. The day was very fine and dry but the wind was very cold. Exercised as usual. No particular occurrences.

Major Edgar informed the Members present he having received from Government an allowance for the Arms and Equipments which had been paid for out of the Fund of the Corps, and also having received the pay which remained due, and discharged the obligations for money borrowed[124] he was desirous a committee should be appointed to Audit the Accounts current, and to settle the same that the exact state

---

[123] The most common reason for resigning was moving too far away to be able travel to musters. B214–B223, copy of a circular letter addressed to the Lord Lieutenant and the defence plan for 'Driving the country' in case of invasion, 1798, moved to follow the letter on A100.

[124] It had taken a long time to repay the money the Troop borrowed to pay the debts resulting from the failure to submit the forms at the right time in 1803.

of the Fund may be known and the accounts of the Corps settled to the present time. A Committee was agreeable to **B225** the Major's request immediately appointed, consisting of Five Members. The same were chosen by the non-commissioned officers and privates (the commissioned Officers not receiving pay and having no claim upon the Fund) Viz [blank]

They were requested by the Major to meet at his House on a day he would very soon appoint for the purpose when the Accounts would be exhibited to them. The Major also reported there was a balance in hand to the amount of about four pounds ten shillings per Man, and wishing to have the opinion of the Members present wether said balance should be applied to their immediate use, or remain over another year, by which time with the additional pay the Fund may probably be so far increased that the greater part of the expense of new clothing may arise from same. The sense of the Members present was taken thereon by a show of hands and by a great majority it was determined the balance, whatever it may be should remain in hand and the increasing amount from this time for one Year viz to Lady Day 1809 added thereto.

Tuesday April 5th 1808 General Muster

The Troops being assembled, marched from Parade to Sutton to a Field in the occupation of Mr Nathaniel Gross. The morning was fine with a fresh Breeze of Wind, which by 12 oClock increased to a perfect hurricane; so much so that the Troops could not possibly go through the Evolutions as they could not Face the Wind or hear the Word of command. We consequently marched from the field in which we intended to have Exercised into a hollow ground under a Hill, and forming in a Circle, the Muster Roll was called over, and a great part of the Troops having attended Four Musters as required by Act of Parliament, it was requested by Major Edgar a time should be fixed upon for the next Meetings when it was unanimously agreed they should commence on the 17th May and that Notice of same be published in the Ipswich Journal as usual.

The Corps was to have been Inspected this day by Colonel Sharpe Inspecting Field Officer, which he was prevented doing by a most unfortunate accident. On Tuesday, the 29th March (this day week) the Colonel being out Woodcock Shooting after having fired off his Double Barrelled Gun on reloading the same unfortunately the Lock of the other Barrel was at the time remaining on the Cock, and when he was raming down the Charge with his hand over the Muzzle of the Gun, his Dog accidentally jumping up his foot caught the Trigger and discharged the Piece, which most unfortunately Shot away the Fingers of the Colonel's Right Hand, which consequently deprived him of the use of same and prevents his attending the Inspections of the Troops in the District at this present Time.

B226 Friday April 22nd 1808 General Muster and Inspection

The Troops being assembled at the time appointed marched from Parade at Kesgrave and exercised in a Field in the occupation of Mr Cotton. About half past twelve or one o'clock, Colonel Watson arrived. The weather unfortunately proved very unfavourable being very quick successions of hail storms, which coming down so very thick with a breeze of wind, the horses heads could not be kept to face the weather, and which also impeded the Evolutions, and consequently they could not be executed with the exactness desirable on occasion of it being a day of Inspection. The General was pleased to express his satisfaction at what was done, and hoped that as it was probable he might attend the next Inspection, the weather would then be more favourable.

(Circular)   **War Office 11th April**

Sir,   His Majesty having been pleased to direct, that a Revision of the Establishments of the Corps of Volunteer Cavalry and Infantry should take place, I have the honour to acquaint you that in consequence thereof, you are to consider the Establishment of the Corps under your command as provisionally limited to the Number of Men actually enrolled, and serving, on the first day of this Month.

I have the honour to be, Sir, Your most obedient humble Servant,

James Pulteney

Major Edgar, Commandant of the Suffolk Volunteer Cavalry

B227 Thursday June 16th 1808 General Muster and Inspection

The four Troops[125] met at Barham at the time appointed and marched from the Parade to a Field belonging to Sir William Middleton[126] and was inspected by Lieutenant Colonel Watson, Inspecting Field Officer (in the absence of Colonel Sharpe), who was pleased to express himself much satisfied with the Evolutions, Sword Exercise etc, etc, and the respectable appearance of the Men, Horses and Equipments etc. The day was very fine and many very respectable persons, Gentlemen and Ladies of the Neighbourhood were in the field who expressed themselves gratified with the Exercise etc of the Troops.

Tuesday June 21st 1808

Many Members of the Troops having from unavoidable Circumstances been prevented attending one Meeting on either of three preceding days of Muster, Major Edgar at our meeting on the 16th instant, fixed upon this day for such Gentlemen as had been absent to attend for the purpose of compleating the Number of days attendance required by Act of Parliament, they accordingly met on Parade at Woodbridge and marched from thence to Kesgrave and Exercised in a field in the occupation of Mr Cotton. About fifty Members being present they formed in one Troop and exercised in the sundry Evolutions and Sword Exercise. The day was very fine and pleasant. No particular occurrence.

Memorandum

Lieutenant Baldry having for a considerable time past (although present in the field on days of Muster) been too unwell to go through the duty of the day, On the 16th June, being then a spectator only, was very suddenly attacked with a fitt, and instantly fell from his Horse. But having the immediate assistance of a Surgeon, he recovered from same, and in the Evening was able to ride home. From such declining state of health the Officers of the Corps were unanimous in their opinions it was advisable, (and most prudent) in him to resign his Commission, and much wished that someone would speak to him on the subject. Not having since seen him at Woodbridge, or had an opportunity of calling upon him at his own house, I addressed him by letter of which as under is a copy.

---

[125] The Babergh Troop under the command of Captain Moore usually met for their musters on Babergh Heath and sometimes at Boxford.

[126] He was the owner of the Shrubland estate.

Dear Sir,   **Woodbridge July 2ⁿᵈ 1808**

With much concern I have for a considerable time past, observed your declining state of health, and your inability in consequence thereof to go through the duty required on days of Muster, and which the last meeting most afflictingly confirmed.

I am well assured that your Spirit of Loyalty and Zeal for the good of your Country induce you to make every exertion possible, but the length of the Journey and the duty required in the Field are most assuredly too great for your Constitution. I cannot help feeling a very great degree of fear and apprehension that **B227** at the time of Exercise your strength may suddenly be so much exhausted as to occasion some fatal accident. I am therefore induced (together with a sincere regard for you from our long acquaintance) to request you will give in your resignation. I am more anxious for your doing it at this time, as the Inspecting Field Officer having been an Eye Witness to the precarious state of your health, it gives you the opportunity of withdrawing with Honour to yourself, and the respect due to the Corps. And I further claim your attention to this request, under this assurance, that from the sincere regard the Officers of the Corps entertain for you, it is their anxious wish you will comply therewith.[127]

I remain Dear Sir, Yours most sincerely,   Cornelius Collett
To Mr J S Baldry   Earl Soham

Woodbridge August 13ᵗʰ 1808

Lieutenant Baldry being too much enervated to write himself, this day waited upon me (at my house) and in the most handsome terms desired I would state to Major Edgar and all the Officers of the Corps, his lively sense of their respect for him expressed in my Letter of 2ⁿᵈ July, and that he was truly sensible of their feelings at the time of his being taken ill in the field on the day of General Muster and Inspection at Barham the 16ᵗʰ June last, which occasioned their deputing me to address him on the propriety of his resignation.

Having been a Member of the Corps from the time of its institution, and from his sincere respect for same, and his Loyalty; together with his good wishes for his Country, he felt himself anxiously desirous of continuing his Services (having also hopes of his indisposition being removed) but since his illness at Barham the 16ᵗʰ July having been twice attacked in a similar way and feeling his constitution so much impaired, together with the opinion of the Gentlemen of the Faculty who attend him that he could not possibly go through the Exercise required of an Officer on days of Muster, he was (however reluctant to his feelings) under the disagreeable necessity of resigning his Lieutenant's commission, which he requested I would signify to Major Edgar that he may make the same known to the Lord Lieutenant of the County in order that the proper arrangements may be made accordingly, which information I immediately communicated by Letter per Post to Major Edgar.

Woodbridge September 13ᵗʰ 1808

This being the first Day of Muster since Lieutenant Baldry's resignation, an arrangement was made for the Nomination of a Lieutenant and other Officers.

---

[127] This is a very sensitive letter from Collett and gives much insight into his character.

197

B229 Copy of an Advertizement in the Ipswich Journal July 9th 1808
Volunteer Corps
By a Letter received from the Secretary of State's Office, Lord Hawkesbury has desired me Officially to call the particular attention of the several Commandants of Yeomanry and Volunteer Corps within the County of Suffolk, to the necessity of transmitting their Returns of Muster Rolls to me, as soon after the 1st day of August next as possible, agreeably to the 9th Section of the Act of 44th Geo 3rd, cap 54, in order that I may be enabled to make out and transmit to His Majesty's Secretary of State the Abstract required by the 14th Section of the said Act. And I am also directed to apprise them, that if they omit sending their Returns within 14 days of the period above mentioned, the Members of the Corps under their Command will not be entitled to any of the privileges enjoyed by effective Volunteers, but will be subject to Ballott, under the Local Militia Act.
Bury 1st July   Philip James Case Clerk of General Meetings of Lieutenancy[128]

Tuesday July 26th 1808
The three Troops met on Parade at Woodbridge at the time appointed and marched from thence to Sutton and Exercised in a Field in the occupation of Lieutenant Nathaniel Gross. Lieutenant Colonel Sharpe did not meet the Corps for Inspection, having a few days since received instructions from the Secretary at War to postpone the Inspection of all Volunteers for the present, (supposed to be on account of the approaching Harvest), there being several very heavy showers of Rain in the Morning between 8 and 10 o'clock, many of the Gentlemen on their way to Woodbridge got very Wet. After 11 o'Clock, the day was very fine.
NB I was not myself on duty this day, being very unwell.[129]
[130]

B233 Regulation   By a Letter from the War Office, 11th April 1808, the Establishment of the Corps of Volunteer Cavalry are not, (until further orders) to exceed the number of Members returned effective the 1st April 1808 if any vacancies occur after that date they may be filled up with new Members but not to increase the number on the return of the 1st April. As under is a statement of the effective Numbers in each Troop of the 2nd Corps of L.S.Y. Cavalry Commanded by Major Edgar.

Establishment of the 2nd Corps Loyal Suffolk Yeomanry Cavalry: from April 5th 1808[131]

2nd Corps: Major Edgar
1st Troop   Captain Theobald
2nd Troop   Captain Collett
3rd Troop   Captain Couperthwaite
4th Troop   Captain Moore

---

[128] This might have been an efficient and time-saving way of sending out orders to the whole county, but it lacked the personal touch that had been so prominent and successful earlier.
[129] Collett made very few remarks about himself throughout the book.
[130] B230–B232, *London Gazette Extraordinary*, Peace with Spain and the Spanish Declaration of War against Napoleon, not included.
[131] Blank form of inspection return and report, omitted.

		1st Troop	2nd Troop	3rd Troop	4th Troop	Corps	Total
	Majors					1	**1**
	Captains	1	1	1	1		**4**
	Lieutenants	1	1	1	1		**4**
	Cornets	1	1	1	1		**4**
Staff	Chaplain					1	**1**
	Surgeon				1		**1**
	Quarter Masters	1	1	1	1		**4**
	Sergeants	3	3	3	3		**12**
Rank and File	Trumpeters	1	1	1			**3**
	Corporals	3	3	3	3		**12**
	Farrier	1					**1**
	Privates	36	37	36	32		**141**
	Totals	**48**	**48**	**47**	**43**	**2**	**188**

B235 Captain Moore's resignation and appointment of Captain Ray

Kentwell Hall July 20th 1808

Owing to the repeated non-attendance of several of the Members belonging to the Babergh Troop of Yeomanry Cavalry, and the Consequent impossibility of going through the different Evolutions, with such a material deficiency in point of Numbers as generally occurs, I must beg leave to resign the Command of the said Troop, which I shall be obliged if you will signify to the Lord Lieutenant, and remain Sir, Your obedient humble Servant

Richard Moore

To Major Edgar

Dear Lord Euston   **Red House July 31st 1808**

Captain Moore having resigned the Command of one of the Troops in the 2nd Corps, it is my duty to apprize your Lordship thereof. I beg leave to recommend Lieutenant Walter Ray of to succeed to the Troop, Cornet Richard Waring of Edwardstone to be Lieutenant vice Ray, and Quarter Master Amos Todd of Acton to be Cornet vice Waring, an arrangement which I am happy to say gives great satisfaction to the whole Corps, and will, I hope, to your Lordship.

I remain, with respect and esteem, Yours truly   Mileson Edgar

---

My Dear Sir,   **Lodge August 2nd 1808**

I have received your communication of 31st Ulto and shall send by this Post to the Secretary of State the new arrangement proposed by you with the Concurrence of your Corps, on Captain Moore's resignation, believe me to be my Dear Sir,

Yours faithfully etc etc   Euston

M Edgar Esq

My Dear Sir,   **Lodge August 6th 1808**

The King has been pleased to approve of the following appointments in the 2nd Corps of Yeomanry Cavalry under your Command. Lieutenant W Ray to be Captain instead of Mr Moore resigned, Cornet Richard Waring to be Lieutenant and Mr Amos Todd to be Cornet. I have directed the Clerk of the Peace to make out the necessary Commissions.

I have the honour to be, your most faithful and most obedient, Euston

M Edgar Esq

Memorandum Captain Moore, having been very Popular consequently raised a very full Troop which was maintained with great Spirit and attention, unfortunately his popularity during the last 12 months has so far declined, that he has very prudently resigned the command.[132]

B236 Tuesday September 13th 1808 General Muster

The three Troops of the Corps being assembled in complyance with Major Edgar's Notice of same in the Ipswich Journal of the 3rd instant, marched from the Parade in Woodbridge to Kesgrave, and Exercised in a field in the occupation of Mr Cotton. The Corps being formed in a Circle, Major Edgar gave notice of the Resignation of Lieutenant Baldry, and after stating the particular cause and reason of same, requested the Members of Captain Collett's Troop (in which Mr Baldry had been Lieutenant), to proceed to the nomination of a Member of the Troop to succeed Mr Baldry and if any further vacancies were occasioned thereby, that they would also nominate such Members of the Troop as they considered eligible to fill up the same. The following arrangement was accordingly made and without a single dissenting voice, each Gentleman so nominated was elected to fill the office as follow Viz Cornet Dikes to be Lieutenant vice Baldry, Quarter Master Whimper to be Cornet vice Dikes, and Major Edgar approving the nomination was requested to signify the same to the Lord Lieutenant of the County, to be by him forwarded to the Secretary at War and by him reported to His Majesty for his approbation, which being obtained, orders will be accordingly given for making out their Commissions. Sergeant Major Hayle was Elected Quarter Master, Sergeant Gross Sergeant Major, Corporal Bates Sergeant, and Jonathan Keer, Corporal, which Election being approved by Major Edgar, the appointments were made accordingly, and to fill up the vacancy in the Troop occasioned by Mr Baldry's resignation, Mr John Blake of Wickham Market was proposed by Lieutenant Dikes and unanimously Elected. After these arrangements were all settled, the Troops Exercised in the usual Evolutions practised on days of General Muster, which terminated about a quarter before three oClock.

There was a very great deal of Rain in the course of the Morning, it clearing up about 8 oClock, the day proved very fine and pleasant.

Major Edgar having advised the Lord Lieutenant of the above arrangements received in answer the following reply (copied as under)

Walnefield Lodge September 23rd 1808[133]

I have the satisfaction to acquaint you that the King has approved of Mr Philip Dikes as Lieutenant and Mr Thurston Whimper as Cornet in the Second Troop of Suffolk Yeomanry Cavalry on the Vacancy made by Lieutenant Baldrys Resignation. I shall direct their Commissions to be made out accordingly.

I have the honour to be, my Dear Sir, Your most faithful and Obedient

Servant, Euston

To M Edgar Esq

---

[132] This is an unusually personal judgement.

[133] Wakefield Lodge (modern spelling) was on Lord Euston's hunting estate in Northamptonshire.

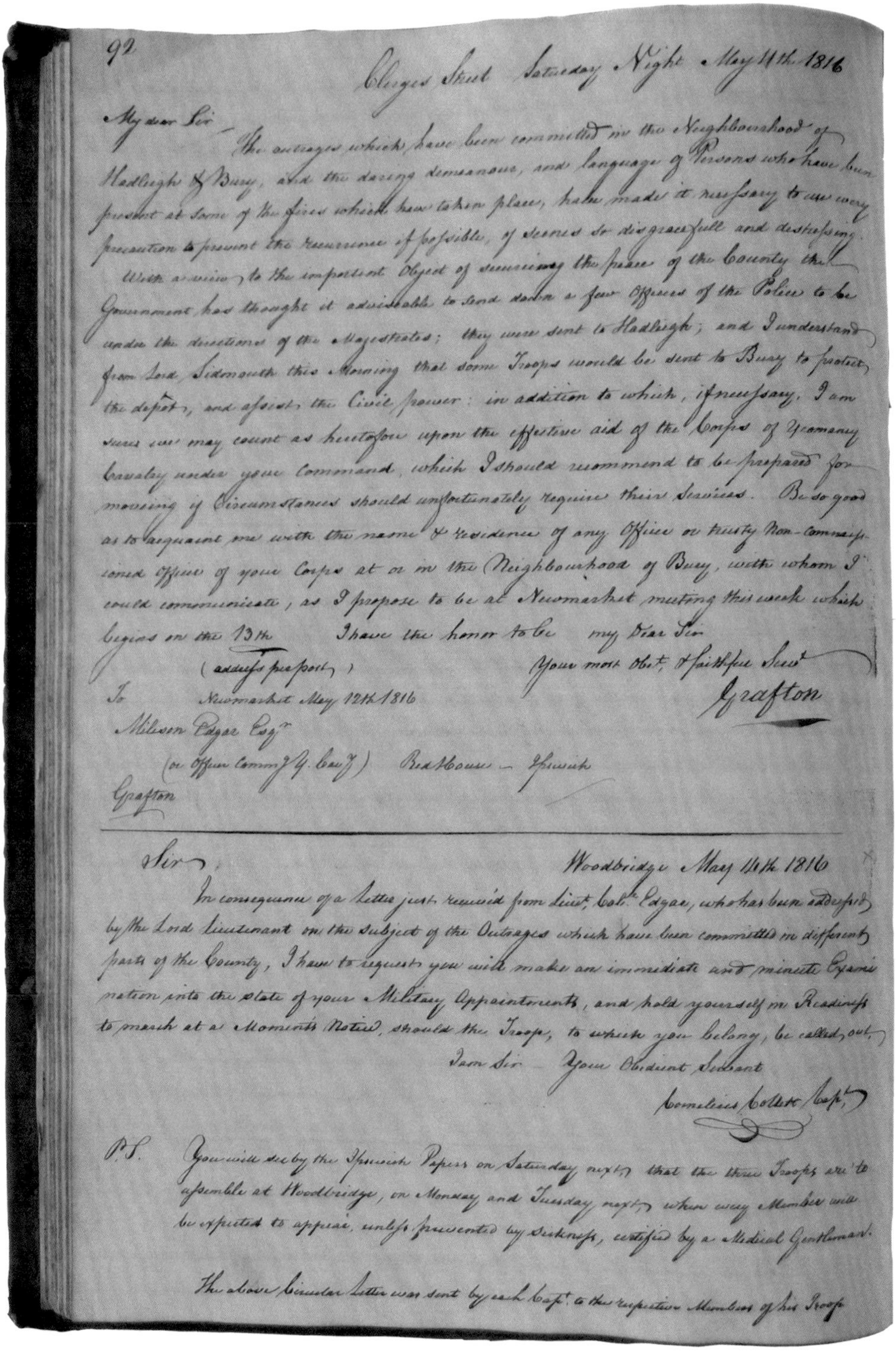

Clarges Street Saturday Night May 11th 1816

My dear Sir,

The outrages which have been committed in the Neighbourhood of Hadleigh & Bury, and the daring demeanour, and language of Persons who have been present at some of the fires which have taken place, have made it necessary to use every precaution to prevent the recurrence if possible, of scenes so disgracefull and destressing.

With a view to the important object of securing the peace of the County the Government has thought it advisable to send down a few Officers of the Police to be under the directions of the Magistrates; they were sent to Hadleigh; and I understand from Lord Sidmouth this Morning that some Troops would be sent to Bury to protect the depôt, and assist the Civil power: in addition to which, if necessary, I am sure we may count as heretofore upon the effective aid of the Corps of Yeomanry Cavalry under your Command, which I should recommend to be prepared for moving if circumstances should unfortunately require their Services. Be so good as to acquaint me with the name & residence of any Officer or trusty Non-commissioned officer of your Corps at or in the Neighbourhood of Bury, with whom I could communicate; as I propose to be at Newmarket meeting this week which begins on the 13th. I have the honor to be my dear Sir

(address prepost)   Your most Obt, & faithfull Servt
To   Newmarket May 12th 1816   Grafton
Milson Edgar Esqr
    (or Officer commg of y Corps)   Red house — Ipswich
Grafton

Sir,   Woodbridge May 14th 1816

In consequence of a letter just received from Lieut. Colt. Edgar, who has been addressed by the Lord Lieutenant on the subject of the Outrages which have been committed in different parts of the County, I have to request you will make an immediate and minute Examination into the state of your Military Appointments, and hold yourself in Readiness to march at a Moments Notice, should the Troops, to which you belong, be called out.

I am Sir — Your Obedient Servant
                                    Cornelius Collett Capt.

P.S.   You will see by the Ipswich Papers on Saturday next that the three Troops are to assemble at Woodbridge, on Monday and Tuesday next when every Member will be expected to appear, unless prevented by sickness, certified by a Medical Gentleman.

The above Circular letter was sent by each Capt. to the respective Members of his Troop

Plate I. A page from Collett's book showing a letter from the Duke of Grafton (formerly Lord Euston), concerning the outbreaks of agrarian protest and violence in Bury and Hadleigh in 1816. © Suffolk and Norfolk Yeomanry Museum Trust

Light Dragoon.

3

This Reg.ᵗ was Created in 1759, & Commanded by Col. John Burgoyn.

Light Dragoon.

4

This Regiment was Created in 1759, & Commanded by Col. Geo. Aug.ˢ Eli

Plate II. Light Dragoons of 1759, two of the coloured prints with which Collett decorated the inside cover of his Volume B. © Suffolk and Norfolk Yeomanry Museum Trust. Photograph by Mike Durrant

Plate III. Mileson Edgar and Cornelius Collett in the first uniform of the Loyal Suffolk Yeomanry Cavalry in the Market Square, Woodbridge. The watercolour was painted after the Yeomanry bought Collett's book in 1953. © Suffolk and Norfolk Yeomanry Museum Trust. Photograph by Gary Walker

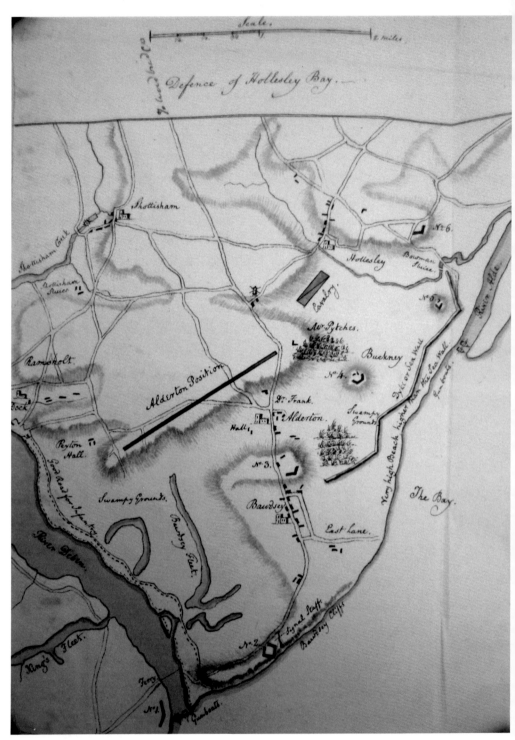

Plate IV. General Sir Eyre Coote's map of his defence plan for Hollesley Bay and the Bawdsey peninsula, August 1803, probably based on Hodskinson's map of 1783. It shows gunboats across the Deben and the Alde, the signal staff at Bawdsey, suggestions for defensive points, and cavalry and infantry positions if the French landed.
© Gloucestershire Archives, D421/X19

B237 Tuesday September 20ᵗʰ 1808

The [Troops] assembled at the usual time and marched from the Parade Woodbridge to Sutton and exercised in a Field in the occupation of Mr Nathaniel Gross. No particular occurrence. They were by Major Edgar, requested to attend at Barham on Tuesday next for inspection by order of Colonel Sharpe Inspecting Field Officer.

NB I could not myself attend this day's meeting in consequence of the sudden ill health of Mr Vertue who was not able to attend on the business at the Bank.[134]

Local Militia

Copy of the Act of Parliament as far as it regards the offer of Services of any of the Corps of Yeomanry Cavalry or Volunteer Infantry for their being attached to same.[135]

48 Geo 3rd Cap 111 29 And be it further enacted, that it shall be lawful for His Majesty to permit any Volunteer Corps of Yeomanry or Artillery to transfer themselves into the Local Militia, upon such Terms and Conditions as to their Establishment and as to allowances for Horses or Accoutrements or other Things, and as to Pay, as His Majesty shall direct, and to be attached to the Local Militia of the County, wherein such Corps shall serve, in such manner as His Majesty shall direct. Provided always, that no Vacancies arising in any such Corps of Yeomanry so transferred as aforesaid, shall be supplied by Ballot under this Act, but all such Vacancies which shall not be supplied by the entering of any Men into such Corps within three Months after such Vacancy occurring in Yeomanry Corps, shall be supplied by Ballot for the Local Militia of the County to which such Yeomanry Corps shall be attached.

Tuesday September 27ᵗʰ 1808 General Muster and Inspection

The Corps four Troops[136] assembled at Barham at the time appointed in Major Edgar's advertisement of the 17ᵗʰ instant, marched from Parade to a field in the occupation of [blank] Major Edgar being confined by means of a sudden violent Cold attended with Fever, was unable to appear on Duty, consequently Captain Theobald commanded the Corps. Colonel Sharpe, Inspecting Field Officer arrived about 12 o'clock and inspected the Corps, who were Exercised in the usual Evolutions etc etc, and the Colonel was pleased to express himself highly gratified with the manner in which every part of same was gone through.

The Morning being wet indicated a very unpleasant day, about 10 o'clock it cleared up, and the remainder of the day was very fine and pleasant.

NB It was the first meeting of the four Troops since the Resignation of Captain Moore and appointment of Captain Ray (vice Moore).

Lord Euston's letter advising His Majesty had approved of the Nomination of Mr Dikes and Mr Whimper, was by order of Major Edgar read to the Corps by Captain Theobald.

---

[134] Another of the rare personal references made by Collett, and interesting because it is the only one in which he referred to his bank in Woodbridge.

[135] It is unclear why yeomanry cavalry should want to transfer to the local militia.

[136] When the four Troops that made up the Corps (the three Woodbridge ones and that of Babergh) met, they did so at Barham, north of Ipswich, which was more central for those from Babergh.

Tuesday November 1st 1808 General Muster

The three Troops met at the Parade Woodbridge and marched from thence to Kesgrave to a Field in the occupation of Mr Cotton. It being the 4th meeting as required by Act of Parliament, the Muster Rolls were called over by Major B239 Edgar for the purpose of ascertaining the respective number of times each member had attended as required by Act of Parliament. At same time, such Gentlemen as were absent on either of the meetings on the 13th, 20th and 27th of September, and this day the 1st of November, were required to attend on Tuesday next the 8th instant. After which, the Troops being formed in a Circle, Major Edgar read to them the clause in a late Act of Parliament respecting an offer of Services from the respective Troops of Volunteer Cavalry throughout the County for their being attached to the Local Militia, and at same time expressed his desire of receiving their answer regarding their own offer of Service by a show of hands. In reply, the Major was informed there was not an Individual who was inclined to make such offer, every one having objected to the proposition.

The sundry arrangements taking up a considerable deal of time and the Major not being quite recovered from his severe indisposition and being his first time of mounting his horse (except for the space of half an hour at each time), we did not go through any of the usual Evolutions practised on days of Muster. The Troops were dismissed about 2 oClock.

NB. A vacancy taking place in Captain Couperthwaite's Troop by the resignation of Lieutenant Robert Scholding of Falkenham, who is going to reside in a Farm in the County of Essex, Mr Robert Lankester proposed his friend Mr Lott Knights of Woodbridge for the choice of the Members of the Corps to supply the place of Lieutenant Scholding, and he was accordingly Elected a Member of the Corps, and directed to join Captain Couperthwaite's Troop.

Tuesday November 8th 1808 General Muster

Such Members of the Corps who had not attended the number of days of exercise required by Act of Parliament, assembled on Parade at Woodbridge in complyance with Major Edgar's Advertizement of the 20th October, and Marched from thence to Sutton and Exercised in a field in the occupation of Mr Thomas Brooks. The day was very fine and the Members present being formed into two Troops, were, by Major Edgar, exercised in the sundry Evolutions practised on days of Muster, which they performed in a manner highly creditable to themselves.

Mr David McCluer in consequence of not having in his present situation an opportunity of continuing the keep of a horse requested to give in his Resignation,[137] which being accepted by Major Edgar, Mr James Fenn of Hemingston was proposed to fill the vacancy and unanimously Elected, and accordingly desired to take the place of Mr McCluer in Captain Collett's Troop.

Such Gentlemen who, from unavoidable Circumstances had been prevented from attending on days of General Muster on 13th September to this day 8th November, the number of days required by Act of Parliament, were by Major Edgar desired to meet him at the times and places which he appointed for the purpose, in order that he may be enabled to make the return of these respective attendances by the time required in the Act of Parliament, at which time those Gentlemen pledged themselves to be present on the days appointed.

---

[137] The stabling and/or costs of keeping a horse were often given as reasons for resignation.

B240 Tuesday March 7th 1809 General Muster

The three Troops being assembled in complyance to the above order, marched from Parade to Martlesham Heath and exercised on the Ground upon the Heath which is occasionally made use of by the Royal Horse Artillery in the Evolutions usually practised on days of General Muster. An unfortunate Circumstance occurred by Mr William Salmon's receiving a violent kick on his Leg from the horse of Mr Nathaniel Bunn. Fortunately the leg was not broken, which it first was by himself thought and those near him considered was the case.

The Troops being formed in a Circle, after the Exercise of the day, Major Edgar gave notice to the Members present, that his having previous to this time for the purpose of accomodating such Gentlemen as did not attend the General Musters, appoint extra days in order that they might attend the number of days required by Act of Parliament, he should decline those meetings in future, having found by experience they were the means of preventing full Musters on days of general Exercise, consequently very prejudicial to the Corps, and particularly to the younger Members, that from this time it is expected every member will comply with the order, otherwise they would be returned ineffective, and thereby be deprived of the exemptions granted by the Act of Parliament; and further, that if anyone did not fully comply with the general orders so as to insure a full meeting on General Muster days, it was the wish of the Major that they would withdraw their Names from the Muster Roll.

Major Edgar reported that the Committee which was chosen for the purpose on the 29th March 1808 at a General Muster on that Day had yesterday investigated his Account Current as settled to that time, which had been procrastinated by means of the unsettled Accounts of Captain Moore late of the Babergh Troop, finding every part of same correct, his Book was settled accordingly, and that he had now the satisfaction to further state the increase of the fund to the present time which statement appeared as under viz

A Balance in Major Edgar's hands of £824 2s 4½ d

To be received from the Babergh Troop, being 1/3 of contingent expenses of the Corps, to be borne by that Troop   £75 18s 9d

Clothing Money for the present year and half a years contingent money to the 24th June next which have been applied for but payment not yet ordered £363

[Total] £1263 1s 1½ d

Major Edgar having been obligated to give his Bond for an Ordnance Debenture of £153 12s 4d it was the unanimous Resolution of the Corps that the amount of same should not be drawn out of his hands or deemed disposable until the Arms were returned to the Board of Ordnance and the Bond cancelled. Consequently the sum applicable to the service of the Corps after the Balance above stated is fully received will amount to £1109s 8s 9½ d

After receiving the above report it was the general wish of the Corps that new Clothing should be provided as soon as conveniently may be, and the Equipments etc put in a proper state of repair.[138] A committee for conducting the Business of same was immediately chosen consisting of the 13 commissioned Officers and twenty other members of the Corps elected from the Non-Commissioned Officers

---

[138] The Corps could now replace their old uniforms, which they could not do before because they were still paying off the money borrowed to cover the muddle over the forms in 1803.

and Privates, with full power to act therein as in their Judgement they should at the Committee Meetings think adviseable. The Committee for transacting Business to consist of not less than 16 Members of which Ten shall be Non-Commissioned Officers and Privates and if any difference of opinion arose in any matter before the Committee, the same should be decided by a Majority of those present at the time. The Committees for the dispatch of Business to be held at such time and place as the Members thereof shall hereafter appoint.

Names of the Committee:

Major Edgar, Captain Theobald, Captain Collett, Captain Couperthwaite, Captain Ray,

Lieutenant Pearson, Lieutenant Dikes, Lieutenant Errington, Lieutenant Waring, Lieutenant Todd vice Waring

Cornet Rodwell, Cornet Whimper, Cornet Brooke, Cornet Frost

Captain Theobald's Troop: Sergeant Major Sexton, Corporal Edwards, Benjamin Cook, William Cockrell, Thomas Bolton

Captain Collett's Troop: Sergeant Bates, Corporal Simpson, Corporal Keer, Thomas Catling, John Flatt

Captain Couperthwaite's Troop: Sergeant Major Hewitt, Sergeant Field, John Cook, Robert London, John Porter

Captain Ray's Troop: Quarter Master Cross, Corporal Stearns, Mr Stead, George Ruffell

The Commissioned Officers have no claim upon the Fund of the Corps they receiving no pay and equip themselves at their own individual expense.

The pay of the Troop received from Government not extending to such Gentlemen as became Members and joined the Corps subsequent to the 24th July 1806[139] they consequently have no claim upon the Fund. The same being submitted to the consideration of those Gentlemen who joined the Corps prior to that date they unanimously voted the sum of Four Guineas each should be paid by those Members so Circumstanced in aid of their expense for new Clothing etc etc etc.

Copy of Major Edgar's obligation for the return of Arms
Counterpart
This Indenture made the Third Day of March 1807, and in the Forty seventh Year of the Reign of our Sovereign Lord, George the Third, by the Grace of God, King of the United Kingdoms of Great Britain and Ireland, Defender of the Faith, and Between the Right Honourable Francis Earl of Moira, Master General of His Majesty's Ordnance and the principal Officer of the same, for and on the behalf of His said Majesty on the one part, and Major Mileson Edgar, Commanding the Woodbridge Troop of Suffolk Yeomanry on the other part, Witnesseth that the said Major Edgar doth acknowledge by those Present, by virtue of Boards order dated 17th of January 1806 to have had and received the value in lieu of the serviceable Arms and Habilaments of War, hereunder specified. For all which **B242** Arms and Habilaments of War the said Major Edgar doth hereby agree and undertake to be accountable, and to maintain and continue the very same Arms in good Repair, and to return and deliver the very same Arms so purchased into His Majesty's said Magazine, fixed and serviceable, when he shall be thereunto required by the Board of Ordnance (the

---

[139] This was one of the cuts imposed by Windham.

Hazard of the War only excepted). And that in case any of the said Arms be lost, by Negligence or by any other Default, that then the said Major Edgar shall and will buy so many good Arms out of His Majesty's Magazine as shall re-supply the Arms so lost, at the Rates usually paid by His Majesty for the like Arms.

Pistols	51	
Sabres and Scabbards	51	
Belts and Knots	122	
Bugles	2	Signed Richard Welbank

Tuesday March 14th 1809 General Muster

The Corps being assembled marched from Parade to Bromswell and exercised in two Troops in a field in the occupation of Mr Walton opposite the Cherry Tree Inn. The day was fine and dry, but rather cold.

Mr James Neeve being removed from Pettistree to Aldeburgh, and being now so far distant from Woodbridge, it became so very inconvenient to him to attend the Musters, he consequently wrote a very respectable Letter to Major Edgar, requesting him to accept his Resignation, the same being accepted Mr Robert Brook of Barham was appointed to supply the place of Mr Neeve.

Several respectable young Men having expressed to Major Edgar a desire of becoming Members of the Corps, in cases of vacancies or on augmentation of the Troops, he signified the same at this meeting, and that they might join the Corps in rotation conformable to their applications, he proposed their respective Names when the undermentioned were unanimously elected to fill such vacancies as should hereafter occur viz

1st	Mr Robert Brook	Barham	March 14th 1809	appointed to the vacancy occasioned by the resignation of Mr James Neewe
2nd	Mr Frederick Cobbold	Ipswich		who on the sudden Illness of his brother left Ipswich and reside at Manchester
3rd	Mr Philip Provart	Hasketon	March 21st	Succeeded Mr Postle Jackson
4th	Mr Philip Dikes Junior	Pettistree	March 21st	Succeeded by Mr Lott Knight
5th	Mr Nathaniel Barthrop Junior	Hacheston	March 21st	Succeeded by Mr John Button
6th	Mr Thomas Roberts	Kirton	June 12th	Succeeded by Mr George Bates
7th	Mr Joshua Thurston	Bramford	June 20th	Succeeded by Mr I Fryatt
8th	Mr Robert Firmin	Sproughton	June 20th	Succeeded by Mr Charles Collett

B243 Tuesday March 28th 1809 General Muster and Inspection

The Troops being assembled as usual, marched to Melton and were met by Colonel Sharpe, Inspecting Field Officer who in consideration of its being a rainy Morning, directed them to Halt there, when he called over the Muster Roll, inspected the

Men, Horses etc, and in consideration of the unfavourable weather, dispensed with the usual Exercise etc.

This being the last day of Muster of the Troops appointed by Major Edgar's advertizement February 26th, the Members present were by the Major requested to fix upon the next days of meeting conformable to Act of Parliament, when it was suggested by several Members that providing the two next days of Muster succeed each other, it would be more convenient, and a Motion was made by Quarter Master Hayles for that purpose and the same being seconded, the sense of the Troops was taken thereon by Show of Hands when it appeared the Majority was in favour of the Motion and Monday and Tuesday, the 1st and 2nd days of May next were fixed upon for the two next Meetings at Woodbridge at the usual time and place.

Major Edgar also informed the Gentlemen present, in consideration of their being soon to have new Clothing and the Equipments of every kind fully repaired and put into good condition, it was requisite to fix upon a day for inspection of arms, Equipments etc of every description, and for the greater conveniency, each Troop would assemble at a time and place most convenient to themselves; at each Meeting he proposed himself to attend and assist the Officers in making a full and minute inspection of each article of Equipment etc distinctly both of Man and Horse. The following days and place of assembly were accordingly fixed upon viz

Captain Theobald's Troop at Barham on Wednesday morning 5th April precisely at 11 oClock

Captain Collett's Troop at Wickham Market, Saturday 8th April precisely at 11 oClock

Captain Couperthwaite's Troop at Rushmere Heath Friday 7th April precisely at 11 oClock

After the above arrangements were agreed upon the Members composing the Committee for conducting the Business of New Clothing etc appointed their first Meeting to be held at the Golden Lion Ipswich on Thursday the 13th day of April next precisely at 11 oClock.

Mr John Button and Mr James Newson this day gave in their Resignations, no particular reasons assigned other than a plea of Inconvenience to their business etc. Mr James Newson appeared at Wickham Market on Saturday the 8th of April, being the Meeting for Inspection of Arms and Equipments, when he informed Major Edgar since the meeting on the 28th March when he gave in his notice for resignation, he had on reconsideration rescinded his former intentions and providing Major Edgar had no objections it was his wish to continue in the Troop, which offer being accepted by the Major, he is continued a member of the Corps.

The Committee met at the Bear and Crown Inn, Ipswich for the purpose of arranging the plan for New Clothing the Members of the Corps, directing the Repair of the sundry Equipments etc etc

---

B244 Tuesday June 20th 1809 General Muster

The Troops being assembled at the usual time and place marched from Parade to Bromeswell and exercised on the Hill opposite the Cherry Tree Inn, a piece of ground in the occupation of Mr Cook. Exercised in three Troops preparatory to the Inspection at Barham on Friday next when the Troops were requested to assemble precisely at 10 o'clock, in the forenoon. A vacancy having taken place by the resignation of Sergeant Bates, Corporal Hunt was unanimously elected Sergeant vice Bates, and Mr Robert Ablett, Corporal vice Hunt, and Mr Thomas Roberts appointed to fill the vacancy occasioned by the resignation of Mr Bates. Mr John

Morgan of Bramford being nominated by Captain Theobald and Mr William Spink of Eyke by myself to supply the next vacancies which may occur in the Troops, were unanimously Elected.

B245 Lieutenant Errington who is obliged to quit his residence at Westerfield at Michaelmas next, and remove to a distance out of the County, and Quarter Master Collett whose health will not permit of his due attention on days of general muster etc have consequently each of them sent in their Resignation and this day the following arrangements took place in Captain Couperthwaite's Troop, occasioned by the above resignations viz

> Cornet Brook elected Lieutenant,
> Quarter Master Hewitt elected Cornet,
> Sergeant Major Sawer elected Quarter Master,
> Sergeant Field elected Sergeant Major,
> Corporal Chapman elected Sergeant,
> Mr Richard Harris and Mr John Cook elected Corporals.

NB Lieutenant Errington continue in the Troop until Michaelmas (when he leave the County) his resignation was announced at this time for the purpose of nominating Officers on account of the new Cloathing of the Troop which will take place prior to Michaelmas, and the commissioned Officer who succeed Lieutenant Errington will have the opportunity of providing his proper Cloathing, as the same in future will materially differ from that of the Privates in the Corps.

Friday June 23rd 1809 General Muster and Inspection
The Troops met at Barham in complyance with Major Edgar's orders in his advertisement of the 9th instant, marched from Parade to a Field belonging to and in the occupation of Sir William Middleton, near to Shrubland Hall. Matters being arranged for the Inspection, about 12 oClock Lieutenant Colonel Sharpe appeared in the Field. After he had inspected the Line which was formed in three Troops, we were Exercised in all the various Evolutions practised on days of Inspection, of which he was pleased to say he was perfectly satisfied with every part of the Duty, very handsomely making allowance for the very great Number of Recruits which appeared on this day, a very great majority of whom had never before been in the field, particularly those of the Babergh Troop. The weather being very dry the day was hot and dusty and might very fairly be said to be fatigueing to Man and Horse. NB Orders were given to the Tailors to have the new Cloathing compleated in the Month of August by which time the Helmets and Horse Equipments were also directed to be repaired that everything may be compleat against the General Inspection, which we were given to understand by Colonel Sharpe would take place in September next.

B246 Proceedings of the Committee for the Affairs of clothing etc
At a Meeting of the Committee appointed by the Second Corps of Loyal Suffolk Yeomanry Cavalry to take into Consideration the proper measures for Cloathing and providing such accoutrements for the Corps as shall be found proper and necessary, holden at the Golden Lion Inn, in Ipswich, on Thursday the 13th April 1809.
Present Major Edgar, Captains Theobald, Collett, Couperthwaite and Ray, Lieutenants Pearson and Todd, Cornets Rodwell, Brook and Whimper. Sergeant Major Hewett, Quarter Master Cross, Sergeant Major Sexton, Sergeants Field and Coaker for Cornet Frost, Corporals Keer, Simpson and Stearns, Privates John Cook, William Cockrell, Robert London, John Cook, John Porter, [blank] Stead, George Ruffle

It appears to this Committee that the Balance in Major Edgars hands amounts to £1209 16s 9½d and that there is a Balance in the Paymaster's hands, due to the Corps, amounting to £35 3s 4d.

It is resolved:

1st That the Corps shall be new cloathed

2nd That it does not appear that new Helmets are generally necessary, and that such as want it shall be repaired, and when absolutely requisite, new ones provided, and that the additional ornament of the Crown shall be added

3rd That Regulation Feathers be provided for the whole Corps

4th That the Colour of the new Jackets shall be dark blue, the facings yellow

5th That the new Jackets shall be made according to the Regulations of the 10th Regiment of Light Dragoons, except as to the quality of the Cloth and Cord

6th That the buttons shall be round, quite plain and white ones

7th That the Corps shall provide the Cloth for the Jackets and that such shall be Yorkshire Broad Cloth

8th That an advertizement shall be inserted in the Ipswich Journal and Bury Papers for proposals for Yorkshire Broad Cloth blue of best quality, patterns to be sent to the Bear and Crown Inn Ipswich before Tuesday 27th April instant

9th That several Members of the Corps having been in the use of wearing Hessian and other boots, different from those originally worn, it is requested the Major will take proper measures to have uniformity in this respect restored, by the use of the round top boots, and further, that the spurs are to be the regimental steel spurs with the Horizontal rowell.

10th That this meeting be adjourned to Thursday the 27th of April instant to be then holden at the Bear and Crown at Ipswich, at 11 o'clock in the forenoon.

11th That the Major sign these Resolutions in the name of the Committee

(Signed) Mileson Edgar

B247 At an adjourned Meeting of the Committee holden at the sign of the Bear and Crown in Ipswich on **Thursday the 27th day of April 1809**

Present

Major Edgar, Captain Theobald, Captain Collett, Lieutenant Pearson, Lieutenant Errington and Lieutenant Todd, Cornet Rodwell, Cornet Whimper, Cornet Brook, Cornet Frost, Quarter Master Cross, Sergeant Major Hewett, Sergeant Major Sexton, Corporal Edwards, Robert London, privates John Cook, John Stearn, William Cockrell, George Ruffell

Resolved

That the price of the Cloth for Clothing the Non-Commissioned Officers and Privates shall not exceed Thirty Shillings a Yard.

That the Cloth for the first three Troops be taken of William Elliston of Ipswich, agreeable to the pattern produced, at thirty shillings a yard, and that the fourth Troop shall procure Cloth at such place as they may think proper, but it is to be according to the pattern both as to quality and colour.

That Silver Lace shall be used upon the Jackett according to the Pattern now produced by Captain Collett at the price of 2s 6d a yard.

That the Jacket shall button into button holes and not into loops as in the pattern Jacket now produced, and the Sheliton lace to be stitched down on the Jacket, the back to be like the 10th Jacket except that where the Prince's feather is, it shall finish as the Old Jackets.

There are to be three rows of Buttons in front to the pattern produced by Captain Collett No 3010 on the card and 3007 the smaller size, the Centre row of Buttons being of the larger size.

That the linings of the new Jackets shall be the same as those of the Old ones.

There are to be fifteen buttons in a row on the Jackets.

That the Jackets for the Trumpeter shall be precisely like the one produced from the 10th Regiment.[140]

That there are to be 134 Jackets for the first three Troops and to be made by the following Persons Mr Elliston, Mr How, Mr Ringrose of Ipswich, and Mr Gross Woodbridge in equal numbers and that the price of making shall be left to the Major.

That the repairs necessary to the Helmets, and the providing new ones, where new ones appear to be necessary, shall be left to the opinion of the Major.

That the Babergh (4th)[141] Troop on being released from the engagement entered into in the year 1805 for defraying a third part of the contingent expenses of the Corps now agree to bear a fourth part of such contingent expenses, so far as they extend to Farriers pay, and expenses of his horse, Agency, Postage of Letters and carriage of parcels.[142]

That the Major sign these resolutions in the name of the Committee (Signed) Mileson Edgar

---

B249 Tuesday October 24ᵗʰ 1809 The three Troops assembled at the time appointed in the above advertizement, marched from the parade to a Field in the Occupation of Mr Pizzey opposite to Farlingay Hall and Exercised in Three Troops in the usual Evolutions practised on days of General Muster.

The day was particularly fine which proved a pleasant Circumstance, it being the first appearance of the Troops in their new Uniform which from scarlet was now exchanged for Blue, and which in appearance etc is considered to be very neat and handsome. A proper distinction is now made in the dress of the respective Officers and Privates, which in the old uniform was not the Case. The former dress was scarlet cloth and Silver Lace Trimmings with light Blue Facings (see Plate III). The present (or new Dress) is Super fine dark Blue Cloth, Yellow facings, and Silver lace to the pattern of the 10th Light Dragoons or Prince of Wales' Regiment.

Major Edgar gave notice of Sundry Resignations in consequence of several of the Members of the Corps leaving their residence at Michaelmas and being removed at too great a distance to attend the future Musters of the Corps etc etc etc.[143]

Many inconveniences, delays and trouble having been occasioned in consequence of the notice of any person wishing to join the Corps being to be sent to Major Edgar for his approbation (from either of the Captains) previous to their admission the Major this day proposed that from this time the respective Captains of Troops should be impowered to admit new Members on the occasion of a vacancy in their Troops care being taken to chose such persons as are respectable and in no respect obnoxious to

---

[140] The Yeomanry Cavalry have often been criticised for their elaborate uniforms but many were merely copying those of the regular army light dragoons. The Corps obviously took great interest in the details of the uniform.

[141] The Babergh Troop was the 4th Troop of the 2nd Woodbridge Corps.

[142] It is interesting to note what made up their expenses.

[143] Michaelmas (29 September) was one of the four quarter days, when rents were due and leases renewed. The number of resignations reflect the increasing uncertainty of agricultural profits and general economic difficulties.

the present Members (or those of the time being). The same being signified to the Members present and proposed, it was their unanimous opinion it should be adopted and by a unanimous vote it was directed that the respective Captains do in future fill up the vacancies which may occur in their Troops signifying the same to Major Edgar to whom the Members so appointed must apply for his signing the Muster Roll and for his taking the Oath of Allegiance etc as required by Act of Parliament.

Conduct of the Trumpeters

On its being determined the Corps should be new Cloathed, a Committee chosen from Members of the respective Troops was appointed for conducting the same and all matters relating thereto was to be decided by them without any interference from other Members **B250** and as the Cloathing of the Corps had been determined upon to be like that of the 10th Light Dragoons, the Committee directed the Trumpeters dresses should be like those of that Regiment and Major Edgar accordingly procured by application to the Colonel three Jackets made by the Regimental Tailor, the Cloth White, light Blue facings and yellow trimmings and which on being received were considered to be very good neat and handsome, and much approved by every member of the Corps who saw them, except the Trumpeters themselves, who, in consequence of their not being trimmed with Silver Lace expressed their disapprobation in terms not very respectful to the Officers and the Committee and a seeming determination to withdraw their services unless an alteration was made in them. Major Edgar, in consequence of their Conduct, at the head of the Corps, called upon them to explain themselves, he not having expected to hear of such behaviour. In reply, they had only to say they considered they ought to have had Silver Braid as well as the Privates of the Corps, and on being questioned respecting the quality of the Cloath (one complaint), they made no reply, of which they certainly could have no reason to complain, and in reply to their being no Silver Cord on the Jackets they were reminded, that in consequence of their receiving Pay at the rate of nine Guineas a Man per Annum[144] out of the Fund of the Corps and every expense of their Equipments paid for from same, they were the Servants of the Corps, and consequently could have no possible reason for Complaint, their Cloathing being in every respect equal to the Princes Regiment. On being further questioned they had not a word to say in defence of their conduct. Major Edgar then informed them, himself as well as the Corps (whose opinion was taken thereon) considered their Conduct very Reprehensible and very unbecoming their situations as Trumpeters of the Corps; that no alteration whatever would be made in the Jackets. He then requested them to withdraw and to reconsider the matter, and provided they Receded their former opinion no further notice would be taken of what had passed, but if otherwise, they must send in their Equipments, and as a proof of the disapprobation of their Conduct, both by himself, the respective Officers, and the Corps, he should strike their names from off the Muster Roll. Being again called upon at the close of the Business of the day, they gave for answer, they had not, (or should), alter their sentiments, and their names were accordingly erased from the Muster Roll, viz Spencer Leek, Thomas Symonds and Spencer Leek Junior.[145] In consequence of the discharge of the Trumpeters a short time after, Mr John Ashfield and Mr John Fox of Coddenham, belonging to Captain Theobald's Troop offered their Services to Major Edgar, and being accepted, the respective Equip-

---

[144] From 1794 trumpeters, replacing the corporal allowed by the government, had been paid.
[145] This would seem to be very unreasonable behaviour given that their duties were far from onerous.

ments, Cloathing etc etc was delivered to them, and being appointed Trumpeters, are to receive Pay to the same amount as was paid to Leek and Symonds, viz: Nine Guineas each per Annum.

The two next meetings of the Corps for Exercise it was agreed upon should be on Monday and Tuesday the 26th and 27th of February 1810

B251 Major Edgar gave notice that Cornet Brooke, who had agreed to accept the promotion to a Lieutenant in the place of Lieutenant Errington who resigned in consequence of leaving the County, had signified to him by Letter his intention of resigning, in consideration he said of his situation being so very far distant from the Fields of Exercise and Head Quarters (18 or 20 miles), and the very great inconvenience in his Business by reason of his absence etc etc of which he considered it most prudent to give Notice at this time to avoid the extra Expense of New Clothing and Horse Equipments which altogether would not be less than from Thirty to Forty Pounds, the Officers equipping themselves at their own expense.[146]

In expectation that Mr Brooke would resign it was necessary to make an arrangement to supply the vacancies etc etc and the Gentlemen as under Members of Captain Couperthwaite's Troop were proposed for same, which proposition being approved by the Members of the Troop (each of which elect their Officers) they were nominated and chosen accordingly viz Cornet Hewett vice Brooke Lieutenant, Quarter Master Field Cornet, and Sergeant Major Sawer Quarter Master. Soon after the above time Lieutenant Brooke sent in his Resignation to Major Edgar, who recommended Mr Hewett and Mr Field to the Lord Lieutenant of the County in order to obtain their Commissions and entered the arrangements as above stated on the Muster Roll of Captain Couperthwaite's Troop.

Friday October 27th 1809 General Muster and Inspection

The Four Troops met at Barham at the time appointed and marched into a field in the occupation of Cornet Rodwell and were inspected by Lieutenant Colonel Sharpe. The day proved very fine and everything was conducted to the satisfaction of the Colonel who was also pleased to express his approbation of the new cloathing. He considered it military, neat and handsome.

Ipswich Journal February 17th 1810 Second Corps of Suffolk Yeomanry Cavalry. The Members of Captain Theobald's, Captain Collett's and Captain Couperthwaite's Troops are requested to assemble at Woodbridge in Field Day Order, on Monday & Tuesday the 26th and 27th instant, and on Monday and Tuesday the 5th and 6th of next month precisely at eleven o'clock.

The weather proving unfavourable, by reason of a severe frost, the meeting intended at the time above stated was postponed and the following advertisement in the Ipswich Journal:

Second Corps Suffolk Yeomanry Cavalry

In consequence of the change in the weather since last week's advertisement, the Corps will not assemble for exercise on the 26th and 27th instant, nor until notice thereof shall be given in the Ipswich paper.[147]

Red House February 22nd   M Edgar Major

---

[146] It is interesting to note the total cost of their uniform and equipment.

[147] This illustrates the problem of communicating quickly with such a sizeable number of members who might have to travel some considerable distance: the local newspaper was the most effective way of overcoming it.

Monday March 5th 1810

The Troops assembled at Woodbridge as ordered by the above advertisement.[148] In the course of the night and early in the morning there was very heavy showers of Rain and the morning was very unpleasant with a prospect of a very dirty day. About 12 oClock the Troops assembled on the Market Hill, marched from there and formed the line on the Turnpike road in Hasketon, and after calling over the Muster Rolls, were dismissed in consequence of the unfavourable weather and not being able to get a field for exercise nearer to Woodbridge than Bromeswell or Sutton. Major Edgar did not attend having been confined to his house for nearly three months with the gout etc, etc, and by reason of the unfavourable weather was fearful of taking cold.

Tuesday March 6th 1810

The day was most unfavourable for the meeting. It rained considerably in the early part of the Morning and about 8 oClock it began to snow and continued to snow very hard until nearly 12 oClock; Captain Theobald was at my house, and with Captain Couperthwaite and myself went into the Market Hall where we met about forty or fifty of the Gentlemen of the Corps, when we called over the respective Muster Rolls. But from the excessive bad state of the weather was prevented going into the Field for the purpose of exercise.[149]

B254 Copy of an Advertizement inserted in the Ipswich Journal March 10th 1810

Suffolk Yeomanry Cavalry and Volunteer Infantry

The Lord Lieutenant desires the Commandants of each Corps of Yeomanry Cavalry, and of such of the following Corps of Volunteer Infantry as have not already done so, forthwith to transmit to the Office of Mr Case, Clerk of the General Meetings of Lieutenancy at Bury St Edmunds, a correct return of the Number of Officers, Sergeants and Rank and File which belonged to their respective Corps, and were inspected or ready to be inspected on or about the first of last December.

Yeomanry Cavalry
First or Blything Troop
Second or Woodbridge Corps
Third or Hoxne Troop
Fourth or Bury Corps
Fifth or Beccles Troop
Seventh or Heveningham Troop
Eighth or Southelmham Troop[150]

Volunteer Infantry:
Bury, Bosmere and Claydon, Benacre and Wrentham, Bungay, Blackbourn Hundred, Dunwich, Eye, Framlingham, Hadleigh, Helmingham, Hartismere Rangers, Ipswich,

---

[148] Omitted.

[149] B253, copy of the muster rolls as arranged by Major Edgar, 7 February 1810. Omitted. The names of Captain Couperthwaite's Troop are missing.

[150] The 6th or Hadleigh Troop is missing from the list, probably a lapse on Collett's part. The old 7th Babergh Troop had been incorporated into the 2nd Corps, and the South Elmham and Heveningham Troops moved up to the 7th and 8th Troops of the Suffolk Yeomanry Cavalry.

Lowestoft, Lakenheath, Southwold, Stoke by Nayland, Sibton and Peasenhall, Saxmundham, Tunstal and Iken, Woodbridge, Yoxford and Darsham[151]
Brook Street March 5th 1810   (Signed) Euston

B255 Tuesday April 3rd 1810

The Troops met at the time appointed in the above Advertizement,[152] but in consequence of its raining all the forenoon, they could not go into the Field for Exercise, and Major Edgar being absent under confinement with the Gout, about 12 oClock, Captain Theobald marched the Troops present to Melton where he was met by Colonel Sharpe who inspected Horses and Equipments etc but in consideration of the badness of the weather he declined their attendance in the Field for Exercise. I was not present myself, being at the time in London.

Tuesday May 8th 1810

The first part of the Morning was very wet and unfavourable after 9 oClock it cleared up and was a very fine day. Captain Theobald was on parade but too unwell to join the Troops. About 12 oClock I ordered them to March to a field in Woodbridge in the occupation of Mr Thomas Frost, where being met by Major Edgar we exercised in two Troops in the usual Evolutions etc etc.

It being represented by many of the Members that our Meetings on the Monday and the following day was by experience found to be very inconvenient, and expensive to such Members who resided at a considerable distance from Woodbridge, it was proposed to alter the days of meeting and from this time to fix them for Tuesday and Friday in the same week, and on the sentiments of the Members present being taken by a show of hands, a very great Majority was in favor of the alteration and the same was decided accordingly.[153] Major Edgar, considering it needful there should be a general inspection of Arms, Equipments etc directed the same should take place at the time and places as follows viz

Captain Theobald's Troop 18th May 12 oClock at Barham,
Captain Collett's 21st May 12 oClock Wickham Market,
Captain Couperthwaite's 28th May 11 oClock at Rushmere

B256 Monday May 14th 1810

The Troops being assembled marched from Parade to a Field in Woodbridge in the occupation of Mr Thomas Frost where I was met by Major Edgar. (Captains Theobald and Couperthwaite being indisposed were not present).

The day was excessive Cold and the wind was very high and it being a plowed Field and very dusty, there was only a small degree of Exercise, being found impracticable by reason of the dust and excessive cold wind.

Particular instructions were given by the Major that each Member attended on the days directed for Inspection of arms Equipments etc, etc.

Copy of an Advertizement in the Ipswich Journal June 2nd 1810

The whole Corps will assemble at Babergh Heath in Field Day Order, on Monday June 4th at eleven oClock, by order of M Edgar, Major.

---

[151] Comparision with Collett's 1803 list clearly illustrates the huge decline in numbers of volunteer infantry troops.
[152] Omitted.
[153] This is another illustration of the problem of having a membership drawn from such a wide radius.

Dinner at the Rose and Crown Inn, Sudbury, at Three oClock. Tickets to be had at the Bar at 10s 6d each.[154]

Monday June 4th 1810

In complyance with the above order, the Corps met at Baburgh Heath at the time appointed but being so great a distance from Woodbridge very few of the Members of Captain Collett's Troop attended. We marched from Baburgh Heath to Acton Park[155] and Exercised in the usual Evolutions practised on days of General Muster; fired three vollies in honour of His Majesty's Birthday. The Spectators were many and very respectable and expressed great satisfaction at seeing the Corps assembled together, it being our first time of meeting the Baburgh Troop in that part of the Country. The day was very fine but being a particular dry season, the Roads etc. were most uncomfortably dusty. The place of exercise was a most beautiful situation and charming ground. From same is a very extensive view of the Country including Long Melford and the neighbourhood for many miles round the same. From the Field of exercise we marched to Sudbury. On our way there, we passed through Long Melford arrived at Sudbury about half past three oClock, Our approach being announced to the Mayor etc etc. we were directed to assemble on the Market Place and requested to fire three rounds (or vollies) in honour of the day which was very well conducted and the firing was truly creditable to the Corps, after which the spectators who were very numerous, joined in three Cheers. The duty of the day being over we all met together and dined at the Rose and Crown Inn, a very handsome dinner being provided on the occasion by Mr Frost, the Landlord, who is a Member of Captain Todd's Troop.

Mr Oliver (the Mayor of Sudbury) with Mr Strutt and some other Gentlemen of the Town dined with us (the party being about 112 in number) Major Edgar in the Chair. B257 Everything was conducted with great regularity and order much to the pleasure and satisfaction of all present and without the least interruption to the Jollity of the day.

Tuesday June 5th 1810

The Members of the Corps who attended yesterday, this morning by order of Major Edgar assembled at Babergh Heath and exercised in the usual Evolutions in two Troops, and after being dismissed returned to our respective homes.[156]

Friday October 19th 1810 Inspection by Colonel Sharpe

The Troops marched from parade (Market Hill Woodbridge) about Eleven oClock (the Morning being wet, did not muster so soon by an hour as was intended). The weather after eleven oClock was very fine and pleasant. We marched into a Field in the occupation of Mr James Smith, Colonel Sharpe attended about 12 oClock and inspected the Troops who were Exercised by Major Edgar in such Evolutions as Colonel Sharpe directed, who expressed his satisfaction and approbation in most respectful Terms. Robert Welton of Pettistree was unanimously elected a Member of the Corps.

---

[154] This was the first meeting of the 2nd Corps at Sudbury to celebrate the King's birthday.

[155] The park was part of the estate of Acton Place built by the Jennens family, the last of whom died intestate in 1798 and long litigation followed. See W. M. Roberts, *Lost Country Houses of Suffolk* (Woodbridge, 2010), pp. 12–15.

[156] Members obviously must have had to stay overnight.

Death of Cornet Whimper

On Saturday November 10th 1810 it blowed a most tremendous Gale of Wind until about two or three o'Clock after noon and during the Gale many ships went on shore upon this Coast in the evening. Mr Thurston Whimper and another Gentleman who was an Officer of Artillery, and at the time on duty at the Works building at Bawdsey etc[157] rode to the Beach for the purpose of rendering any assistance in their power to the unfortunate persons who had suffered Shipwreck and to protect the wreck or Goods which came on shore, and being too much engaged **B258** by the humane object they had in view, they remained on the shore till the tide, which was unusually high, came in, and beating over the beach in a tremendous manner, and in some places making breaches in it, impeded their retreat. The Officer, by the strength and spirit of his horse, escaped, though very narrowly, with his life. But Mr Whimper's horse which was only a pony was not able to make its way against the Tide, in crossing which it fell down. On recovering from the fall he again mounted the pony, in pursuing his endeavours to cross the tide which was then running out very strong the pony again fell down and Mr Whimper falling off, it got away from him and making its way towards the marshes, was secured by some persons who were upon the inner wall. Mr Whimper then endeavoured to walk to those persons and got within a short distance from them and requested their assistance. There being a wide marsh ditch between him and the men they could not assist him but requested of him to remain steadfast in his then situation, the tide being falling, probably the water would soon be so far reduced that he might remain there in safety until such time as they could provide means for taking him off, but unfortunately, from appearances, he was too much exhausted to support himself (being at the time up to his armpits in water) and moving forward, its considered he stepped into a place where the earth had been dug out for the purpose of raising the inner wall[158] and immediately disappeared and thus fell a sacrifice, in the prime of life, and full enjoyment of health, to the benevolent design of affording aid to his fellow creatures, suffering under the afflicting circumstances of shipwreck. His body was found next morning. He has left a young widow to bewail his untimely fate, and irreparable loss, with two infant daughters (unfortunately he could not swim, otherwise in all probability, his life would have been preserved). He joined the Corps on its original institution in July 1794. He was a young man very much respected by all his acquaintances etc

Friday March 8th 1811

The three Troops assembled on Parade on Market Hill, Woodbridge, and marched from thence to Kesgrave into a Field in the occupation of Mr Weeding. After calling the Muster Roll, in consequence of the death of Cornet Whimper, Major Edgar ordered the 2nd Troop (Captain Collett's) to **B258** withdraw and elect a Member of the Troop to supply the vacancy of Cornet occasioned by the death of Cornet Whimper, and to fill up the vacancies occasioned by promotion and a Corporal in place of Corporal Ablitt who has quitted the Troop (having taken a Farming Business in the County of Essex). The following arrangements were accordingly reported to Major

---

[157] The construction of the line of Martello Towers along this section of the east coast had been underway for some time by this date.

[158] This may have taken place as part of the defence works to protect this stretch of the Hollesley Bay coastline from French invasion.

Edgar: Quarter Master Hayle to be Cornet vice Whimper deceased; Sergeant Major Gross Quarter Master; Sergeant Kemp Sergeant Major; Corporal Simpson Sergeant; Thomas Catling and Jonathan Thredkell Corporals. The reports being made of the nominations and choice by Captain Collett to Major Edgar and meeting with his entire approbation, he said he should report the choice of Cornet Hayle to the Lord Lieutenant of the County for his approbation and appointment for obtaining the Commission, at same time confirmed the appointment of the Non-Commissioned Officers.

Just at the time of reporting the choice of Officers it began to rain and continued untill such time as we were obliged to quit the Field without any further duty. The remainder of the day was nearly a continual Rain.

Mr William Damant of Hacheston and Mr John Kirby of Pettistree were this day reported by Major Edgar as being by himself appointed Members of the Corps and having signed the Muster Roll were directed to join Captain Collett's Troop also Mr William Studd of Woodbridge who was appointed to Captain Couperthwaite's Troop.

Friday March 15th 1811

The three Troops assembled at the time and place directed in the advertizement above,[159] marched from thence to Kesgrave and exercised in a Field in the occupation of Mr William Weeding. The day was particularly fine and pleasant.

We exercised in two Troops and were inspected by [blank] German Legion (an experienced old Officer) who was pleased to express himself much pleased with the manner in which the Troops went through the various Evolutions etc.

Tuesday May 28th 1811 The Troops assembled and Marched from Parade at 12 oClock the morning being wet prevented an earlier attendance. About half past eleven it cleared up and the remainder of the day was very fine and pleasant. We marched to Bromswell and exercised in a Field in the occupation of Mr John Wolton. The Muster being well attended the exercise was altogether performed with great precision and credit to the Corps; also the firing, being in practice for the 4th of June.

Tuesday June 4th 1811 His Majesty's Birthday

The four Troops of Major Edgar's Corps, viz Captain Theobalds, Colletts, Couperthwaites and Todds (or Baburgh Troop), assembled at Ipswich at the time appointed in the Advertizement above, the proceedings of the day are copied as under from the Ipswich Journal of the 8th June 1811.

His Majesty's Birthday was observed here on Tuesday last by ringing of **B261** Bells and other demonstrations of joy. At noon the Corporation went to St Lawrence church where a sermon was preached by the Reverend Mr Howarth, from the 2nd chapter 26 Chronicles verse 11.

About 11 o'Clock the 2nd Corps Loyal Suffolk Yeomanry Cavalry (4 Troops), commanded by Major Edgar, and the Loyal Ipswich Volunteers, commanded by Lieutenant Colonel Jackaman, mustered on the Cornhill, and shortly afterwards marched for Rushmere Heath where they joined the Troops from the Garrisons of this town and Woodbridge. At 12 o'clock the whole formed into line; two Troops of

---

[159] Omitted.

Royal Horse Artillery and the 3rd German Huzzars (10 Troops) were on the right; the South Lincoln and Hertford Militias, Loyal Ipswich Volunteers, Berwick and Dumfries Regiments of Militia formed the centre; two Troops of the Royal Horse Artillery and the 2nd Suffolk Yeomanry were on the left. The Foot Artillery with their Field Pieces, were stationed about 100 yards in front of the infantry where they fired a Royal Salute, which was followed by three vollies from each Regiment of infantry.

The whole then presented arms, the bands playing God Save the King. The line afterwards wheeled into column, and passed the Commanding Officer (Colonel Fowle) in Review Order. All the troops then marched off the heath, except Major Edgar's Cavalry who had a Field day. They made a fine appearance and performed all the manoeuvres of a light horse Regiment with great exactness. The Corporation with a large party of Gentlemen, dined at the Bear and Crown, at the Great White Horse an elegant dinner was provided for the Yeomanry Cavalry; 157 of whom were present, and the Volunteers dined at different Inns.

Tuesday October 22nd 1811

The three troops being assembled at the time appointed in the Advertizement[160] marched from Parade to a Field belonging to myself in Woodbridge, and exercised under command of Major Edgar in the usual Evolutions, preparatory to their being inspected by Lieutenant Colonel Sharpe on Friday next.

George Loft, in consequence of Bodily infirmity, was necessitated to decline riding on horseback, and consequently this day sent in his resignation, which was signified to the Members present by Major Edgar.

Mr Charles Ablett of Alderton being proposed a Member of the Corps by Mr Thomas Miller, was nominated by Major Edgar and unanimously elected and ordered to attend on Friday next, and attached to my troop. The day was fine. No particular occurrence.

Was not on duty myself having a violent attack of Rheumatism in my Arm and Shoulder which rendered me incapable of directing my horse, having no use of the Arm etc.

[161]

B274 Friday October 25th 1811

The Corps 3 Troops being at the time and place appointed marched from parade under the command of Major Edgar was inspected by Lieutenant Colonel Sharpe, but from being late in the Field and Colonel Sharpe being much engaged were not long under his inspection. He expressed a desire that in the future earlier attendance would be given on days of inspection otherwise he should be much disappointed, punctuality in attendance being highly requisite, those Gentlemen who in future were not strictly punctual would be by him considered absentees. The day was fine. No particular occurrence. I was myself absent in consequence of a continued indisposition from Rheumatism, not having the use of my arm.[162]

---

[160] Omitted.

[161] B262–B273, muster rolls of the 2nd Troop commanded by Captain Collett from 1811 to 1816 in Major, later Lieutenant Colonel, Edgar's Woodbridge Corps. This might indicate that Collett was writing this part in 1816. See Plate 7 for a typical page of a muster roll. The other pages have been omitted.

[162] Although Collett rarely mentioned his health, his sufferings were unsurprising since he was sixty-four at this date. Mileson Edgar, who suffered from gout, was often forced to miss musters.

Tuesday March 24th 1812

The Troops met at the usual time and place. The weather was very unfavourable, it having rained all Night and Morning until 12 o'Clock, when the storm ceasing, we assembled on the Market Hill, marched from thence a short distance from the town and called over the Muster Rolls. The land being so very wet, we could not Exercise, and fresh storms of rain etc appearing, Major Edgar and Captain Theobald being absent, I discharged the Troops present, hoping to have more favourable weather on Thursday.

B275 Thursday March 26th 1812

The Troops assembled at the usual time and place, the day being very fine. They marched into a Field in Woodbridge in the occupation of Mr James Hayward and exercised in the usual Evolutions practised on days of General Muster. No particular occurrence. Sundry new Members having recently been elected, the Corps three Troops are now compleat.

Lieutenant Colonel Sharpe, our late Inspecting Field Officer, having been promoted to the Rank of General, addressed a Letter to Major Edgar expressive of his very high opinion of the Corps for their uniform attention and military discipline etc etc in which he was pleased to bestow great encomiums, and wishing health and happiness to each member thereof.

Lieutenant Colonel McLeroth is now appointed Inspecting Field Officer of the Eastern District.

Tuesday April 7th 1812 Inspection by Lieutenant Colonel McLeroth

The three Troops being assembled as order, per Advertisement 14th March, marched from Parade to a Field in Woodbridge in the occupation of Mr James Hayward. Soon after the Troops were formed etc Lieutenant Colonel McLeroth, Inspecting Field Officer (successor to Lieutenant Colonel Sharpe) appeared in the Field, and was received by the Troops in the usual form, and passing the Line, having minutely inspected the Horses, Arms, Equipments etc etc after which the Troops exercised in his presence in the sundry Evolutions, commanded by Major Edgar. Everything being gone through, Lieutenant Colonel McLeroth was pleased to express his approbation in very high terms of the exactness which every Evolution was performed, and declared, that although he had heard Colonel Sharpe speak of the Corps in very high terms they certainly very far exceeded his expectation or of whatever he had before seen of Volunteer Troops. The day was fortunately very fine.

Tuesday 19th May 1812

The Troops being assembled at the time requested, marched from Parade to Kesgrave and Exercised in a Field in the occupation of Mr William Wheeding. After the exercise was over, Major Edgar proposed that the Members of Captain Theobald's, Collett's and Couperthwaite's Troops should on the 4th of June, meet the 4th or Captain Todd's Troop at Baburgh Heath and after Exercising there march to Sudbury and dine together it being His Majesty's Birthday, to which proposal the majority of Members present acceeded but many of Captain Collett's Troop in consideration of the very great distance declined the invitation. The majority being in favour of a meeting, the same was by Major Edgar ordered accordingly.

B276 Thursday June 4th 1812

The Corps assembled at Baburgh heath between Eleven and Twelve oClock, and being formed in three Troops Exercised in the usual Evolutions, Firing etc. After the exercise of the day was over we marched through Long Melford to Sudbury, formed on the Market Place and fired three vollies in honour of His Majesty's Birth Day, after which a dinner being provided for us by Mr [blank] of the [blank] Inn (he being a Member of the Corps), we dined together in a large building fitted up for our reception and accommodation.

The Mayor of the Corporation, [Mr] Strutt Esq with several other respectable Gentlemen, of the Town dined with us and a Band of Music attended (being previously placed on a gallery erected for their reception) a very good dinner was provided with a full supply of wine etc. After dinner the King's health was first drunk, then the Prince Regent and others of the Royal Family, then followed a number of Constitutional Toasts, accompanied by many good songs. The meeting was altogether well conducted and terminated exceedingly pleasant to all present, and the day was very fine. All the company retired about 10 oClock. (120 Members of the Corps present)

Friday June 5th 1812

The Members of the Corps who attended yesterday, assembled this morning at Sudbury at 10 oClock, and marched from thence to Baburgh Heath, and after exercising about one hour, where dismissed and each returned to their respective homes. This day was also very fine.

Copy of an Advertizement in the Ipswich Journal July 18th 1812

2nd Corps Suffolk Yeomanry Cavalry

Those Members of Captain Theobald's, Captain Collett's and Captain Couperthwaite's Troops who did not attend the muster of the Corps on the 4th and 5th of June at Sudbury, are requested to assemble at Woodbridge on Monday the 20th and Monday the 27th instant at 11 oClock precisely, in Field Day Order.

M Edgar, Major

Having myself attended at Sudbury, and also the other commissioned Officers of my Troop, we were none of us present on either of these days. By Major Edgar's report, the respective Members who were at that time absent, made good their attendance by being present on these days.

Friday October 16th 1812

The Troops being assembled, marched from Parade to [blank] and exercised in a Field in the occupation of [blank].

The day was very fine. No particular occurrence. Was not myself present in the Field in consequence of my horse being lame from a wound he received in his foreleg in a way I cannot account for.

B277 Tuesday October 20th 1812

The Troops being assembled at the usual time and place, marched to a Field in the occupation of Mr Frost in Martlesham, and exercised in the usual Evolutions. No particular occurence. The day was very fine excepting a shower of rain just at the time we quitted the Field. The wind blowing a strong gale, it did not rain long, only about 10 minutes. The exercise was performed with great exactness.

Tuesday October 27ᵗʰ 1812

The three Troops being assembled, marched from Parade about a quarter past Eleven oClock to a Field in Martlesham near the Barrack Ground in Woodbridge, in the occupation of Mr Frost. About 12 oClock, Lieutenant Colonel McLeroth made his appearance being the day he had appointed for inspecting the Corps and was received in the accustomed form as usual upon such occasions. Having passed the line and inspected the same, he took his Station, when the Troop were exercised in the accustomed evolutions, Commanded by Major Edgar. The same being finished, the Colonel addressed the Corps, expressive of his great satisfaction of their appearance and of the soldierlike manner in which every part of the Exercise was performed. He expressed himself most highly gratified and declared he should make his return accordingly.

The day was very fine until about two oClock just after we were dismissed when it began to Rain and continued the remainder of the day. After 6 oClock and during the whole of the night it blowed a most tremendous Gale and a very great deal of damage was done to the Shipping etc etc. Very many ships were lost upon the various coasts etc of the Kingdom.

On examining and calling over the Muster Roll by Major Edgar Mr Richard Rope it appeared had not attended since 3ʳᵈ April last, and that his report of illness was fictitious, the same being occasioned by Inebriety – in short he was become a common drunkard. He was consequently adjudged a very unfit person to continue in the Corps, and his name was struck off the Muster Roll.

Robert Roper, whose attendance had been very irregular, and his excesses not admissible, and being spoken to on the occasion by Major Edgar at our last Muster Day, was very indignant on the Occasion, expressing himself in a manner of indifference wether he should again attend, and not being present this day, the Major ordered he should send in all his Equipments etc etc for that he should not continue him any longer a Member of the Corps.

R. Roper, having on the 20ᵗʰ of November apologised to the Major for his Conduct, was in consequence of same readmitted a Member of the Corps.

Tuesday March 9ᵗʰ 1813

The three Troops assembled at the time appointed by Major Edgar in his Letter of 25 February above.[163] A general inspection of Arms and Equipments occupied the attention of the Major and Officers during the day. Were repairs were needful, directions where given to have them done, and the Horse Equipments being altogether worn out, a compleat set of new Saddles, Bridles, and other Equipments of Horse Furniture was directed to be ordered and procured as soon as conveniently can be for each Member of the three Troops (excepting the commissioned Officers who find their own equipments etc.) and the same to be paid for out of the Fund of the Corps. We had the use of a Barn in the occupation of Mr Couperthwaite for the convenience of Inspecting the Sundry articles in case of its being a Rainy day but fortunately the day proved very fine.

Friday March 12ᵗʰ 1813

The three Troops met on the Parade at the time appointed. There having been a considerable fall of Snow during the Night it was impossible we could ride in

---

[163] Omitted.

the Field to Exercise by reason of same. A letter was received by the Officer Commanding from Major Edgar, stating he at this time experienced many Gouty Pains and Achs **B279** that he dare not face the cold Northerly Wind this morning, fearing the consequences would be a six or eight weeks confinement. Captain Theobald being present, ordered the Troops to march a short distance out of the Town and after the Muster Rolls were called over, they were dismissed.

In consequence of the death of Sergeant Major Kemp, Sergeant Simpson was unanimously elected Sergeant Major, Corporal Keer, Sergeant, and Thomas Miller a Corporal in Captain Collett's Troop.

Tuesday March 16th 1813
The Troops being assembled, marched from Parade to a Field in Woodbridge in the occupation of Mr James Hayward, and Exercised under the command of Major Edgar in the usual Evolutions. The day was very fine and pleasant. Major Edgar read to the members present Letters which he had just received from Mr John Welham of Martlesham, Mr Robert Blomfield of Hemley and Mr John Stannard of Bucklesham wherein they requested the Major to accept their resignation, merely assigning as a reason for their withdrawing from their Services in the Corps that they differed from the Major in opinion respecting an application that was about to be made to Parliament, for a Bill to equalize the assessments in the sundry parishes in the Incorporated Hundreds of Colneis and Carlford. (Reasons the most ridiculous and absurd possible and in respect to themselves (was considered by all present) most disgraceful being on matters of Public Business and totally unconnected with their engagement in the Corps and duty as Soldiers, and a self sufficient consequence pitiful in the extreme.)

March 19th   Major Edgar read a Letter to the Corps from Mr John Hyam Martlesham requesting he would accept his resignation for reasons as above stated by Mr R Blomfield etc etc of which every Member present expressed his disapprobation of such low and mean Conduct, with Contempt.

John Last of Otley also sent in his resignation for the same reasons stated above whose conduct was considered equally contemptible and Futile in extreme.

Friday March 19th 1813
The Troops marched from Parade at the time appointed and exercised in a Field in Woodbridge in the occupation of Mr James Hayward (Commanded by Major Edgar). The day was very fine. No particular occurrence. Such of the Members who had not attended the four days of Muster were directed to assemble on Tuesday next being the day appointed for that purpose. Major Edgar informed the Members of the Corps for the purpose of ensuring a due and full attendance on the days of General Muster, and for the better regulation of the Corps; if from this time anyone was absent three succeeding Muster days and did not send to him Certificates of Sickness or assign any satisfactory reason for such his absence previous to the next General Muster, he should be considered as having withdrawn himself from his Services in the Corps, and his Name would consequently be erased from the Muster Roll, and that he the Major should require his sending in his Equipments.

March 23rd This being an extra meeting of absentees on the 4 prior meetings, I have no account of the Muster.

Tuesday June 4th 1813

The three Troops as per above Advertisement[164] assembled at the time requested, at Ipswich, and being there joined by the Baburgh, Captain Todds or 4th Troop the whole under the command of Major Edgar formed on the Cornhill. The Body Corporate of the Town being assembled as customary on His Majesty's Birth Day, the Troops were arranged in proper order, paying them proper respect as they passed on their way to Church, who being preceded by a Band of Music and followed by the Charity Children in proper order. The whole as they passed the Line of the Yeomanry Cavalry had a very pleasing effect, and the day being very fine the assembly of Spectators was very numerous and most respectable. The Troops remained on the Ground until the return of the Body Corporate from Church and received them in form on their return. For further particulars of the proceedings I have as under copied an account thereof from the Ipswich Journal of the 5th June 1813 (being myself absent from duty on my journey to Warwickshire on Business for the Troops).

Copy from the Ipswich Journal

The Birthday of our revered Monarch was observed here yesterday by the Bells ringing at an early hour. The Corporation, attended by the Recorder, R Alderson Esq, and preceded by a Band of Music, went to St. Mary Tower Church, where an appropriate discourse was delivered by the Reverend Mr Howorth from 2nd Chapter 1st Epistle of Paul to Timothy 2nd verse.

The 2nd Corps of Suffolk Yeomanry Cavalry, commanded by Major Edgar, consisting of four Troops, mustered on the Corn Hill about 11 o'Clock. The neatness of their appearance and steady conduct under arms attracted general attention, and justly realised the opinion which rank them with the foremost of our Yeomanry establishments. They marched from the hill to the parade field behind the King's Barracks, where they went through the different cavalry Manoeuvres with great exactness.

The Artillery fired a Royal Salute on Rushmere heath, and the 63rd Regiment three vollies, in honor of the day. The Corporation and a large party of their friends, dined at the Bear and Crown, and the Yeomanry had a dinner served up from the Golden Lion in the Council Chamber of the Old Town Hall, where upwards of 150 sat down to table.

NB The Yeomanry in the field fired three vollies in honor of the day, and after dinner drank his Majesty's health, the Army and Navy etc etc and spent a very agreeable afternoon and Evening, and I understand the whole was pleasant and comfortably conducted.[165]

B284 Thursday July 29th 1813

The Corps being assembled marched from parade to Bromeswell and exercised in a field in the occupation of Mr John Wolton. The day was very fine and the Corps exercised in the usual evolutions practised on days of general muster. No particular occurrence excepting that of the General commanding at the Barracks here sending for Major Edgar, and demanding of him in a high tone of self-consequence, why he dared to assemble a body of Troops in the town without having first applied to

---

[164] Omitted.
[165] B281–B283, *London Gazette Extraordinary.* The account of the battle between the Shannon and the Chesapeake 10 July 1813 is omitted. The commanding officer of the Shannon was the son of the Troop's first captain, Philip Bowes Broke.

him as General commanding the Garrison at the Barracks etc etc. Major Edgar in answer replied he was not aware of any occasion for his giving such information the same never having before been required of him by any of the Generals who had previously commanded and that in his Major Edgar's consideration, the General had no command whatever over the Yeomanry Volunteer Cavalry who assemble for exercise, they not at the time being on pay or permanent duty that they were raised by Act of Parliament and exercised thereby under the orders of the Lord Lieutenant of the County for purposes particularised in said Act. The General's treatment not being very respectful to Major Edgar, he determined on making the needful enquiry by application to the Lord Lieutenant and the General Officers of his acquaintance that the matter being properly stated he may receive the needful instructions against the time of our next meetings.

Friday July 30th 1813

The three Troops marched from Parade to Martlesham. About twelve o'Clock Lieutenant Colonel McLeroth appeared in the field, and inspected the Corps and was pleased to express himself much gratified at the appearance of the Corps and of the manner in which they went through the several duties of the day. The field in which we exercised was in the occupation of Mr William Weeden, a Member of the Corps. The day was very fine; no particular occurrence. Mr M Tyrrell of Woodbridge was elected a member and desired to join Captain Couperthwaite's Troop.

B285 Major Edgar considering the Corps (and more particularly himself) most disrespectfully treated by General Hawker on the 29th of July, was particularly desirous to know wether the General had any authority or command over the volunteer Yeomanry Cavalry when assembled for the purpose of exercise. He accordingly personally stated to Earl Chatham who command the Eastern District, the particulars of the conversation which passed between General Hawker and himself, and on the 16th September 1813 received a letter from his Lordship in explanation, of which as under is a copy.

Dear Sir   **Colchester September 15th 1813**

After I saw you I lost no time in communicating with Major General Hawker on the subject of the representation you had made to me. I have fully explained to the Major General that the Corps of Yeomanry meeting for the purpose of Exercise, are not liable to any interference of the General Officer Commanding in the vicinity of the place where they may assemble, and you may be satisfied that in future, you will receive no Interruption to your proceeding as you have always hitherto done in this District. I beg at the same time to acquaint you that Major General Hawker has assured me that owing to the circumstance of his having almost immediately after his appointment to the Staff, been sent into the disturbed Counties, when he found the Corps of Yeomanry in constant intercourse with the General Officer, and referring to him on all occasions, he had certainly not sufficiently attended to the nature and constitution of these Corps, and had been therefore led to act upon what he had conceived to be the general Custom of the service, and he has further desired me to express his regret that this misapprehension on his part should have occasioned any uneasiness to you or your Corps.

I will only add that it will give me great pleasure to learn that this Explanation is satisfactory to your feelings personally, as well as to all those of a Description of

Force, the value of whose Services no one can appreciate more highly than I do, and that, I am, my dear Sir,

Your very faithful Humble Servant   Chatham

To Major Edgar Red House Ipswich

Copy of a Letter from Major Edgar to Lord Chatham in reply to the above

My Lord,   **Red House September 19ᵗʰ 1813**

I lose no time in acknowledging your Lordship's most kind and friendly letter which has raised in my mind such feelings of Gratitude and Respect, as are not to be erased by Time, or Circumstances. Permit me to assure your Lordship that if the Zeal and Perseverance of the Suffolk Yeomanry Cavalry in their Country's Cause received some little Check in Consequence of Major General Hawker's conduct to me, it cannot fail of being restored to its full Vigour through your Lordship's kind and official Interference. I have also to observe that no greater Stimulus to their Exertions can be given than the Knowledge of their Services being well appreciated by your Lordship. In the hope that I may ere long have an opportunity of making my acknowledgments in Person, I have only to assure your Lordship, that I am with the greatest Respect and Esteem.

Your most faithful and humble Servant   Mileson Edgar

To Lord Chatham etc etc

B286 NB The Quarter Masters, Non-commissioned Officers and Privates are desired to apply at Captain Colletts for their New Horse Appointments before the 22nd instant. [166]

B287 Friday October 29ᵗʰ 1813

The morning was Rainy and indicated a bad day. About 11 o'clock it cleared up and the remaining part of the day was particularly fine and pleasant, and the Troops being assembled marched from Parade about 12 o'Clock to the field above mentioned in the occupation of Mr John Newson. Major Edgar being present, exercised the Troops in the usual Evolutions etc. Mr Whitmore Pennington of Barking was elected a member of the Corps vice Mr Robert Rudland of Claydon who resigned in consequence of having been so unfortunate as to lose two Riding Horses in the course of the year, it was not convenient to supply the loss. This day information was received of the death of Mr William Orford of Marlesford a Member of my Troop who came into the Troop in July 1803 He was a very worthy man and highly respected and really beloved by all his Neighbours.

Tuesday, November 2ⁿᵈ 1813

The meeting on the 29ᵗʰ October being the time for which those members who were constant attendants completed the number of days required by Act of Parliament for exercise during the year, the meeting of this day and the one appointed on Friday next are attended by those members only, who being absent on former meetings were required to make up the deficiency by their attendance on these two days to enable the Major to make his return of their being efficient. Such members being assembled marched from the parade to the field hired of Mr Newson and were

---

[166] Names omitted.

exercised under the command of Major Edgar in evolutions practised by a single Troop. The day was very fine.

The letter from Lord Sidmouth[167] not having been officially communicated to Major Edgar by the Lord Lieutenant, he only noticed to the Troops its appearance in the London News Papers, and after reading the Contents signified that as soon as he heard from the Lord Lieutenant he should convene the Corps to ascertain their sentiments etc etc in forwarding the wishes of government. Mr Jonathan Kirby Moore of Badley was elected a member of the Corps.

B288 The following Circular Letter was transmitted to the Lord Lieutenant of the different Counties

My Lord,   **Whitehall October 29ᵗʰ 1813**

I have the honour to inform your Grace, that it has been deemed expedient by His Majesty's Government to take measures, with a due regard to considerations of economy, for giving increased efficiency to that valuable part of our defensive force, the Yeomanry Cavalry of Great Britain.

With a view to this important object, it appears highly desirable to afford every degree of encouragement for the formation of the separate Troops and small Corps now serving in the different counties, into Regiments, consisting of not less than six Troops, where there are so many in the County; and that each Regiment should perform its annual exercise of twelve days as Permanent Duty, at one and the same period, and be subject during that time to one inspection.

I need not point out to your Grace, that although in some parts of the kingdom the former object has already been partially accomplished through the zeal of the individuals composing certain troops of Yeomanry Cavalry, yet, even there, objections have occurred to the attainment of the second, from the inadequacy of the allowances granted for some years past to meet the expenses necessarily incurred during such service.

It is therefore proposed, subject in each instance to the special approbation of the Prince Regent, to be signified to the Lord Lieutenant by the Secretary of State, that Corps so formed, and consenting to assemble annually for the period above mentioned, should, in future, in lieu of the present allowances, receive the same pay and allowances as are granted to regular cavalry.

In those cases where a county does not furnish six Troops, these Regulations may be carried into effect, provided the whole number, not being less than three, shall consent to the conditions herein specified. In those counties where there are single troops unattached to any regiment, such troops will be required, to entitle them to the benefit of these allowances, either to become part of such existing Regiments, or to form themselves into new Corps consisting of not less than three Troops each. I have therefore to request that your Grace will cause these intentions of Government to be made known without delay to the Commanding Officers of the different Corps and Troops of Yeomanry Cavalry of the County over which you preside, and that you will exert your utmost endeavours to give full effect to Regulations which promise to be attended with the most beneficial consequences.

You will please to report to me whatever propositions may be made to your Grace with a view to this object, and of which you would recommend the adoption, that

---

[167] Lord Sidmouth, as Henry Addington, had been Prime Minister 1801–1804, and responsible for the Truce of Amiens. He was Home Secretary from 1812 to 1822.

they may be submitted without delay to the consideration of His Royal Highness the Prince Regent.

I have the honour to be my Lord, Your Grace's most obedient humble servant

Sidmouth

His Majesty's Lieutenant of the County of [blank]

Copy of an Advertizement in the Ipswich Journal November 27th 1813

Second Corps Loyal Suffolk Yeomanry Cavalry

Major Edgar particularly requests all the Officers, Non-commissioned Officers, and Privates of the Corps, to meet him at the Golden Lion in Ipswich, on Friday December 10th at Twelve o'clock precisely, out of uniform, in order that he may submit to them the Secretary of State's letter respecting the Yeomanry Cavalry, as well as the communications which have been made to him since the receipt thereof. Red House, November 25th 1813
¹⁶⁸

B292 Friday December 10th 1813

In complyance with Major Edgar's Advertisement of the 27th November, One hundred Members, exclusive of the Commissioned Officers of Captain Theobald's, Captain Collett's and Captain Couperthwaite's Troops, and Captain Todd's on the part of his or Baburgh Troop, which four Troops compose the Corps of Suffolk Yeomanry Cavalry under the command of Major Edgar, met at Ipswich and assembled at the Town Hall for the purpose of taking into consideration the Circular Letter of Lord Sidmouth of the 29th October, to the Lord Lieutenant of the County.

Major Edgar addressed the Corps in an eloquent speech of considerable length. He apologised for not calling them sooner together on the occasion, which amongst other reasons was owing, he said, to his wish that other Corps or Troops might previously meet and determine on the propriety of joining them, as he considered the Second Corps, being the largest (consisting already of four Troops), the rallying point upon which the smaller Corps or Troops were to form a Regiment. After reading letters which he had received from the Duke of Grafton and Mr Heley B300 elucidating certain parts of Lord Sidmouth's Circular relative to the allowance to the Corps, and which he satisfactorily explained, he took an extensive view of the Volunteer system from its first dawning to the present time. The same feelings, he remarked, which originally drew forth the Corps, had now burst forth on the continent, and broken asunder the fetters which the merciless tyrant of France had endeavoured more closely to rivet, and by which Europe had been so long enchained. He congratulated them most cordially on the present prospect of affairs, and said that to them, in common with the other volunteer corps of Great Britain, might, in no inconsiderable degree, be attributed the change, the establishment of those corps in all parts of the kingdom having placed 500,000 soldiers at the disposal of Government. Although great sacrifices might still be required, he trusted that the time was not far distant when their services would be no longer required; when they might lay aside their sabres with the proud reflection of having eminently contributed to the preservation of the constitution of their country, and of the liberation of Europe from tyranny. Alluding more particularly to the business upon which they now met, he observed that in the spring, to reinforce our armies upon the Continent, all the disposable force of the country would probably

---

¹⁶⁸ B289–B291, *London Gazette Extraordinary.* The insurrection in Holland is omitted.

be required, consequently the internal defence of the country must devolve upon those regiments which are more particularly formed for that purpose. They must be aware, he said, that however well the exercise might be performed in small corps, their efficiency nevertheless depended upon their being accustomed to manoeuvre in large bodies; and that assembling upon Permanent Duty for twelve days must be essentially conducive to that efficiency. Their steady and long-tried loyalty had been so fully demonstrated that any inconvenience arising from considerations of a personal or a pecuniary nature, he was assured, would not have sufficient weight to induce them to reject the proposed measure. The proposal to assemble on permanent duty twelve days in the year, alternately in Ipswich and Bury (the first Muster to be held at Ipswich in May next), was then agreed unanimously.

Captain Wythe of Eye, on behalf of the third Troop, attended to express the desire of that Troop to be incorporated with the Second Corps, and a letter was read from Captain Cook of the Fourth Troop, expressive of a similar desire.[169] It was intimated that the Beccles Troop also were desirous of joining, but no official communication was made upon the subject.

The Quarter Master of the Bury Troop was present and signified the wish and desire of that Troop, to be regimented with us, and their services were accepted, but from the circumstances of that Troop at this time, not having their commissioned Officers appointed, they cannot at present be considered complete, consequently are not included in the Regiment at the present time.[170] When Officers are commissioned and appointed, a return of the Troop, its understood, will be sent to Major Edgar for the purpose of his annexing them to the regiment.

The assembly, on the arrangement of the Business of the day being gone through, then broke up with three times three cheers to "God bless the King".

B293 Copies of Sundry Letters[171] to and from His Grace the Duke of Grafton,[172] Lord Lieutenant of the County Of Suffolk, Major Edgar and the Captains Of the Troops of Loyal Suffolk Yeomanry Cavalry respecting forming said Troops into Regiments, in reply to Lord Sidmouth's Circular Letter dated 29th October 1813

Memorandum   These letters respecting the Bury Troops being attached to the present Corps under the command of Major Edgar were in correspondence previous to Lord Sidmouth's Letter, said the Troop being desirous of joining our Corps on the same terms with the Baburgh Troop requested Captain Todd to apply to Major Edgar for that purpose who after personally applying to the Major, advise of their proceedings as follows:

My dear Sir   **Bury   September 24th 1813**
I have this morning attended at Eldo heath for the purpose of obtaining the unanimous Voice of the Members, appointing their Officers and keeping up the establishment of the 4th Troop, Exercising with mine, and becoming a Troop of the 2nd

---

[169] Captain Cook commanded the 6th Hadleigh Troop, not the 4th.
[170] It is unclear why this situation had arisen. Under Captain Lord Brome and Captain Fowkes the force had very successfully been built up to a Corps of three Troops.
[171] These letters show that the Bury Troop had decided to unite with the Woodbridge Corps under the leadership of Mileson Edgar some weeks before Sidmouth's letter.
[172] Lord Euston became the 4th Duke of Grafton on the death of his father in 1811 and continued as Lord Lieutenant.

Corps under your command, also requesting of you to accept their Services under the same restrictions and regulation as the Baburgh Troop at the same time beging of you to recommend to His Grace the Duke of Grafton the following Gentlemen as being nominated and appointed by the Members as their Officers. The troop are to be Clothed like the rest of the Corps, but wait the officers receiving their Commissions to obtain the contingent Money for that purpose.[173] The persons nominated for Officers are, Mr William Frost of Brent Ely to be Captain, Mr John Parkinson De Carle of Rushbrook, Lieutenant, Mr William Fisher of Reed, Cornet.

I remain Dear Sir, Your Obedient humble Servant,   Amos Todd

My Lord   **Norwich 7th October 1813**

It is of course well known to your Grace that the Bury Troop of Yeomanry Cavalry is and has for some time been, without Officers. On the 29th Ult I find the Members of it met for the purpose of taking under their consideration some plan for organizing their Troop and making it more efficient. The result of their meeting was that they unanimously wished to be joined to the 2nd Corps under my Command and that I would write to your Grace on the Subject. At the same time they made a request that I would recommend to you the following Gentlemen to be their Officers viz Mr William Frost of Brent Eleigh as Captain, Mr John Parkinson De Carle of Rushbrook as Lieutenant, and Mr William Fisher of Reed Cornet. If therefore your Grace should think fit to comply with their wishes, I have only to say that no exertions shall be wanting on my part to render their Services Efficient. I shall return to Red House on Saturday and shall be happy in being favoured with your Grace's Sentiments.

I remain my Dear Lord with the greatest respect and esteem Yours

Mileson Edgar

My dear Lord   **Red House November 29th 1813**

On the 6th instant, I received a letter from Mr Boston enclosing a copy of one addressed to your Grace by Lord Sidmouth respecting the Yeomanry Cavalry. Having for a Month past been suffering from Gouty Spasm in my Chest, which has made me almost a close prisoner to the House, I have not till now dared to fix a day for meeting the Corps on the Subject. I have however just sent off an Advertisement to the Ipswich papers calling them together on the 10th of next month for that purpose, and as I would wish to make them clearly understand what is proposed, I have taken the liberty of addressing a few Lines to your Grace previous thereto. The part of Lord Sidmouth's letter on which I wish for a little information, is that wherein he says "that Corps so formed and consenting to assemble annually for the period above mentioned, should, in future, in Lieu of **B294** the present allowance, receive the same pay and allowance as are granted to the Regular Cavalry". Does His Lordship's expression "in lieu of the present allowances" apply to the £4 per Man at present issued annually for Clothing and Contingent money, or do they apply only to the Pay which under the 48 Clause of the Volunteer Act of 1804 every Commanding Officer is allowed to draw when his Corps or Troop is on permanent Duty, of two shillings per day for every Volunteer and 1s 4d per day for every Horse.

---

[173] In 1794, the separate Troops of the Suffolk Yeomanry Cavalry all had the same uniform, but as they became worn and funds became available, the uniform was changed individually by each Troop. Since the Woodbridge Corps was made up of four Troops, the other Troops joining them copied their uniform.

I am certain the Corps I have the Honour to command are well disposed on all occasions to meet the wishes of Government and to conform to any Regulations which are calculated to increase their Use and Efficiency. I entertain no doubt therefore of the Measure when rightly understood being readily acceeded to. Captain Cook who commands the Hadleigh Troop, has been with me to say he entertain no Doubts of a Disposition among his Men to join my Corps, and as I informed your Grace by Letter 6 or 7 weeks back, the Bury Troops have requested me to make application to you for that purpose. With the addition of these Troops my Corps would become a Regiment of Six Troops agreeable to the regulations of Lord Sidmouths Letter. There are, as your Grace knows, four other Troops in the County, from the commanders of which I have heard nothing, so that I should suppose they will form themselves into a Corps. I shall be happy to hear from your Grace any time between this and the 10th of next month, and I need not add that I trust that I shall be most ready to attend to any suggestions you may wish to make to me. I was sorry to hear some time ago that your Grace was severely attacked by Rheumatism, from which I hope however you are completely recovered.

I am etc etc etc   Mileson Edgar

To his Grace the Duke of Grafton Lord Lieutenant of the County of Suffolk

---

My Dear Sir   **Thursday December 9th 1813**

Not having been able as I intended to see Lord Sidmouth yesterday, and being obliged on business to leave Town this morning, I have written to Mr Heley Addington, begging he would answer the Questions contained in your Letter, by this Night's Post directed to you near Ipswich. The plan of forming a Corps of Six Troops is one which can't fail to give greater efficiency to the same number of Men, than that of smaller Corps. Eight would be still better in good hands such as yours. I shall be both ready to receive your communication and glad to forward any plans offered for the benefit of the public service, an object of which I hope and believe neither of us shall ever lose sight of my dear Sir.

Yours truly, Grafton

Mileson Edgar Esq   Red House Ipswich

Sir,   **Whitehall 9th December 1813**

In consequence of a communication from His Grace the Duke of Grafton, I have received Lord Sidmouth's directions to acquaint you that no alteration is intended to be made in the present allowances of the Yeomanry Cavalry for Clothing and Contingencies. The Expression in Lord Sidmouth's Circular Letter of the 29th October last, "in lieu of the present allowances" has reference only to the proposed period of permanent Duty, when such Corps, as may be actually called out on that duty, will be entitled for the Officers as well as the Men, to the same amount of pay and allowances as the Regular Cavalry.

I am Sir Your most obedient humble Servant   I H Addington

To Major Edgar Red House Ipswich

My dear Lord   **Red House December 17th 1813**

I am happy in being able to make a favourable report to your Grace of the meeting of my Corps on Friday last, for the purpose of taking under consideration Lord Sidmouth's Letter. A perfect unanimity prevailed, and a ready concurrence **B295** took place in every Regulation contained in the letter, I have only to express a wish that we may be assembled at Ipswich and Bury alternately, as best calculated to meet the convenience of the Troops of which the Regiment is likely to be composed, and if we are to have any choice as to the time of going out, we should wish it to take place in the latter part of May, so that the 4th of June may be included in the 12 days we are to be on duty.

Captain Wythe attended the meeting on the part of the 3rd Troop, which had been previously called together, and expressed an anxious desire to be regimented with us. Mr De Carle also attended on the part of the Bury Troop, and confirmed the wishes of the Troop as reported to me several weeks ago, and by me communicated to your Grace, to become a Troop of the Second Corps. With this addition, the Corps or Regiment will consist of Six Troops. At the meeting on Friday it was suggested that the Beccles Troops had assembled, and expressed a wish to be Regimented with us, but at present no communication of the kind has been made to me. I have received a letter from Captain Cook who command the Hadleigh Troop, to say he should immediately call together his men and forward the result of the meeting to your Grace. This morning's post brought me a letter from Captain Crabtree of the first Troop, to say that he had assembled his men on the 6th instant, "who had unanimously agreed to meet the wishes of Government in any plan which appears best calculated to increase the efficiency of their Services". I sincerely congratulate your Grace on the Patriotic spirit displayed by your Countrymen, well knowing the warm Interest you feel, as well as myself in everything that effects the credit and prosperity of Suffolk. In a former letter more immediately written on the subject of the Bury Troops wish to be joined to the 2nd Corps, I signified to your Grace that it had no Commissioned Officers having for a long time past assembled under and been exercised by Mr De Carle, their Quarter Master. I would wish to recommend the following Gentlemen to be their Officers, if it meets with your Grace's approbation, viz Mr William Frost of Brent Ely, to be Captain, Mr John Parker De Carle of Rushbrook (the present Quarter Master) to be Lieutenant, and Mr William Fisher of Reed, to be Cornet.

I have now, I believe, made every Military communication to your Grace which is necessary at the present moment, and shall at all times be ready to attend to any instructions or directions I may receive from you.

With every good wish etc, believe me my dear Lord, most sincerely and respectfully yours,

Mileson Edgar

To His Grace the Duke of Grafton

My dear Lord   **December 19th 1813**

I think the details of the arrangement for forming a Regiment of Yeomanry Cavalry under your Command are not sufficiently distinctly before me to put the matter in such a shape that it can be laid Officially before the Secretary of State. I understand from your letter that three Troops are disposed to join the three already under your Command, but I have not heard this (a necessary preliminary to further proceedings) from any of the Captains Commandants, except Captain Waythe. Be so good as to let me receive the particulars of your proposition for forming a Regiment of Yeomanry Cavalry according to the terms of Lord Sidmouth's Letter, and you must also se the necessity for my being informed by the Commandants themselves of the Troops which propose to act under your Command.

I have the honour to be my dear Sir, Your faithful and obedient,   Grafton

To Major Edgar, Red House, Ipswich

My dear Lord   **December 21ˢᵗ 1813**
I am just favoured with your Grace's letter and lose no time in giving that explanation to what has hitherto taken place within my knowledge touching the regimenting the Yeomanry Cavalry of this County, which I am sorry to find my last
letter did not **B296** contain. In the first place I must state to your Grace that my
Corps consist of four Troops, and has done ever since the year 1804, when it
was joined by the Baburgh Troop, at that time commanded by Captain Moore. I
am happy to find Captain Waythe has not failed to make the necessary communication to your Grace. As to the Bury Troop, I know not how your Grace is to
receive their wishes in a more regular way than through me, as they have no
officers, and the Quarter Master attended the meeting on behalf of the members
of the Troop, and desired I would make the report I did to your Grace. But if you
would wish such a communication to be made by the Quarter Master, it shall be
done immediately. From the statement now made, your Grace will se how the six
Troops are accounted for, I suppose a few days will put your Grace in possession
of the sentiments of all the Troops within the County, and I have only to say if a
Regiment is formed, I shall have no objection whatever to the Command being
given to any person your Grace should appoint or recommend to be appointed,
and shall be most happy to serve under him. There are many Gentlemen in the
County better qualified in every respect for the situation, and my only wish is to
make myself serviceable to my King and Country so long as I have the health
and strength to do it. I beg therefore your Grace will dispose of me in any way
you shall think fit, and rest assured that you will ever find me attentive to your
wishes and commands.

                              I am etc   Mileson Edgar
To His Grace the Duke of Grafton

My dear Sir   **Euston   December 25ᵗʰ 1813**
My mistake as to the Number of the Troops in your present Corps arises from the
manner in which the General Return is made out, in which the Corps under your
command is described as consisting of three Troops, The Baburgh being described
as a separate Troop. I now however understand from you that it consists of four
Troops including the Baburgh. To these it is then proposed to add the 4th or Bury
Troop, and to be officered according to your letter of the 7ᵗʰ and the 3rd Troop
commanded by Captain Wythe, and the 6th by Captain Cooke; whose proposition
to this effect I have this day received. Now what I wish to receive through you, who
will of course apply to the Inspecting Field Officer for them, are the Returns of the
Troops proposed to form part of the Regiment under your Command, as to their
numbers at the latest Inspection; as well as a Return of your own Corps as taken
at the same date; from which I shall be able to lay before the Secretary of State an
intelligible account of the strength of the Regiment proposed to be formed, with the
Names of its Officers.

        I have the honour to be, my dear Sir, Your faithful Servant,   Grafton
Mileson Edgar Esq   Red House Ipswich

Dear Sir   **Theberton Hall December 24ᵗʰ 1813**
I collected the sentiments of my Troop on Monday last, and I have the pleasure of
saying they agreed to the proposals of Government as expressed in Lord Sidmouth's
Letter of the 29ᵗʰ October, and to be Regimented with the other Volunteer Yeomanry
at Ipswich.

I have written to the Lord Lieutenant the result of the meeting.

Yours truely   F W Cooke

Mileson Edgar Esq Red House, Ipswich

My dear Sir   **Red House December 27ᵗʰ 1813**

You are of course no stranger to what is going on respecting the Regimenting the Yeomanry Cavalry of this County. My Corps, consists as you know, of four Troops, is to be joined by the Bury Troop, by the Eye Troop commanded by Captain Wythe, and by the Hadleigh Troop commanded by Captain Cooke, so that it will then become a Regiment of Seven Troops. This Communication is made to me this morning by the Lord Lieutenant, who wishes me to furnish him with Returns of the Bury, the Eye and the Hadleigh Troops, as to their Numbers when last Inspected, and desires me to apply to you for them. I have therefore to request you to furnish me with a Return of each of the 3 Troops above mentioned, as made up of Commissioned Officers, Non-commissioned Officers, **B297** Quarter Masters, Trumpeters and Privates, with the addition of the Commissioned Officers' Names. The return of my own Corps I can make out and need not trouble you for. I suppose the remaining Troops of Suffolk Yeomanry viz Crabtrees, Reedes and Adair's will become a Corps, but I know nothing of what is going on. Requesting to hear from you as soon as you conveniently can.

I remain my dear Sir, truly yours   Mileson Edgar

Lieutenant Colonel McLeroth

Dear Sir[174]   **Red House December 27ᵗʰ 1813**

You cannot be a stranger to what is going on respecting Regimenting the Yeomanry Cavalry of the County. Our Corps is to be joined by the Bury, the Eye and the Hadleigh Troops, and the Lord Lieutenant in making the Communication to me by this Morning's Post desires I will furnish him with the Returns of the strengths of the seven Troops, together with the Officers names. It is impossible for me to return your Name as Cornet of a Troop, which perhaps you have not seen for nearly two years, neither have you thought fit to furnish me with any medical Certificate, or satisfactory reason for your absence. I must therefore request you will send in your Resignation, or give me an assurance that you will in future be at your Post. I was in hopes, after the Conversation we had at the Lamb Fair on the subject, I should not have been under the painful necessity of writing this Letter. I shall hope to hear from you immediately on receipt of this, as I must write to the Lord Lieutenant in two or three days.

With best Compliments of the Season, I remain much yours

Mileson Edgar

To Mr John Field Gedgrave

Dear Sir   **Gedgrave December 30ᵗʰ 1813**

I have deferred writing to you respecting my absence from the Troop under an Idea that I should be once more able to join you, but the distance is so great, it would fatigue me too much and I am obliged to be so careful of cold. Therefore I think it

---

[174] This letter and the following one occur on B322 having obviously been found later and put into the account of Napoleon's downfall, which Collett was copying at the time. It has been moved here for chronological convenience.

would be most prudent of me to resign at once, although very reluctantly. My heart will be with you on all occasions; and I can assure you Major, that no one Love his King and Country better than myself or would do more to support it as far as my situation and circumstances would allow me.

I saw an advertisement respecting the Troops meeting at Ipswich but never knew for that purpose (I do not se the Old Ipswich paper). If the Troops in this County should meet at Ipswich it will be a most gratifying time for you Major. I hope everything will pass as pleasantly as at Bury. I shall certainly come to Ipswich in the time of your hard Service. I have sent not an excuse but the real reason of my absence for the last two years from the Surgeon who have attended me, which I hope will be satisfactory to you.

I remain Sir Your Obedient Servant   John Field

Major Edgar Red House Ipswich

Copy of Certificate

I John Randall, of Orford in the County of Suffolk, Surgeon, do hereby certify, that, Mr John Field of Gedgrave has not been able to attend the duty of the Troop to which he belongs, on account of Ill Health.

Given under my hand, the 30th day of December 1813

Signed John Randall

My dear Sir   **Bury December 29th 1813**

On the other side I furnish you with a Return of the three Troops together with the names of the commissioned Officers, for the Lord Lieutenant, and congratulate you and them on the intended junction, with every good wish, I am always faithfully Yours,   H McLeroth

To Mileson Edgar Esq etc etc

Corps	Commandant	No. of Troops	Field Officers	Captains	Subalterns	Staff	Quarter Masters	Sergeants	Trumpeters	Privates	
Bury	Quarter Master de Carle	1					1	2	1	38	
Eye	Captain Wythe	1		1	2	1		2	1	55	John Wythe Captain Blomfield Cornet
Hadleigh	Captain Cooke	1		1	2		1	3	1	49	Thomas William Cook Captain Charles Reeve Lieutenant William Chapling Cornet

H M'Leroth Lieutenant Colonel Inspecting Field Officer

Eye January 5th 1814

Dear Sir,

Being from home when your favour of the 31 Ulto came to Eye I take the earliest opportunity of answering it. The Lieutenant when Captain Smith Commanded the Troop F Leake Esq of Maxley Hall has resigned and I have nominated Mr George Clabon of Feanecon to succeed him, but have not sent his name to the Duke of Grafton for his approbation. I made a return to the Secretary of State on the 13th December last my Troop being then Complete; the Establishment is as stated by Colonel McLeroth 63, I send you on the other side a Copy of the return I made my Troop being full, I have several supernumerys.

I am my dear Sir Yours truly John Wythe

To Mileson Edgar Esq etc etc

Establishment figures

Captain J. Wythe

	Captains	Lieutenants	Cornets	Quarter Masters	Sergeants	Corporals	Trumpeters	Privates
Now serving	1	1	1	1	3	3	1	52
Wanting to complete	-	-	-	-	-	-	-	-
Total Establishment	**1**	**1**	**1**	**1**	**3**	**3**	**1**	**52**

I certify this to be a correct Return John Wythe Captain

Captain T. W. Cooke's Return January 7th

	Captains	Lieutenants	Cornets	Quarter Masters	Sergeants	Corporals	Trumpeters	Privates
Serving	1	1	1	1	3	3	1	49
Wanting	-	-	-	-	-	-	-	Including Farrier
Total Establishment	**1**	**1**	**1**	**1**	**3**	**3**	**1**	**49**

Thomas William Cooke Captain

B298 My dear Sir   **Euston January 17ᵗʰ 1814**

Although I have received no return of the strength of the different Corps which are proposed to form the Regiment of Yeomanry Cavalry under your Command, except from Captain Cooke whose return has been regularly transmitted to me; I have nevertheless Submitted to the Secretary of State, for the Prince Regents approbation, a Proposition for uniting the 4 Troops already under your Command with the 3rd, 4th and 6th Troops, so as to form a Regiment of 7 Troops under your command as Lieutenant Colonel. The Captains Commanding the 3rd and 6th having distinctly expressed themselves to me, on behalf of their respective Troops, but the 4th (having no Officers) through yourself as not only acceeding generally to the proposition contained in Lord Sidmouth's Letter of the 29ᵗʰ October but as being desirous henceforward of forming a part of the Corps under your Command.

I have the honor to be my dear Sir Your most obedient and faithful servant

Grafton

To Mileson Edgar Esq etc etc

My dear Lord   **Red House 18ᵗʰ January 1814**

I herewith inclose a return of the 2nd Corps under my Command as also of the three Troops which from your Grace's letter I find are to be Regimented with it, but as I knew some resignations had taken place, and others were intended, I wished to make the necessary arrangements for recommendations of Officers to fill their place before I wrote to your Grace. In the 2nd Corps I wish to recommend Quarter Master Robert Sexton to be Cornet in Captain Couperthwaites Troop, vice John Field, Cornet Robert Cross to be Lieutenant in Captain Todds Troop, vice Mr Frost and John Sidney Coker to be Cornet vice Francis Leake. In the Bury Troop I wish only to confirm the recommendation I made to your Grace by Letter, bearing the date October 7ᵗʰ. As I have noticed on the return made of my Corps, and of Hadleigh Troop, the vacancies in the number of privates were filled up previous to the last return sent to the Secretary of State and to your Grace, so that I suppose their present strength agrees with their Establishment, as fixed by Government on the first of April 1808. But I am given to understand it is not so with the Bury Troop, for subsequent to that period it was, including Officers, more than 80 strong. I should wish to know from your Grace whether that Troop may be increased to Regulation Strength of April 1 1808 as in that case it will be done in a very short space of time, having always a supplementary list for filling up vacancies which arise. I hope I have complied with everything your Grace wished for in your last letter, if not, upon its being pointed out, it shall be immediately done.

I am etc etc   Mileson Edgar

To His Grace the Duke of Grafton

Corps of Troops

Corps	No. of Troops	Field Officer	Captains	Lieutenants	Corporals	Surgeons	Quarter Masters	Sergeants	Corporals	Trumpeters	Farriers	Privates
2nd or Woodbridge Corps	4	1	4	4	4	1	4	12	12	3	1	140
4th or Bury Troop	1						1	2	2	1	-	38
3rd or Eye Troop	1		1	1	1		1	3	3	1	-	52
[blank] or Hadleigh Troop	1		1	1	1		1	3	3	1		45
TOTAL	**7**	**1**	**6**	**6**	**6**	**1**	**7**	**20**	**20**	**6**	**1**	**275**

6th or Hadleigh Troop Captain Thomas Wm Cooke Lieutenant Charles Reeve
Cornet William Chaplin
Red House January 1814 Mileson Edgar Major

Wanted to complete in the 2nd Corps when last Inspected One Private, ditto in the Bury Troop 1 Captain, Lieutenant and Cornet, ditto in the Hadleigh Troop 3 Privates - but of the last returns to the Secretary of State and to your Grace, the 4 privates were added to the Corps of the Hadleigh Troop.
Names of Officers
2nd Corps   Major Edgar, Captains John Meadows Theobald, Cornelius Collett, John Couperthwaite, Amos Todd,   Lieutenants William Pearson, Philip Dikes, William Hewitt, William Frost, Cornets John Meadows Rodwell, Frances Hayle, John Field, Robert Cross
3rd or Eye Troop   Captain John Wythe, Lieutenant Francis Leake, Cornet Blomfield

---

B299 My dear Sir   **Euston February 4th 1814**
Calculating the 4th Troop of Yeomanry Cavalry at 41 Rank and File, and the other Troops according to their Numbers on the last Return, the Corps to be formed by the consolidation of the seven Troops (2nd Corps of four Troops, 3rd 4th and 6th Troops) will consist of 296 Rank and file.
The strength of the Corps will entitle it to two Field Officers, viz One Lieutenant Colonel and one Major, it will likewise be allowed an Adjutant, who if he be duly Qualified, will receive constant pay. Sergeants may be appointed at the rate of one for every 20 private men, and one Quarter Master and one Trumpeter may be placed on the Establishment of each Troop. The Corps will be entered in the Books of the Secretary of State, as well as in those of the Clerk of the Peace, by the name of the first Regiment of Loyal Suffolk Cavalry.
You shall hear from me Officially, if I have time, by this Post, on the same subject but this Letter contains in brief, all that an official one will communicate to you.
        I am dear Sir Your most faithful and Obedient Servant   Grafton
To M Edgar etc etc

Sir   **Euston February 4th 1814**

I have to acquaint you that in Consolidating the following Troops of Yeomanry Cavalry into one Corps under your command with the Rank of Lieutenant Colonel has been approved by HRH the Prince Regent viz 2nd Corps consisting of 4 troops, 3rd Troop, 4th Troop, 6th Troop forming altogether a Regiment of 296 Rank and File as follows

2nd Corps consists of 4 Troops of 38 Rank and File		152
3rd Troop ..	..	55
4th Troop ..	..	41
6th Troop ..	..	48
		296

The strength of this Corps will entitle it to two Field Officers, viz one Lieutenant Colonel and a Major – it will likewise be allowed an Adjutant who is to be duly qualified according to the Established regulations of the Volunteer Service, will be allowed constant pay, at the rate of Eight Shillings per diem. Sergeants may be appointed at the rate of one for every 20 private men, and one Quarter Master and one Trumpeter may be placed on the Establishment of each Troop.

The Corps will be entered in the books of the Secretary of States Office by the name of the 1st Regiment of Loyal Suffolk Cavalry.

           I have the honor to be Sir your most obedient Humble Servant
                                         Grafton

PS I have to signify to you the following appointments in the above described Corps under your command. Major Edgar to be Lieutenant Colonel, Mr William Frost to be Captain, John de Carle Lieutenant, William Parker Cornet in the Troop at present known by the name of the 4th Troop.

You will be so good as to signify the same to these Gentlemen, as well as that their Commissions will be ordered to be made out forthwith.

Drawing of epergne[175]

---

[175] The sketch of the silver epergne and the related letters were moved from C63 for chronological relevance. Three sketches of it survive: one drawn in Collett's book (illustrated here), one by Isaac Johnson (SROI HD 480/4 folio 98 sketch 98, illustrated in Blatchly, *Isaac Johnson*, p. 27) and one

The above is the Design of a Piece of Plate presented to General Sharpe by the Sundry Troops of the Loyal Suffolk Yeomanry Cavalry on which was engraved the following Inscription

Presented to Major General Sharpe by the Yeomanry Cavalry of Suffolk of whom he was for many years Inspecting Field Officer, in grateful Testimony of the able assistance which he afforded them in Discharge of their Military Duty and of the Gentlemanly and conciliatory manner in which it was uniformly rendered. It was accompanied by the following letter from Major Edgar, the senior Officer.[176]

Red House January 31ˢᵗ 1814

My dear General,
Believe me, 'till the present moment I have never known how to appreciate justly the Rank I hold in that respectable Body of Men, the Yeomanry Cavalry of this County. Nor could any event so strongly have pointed out to me its value, as being deputed in Consequence of that Rank, to present to you on Behalf of my Brethren in Arms, this small tribute of our Gratitude and Esteem. The inscription which appears upon it conveys but a faint Expression of our Feelings; they are, I can assure you, much too deeply engraven on our Hearts ever to be erased by Time or Circumstance. I can not my Dear General remove my Pen from the Paper without expressing a hope, and an anxious one too, that the Friendship I have so long experienced from you may, notwithstanding the Dissolution of our Military Connection, cease only with our Lives, and that you will ever believe me, with every Sentiment of Respect and Esteem.   Yours Mileson Edgar

---

My Dear Major   **Darsham House 4ᵗʰ February 1814**
The very distinguished favor conferred on me by the Yeomanry Cavalry of Suffolk, could only have received additional value in my estimation, from the kind and handsome manner in which it has been presented by you. Sensible how unable I am to express my acknowledgements in adequate terms, it is a source of infinite satisfaction to me that I have to convey them through a friend who will do justice to my feelings.
I beg you to offer my grateful thanks, with the assurance how justly I value and appreciate the approbation of so highly respectable a body of men. The expression of their esteem conveyed in such flattering sentiments is an honor, I owe solely to their kind partiality, not to any merit of my own.
The Loyalty, Zeal and Intelligence uniformly displayed by the Suffolk Yeomanry left little for me to require. That little was always attended to with such marked alacrity and good will that almost the only point of duty left me to perform was that most satisfactory one, to command.

---

in the Mileson Edgar papers (SROI HA247/5/25). Collett commissioned many sketches and maps from Johnson so it is very likely that he employed him to draw two more, one directly in his volume. With the sketch in the Edgar papers is the original receipt from Rundell, Bridge and Rundell, the most important silver retailers in London of the time. A similar one by Paul Storr now in the National Museum of Wales measures 48.9 cm, plus the glass bowl.

[176] The collection of donations from the different Troops of the Suffolk Yeomanry and the organisation involved in the purchase of the silver with its inscription had taken some time, since the last communication Collett recorded with Colonel Sharpe was just after his promotion.

If I have any claim to remembrance, it is in the sincere anxiety I always felt for their pre-eminence. The kindness I constantly experienced from them individually will ever form a part of the most pleasing recollections of my life. It has created in my breast an attachment to the County of Suffolk, which time cannot efface. The obligations I am under to yourself as an Officer and a friend, I can never sufficiently acknowledge. I shall only assure you of the perfect esteem and regard with which I shall remain, My dear Major, ever truly Yours

M Sharpe Major General

To Major Edgar etc etc Red House Ipswich

Copy from the Ipswich Journal February 26th 1814 Inserted by order of Major General Sharpe, (Inspecting Field Officer)
The Yeomanry Cavalry of the County of Suffolk have presented to Major General Sharpe an elegant piece of Plate. It is a centre ornament for the table, richly chased and of most beautiful workmanship.
On the base is this inscription: Presented to Major General Sharpe by the Yeomanry Cavalry of Suffolk of whom he was for many years Inspecting Field Officer, in grateful Testimony of the able assistance which he afforded them in Discharge of their Military Duty and of the Gentlemanly and conciliatory manner in which it was uniformly rendered.

Cost of the Piece of Plate
Mileson Edgar Esq
Bought of Rundell, Bridge and Rundell, 32, Ludgate Hill
November 24th 1813

	£	s	d
A Silver Tripod Epergne, with three Female Figures supporting a Basket 180ozs 12 [?]div, [?]fastrion 12s 6d an oz	124	10	7
Engraving inscription on ditto, Arms and Crest	3	15	0
a Glass Bason for ditto (handsome cut glass)	3	10	0
A set of artificial Flowers for ditto	3	3	0
A Wainscot Case for the above, Matting and Cordage etc	2	12	6
A Wire frame for Flowers, 18s a box for ditto 3s	1	1	0
	138	12	1

(With Carriage, Postage and the full cost was £140)

The above piece of plate was of most Elegant Workmanship and when the Cutt Glass and Flowers were fixed in the Basket it had a beautiful appearance in the Centre of the Table.

My dear Sir   **Red House February 7th 1814**
I had the honor of receiving two Letters from your Grace yesterday morning with Military communications, on some of which I am anxious to obtain a little Information and on others a little correction. With respect to the strength of the Regiment, as to the Rank and File, as detailed in your Grace's letter, am I to consider that as the Establishment from this moment instead of the one of April 1st 1808 when the Troops which compose it were certainly stronger but of course would now be struck off. Is the Surgeon who has been attached to the Troop without pay to be struck off or continued? May not the six sergeants who exceed the Number allowable (being

20 instead of 14) be continued in the Regiment as Privates, and are the Farriers, **B300** of which there are two to be struck off?

The 2nd Corps reducing 4 of its Sergeants and taking the Farrier as a Private would have 157 instead of 152 Rank and File and having recruited the one private wanting to complete at the June Inspection previous to the December Return made to your Grace and the Secretary of State, I should suppose he would be allowed and in that case the strength would be 158. In the 3rd Troop one Sergeant being reduced to a Private would make the number of Rank and File 56 instead of 55. In the 4th Troop the Number of Rank and File is only 40 instead of 41 unless your Grace thinks they may be augmented to the Establishment of 1808 in which case it would be at least 60. In the 6th Troop one Sergeant being reduced to a private and taking the Farrier also as one of the Number of Rank and File would be 50 instead of 48, and this Troop having also recruited the three Privates wanting to complete at their last Inspection previous to making the December return to your Grace and the Secretary of State may possibly be thought entitled to 53 Rank and File instead of 48.

The great inducement with me for stating these Circumstances so strongly to your Grace is that the 2nd Corps, 3rd and 6th Troops are full, and in the event of the Number of Rank and File standing as detailed in your Grace's letter, I shall have to dismiss 5 or 6 men out of the 2nd Corps, 4 or 5 out of the 6th Troop and one man out of the 3rd Troop. By referring to the Regulations of July 12th 1808 I perceive that a Corps must consist of 300 Rank and File to have an Adjutant. I suppose I am to recommend to your Grace both the Major and the Adjutant. Having now stated the matters on which I have ventured to trouble your Grace for Information, I have to observe that the Gentleman recommended as Cornet in the 4th Troop is Mr William Fisher and not William Parker, and that Mr De Carle has two Christian names, John and Parkeson. I fear your Grace will think my letter a very troublesome one, but I trust you will impute it to a wish of discharging my Duty regularly and satisfactorily.

I am my dear Lord, with the greatest respect and Esteem, Yours,

Mileson Edgar

To his Grace the Duke of Grafton

My Dear Sir   **Euston February 10th 1814**

The Establishment of the Regiment of Yeomanry Cavalry which it is proposed you should command is taken as to Rank and File, correctly from the last Returns; but I can have no doubt of the Sergeants which at present exist beyond the number allowed by the Secretary of State's letter, being still admitted to form part of the strength of the Regiment as Rank and File, and in like manner the Farriers. The principle upon which Government have proceeded I understand to be that of rendering more Effective the actually existing force of Yeomanry Cavalry, not of increasing it. I will therefore, beg the favour of you to send me such a return of the Establishment of the Regiment in question as will satisfy yourself inasmuch as it may contain the Excess of Sergeants and Farriers converted into Rank and File; which seemed if I collected your meaning, with correctness, to be one of the objects you had in your contemplation, and to which arrangement I can see no likelihood of any objections being made by Government. A Surgeon I conclude, may form a part of the Establishment, but I imagine no pay will be allowed him from Government.

I am, Dear Sir, very respectfully yours etc   Grafton

M Edgar Esq etc

My dear Lord   **Red House February 17th 1814**

I am happy to find by your Grace's letter that the Sergeants exceeding the number allowed by the Secretary of State's letter may, together with the Farriers, be admitted to form part of the strength of the Regiment as Rank and File, as in such case I shall have no men to discharge. Enclosed is a return of the Establishment of the Regiment, and at the foot of it I have made such Remarks as will, I trust, be satisfactory to your Grace. **B301** In my next Letter I shall have the Honor of recommending a Major and Adjutant for your Grace's approbation, as well as of Officers to supply the vacancies made by such promotion. I shall be glad to hear from your Grace that the return now made is satisfactory, after which I shall proceed to make the necessary arrangement in the different Troops.

I am my dear Lord, with the greatest respect and Esteem, most truly yours,

Mileson Edgar

To His Grace the Duke of Grafton

Establishment of the 1st Regiment of Loyal Suffolk Yeomanry Cavalry

Number of Troops 7, Field Officers 2, Captains 7, Lieutenants 7, Cornets 7, Surgeon 1, Adjutant 1, Quarter Masters 7, Serjeants 15, Trumpeters 7, Rank and File 302. Total Strength 356

Remarks (as memorandums) The Surgeon receives no pay from Government.

The five Sergeants exceeding the number allowed, now reduced to the Ranks, together with the two Farriers, make the number of Rank and File 302 instead of 296 In this Return I have taken one Rank and File off the Bury Troop (40 not 41 being the number), otherwise the total Rank and File would have been 303. M.E.

My dear Sir   **Euston February 24th 1814**

I have transmitted your Return (with a single alteration of Number of Rank and File from 302 to 303, in order that the Bury Troop may not be unnecessarily reduced), to the Secretary of State; and you shall hear from me whenever I have received his answer.

I am my dear Sir faithfully   Grafton

M Edgar Esq etc

Dear Ray   **Red House February 24th 1814**

You may probably not have heard what has been going on in this County since Lord Sidmouth's circular letter, respecting Regimenting the Yeomanry Cavalry, and taking them out on permanent duty for 12 days in the year. This letter will not only give you that information but also prove that the old saying "out of sight, out of mind" is not applicable to me. You are to know that the old 2nd Corps of 4 Troops as you remember it, has been joined by the Eye, the Bury and the Hadleigh Troops, and is now become the 1st Regiment of Loyal Suffolk Yeomanry Cavalry consisting of 7 Troops, and that we have agreed to go out in the month of May for 12 days agreeable to Lord Sidmouth's letter, to Ipswich and Bury alternately.

The Regiment is, I find in a letter from the Lord Lieutenant, entitled to have an Adjutant, and should such an appointment be as desirable to you, now as it were 8 or 9 years ago when I made an unsuccessful application on your Behalf, I shall have great pleasure in recommending it. The pay is 8s per day which certainly appears no bad thing considering the Duty not to be very Severe. It is necessary that the person recommended to the situation should have been Commissioned Officer for

4 years at least in the Regulars or Militia, in the former of which you were I think for a much longer time. Although it is desirable that I should receive your answer in a few days, you will I trust, bestow such a portion of thought upon it as to satisfy yourself that the appointment will be in every point of view what you will like, for which purpose I request you, my Friend, to dismiss from your mind all complimentary feelings towards me.

Believe me, ever, Yours truly, Mileson Edgar

Mr Walter Ray Wortham

B302 Memorandum

Mr W Ray in his reply to Colonel Edgar's letter of 23rd February, declines the acceptance of the Adjutancy of the Regiment, and recommends his Brother Philip. I had not the opportunity of copying Mr Ray's letter, Colonel Edgar having sent it to Mr Elrington as appears by the following letter from Colonel Edgar to Mr Elrington.

After writing the above Memorandum, Mr Ray's letter came to hand, of which as under is a copy.[177]

Wortham February 25th 1814

Many thanks my dear Sir, for your very kind and friendly letter received yesterday. Lord Sidmouth's circular Letter I had seen, but did not know what steps had been taken, for Regimenting the different Troops. Your promotion was announced in the Bury Paper, on which I beg leave to congratulate you. How came the Majority not mentioned, Theobald I suppose will fill that Station. The addition of three Troops to your present Muster will give effect to Dundas's system.[178] I have given due consideration to the Adjutancy, and was I placed in a good Farm near the Red House, under so able and judicious a commander as yourself, I should like much to be a candidate for the Commission, with the uncertainty what direction I may take when Michaelmas arrives prevents my accepting your very handsome offer, as I should be unwilling to undertake it if at any great distance from Ipswich or Bury. I am requested by my Brother, to whom I made known the contents of your Letter to say if you have not any particular Friend you would wish to oblige, he would be very happy to take my place. I have only to observe from his quitting the Army so recently and having been sometime upon the Staff, I think him better qualified for the situation than myself, he is now upon half pay as Captain, with the rank of Major by Brevet,[179] from the smallness of his occupation, much time upon his hands.[180]

I remain my dear Sir, Yours most truly, Walter Ray

---

[177] Another example of Collett's method of working. It is obvious that Mileson Edgar was happy to co-operate with him by passing on his letters for him to transcribe, and shows that by this date at least he was up to date with copying his material.

[178] In 1803, for example, the Norfolk Yeomanry with 23 Troops had been organised into three regiments, Western, Eastern and Midland. See J. Bastin, *The Norfolk Yeomanry in Peace and in War* (Fakenham, 1986), p. 7.

[179] In the army this was the promotion of an officer to a higher rank without the corresponding increase in pay.

[180] An illustration of the difficulty that was faced by officers in the army, and indeed the navy, returning to settle down after many years of fighting. Younger sons often joined the armed forces because many estates were entailed, to be inherited by the eldest son, in order to prevent the fragmentation of the estate.

Dear Sir

I yesterday convened the 5th Troop under my Command, the result of which meeting was, after a very considerable resignation which reduces the Number of its Members including Officers to forty one or two, to propose to you to become a part of your Regiment should it meet with your approbation. In that Instance I should thank you to inform me whether a change of Uniform will be necessary, our present one being Scarlet with Helmet and Scarlet Feather tipted with white[181] and what will be the precise time and place of meeting as the farming Members wish as early Information on that point as possible that they may arrange their business accordingly.

I am dear Sir, very faithfully, Your obliged Humble Servant   R Rede

Beccles 26th February 1814

Lieutenant Colonel Edgar, Red House, Ipswich

Dear Sir   **Red House February 27th 1814**

I lose no time in acknowledging the receipt of your letter, and in saying that I shall be most happy to have your Troop as part of my Regiment, knowing that there can be no objection or difficulty raised on the part of the Secretary of State or the Lord Lieutenant to such a Measure in consequence of its not having taken place in an earlier Stage of the Business. I shall write to the Duke of Grafton to Night on the Subject in order to prepare him for a Letter from you which I trust you will be able to send off by to morrows post. In that letter you will be kind enough to state the Strength of your Troop, as it was at the last return made by you in December to his Grace and the Secretary of State, and not as it is in its present reduced state, because whatever that strength was, it may be completed to the same again, and were it returned according to its present strength, it could never be increased beyond it. As to the Clothing, it will be a matter for future consideration when other arrangements are made. We shall I apprehend, assemble at Ipswich and about the middle of May, which will be a leisure time for Farmers. You will bear in mind that in your return there can be only two Sergeants because Government will allow one Sergeant to 20 Rank and File consisting of Corporals and Privates. You will therefore if you please, make your return as follows **B303**

1 Captain
1 Lieutenant
1 Cornet
1 Quarter Master
2 Sergeants
1 Trumpeter
[blank] Rank and File
Total [blank]

The numbers of Rank and File will be made up of any Sergeants you have or had at the date of your last return beyond the two above mentioned, and your Corporals and Privates. You will add at the foot of the return the names of the Officers. I will thank you to send me a copy of the Return you furnish to the Lord Lieutenant and with it the Date of Your and Your Officers present Commissions as Captain, Lieutenant and Cornet, as promotion in the Regiment will in future take place by seniority without respect to the Troop in which the Vacancy may happen to have been made. Excuse haste and believe me, my dear Sir,   Yours truly,

Mileson Edgar

R Rede Esq Beccles

---

[181] The 5th (Beccles) Troop had also changed its uniforms to its own designs from the original 1794 one.

Red House   February 28th 1814

My Dear Elrington
The best thing I have discovered as arising from my Military Promotion is, that I have an opportunity of recommending an Adjutant for the Lord Lieutenant's appointment to the Regiment of Yeomanry I am to have the honor of commanding. Having in the year 1804 made an unsuccessful application on behalf of one of the Captains of the Corps, who had been an old Dragoon Officer, I thought it but right to make him the first offer of the Adjutancy now there appeared reason to suppose my Recommendation would be attended to. I inclose you his Letter in which he declines it, but recommends his brother to me, with whom I am also well acquainted. Feeling myself however quite at Liberty as to the second offer of the Adjutancy, I beg leave to say, that should such an appointment appear to you desirable, I shall have great pleasure in recommending you to the Duke of Grafton. The person who fills the situation must have been a Commissioned Officer for four years at least, in the Regulars or Militia, in the former of which you were I think for a much longer time. The pay is 8s per day, constant, which does not appear a very bad thing as I consider the duty will not be severe. Although it is desirable that I should receive your answer with as little delay as possible, you will I trust give it such a portion of Thought as to satisfy yourself that the appointment will be in every point of View what you will like, for which purpose, my good Friend, I request you to dismiss from your mind all Complimentary Feelings towards me. I shall be happy to receive a favourable Bulletin of all your Family etc and believe me, ever
Yours most Truly   Mileson Edgar
To Captain Elrington, Ipswich

My Dear Edgar   **Ipswich March 1st 1814**
I feel particularly obliged by your kind offer of the Adjutancy of your Corps, and had I been fortunate enough to procure a permanent residence in the neighbourhood of Ipswich, I should have had great pleasure in serving under your command and, but the uncertainty where, or in what County I shall be able to find a suitable habitation for my family, compels me, reluctantly to decline your friendly proposition. However, my dear Sir, let my abode be where it may, I shall always rejoice to hear of the prosperity of you and your Corps, and when a desirable Peace renders your services no longer necessary, I trust you will find in the gratitude of the Country an ample reward for all your patriotic exertions.
With sincere regard, believe me, Your obliged and faithfull,   J M Elrington
Lieutenant Colonel Edgar etc etc Red House

B304 Dear Sir   **Euston   March 2nd 1814**
I have to acquaint you that your Regiment of Yeomanry Cavalry will consist of 303 Rank and File instead of 296 the same having been approved of by H,R,H the Prince Regent. I have not heard from Captain Rede; his proposition shall be attended to when I receive it, and I conclude there will not only be no difficulty on the Subject of this accession of Strength to your Corps, but that it will be considered advantageous to the public Service that it should take place. I conclude you propose that the Head Quarters of the Regiment should be at Ipswich.
                    I am dear Sir very faithfully etc Yours   Grafton
M Edgar Esq Red House Ipswich

DATE OF OFFICERS' COMMISSIONS

Name of Officer	Date of Commission
Lieutenant Colonel Edgar	February 1814
Major Theobald	
Captain Collett	September 5 1803
Captain Couperthwaite	September 5 1803
Captain Rede	February 15 1806
Captain Cooke	July 13 1809
Captain Todd	July 31 1810
Captain Wythe	
Captain Frost	February 1 1814
Captain Pearson	
Adjutant Philip Ray	May 1 1814
Lieutenant Dikes	September 10 1808
Lieutenant Reeve	July 13 1809
Lieutenant Hewitt	July 31 1810
Lieutenant Farr	January 1 1812
Lieutenant De Carle	February 1 1814
Lieutenant Rodwell	March 31 1814
Lieutenant Clabon	March 31 1814
Lieutenant Cross	March 31 1814
Cornet Chaplin	July 13 1809
Cornet Glasspole	January 1 1812
Cornet Hayle	February 10 1812
Cornet Taylor	March 31 1814
Cornet Fisher	February 1 1814
Cornet Sexton	March 31 1814
Cornet Coker	March 31 1814
Cornet Simpson	March 31 1814

Establishment of the 1st Regiment of Loyal Suffolk Yeomanry Cavalry: March 11th 1814

Number of Troops: 8	
Field Officers	2
Captains	8
Lieutenants	8
Cornets	8
Surgeon	1
Adjutant	1
Quarter Masters	8
Sergeants	17
Trumpeters	8
Rank and File	354
Total strength	**415**

Remarks: The Surgeon receive no pay.
The Adjutant constant pay of 8s per day, 6s for himself and 2s for his horse
One of the Sergeants will be Sergeant Major with the Regular Constant Pay
Of the Rank and File there will be 16 Corporals and two Farriers

Philip Ray of Wortham, Suffolk, appointed Adjutant, his commission dated 1st May 1814 se his letter to Colonel Edgar March 3 1814 stating his Rank in the Army which qualify him for the appointment to the Agency which require his having served in the Army.

Memorandum: The Cavalry being now Regimented, Promotion will in future take place according to Seniority without reference to the Troop in which the Vacancy may happen to have been made. The Seniority takes place from the dates of the respective commissions.

B305[182] My Dear Sir   **Wortham March 3rd 1814**
In reply to your letter with respect to the length of Service as it seems are considered necessary to qualify for the Adjutancy; I joined the Kings Dragoon Guards on the 1st June 1796 and continued in that Regiment till the 24th June 1802 when that abominable Peace had the effects of placing two Troops of every Regiment on half pay, and myself as the Junior Captain was one of the unfortunate sufferers. In the following Spring I had the honor of being presented with a Company in the West Suffolk Militia, and had the pleasure of serving under the Duke of Grafton[183] for about 17 months and was then appointed Brigade Major to Brigadier General Warde to whom I was attached for about 8 months, after which I was again restored to my Troop in the Kings Dragoon Guards and continued on full pay in the Service till the early part of 1812, when finding that five young Children and an establishment of Servants were no trifling expense to move from Quarter to Quarter, I determined if possible to accomplish an exchange to half pay (having previously attained the rank of Brevet Major) and which I was fortunate enough to effect, and am now on half pay of the 3rd Foot Guards. I conclude all the above is unnecessary, but of course you will take out such parts of it as you may deem sufficient for the recommendation. The appointment of the Adjutancy I trust will not interfere with my half pay as, in the case of all Staff situations, of which nature I consider the present, neither Regimental or half pay is withheld.
                        I remain Dear Sir Yours very truly   P Ray
To Lieutenant Colonel Edgar Red House, Ipswich

Dear Sir   **Beccles 9th March 1814**
I awaited the Duke of Grafton's reply to my letter before I answered yours. His Grace says it is a measure in which he entirely concurs, and to which he says he has no doubt the Secretary of States answer will soon enable him to give effect. The date of my Commission is the 15th February 1806, those of my Officers I will send you as soon as I can learn them, and the Copy of the Return which I sent to the Duke you have on the other side. I suppose I am correct in having applied for the years

---

[182] There is a note in the margin in a later hand: Lieutenant Colonel Ray resided for many years at Eldo House near Bury St Edmunds and died there.
[183] The Duke of Grafton was Lord Euston when he commanded the West Suffolk Militia.

Clothing Allowance and that for the Half years Contingencies notwithstanding the present Arrangements.

I am Dear Sir very faithfully Yours, R Rede

Lieutenant Colonel Edgar Red House Ipswich

Sir   **Clerges March 10th 1814**

I have to acquaint you that H,R,H the Prince Regent has been pleased to approve of the 5th Troop of Yeomanry Cavalry, commanded by Captain Rede being united to the 1st Regiment of Loyal Suffolk Yeomanry Cavalry under your command.

The Troop consists of 1 Captain, 1 Lieutenant, 1 Cornet, 1 Quarter Master, 2 Sergeants, 1 Trumpeter, 51 Rank and File, which will hence forward, make a part of the Establishment of your Regiment.

I have the honor to be, Sir, Your most Obedient Humble Servant,

Grafton

To Lieutenant Colonel Edgar Commanding 1 Regiment Yeomanry Cavalry Red House, Ipswich

---

My dear Lord   **Red House 13th March 1814**

I am happy to find that by your Grace's letter the Prince Regent has approved the addition to the Regiment of Captain Rede's Troop of which I lose no time in advising him. I have now to furnish your Grace with a long list of recommendations for promotion in the Regiment, having waited till I could ascertain the seniority in the different ranks to be promoted viz Captain John Meadows Theobald to be Major; Lieutenant William Pearson to be Captain, Mr John Clabon, Mr Robert Cross and Mr John Meadows Rodwell to be Lieutenants; John Sidney Coker, Robert Sexton, Thomas Simpson, Cornets; Captain Philip Ray, Adjutant. Captain Ray is not only qualified by the length of his services as an Officer in the **B305** Regulars and Militia agreeable to the regulations of Government for the appointment of an Adjutant to the Yeomanry, but is also from his military knowledge and conciliatory manners particularly well suited to the situation. He served more than 10 years in the King's Dragoon Guards and for 17 months had a Company in the West Suffolk Militia during the time your Grace commanded it. I have therefore to request a recommendation of him to the Secretary of State through your Grace, agreeable to the regulations of 1806.

I have now further to request information of your Grace as to what returns are henceforth to be made to the Secretary of State and to your Grace, as whilst in distinct Corps or Troops we have been directed to make 3 periodical returns within 14 days after the 1st of April, the 1st of August and the 1st of December in every year. I conclude your Grace has heard from the Clerk of the Peace that the names of Mr Woodcock as Lieutenant and of Mr Plant as Cornet, which appeared in the Provincial Papers as Officers in my Regiment, were intended for their respective situations in Captain Crabtree's Troop of Yeomanry, which is not attached to me.

I am etc etc   Mileson Edgar

To his Grace the Duke of Grafton

Dear Sir   **Red House March 13th 1814**

I perceive by the Ipswich Paper of Yesterday that you have called your Troop together this week, on Friday next. I wish therefore to address a letter to you upon regimental Business, to which you will be kind enough to call the attention of the Troop when assembled.

In the first place I shall give you a statement of the component Parts of your Troop in order that you may make the necessary arrangements.

1 Captain, 1 Lieutenant 1 Cornet, 1 Quarter Master, 2 Sergeants, 1 Trumpeter, 2 Corporals, 39 Privates, Total 48

If you should have more Sergeants or Corporals than those mentioned, they must again become Privates until an opportunity offers of Promoting them. It will certainly be necessary that the Regiment should be Clothed alike which I have signified to the Captains of all the Troops which have joined the Regiment. The Fund of every Troop must be fully equal to such an expense, unless there has been some abuse in the management of it. If a Commander of a Troop has ever suffered a Distribution or a Partition of money to be made amongst its Members, he has in so doing been guilty of a most irregular act, and one which is subversive of the purposes for which the issue of money were made by Government. This I am the more induced to notice because, as several of the Bury Troop are gone out, they may have formed Ideas to themselves of taking out a certain proportion of the fund. They must bear in mind that the Clothing and Contingent Money is not issued for the individual use and benefit of any man in a Troop, any longer than he is a Member of that Troop, and then only in the furnishing and providing the necessary equipments.

I have this morning received a letter from Mr Shillito for information how the balance of the Fund is to be transferred. I shall by this Post request him to transfer it into your name as Captain of the Troop, being thoroughly sensible you will feel the responsibility of such a trust, and not suffer one farthing to be applied for other than the purposes of the Service and with which you will previously make me acquainted.

Although on Monday sennight the 21st instant I should wish to meet your Troop at Stowmarket in Marching order at 12 o'clock, when I will inspect the Men and Horses, after which we can adjourn to the Inn and finish matters we may have to talk about.

I wish to be furnished with an account of the Number of Sabres, Waist-belts, and Pistols, Camp Kettles, Billhooks, Trumpets, Bugles and Sadlery, in short every Military appointment issued by Government, as responsibility will from this moment rest on me. I hope your Trumpeter is a pretty good one as he will have to blow both on the bugle and trumpet with some who are very good.

I am dear Sir Yours etc etc   Mileson Edgar

To Captain Frost Loyal Suffolk Yeomanry Cavalry Brent Ely

B307 Copy of a Letter from Lord Sidmouth to His Grace the Duke of Grafton

My Lord   **Whitehall 25th March 1814**

I have laid before His Royal Highness the Prince Regent, your Grace's recommendation dated the 15th instant of Captain John Meadows Theobald to be Major, and Lieutenant William Pearson to be Captain in the first Regiment of Suffolk Yeomanry Cavalry, and I have the satisfaction of informing your Grace that His Royal Highness in the name and on the behalf of His Majesty, does not disapprove thereof. As I am not aware of more than one vacant Lieutenancy in the said Regiment, I must trouble your Grace to inform me in whose room the gentlemen recommended for

Subalterns' commissions are to be appointed before their names can be submitted for the Royal Approbation.

I have the honor to be My Lord, Your Grace's most obedient

humble Servant   Sidmouth

His Grace the Duke of Grafton

Dear Sir   **March 28th 1814**

I inclose the copy of a letter from the Secretary of state and will beg of you to enable me to answer the question therein contained respecting the Subaltern Appointments etc.

The Commission for Major Theobald and Captain Pearson are ordered to be made out for my Signature.

I am, dear Sir, faithfully etc., Yours,   Grafton

M Edgar Esq etc

My Dear Lord   **Red House March 31st 1814**

I received your Grace's letter yesterday with a Copy of Lord Sidmouth's Letter respecting the Subaltern Appointments in the Regiment. I am sorry I did not state in my Letter to your Grace of the 13th instant how the vacancies were made to which I recommended Officers to be appointed, which certainly should have done had I not in a letter written on the 18th of January made a full statement of them to your Grace. I will now however correctly detail them, and I trust the explanation will be satisfactory to your Grace and to the Secretary of State.

To be Lieutenants Cornet John Meadows Rodwell vice William Pearson promoted

to be Captain,

Cornet Robert Cross vice William Frost   ditto

Mr George Clabon vice Francis Leake resigned

To be Cornets John Sidney Coker vice Robert Cross recommended to a Lieutenancy

Thomas Simpson vice John Field resigned

Robert Sexton vice J M Rodwell recommended to a Lieutenancy

Robert Taylor vice John Edwards resigned

The last mentioned name (Mr Taylor) is a fresh recommendation, as I find that the Eye Troop has neither a Lieutenant or Cornet, although Lieutenant Colonel McLeroth in his return to me mentions their having a Captain and Cornet which I find is not the case, (Mr Edwards having long since resigned).

The resignation of Mr John Field is in consequence of very bad health. The resignation of Lieutenant Francis Leek, of the Eye Troop took place in the Autumn I believe. The Regiment will, when the above Promotion of Officers takes place, be complete, but in your Grace's letter no mention is made of Captain Ray's appointment to the Adjutancy.

I am, my Dear Lord, most sincerely yours,   Mileson Edgar

To his Grace The Duke of Grafton

My dear Sir,   **Halesworth 28th March 1814**

I was extremely surprised to be informed by Mr Davy of Yoxford whilst at the Assizes, that he had seen you at Stowmarket, and that you had inform'd him, mine was the only Troop in the County which was not to be under your Command. I had conceived that after my Letter to the Lord Lieutenant and my conference with you at your own house, there could be no misunderstanding **B308** on this subject, and

I was therefore quite unable to account for what I heard. Do my dear Sir have the goodness to favor me with a Line in Explanation that the matter may be cleared up.

I am, Dear Sir, Yours very faithfully,   Robert Crabtree

Lieutenant Colonel Edgar, Red House, Ipswich

My Dear Sir   **Red House March 29th 1814**

I loose no time in answering your letter received this Morning which has, I assure you surprised me as much as my Friend Davy's Communication at the Assizes possibly could you.

After the letter which I received from you and the Conference we had, I expected to have heard from the Lord Lieutenant that you had communicated to him a Wish on the Part of your Troop to be placed under my Command. This was the Step (and an indispensable necessary one) taken by the Commanders of the Eye, Hadleigh, and Beccles Troops. Delicacy prevented my making any suggestions on the subject as it might appear arrogant and presumptuous, conveying as it were a wish to Command all the Yeomanry of the County. Indeed it occurred to me that probably some change had taken place in your Mens minds, in consequence of your distance from Ipswich and Bury and that it was the Wish of the Troop to remain unattached. In short, circumstanced as I was, I dare not move in the Business, or believe me, your Troop would have been among those which form the Regiment.

I will hope however that it may not be too late to have it now, and trust that you will by to Morrows post, write to the Duke of Grafton on the Subject. On the 19th January I received a Letter from His Grace from which I will give you an Extract, to prove how necessary it was for the Commanders of the Troops to make the Communication I have alluded to. "I have submitted to the Secretary of State for the Prince Regent's approbation, a Proposition for uniting to the 4 Troops already under your command as Lieutenant Colonel the 3rd, 4th and 6th Troops so as to form a Regiment of 7 Troops. The Captains commanding the 3rd and 6th having distinctly expressed themselves to me on behalf of their respective Troops, and the 4th (having no officers), through yourself, as not only acceeding generally to the proposition contained in Lord Sidmouth's letter of the 29th October, but as being desirous henceforward of forming a part of the Regiment under your command." On the 11th instant I received a Letter from His Grace to say that the Prince Regent had approved the addition of Captain Rede's Troop to the Regiment (he having on the 27th ult. made on the Part of his Troop the first Communication to me on the subject and immediately after to the Lord Lieutenant. The Regiment now therefore consists of 8 Troops, and I sincerely hope it will with as little loss of time as possible be permitted to have Nine. I trust my dear Sir you will aquit me of any inattention to your wishes and those of your Troop, and perceive that they could only be made known to the Lord Lieutenant but by yourself. I shall be very anxious to hear again from you. The Duke is in Town, and his address is Clerges Street, Piccadilly.

I am my dear Sir, truly yours,   Mileson Edgar

R Crabtree Esq Halesworth

My dear Sir,   **Halesworth 1st April 1814**

I beg to acknowledge the receipt of your obliging favor of 29th March and to assure you that I do most sincerely acquit you of any the least Inattention to my Wishes or those of my Troop. On the contrary, I with the utmost pleasure acknowledge the uniform kindness, politeness and attention with which you have at all times favoured me.

I cannot however but regret that a sense of delicacy should have prevented your suggesting to me the necessity for my communicating to the Lord Lieutenant, a Wish on the part of the First Troop to be placed under your Command, as you were aware of my having acquainted His Grace with the Resolution of the Troop to acceede to the Wishes of His Majesty's Government by consenting to their formation with the other Troops of the County into a Regiment and that the object of my calling upon you was to state to you the Wish and Intention of the Troop to be placed under your Command. If you had given me the least hint of any further Communication to His Grace being necessary, I should instantly have made it, but not being at all aware of the necessity of so doing, I took it for granted that the First **B309** Troop would, as a matter of course, have been included in the arrangement for the original formation of the Regiment, and which I also presumed would have entitled it to the same rank in the Regiment as the period of its original formation intitled it to in the County, and I confess I was extremely surprized and disappointed at finding we had been left out altogether, but I have certainly only my own ignorance to blame for the misunderstanding. I now beg to say that we shall be much happy to be placed under your Command, provided that we can be placed in the same situation as to precedence as we should have stood in had we been included in the original Proposition for the formation of the Regiment. For myself this is a Point of no Importance, but in matters of this kind, you are aware how necessary it is to consult the feelings of Individuals, and I know there is amongst my Men esprit de corps, that feeling of pride in being designated the First Troop, which would utterly disincline them to any Proposition tending to deprive them of that imaginary distinction. I shall be happy to hear from you on this Subject, and till I am favoured with your reply think it will be better to defer writing to the Lord Lieutenant.

I am Dear Sir Yours most faithfully   R Crabtree
Lieutenant Colonel Edgar, Red House, Ipswich

B310 Dear Sir   **Beccles April 13th 1814**
Although my mind has within the last Week been too much occupied by the melancholy cause of my Journey hither viz the serious Illness and death of Mrs Edgar's sister, I take much Interest in the Public good News which in that time has arrived.[184]
Yet has it occurred to me that amongst the many changes and economical arrangements which will speedily take place, Government may probably discontinue the services of the Yeomanry. Under the Influence of such an idea I have taken up my Pen to say that I think it would be better to stay all further Proceeding touching the New Clothing and other appointments of the Troop, till I have used my Endeavours to ascertain whether such a Measure is likely or not to take place. Should the Services of the Yeomanry be continued, and upon their present Footing, we shall only have to defer the Period of our going out a little. Should your opinion concur with mine, you will be kind enough to take the necessary steps for giving effect to

---

[184] After his retreat from Russia Napoleon was decisively defeated at the battle of Leipzig in October 1813, leading to the capture of Paris at the end of March 1814. He was forced to abdicate early in April and exiled to Elba. Since it was peacetime, no musters were held in 1814 and the Yeomanry was unsure of its future.

it. I shall return home on Tuesday next, and shall be glad to have your Sentiments on the Subject, as soon as you can conveniently.

In the mean time, believe me, most truly yours   Mileson Edgar
The above Letter was sent to Captains Cooke, Frost, Wythe and Rede respectively.

Dear Sir   **Theberton Hall April 9th 1814**
Your letter met my perfect concurrence and had I not received it, I should have written by the same Post to Goldsmith and Gray to suspend further proceedings relative to our Clothing etc until I had received some communication from you, as thinking it very probable, from the complete unexpected change of affairs our Services would probably be dispensed with. As soon as you learn anything of it I shall be glad to hear from you.

Believe me to be, dear Sir, yours truly,   F W Cooke
Lieutenant Colonel Edgar Red House Ipswich

Dear Sir
Yours I received and am sorry to find your time occupied upon so melancholy Occasion at Beccles. I instantly wrote to Goldsmith the Taylor likewise to the two Saddlers to stop further proceeding respecting the necessary appointments, am sorry to say that Goldsmith has completed the Jacketts and Stable ditto. The Sadlers I have not heard from. I wrote to De Carle to see them, which I expect he have. Goldsmith called upon me, he says that Mr Houblin Member for Essex communicated with Captain Bulieu last week respecting the Clothing wanted for his Troop which Goldsmith has to do. Mr Houblin said the Yeomanry would be continued in the same way it usually has been. All this is hearsay, but coming from a Member of Parliament, or should not have mentioned it. Your further orders will strictly attend to.   Remain Dear Sir, Your obedient, humble servant,   W Frost
Lieutenant Colonel Edgar Red House Ipswich

My Dear Lord   **Red House April 25th 1814**
I should have troubled your Grace sooner on the Business which form the Subject of this Letter, but for the melancholy call I have lately had from home in consequence of the very serious Illness and consequent Death of Mrs Edgar's sister. In the first place, although I have received from Mr Borton the Officers' Commissions for which I had applied to your Grace, Yet have I been favoured with no Communication as to the request I made to be allowed an Adjutant, and my friend Captain Ray, in whose behalf it was preferred is naturally enough anxious to know whether he is to have the Situation. I conclude your Grace has been kind enough to apply to Lord Sidmouth, and probably the cause of my not hearing is that Government may in consequence of the happy change in public Affairs which has certainly taken place to an extent unexpected, and with a rapidity hardly to be credited, meditate on the discontinuance of the services of the Yeomanry among the Economical arrangements which will necessarily take Place. Under the influence of such an Idea, I wrote about two days ago to the Captains of the Troops now Regimented **B311** under my Command desiring them to suspend all further proceedings touching their military Equipments till I had endeavoured to ascertain from your Grace whether it were probable our services would be continued, as some of the Troops were deficient in marching order appointments, and the Bury Troop are without either Clothing or Sadlery fit to come out with, considerable orders were given for Equipments which

252

I should be very sorry to have executed to their full Extent were our services no longer required.

In the event of our going out I have one matter more to refer to your Grace, which is the numbering of the Troops, or in effect the placing them in Line. I find from a little conversation with the Captains, they are of opinion they should be placed as they were raised, whereas my opinion is that the 2nd Corps as well from its superior strength as from its being the Basis or rallying point for the other Troops, should take the Right, and the other Troops stand in the order in which they signified their wishes to join the 2nd Corps.

It is a matter of no moment; and whatever your Graces Idea may be on the subject will be conclusive and satisfactory to us all. I hope your Grace will pardon the trouble I am giving you and that I shall soon have the Honour of hearing from you.

I am my dear Lord most sincerely yours
Mileson Edgar

His Grace the Duke of Grafton

Dear Sir   **Bury May 4th 1814**

Copy of A Letter (transmitted to me) from Lord Sidmouth, Secretary of State to Colonel Torrens Secretary to His Royal Highness the Commander in Chief

Sir   Whitehall 28th April 1814

Referring you to my letter of the 2nd February last, I am directed by Lord Sidmouth to acquaint you, for the Information of His Royal Highness the Commander in Chief, that it is no longer judged expedient to Assemble Corps of Yeomanry Cavalry on Permanent Duty in the present year.

I am etc signed H Addington

I am Dear Sir Yours faithfully,
H M'Leroth Lieutenant Colonel Inspecting Field Officer

To Lieutenant Colonel Edgar
185

Dear Sir   **Head Quarters Woodbridge May 9th 1814**

I am instructed by Lieutenant Colonel Edgar to inform you, he has received a Letter from the Lord Lieutenant to say, that it is not the intention of Government to assemble the Yeomanry Cavalry upon permanent duty in the present year. The Lieutenant Colonel particularly requests you will be attentive to the state of your military appointments, by frequent inspection of the same to preserve them from moths and rust etc. In the event of their not going out by Troops or Regimentally this year, the Adjutant of the Regiment will in the autumn make an inspection of arms and appointments.

Captain [blank]

(The above Circular Letter was sent by the respective Captains to each member of their Troop)

To Lieutenant Colonel Edgar etc etc

---

185 B312–B348, *London Gazette Extraordinary*. The downfall of Napoleon, capitulation of Paris, entrance of the King of France into London, entrance of the King of France into Paris, proclamation of peace, are all omitted.

My dear Sir,   **Clerges Street May 5th 1814**
An Adjutant's Commission is making out for Captain Ray. You will have been informed by Colonel M'Leroth that it is not considered as necessary to assemble your Yeomanry Cavalry Corps on permanent Duty in the present year.

The arrangement of the different Troops consists in a matter which does not press at this moment. The natural way as it appears to me, of posting them, and their usual way is from flanks to Centre, according to Seniority.

I sincerely congratulate you upon the happy and Providential termination of a war which, until very lately, looked as if it might have continued for years.

        Believe me, my dear sir, very faithfully yours,   Grafton
Major Edgar Esq Red House, Ipswich

VOLUME C

C59[1] **Thanks of the House of Commons to the Volunteers**[2]
Mercury 60 die Julii, 1814
Resolved, Nemine Contradicente,
That the Thanks of this House be given to the Officers of the several Corps of Yeomanry and Voluntary Cavalry and Infantry which have been formed in Great Britain and Ireland during the course of the War, for the meritorious and eminent Services which they have rendered to their King and Country.
Resolved, Nemine Contradicente,
That this House doth highly approve and acknowledge the Services of the Non-Commissioned Officers and Men of the several Corps of Yeomanry and Volunteer Cavalry and Infantry, which have been formed in Great Britain and Ireland during the course of the War; and that the same be communicated to Them by the Colonels and other commanding Officers of the several Corps, who are desired to thank them for their meritorious Conduct.
Ordered:
That Mr Speaker do signify the said Resolutions, to His Majesty's Lieutenant of each County, Riding and Place, in Great Britain, and to his Excellency the Lord Lieutenant of that part of the United Kingdom called Ireland.

J Dyson A.D. Dom.Com.

Circular
Sir   **Horse Guards 13**[th] **July 1814**
The Lord Chancellor and the Speaker of the Honourable House of Commons having transmitted in Letters to me the Resolutions of the Houses of Parliament to give their Thanks to the Officers, Non-Commissioned Officers and Men, employed in the Army, for the meritorious and Eminent Services they have rendered to their King and Country during the course of the War, I have the pleasure to send you herewith, copies of the said Letters and Resolutions, which you will communicate to the several descriptions of Troops under your command.
The good conduct, courage and zeal of the Officers, Non-Commissioned Officers and soldiers of His Majesty's Regular, Militia, Yeomanry and Volunteer Forces so uniformly exerted for the Glory and Honor of the Nation afford me an opportunity of expressing the great Satisfaction I feel in communicating through you this Public Mark of Honour conferred upon them.
            I have etc etc   Frederick, Commander in Chief
To the Officers commanding the Troops in the Eastern District

---

[1] C1–C58, *London Gazette Extraordinary* from 10 June 1814 onwards. The Proclamation of Peace and the huge national celebrations. Omitted.
[2] The thanks of the House of Lords followed but has been omitted because it is a repetition of that of the Commons.

C60   **Head Quarters Colchester 18th July 1814**

Major General Wilder feels particular pleasure in publishing the following Letter from the Commander in Chief, transmitting the thanks of both Houses of Parliament and expressive of His Royal Highness's approbation of the Conduct of the Army during the Late War, which the Major General directs may be inserted in the Orderly Books, and Read at the Head of every Corps in the District.

D. Faller, Major, Acting A.A.G

Lieutenant Colonel McLeroth Inspecting Field Officer

C61   **Bury July 22nd 1814**

Sir

I am Commanded by the General Officer Commanding the Eastern District to transmit to you Copies of the above letters etc.

I have the Honor to be Sir, your most obedient servant

        H M'Leroth Lieutenant Colonel Inspecting Field Officer

Lieutenant Colonel Edgar Red House Ipswich

C62 Proceedings of the Regiment of Loyal Suffolk Yeomanry Cavalry Commanded by Lieutenant Colonel Edgar Continued from Letter B or Volume B

Advertisement Copied from the Ipswich Journal March 4th 1815

1st Regiment Suffolk Yeomanry Cavalry

The members of Captain Collett's, Captain Couperthwaite's and Captain Pearson's Troops are requested to assemble at Woodbridge, and the Members of the other Five Troops are requested to assemble at their usual places of Exercise, on the undermentioned days at Eleven o'clock precisely, in Field Day Order viz

1	Thursday	March	9th	5	Friday	March	17th	9	Wednesday	March	29th
2	Friday	March	10th	6	Monday	March	20th	10	Monday	April	3rd
3	Tuesday	March	14th	7	Tuesday	March	21st	11	Tuesday	April	4th
4	Thursday	March	16th	8	Thursday	March	23rd	12	Wednesday	April	5th

           M Edgar, Lieutenant Colonel

Red House March 2nd 1815

General Muster Thursday March 9th 1815[3]

The three Troops met at the time appointed. Unfortunately the forenoon after 9 o'clock proved very wet and the rain continuing so as to prevent our exercise in the Field, the Colonel after waiting till near one o'clock, was pleased to dispense with same, and the horses being taken care of the members adjourned to the Market Hall, when the Colonel informed us that in order for him to make a legal return and also to impower him to draw for the Government allowance for Clothing, and which return was also required for the exemptions from Taxes etc although Government had declined embodying the Regiment for 12 days, yet their attendance for the 12 days previous to 6th of April next could not be dispensed with and for which reason he had now called upon the Regiment for the fulfilment of same on the days respec-

---

[3]   This was the first general muster since November 1813.

tively nominated. Yet he was desirous of C66 altering the days of meeting providing it would insure full attendance etc.

After debating the matter for some time, it was suggested, the time being short and the distance of the situation of a Majority of the Members from Head Quarters was such it appeared almost impossible it could be effected at General Meetings, that provided they were allowed to exercise in four divisions under the Command of the Major and the three Captains it would insure the meeting of each member the few Number of days required. This proposition being considered of and approved by the Colonel, was consequently adopted, and Major Theobald, Captains Collett, Couperthwaite and Pearson were required to fix on such places of meeting as were most convenient to the members who might attend at either of the places most convenient for distance etc from their respective Habitations.

The following places were agreed upon and the days of Muster at each on days respectively appointed, Major Theobald at Coddenham, Captain Collett at Woodbridge, Captain Couperthwaite or Lieutenant Dikes at Wickham Market, Captain Pearson at Rushmere Heath near Ipswich, with the exception that the 3 Troops meet at Head Quarters Woodbridge in a General Muster for a field day Commanded by Colonel Edgar on Tuesday next the 14th instant under the promise of a full attendance and to meet precisely at 11 o'clock.

After the arrangement above stated, the Colonel addressed the Members present on the subject of their engagements of Services, which terminated with the War on the Continent, that on the declaration of Peace, each Member was most honourably exonerated from any further obligation of Service and at full liberty to withdraw if he though proper. At same time the Colonel also expressed a wish that our Services should be continued for the present, as he had been given to understand that it was much the wish of Government to continue the Services of the Yeomanry Cavalry in the time of peace, and that he daily expected an Official Communication thereon, that we should be immediately apprised of same on his receipt thereof. There were only three or four members who expressed any intention of withdrawing, and there were five new members elected in the place of that Number who had quitted the Troop by reason of a removal from their situations including two who died since our last General Muster in November 1813.

Tuesday March 14th 1815 General Muster

This day the Troops met at Woodbridge and marched from Parade to Melton to a field belonging to Mr W Whimper Commanded by Colonel Edgar and being a full attendance exercised in the Evolutions usually practised in days of General Muster. The day was unpleasant the Wind being very high accompanied by with sundry storms of Hail and Rain and was very cold. No particular occurrence. The meetings in divisions was directed to be continued until such time as the twelve days attendance were completed.[4] Those members who at the Meeting on the 9th instant signified a desire of withdrawing, this day respectively informed the Colonel they had declined such intentions and should continue in their posts.

The remaining 10 meetings were in divisions.[5]

---

4 Divisions, the smaller groups of members living closer together, were the only way that the sizeable number of requisite general musters could be fitted in quickly, since the government had said there was to be no permanent duty that year, which is when they had expected to fit them in.
5 C67–C74, *London Gazette Extraordinary*. Peace with America. Omitted. C75–C85 are blank pages.

Advertisement Copied from the Ipswich Journal July 15th 1815

First Regiment Suffolk Yeomanry Cavalry

The Members of Captains Collett Couperthwaite and Pearson are requested to assemble at Woodbridge at Eleven oClock precisely on the undermentioned days July 25th Friday July 28th Tuesday August 1st Friday August 4th

NB On the third day to appear in Marching Order and on the other 3 days, in Field-day order. The Captains of the other five Troops to assemble their Men for exercise, on any four days prior to 5th of August, and at any place they should think fit.[6]

M Edgar Lieutenant Colonel

Red House July 13th 1815

Tuesday July 25th 1815

The Troops being assembled at the time appointed marched from the Parade to the Horse Parade Ground, on land belonging to Admiral Carthew in Woodbridge and hired of him by the Commissioners for the Affairs at the Barracks. Being the first meeting for the present year (from Lady Day to Lady Day 1816) Colonel Edgar after the Muster Roll had been called over addressed the Members present noting that whereas Bouneparte had surrendered himself a Prisoner to the British[7] and peace having been declared with America,[8] there was every prospect of a general peace throughout the universe by means of the Exertions of the United Powers of Europe;[9] he trusted that such members as now belonged to the Troop present would continue their services until such time as he might have official accounts from Government since it had been hinted that a continuation of their services would be very acceptable. At the same time he wishes it to be understood the Troops having pledged themselves to serve during the war only, providing it was their wish to retire they were fully at liberty to do it, having most honourably fulfilled their engagements.[10]

The time of the day being far advanced in the arrangement for appointing officers in place of those who had retired under various Circumstances and occurences respecting Equipments, electing new Members in place of those who had withdrawn etc etc the Colonel dismissed the Troops without requiring their going through the usual Exercise of the day.

NB the weather was very dry, hot and dusty.

Friday July 28th 1815

The Troops marched from Parade to the Ground occupied on the 25th and were exercised by Colonel Edgar in the usual Evolutions. There being sundry new officers and recruits, the exercise was done in a manner full as correct as could

---

6   In many ways this shows the Yeomanry reverting to their former independent way of operating, but now under the overall command of Lieutenant Colonel Edgar.

7   After his defeat at Waterloo on 18 June 1815, Napoleon abdicated on 22 June. He left Paris and embarked on a French frigate, hoping to reach America, but was forced to surrender to the British, arriving in Torbay Bay on 24 June aboard HMS *Bellerophon*.

8   The American War, fought between 18 June 1812 and 17 February 1815 arose both from the attempts of the British to enforce their French blockade by preventing trade with neutral countries such as America, and preventing the Americans from invading Canada.

9   Collett recognised that the war had not been just a European one but one fought across the world in places as far apart as India and the West Indies. The European powers met in Vienna to draw up a treaty that basically established peace in Europe for a hundred years.

10   The names of those who did withdraw appear on B209. Omitted.

be expected under all disadvantages.[11] The day was very dry, hot and dusty – no particular occurrences.

C87 **Sunday August 4ᵗʰ 1815**

The Troops marched from the Parade, Market Hill, Woodbridge, to the Barrack Ground. After calling over the Muster Rolls and sundry arrangements being made for the purpose of a General Inspection of Horses and Arms and Equipments of every sort took place, which occupied the greater part of the day and which being appropriated to that purpose no exercise was required.

After the Muster Rolls were called over, and previous to the Inspection, Henry Garnham of Grundisburgh (of Captain Couperthwaite's Troop) withdrew from the Ranks and rode off without Leave or any notice whatever being given by him to any of the Officers. One of the privates went after him, requesting his return but he would not and on further enquiry by the Colonel the occasion of his so absenting himself, he was informed it was his common practice although it had not been before noticed by his Officers, and that he invariably did it in defiance of the non-commissioned officers or Privates. His Conduct on investigation, was by all considered most daringly Insulting, the Colonel consequently immediately erased his name from the Muster Roll and discharged him from the Regiment for Misconduct, and not worthy of being a Member of same, an opinion in which all the Members present fully concurred.

Tuesday October 24ᵗʰ 1815

The three Troops being assembled, about 12 o'clock marched from the Parade (Market Place, Woodbridge) to a piece of land belonging to myself, late in the occupation of the Commissioners for the Affairs of Barracks,[12] and exercised on that part which was recently used for the Infantry Parade Ground.

Lieutenant Colonel Edgar being too unwell to attend, the Command devolved on Major Theobald. The morning was wet and stormy, but during the time we were out it was very fine and pleasant. The Troops Exercised in the usual Evolutions practised on days of Muster without any particular occurrence. Dispersed about 2 o'clock.

Mr Nathaniel Barthrop was appointed Sergeant vice Thredkell who quitted the Troop by reason of ill health. Mr Samuel Webber of Friston was unanimously elected a member of the Regiment. Mr John Kirby having left Mr Welton of Eyke and taken a small Business (a distance he says of nearly 20 miles from Woodbridge) requested to withdraw his services and as he further say the distance is not the only object, but from being in a small occupation he do not consider it prudent to keep a horse proper to ride in the Troop.[13]

---

11 The war against the French might be over but the unrest in Suffolk and other East Anglian counties with escalating protests and riots amounted to what has been described as a rural war at home. See Archer, 'Rural Protest', in Dymond and Martin, *Historical Atlas of Suffolk*, p. 124. In the absence of any police force the Yeomanry, drawn largely from farmers, would be even more necessary.

12 An indication of how soon the military left Woodbridge. With the withdrawal of the army the barracks were removed and the land sold off. See Plate 2.

13 Ownership of a horse was more difficult in the straitened circumstances of the economic recession after the war.

C88 Friday October 27th 1815

The Troops marched from Parade about 12 o'Clock to the same field on which we Exercised on Tuesday the 24th instant after forming in Line, wheeled into circle when the Colonel himself called over the respective Muster Rolls for the purpose of ascertaining the present residence of each member to enable him to make out a correct return to the Commissioners whereby they may ascertain the names of those members who are effective for the purpose of excluding their services under the Militia Act, and payment of the duty on their riding Horse used in their Service in the Yeomanry Cavalry.

The morning and forenoon was particularly fine and pleasant, after one o'clock there was every appearance of a wet afternoon. The day being far advanced and the Colonel himself unwell, for fear of increasing his cold in the risk of getting wet, about two o'clock dismissed the Troops, soon after which it began to rain and the remainder of the day was very wet and stormy.

At the Colonel's request the Meetings advertised on Tuesday and Friday in next week were altered to Monday and Thursday on which days the Troops will meet at the usual time and place.

William Wase of Bredfield who had withdrawn his services in my Troop in consequence of his expected engagement to superintend a business in another County, this day applied to Colonel Edgar to be readmitted, having he say, being disappointed in his undertaking in which he say he was positively engaged but the Gentlemen whose business he was to superintend having changed his mind, had informed him he should not now have occasion for employing him and no reason whatever was assigned for so doing. Wase consequently now resides with his Father as heretofore. From the occasion of the sudden exchange in the times and removals from their residence (being Michaelmas season) sundry Members have quitted the Troops as will fully appear on the Muster Rolls and explained in my General List of the Members.[14]

There being a General Peace many Members who had engaged to serve during the war being at full liberty to withdraw their services, have occasioned their so doing, and on the pressure of the present time many have declined keeping a horse.[15]

Monday October 30th 1815

The Troops assembled this day at the particular request of Colonel Edgar in lieu of the 31st as ordered by advertisement, marched from Parade to the field belonging to myself in which we exercised last week. The Colonel being too unwell to attend Major Theobald commanded. We exercised in the Evolutions as on former days of practice. No particular occurrence. The day was favourable.

Mr John Fox of Coddenham on withdrawing his services, addressed Colonel Edgar by Letter of which the following is a Copy.

Sir   **Coddenham October 29th 1815**

After a Servitude of upwards of ten years under your command, at a time when the Country was strenuously engaged in war with France, and which I trust has now terminated, I doubt not but you will readily consent to my resignation. But as I am unacquainted with the fund establishment of the Corps, I trust you **C89** will not

---

[14] It also reflects the economic recession at the end of the war and the uncertainty of agriculture. The Corn Laws exacerbated the problems.

[15] Another clear indicator of economic recession.

be offended at the following questions which are, first, whether or not, should the Troop be disbanded, the members would become sharers of the money in hand? and secondly, whether Gentlemen are not entitled to their accoutrements on quitting the corps? because if I am not misinformed, we were equipped at our own expense, and it appears the more likely by recruits paying four guineas at their joining the troop soon after we had new Jackets. I trust you will not consider these questions absurd, as I think there are many members desirous of having an explanation. However, if it appears to you, there is no balance of account due to me after serving ten years, I must submit, and if you conceive I am not entitled to my accoutrements, will send them to you in due course.

I am Sir Your Obedient Servant   John Fox

To Lieutenant Colonel Edgar

Thursday November 2nd 1815
This day was very fine and pleasant, the Troops being assembled marched from parade to the field belonging to myself in which we had exercised the three previous meetings, and were exercised under the command of Lieutenant Colonel Edgar in evolutions generally practised on days of Muster. The Troops present after the exercise of the day formed in a Circle and Colonel Edgar addressed them on the questions in Mr Fox's letter. (se copy as above) He first observed he did not think a reply by letter was needfull, the letter implicating other members of the Troops in the questions therein asked, it was in his consideration more correct to reply thereto in the presence of all the Members assembled which would give a full opportunity to anyone who may have urged Mr Fox to such a measure to state their reasons for so doing and to satisfy their minds on the subject. He first observed he did not consider the Troops would be disbanded, Government having at all times expressed a strong desire to retain the services of the Yeomanry Cavalry, and that in all probability that matter would be brought forward on the next meeting of Parliament.

Providing they were hereafter disbanded, Mr Fox or any other member who may previously withdraw their services cannot possibly have a claim on the subsequent fund of the Troops, that Mr Fox should conceive such an idea, is most extraordinary, he having been appointed one of the Trumpeters, actually received pay for his services. It was also to be remembered that the Troops being Regimented, the allowance from Government granted to distinct troops heretofore, is now consolidated and consequently applied to the aid of all in the Regiment and considered as one fund. A further consideration was the fund of the troops of the Second Corps a few years since were to a very considerable amount indebted to the then treasurer for payment of same,[16] a sum of money was subscribed by the Officers and others, then Members of the Corps, which amount, if a distribution should ever take place, should most assuredly be previously returned to the sundry subscribers. Also that such Members who in consideration of the state of the fund on their joining the Corps did actually pay in aid of same the sum of four Guineas each, should each be repaid that amount. Their subsequent resignation is by no means to exclude the claim. With respect to the Clothing and Equipments, the Acts of Parliament demand their being given up by everyone who quit the Troop.

---

[16] No accounts or any financial dealings were included by Collett, nor was the treasurer ever named, but it was obviously he who lent the Corps most of the money when the government refused to pay an allowance for the additional members.

Thursday March 14ᵗʰ 1816

The three Troops assembled about twelve o'Clock on the Parade at Woodbridge. The morning being very wet prevented our marching to the field for exercise. The Troops were under my command being the senior officer present. Receiving a note of which as under is a copy (from Lieutenant Colonel Edgar) after calling over the Muster Rolls, the Troops were dismissed in complyance with his orders.

My Dear Sir

As the day is so wet I dare not venture out. Unless a great alteration takes place in the weather at the time of assembling, you will of course only take down the Names of those present and disperse. Nothing but as bad a day as this will prevent my being at my post to Morrow. I am my dear Sir, Yours most truly   Mileson Edgar

Red House   Thursday Morning March 14ᵗʰ 1816

To Major Theobald or Officer Commanding, 1st Regiment Suffolk Yeomanry Cavalry Woodbridge

---

Friday March 15ᵗʰ 1816

The Troops being assembled about 12 o'Clock marched from the Parade (Market Hill Woodbridge) to my field (late Barrack Parade Ground). This day was also very unfavourable for Cavalry Exercise, it being a perfect Gale during the whole of the day, and so high was the wind that although we had so much rain yesterday, the Soil from off the Plowed Lands between Martlesham Bridge and Woodbridge River was carried over the River and lodged on the Lands at Sutton, and with the light soil of Sutton, Bromeswell, Eyke, Butley etc, formed a complete Column of drifted soil, which extended as far as the view from the Eye could carry you towards Butley and Orford etc etc.

Having formed the Troops I called over the respective Muster Rolls, and proposed to have Exercised in sundry evolutions which was rendered impracticable by reason the wind blowing so very hard the word of Command could not be heard by the Officers of the respective Troops or by the Troops themselves, that I was under the necessity of dismissing them in consequence of those impediments. Colonel Edgar and Major Theobald were prevented from attending, from which circumstance, being the next senior Officer, the command revolved on myself, (being Senior Captain). The Members present far exceeded in numbers my expectation judging from the state of the weather and the unfortunate situation of the present times so truly distressing to the Agricultural Interest of the Kingdom and consequently to the landlords, Merchants, Tradesmen and Labourers of all descriptions.[17]

C91 Monday March 18ᵗʰ 1816

The third Meeting which, as the two preceding, was truly unfavourable. The Morning was a continued Rain from 8 o'Clock until one P. M. Colonel Edgar and Major Theobald being each of them Unwell could not attend, the command consequently devolved on myself. There being no prospect whatever of a change in the weather as to admit of our marching into the field for Exercise, about quarter past twelve o'clock I ordered those Gentlemen who were in the Town to assemble dismounted on the Market Hall. The Numbers present far exceeded my expectation, many of

---

[17] Collett has included all the classes affected by the agricultural distress caused by the economic recession.

them got very wet on their Journey. After calling over the Muster Rolls of the three Troops, having answered to their Names, I dismissed them from any further duty on this day, with the orders to assemble again tomorrow morning at the usual time.

Tuesday March 19th 1816

The Morning was dry, the Wind very high. The Troops mustered about half past eleven o'clock. Colonel Edgar and Major Theobold although they had been prevented attending the three preceeding Musters by reason of indisposition and bad weather, this morning appeared at their Posts. We marched from the Parade Ground to my field late the Barrack Parade about 12 o' clock and exercised in sundry Evolutions much to the satisfaction of the Colonel. The wind blowing a strong Gale with light squals of rain. We returned from the field to the parade when the Troops dispersed for the purpose of taking care of their Horses and very soon assembled on foot at the Market Hall to call over the Muster Rolls, and it being the last General Muster day in the year to ascertain the attendance of each Member for the Colonel to make out a correct list of effective services. The Colonel on making up the list discovered many names who were non Effective, wishing they should appear on the Effective list, he very obligingly appointed sundry extra days for their meeting for that purpose, which arrangement he hoped and trusted would be particularly regarded and that in future he should not have occasion for such arrangement. It assuredly was a very polite indulgence on the part of the Colonel but I cannot help considering a repetition thereof will be attended with much prejudice to the discipline of the Troops as it tends to encourage non-attendance on days of General Muster.[18]

Mr James Woods of Kettleburgh and Mr William Glanfield of Trimley were each unanimously elected Members of the Regiment.

Commotions or Outrages

C92 My dear Sir,   **Clerges Street, Saturday Night May 11th 1816**

The outrages which have been committed in the Neighbourhood of Hadleigh and Bury, and the daring demeanour and language of Persons who have been present at some of the fires which have taken place, have made it necessary to use every precaution to prevent the recurrence if possible, of scenes so disgraceful and distressing. With a view to the important Object of securing the Peace of the County the Government has thought it advisable to send down a few Officers of the Police to be under the directions of the Magistrates. They were sent to Hadleigh, and I understand from Lord Sidmouth this morning that some Troops would be sent to Bury to protect the depot and assist the Civil power. In addition to which, if necessary, I am sure we may count as heretofore upon the effective aid of the Corps of Yeomanry Cavalry under your command, which I should recommend to be prepared for moving if Circumstances should unfortunately require their Services.

Be so good as to acquaint me with the name and residence of any Officer or trusty Non-commissioned Officer of your Corps, at or in the Neighbourhood of Bury, with whom I could communicate, as I propose to be at Newmarket meeting[19] this week which begins on the 13th.

---

18   One of Collett's very rare critical comments of Edgar.
19   The 4th Duke of Grafton was famous for his racing and horse breeding, as was his father.

I have the honor to be, my Dear Sir,

Your most obedient and faithful Servant   Grafton

(address per post)   Newmarket May 12th 1816

To Mileson Edgar Esq (or Officer Commanding Yeomanry Cavalry) Red House, Ipswich[20]

Sir   **Woodbridge May 14th 1816**

In consequence of a Letter just received from Lieutenant Colonel Edgar, who has been addressed by the Lord Lieutenant on the subject of the Outrages which have been committed in different parts of the County, I have to request you will make an immediate and minute Examination into the state of your Military Appointments, and hold yourself in Readiness to march at a Moment's Notice, should the Troop to which you belong, be called out.

I am your most obedient Servant   Cornelius Collett, Captain

PS You will see by the Ipswich Papers on Saturday next that the three Troops are to assemble at Woodbridge on Monday and Tuesday next, when every Member will be expected to appear unless prevented by sickness, certified by a Medical Gentleman. The above Circular Letter was sent by each Captain to the respective Members of his Troop.

C93 The Circumstances which occasioned the preceeding Letter from the Duke of Grafton, Lord Lieutenant of the County, appear to have originated in the unfortunate depression of both the agricultural and commercial classes. Owing to the very low prices of Grain of all kinds, the Finances of the Farmers had been much reduced, and from this, in an Agricultural County, a stagnation in Trade followed, hence numerous failures in all lines of Business.

The Labouring Poor in the County who had heretofore been employed by the Farmers, were any of them unable to get work, and of the smaller Mechanicks, great numbers from the dullness of trade in general, were thrown out of employ. The number of both Classes, thus unfortunately driven to seek Parish Relief was increased by the reduction of the Army which brought home to their respective Parishes many individuals of loose habits and little principle.[21] In consequence of these combined causes, considerable discontent was manifest and several fires in different parts of the County were, with too much reason, attributed to incendiary outrage.[22] At some of them the behaviour and language of the bystanders was such as to occasion a fear of the evil becoming more extensive, and the vigilence of those most interested being called forth, the interference of Government was deemed necessary.[23]

---

20 When considering Collett's method of working it is interesting to note that Edgar's reply to this letter was not included by him in his account, although the reply can be found in Edgar's own correspondence (SROI HA247/5/49). Collett was obviously told later in general terms what the reply contained but without the detail and added his Memorandum of 14 May.

21 Around a quarter of a million men, who had been recruited or press-ganged into the army or navy during the war, were no longer needed in 1815. On returning home they found little work available and were often forced to seek poor relief, only available in the parish where they had right of settlement.

22 Incendiarism was greatly feared since the attacks on barns and ricks happened at night and the culprits were difficult to identify. The situation was soon to escalate.

23 Collett encapsulated in this brief but detailed synopsis a realistic assessment of the situation in Suffolk. It was also his own opinion, which he rarely allowed to intrude on his account, but an

Monday May 20ᵗʰ 1816
The three Troops met as above directed, the Colonel being present himself and the Commissioned Officers inspected the Horses with all their equipments, and afterwards the Arms and equipments of each Man, and such as were deficient were ordered to be made up compleat that every member may be prepared to march on the shortest notice, in complyance with any order for that purpose either from the Lord Lieutenant or the Magistracy of the County.

Tuesday May 21ˢᵗ 1816
The Three Troops being assembled marched from Parade to my Field, late the Barrack Parade, and Exercised in Evolutions requisite to practice in case of our being called upon to repel a Mob.[24] It being considered, and signified by the Lord Lieutenant of the County (the Duke of Grafton), that there was every reason to consider that himself (or the Magistracy) may have occasion to call upon us for our services. The Colonel fully explained the conduct needful to be observed by each Member as a Soldier in case our Services are required.

For the service required for 1818 the Regiment was Imbodied and Quartered at Ipswich for the time required.[25]

C98 Attendence on the Magistracy if required
Lieutenant Colonel Edgar having formed the three Woodbridge Troops in four Divisions for the purpose of affording Prompt Assistance to the Magistracy should circumstances require it, the Division allotted to myself or Captain Couperthwaite to assemble consist of the following Members.[26]

C99 My dear Sir,   Secretary of State's Office   Friday May 24ᵗʰ 1816
I had hoped that the proceedings of the Malevolent and discontented would have been effectually checked before this time. But though they may have been met manfully in Suffolk, and thereby perhaps somewhat stopped in their progress, the accounts by this day's Posts which have been received from the Neighbouring Counties of Cambridge and Norfolk are of a Nature to make the utmost vigilance necessary in Suffolk. It is therefore particularly to be wished that the Yeomanry Cavalry under your Command should be perfectly prepared, as they may receive a very early call, unless matters soon wear a very different form from the present aspect. You shall hear again by tomorrow's post. The less is said on these occasions the better providing preparation is quietly making to give an effectual blow if necessary to the Malevolent Spirit which is at work to mislead the better intentioned.
                Believe me dear Sir, most faithfully yours   Grafton

---

informed one since as a banker he must have been very aware of farmers' financial problems and those of the community as a whole.
24 The fact that Edgar was training his forces to control a riot and instructing them on their behaviour in such a situation is important given the disaster three years later at Peterloo, where 18 people died and over 700 were injured.
25 C94–C97, the muster roll of Collett's Troop in 1816, has been omitted, together with the list of members of other Troops. It is unclear why Collett should have included this information here, particularly since by then he had made his last proper entry at the end of the book.
26 The members are not included.

Memorandum May 14th Lieutenant Colonel Edgar addressed the Duke of Grafton in reply to his Letter of 11th May, advising that such arrangements were made by himself and the Captain of Troops, that the Regiment or any part thereof would be in readiness to march on the shortest notice, should their Services be required either by himself as Lord Lieutenant or the Magistracy of the County.

Saturday May 25th 1816
Lieutenant Colonel Edgar on receiving the above letter from the Duke of Grafton (having previously seen Captain Pearson) wrote to Major Theobald, myself, Captain Couperthwaite and Lieutenant Dikes, requesting our attendance at his House tomorrow Sunday Morning 11 o'clock for the purpose of our making further arrangement for mustering the Troops as soon as possible in case of being called upon for our Services. It so happened there was no further Letter from the Lord Lieutenant of the County, consequently no further matter for our information. Having arranged our plan for assembling the Troops, we sent the following Circular Letter to the respective members in each division to prepare them for receiving further orders and that they may attend to same.
Sir   May 25th 1816
In consequence of a Letter received this morning by Lieutenant Colonel Edgar, from the Lord Lieutenant, he has directed me to request you to be in a state of preparation for marching on the shortest notice and to attend to the undermentioned order.

I am Sir, Your obedient Servant Captain [blank][27]

First Regiment Suffolk Yeomanry Cavalry   When ordered out in Marching Order, every non-commissioned Officer or Private is to carry in his Saddle Bags as under:
One Shirt, one pair of Stockings, One pair of Shoes, Razor, Comb, Brushes, Curry Comb and Brush, Mane Comb with Sponge, Horse Picker and Nose Bag, Stable Waistcoat and Cape.

From the London Gazette A Proclamation
                                                                          Whitehall May 25th 1816
Whereas it has been humbly represented to the Prince Regent, that a number of persons have, for some time past, unlawfully assembled themselves together in divers parts of the counties of Norfolk, Suffolk, Huntingdon and Cambridge, and have circulated threatening letters and incendiary handbills, held nightly meetings and set fire to several dwelling houses, barns, outbuildings and stacks of corn, and have destroyed cattle, corn, threshing machines and other instruments of husbandry. His Royal Highness seeing the mischievous consequences which must inevitably ensue, as well to the peace of the kingdom as to the lives and property of His Majesty's subjects, from such illegal and dangerous proceedings, if not speedily suppressed, and being firmly resolved to cause the laws to be put in execution for the punishment of such as offend against them, is hereby pleased, in the Name and on the behalf of his Majesty, to promise and declare that any person or persons

---

[27] Correspondence between Grafton and Edgar took place and a meeting of magistrates was organised but because Edgar was involved in his capacity as a magistrate and not as a yeomanry officer, Collett did not have access to it (SROI HA247/5/54).

who shall discover and apprehend or cause to be discovered and apprehended, the authors, abettors or perpetrators of any of the felonies or outrages above mentioned, so that they or any of them may be duly convicted thereof, shall be entitled to the sum of one hundred pounds for each and every person who shall be convicted of any of the aforesaid felonies.

And His Royal Highness is further pleased to promise his most gracious pardon to any person or persons concerned in the violent and illegal proceedings in question, upon making such discovery as aforesaid, except any person who shall have been a principal in the commission of any of the felonious offences above mentioned.

The said reward of One hundred pounds to be paid by the Lords Comissioners of His Majesty's Treasury.

C102 Thursday October 31st and Friday November 1st 1816

Each Day was very fine and pleasant. The Troops being assembled marched from Parade, Market Hill, Woodbridge, to Melton, and exercised in a field belonging to Mr William Whincopp, under the command of Major Theobald, Lieutenant Colonel Edgar being confined to his room with a severe fit of the gout, no particular occurrence.

The harvest having been very late and unfavourable, and those Members who are in Farming Business being at this time very busy in planting and sowing Wheat, the attendance was much more deficient in numbers than usual.

Memorandum

The Season of the Year has been most unfavourable to the ripening of Grain of every kind; consequently the Harvest was in all parts of the Country very much later than has in any previous year been remembered. I am not aware of an instance of anyone having finished their harvest previous to Michaelmas Day (11 October),[28] and I know of one Instance of a field of Wheat being reaped in the course of the present Week when at same time in another place the Wheat has been planted and out of the Ground for the Crop of next year. October 31 1816

Tuesday November 5th 1816

The morning was unfortunately very unfavourable being Wet and Stormy. About 12 o'clock: it appeared to clear up and we marched to a field in Melton belonging to Mr Whincopp. In the midst of our Exercise, a heavy shower of Rain coming on we were obliged to quit the field in the midst of same which was very unlucky as the Troops were Exercising in a masterly stile, much to the satisfaction of the officers commanding and creditable to themselves.

Lieutenant Colonel Edgar being still confined with the gout was unable to attend.

C103 Act of Parliament Annos Quinquagesima Sexto Georgii 3rd Regis. Cap 39

An Act to reduce the Number of Days of Muster, or Exercise of Yeomanry and Volunteer Cavalry

21st May 1816

Whereas it is expedient that the Number of Days Attendance at Muster or Exercise necessary to entitle Persons serving in any Corps of Yeomanry or Volunteer Cavalry to be returned or certified as effective Members of such Corps, should be reduced; be it therefore enacted, by the King's most Excellent Majesty, by and

---

[28] This is an unusual slip on Collett's part since he knew Michaelmas Day was 29 September.

with the Advice and Consent of the Lord Spiritual and Temporal and Commons in this present Parliament assembled, and by the Authority of the same, That from and after the passing of this Act, the Number of Days attendance at Muster or Exercise of Corps of Yeomanry or Volunteer Cavalry, to entitle any person serving in such Corps to be returned or certified as an effective Member thereof, shall be six in each year, anything in any Act passed in the Forty fourth Year of the Reign of his present Majesty, relating to Volunteer Corps, to the contrary notwithstanding; and the said Act shall be construed, as to all Returns and Certificates of Commanding Officers of such Corps, or others, as if the Number of Days Attendance at Muster or Exercise specified in the said Act as necessary to entitle Persons serving in Corps of Yeomanry or Volunteer Cavalry to be returned or certified as effective, has been six instead of twelve in each year, and such Number of Six Days shall in like Manner be divided into Two Days, or three equal Parts in each Four months, instead of four Days as in the said Act provided, with such Provisions as to making good any Number of Days at different Periods as are contained in the said Act in relation to the Days of Muster or Exercise specified in the said Act.

And be it further enacted, That in any case where a Corps of Yeomanry or Volunteer Cavalry should attend at Muster or Exercise, five days successively, such Five Days successive Attendance shall entitle each Individual so attending to be returned or certified as effective, the same as if he had attended the whole Number of Six Days according to the Provisions of this Act.

Commissions

The Members of the Troops in the Woodbridge Division having been recommended to the Lord Lieutenant by Colonel Edgar as proper persons to be appointed Commissioned Officers on the 1st June 1816 their commissions were signed by the Duke of Grafton Lord Lieutenant of the County.

Cornet Francis Hayle, Lieutenant vice Rodwell resigned
Cornet Simpson, Lieutenant vice Hewitt resigned
Thomas Bolton, Cornet, vice Simpson promoted
Robert Welham, Cornet vice Sexton resigned
William Colchester, Cornet vice Hayle promoted

C104   Red House   Monday Morning **4th November 1816**
My Dear Sir

I am truly sorry that my amendment has been so slow, as to render it, impossible for me to join you in the Field to Day, for I have not yet ventured outside the Doors. It gives me also much concern to find by the Returns that have been sent to me, that the Musters have been very thin and ineffective. By ineffective I mean that many Gentlemen have attended without Horses. I wish strongly to impress upon the minds of the Troops that there never has been a Period since the year 1794 when the Yeomanry were first raised, in which their Services were more important to their Country, or when it was more desirable to keep them in an effective State, than the present. I wish it also to be clearly understood by those Gentlemen who attend without Horses, that unless they intend to furnish themselves with Horses, either by Purchase or the Loan of a Friend, in which latter case their friend will have the Exemption from the Horse Tax, I must request them to withdraw from the Regiment, for I cannot think of returning

Men to the Lord Lieutenant and Secretary of State who are not fit to turn out in case of Riot.[29]
I should be very sorry to diminish the Strength of the three Woodbridge Troops, but if their Numbers fall off, it must be done, and I must write to the Captains of the other five Troops to add Men to theirs. I shall write my Sentiments fully to those Gentlemen who have been absent on the late Days of Exercise. I must request you to form the Circle and read to the Troops this Letter.

I remain etc etc   Mileson Edgar

To Major Theobald 1st Regiment Suffolk Yeomanry Cavalry
November 4th 1816 Major Theobald being present the above Letter was read to the Troops who attended the Muster on this day.

Copy
My Lord   **Whitehall January 11th 1817**
It being deemed expedient under the present circumstances, that the Civil Power should be strengthened in the County under your Lordship's charge, I have to request that you will recommend it to the Magistrates in the principal towns within the same (in which the measure is not already adopted) to encourage the enrolment of respectable householders to act as occasion may require, as Special Constables, for a fixed period of time, not less than three months. And I have further to request that your Lordship will communicate to the Commanding Officers of the several Yeomanry Corps within the County of [blank] the wish of His Majesty's Government, that they would hold themselves, and the Corps under their respective commands in a state of preparation to afford prompt assistance to the Civil Authorities in case of necessity.
I have etc etc   Sidmouth
To the Lord Lieutenant of the County of [blank]

Advertisement copied from the Ipswich Journal 6th March 1817
First Regiment of Suffolk Yeomanry Cavalry
The lately enrolled, and such other Members of Captain Collett's, Captain Couperthwaite's and Captain Pearson's Troops as have been unavoidably prevented completing their days of exercise, are requested to assemble at Woodbridge on the under-mentioned days in Field Day Order, at Eleven o'Clock precisely – viz Monday March 17th, Thursday 20th, Friday 21st.

M Edgar Lieutenant Colonel

Red House, March 6th 1817

Advertisement copied from the Ipswich Journal 19th April 1817
First Regiment of Suffolk Yeomanry Cavalry
The members of Captain Collett's, Captain Couperthwaite's and Captain Pearson's Troops are requested to assemble at Woodbridge in Field Day Order on Tuesday the 29th instant, and on Thursday May 1st at Eleven o'Clock precisely.

M Edgar Lieutenant Colonel
Red House April 17th 1817

PS No excuse will be admitted for non attendance but illness

---

[29] This is yet another sign of the serious social effects of the economic recession.

The Troops Assembled on the days above required 29th April and 1st May and were Exercised in a field belonging to Mr William Whincopp in Woodbridge by Lieutenant Colonel Edgar, being myself obliged to be in London I did not attend either of the Musters; and am not informed of any particular occurrence further than each Member was requested to hold himself in readiness to attend on the shortest notice, should occasion require immediate service. [30]

C107 On the first day of Muster, after an Inspection of Arms etc the sense of the Troops present was taken wether they should for the time required for their service this year be Regimented and Imbodied as last year, or remain at home and meet for the 6 days, and the three Troops to exercise together as they previously have done when not Regimented. On a show of hands it was the unanimous sense of the Troops they should not be imbodied, in consideration that the present value of Farming Property did not justify the extra expense unavoidably incurred in the attendance on the Regiment being Imbodied.[31]

C108 Monday July 21st

The Troops assembled at the time required and by order of Lieutenant Colonel Edgar after the Horses with their Equipments and the Arms had been inspected on the Parade, the Men being dismounted adjourned to the Market Hall where the Equipments of every kind were all inspected and such as were out of condition ordered to be repaired and put into a proper state for immediate use should our services be required on the shortest notice. Being a day of general Inspection our services were not required in the field for exercise.

Friday July 25th 1817

The Troops marched from Parade to Martlesham and exercised on a part of the Heath Land in the occupation of Mr James Glanfield in the usual evolutions and we were very fortunate in having a very fine day although from appearances were apprehensive of much rain. The Exercise was in the usual Evolutions and very satisfactory. No particular occurrence.

Tuesday July 29th 1817

The Troops marched from Parade to Bromeswell and exercised in the same field as on Thursday the 24th instant with the same satisfaction to the Colonel. It having been intimated that providing the Troops were inclined to do the Exercise required by the act of Parliament for the year in six succeeding days and were for that purpose Regimented, Government would allow pay for the time. It was at a previous meeting intimated and requested to be considered of and the opinions of the Troops present this day, to give their opinions of the measure. It has consequently this day put to the vote that each Member might express his approval or disapprobation of the measure. On a show of hands it was unanimously determined without a dissenting voice that providing the other Troops of the Regiment agree to the measure, the regiment would be next year embodied for the time, at such time and place as should be appointed by Lieutenant Colonel Edgar.

---

[30] C106–C107, the muster roll of Collett's Troop of 1817/1818, is omitted.
[31] Another example of how seriously many farmers were being affected by the economic downturn.

NB There cannot remain the least doubt if the Plan is carried into effect, that it will be of the greatest possible service to the discipline and improvement of the Regiment, particularly if they should at any time hereafter be called upon to act in a Body etc etc

C109 Copied from the Bury Post of 6th August 1817 Advertisement
A Caution

To Members of Troops, Corps or Regiments of Yeomanry Cavalry

Whereas I was this day summoned before John Benjafield Esquire one of His Majesty's Justices of the Peace for the County of Suffolk, on a complaint preferred against me by Lieutenant Colonel Edgar, for not returning my Arms and other Military appointments into Store on my quitting the Regiment, but all further proceedings of conviction of the penalty incurred under the Act of the 5th of his present Majesty, and of levying double the amount in value of the Appointments so witheld, have been stopped on condition of my making a public acknowledgement of my error in the three provincial papers.

Now I do hereby thus publicly acknowledge my error, and the kindness which has been shown me, and trust it may operate as a warning to all the Members of the Regiment, not to withhold any of their appointments on their Resignations being accepted, but to return the same in a proper and soldier like manner.

Robert Goodchild of Higham late Sergeant 4th Troop[32]

Witness to the signature of Robert Goodchild, William Frost Captain
Bury St Edmunds 2nd August 1817

First Regiment of Loyal Suffolk Yeomanry Cavalry

It having been stated to me, that the Arms and other Appointments of several Members who have retired from the Regiment, are not returned into Store, the Captains of the different Troops are hereby requested to apply for the same, and to report all Cases of inattention to such application.

Red House August 4th 1817   M Edgar Lieutenant Colonel

As a minute inspection of all the Military Appointments will take place, and a question of importance will be submitted to the consideration of the Troops, no excuse will be admitted for non-attendance but illness.

Red House April 23rd 1818   M Edgar Lieutenant Colonel

C110 Thursday April 17th 1818

The Meeting of the Troops this day was very fully attended, those absent were occasioned by illness as appeared by Certificates. The business of the day was for Inspection of Arms and Equipments of every kind preparatory to going out for Annual exercise and the whole of the Regiment to be Imbodied for a certain number of days and for such Members who approved of the plan or otherwise were to declare their sentiments. To obtain the same a show of hands was required of those in favour of the plan when only one member that I saw dissented from same and the whole gave in their signatures as a pledge and engagement for their due attendance at the time and place hereafter to be appointed. Ipswich was nominated for the Regiment to assemble at and the 9th day of June next for the time of meeting

---

[32] This is an effective and imaginative way of ensuring the return of uniform.

and Lieutenant Colonel Edgar is to signify the same to the Lord Lieutenant of the County who will forward it to the War Office and from thence to the Prince Regent for his approbation and assent or orders, in complyance with the Instructions received officially by Lieutenant Colonel Edgar for that purpose.

Names of the Members present who signed an engagement for their attendance[33]

May 7ᵗʰ 1818 All the Members of my Troop assembled this day in complyance with Lieutenant Colonel Edgar's advertisement excepting James Bendall, William Wase and William Glanfield and respectively signified their desire to go out with the Regiment and signed their names to be presented to the Colonel in pledge of same.

C116 Captain Colletts Troop[34]

C117 Captain Couperthwaite's Troop [blank]
C118 Captain Pearsons Troop [blank]
C119–C120 Missing page cut out
C121 Captain Todd's Troop   Ranks only, no names
C122 Captain Frosts's Troop A few ranks listed, no names
C123 Captain Farr's Troop Beccles A few ranks only
C124 Captain [blank] Eye in pencil
C125 Captain Cook in pencil

C127 **Muster Roll of Captain Collett's Troop 1820**[35]
1 Captain Collett
2 Lieutenant Dykes
3 Cornet Dykes
4 Quarter Master Miller
5 Trumpeter Ackfield
6 Sergeant Churchyard
7 Sergeant Lewin
8 Corporal Wright
9 Corporal Lankester
10 John Easter
11 Philip Pierce
12 William Cooper
13 James Bendall
14 William Spink
15 William Damant
16 Simon Fenn
17 Charles Ablett
18 William Lankester
19 John Garnham
20 Charles Jackson

---

[33] Omitted.
[34] These were not included as they are much the same as the final entry.
[35] This was Collett's final entry, although several more pages had ruled lines. He resigned in October 1820 with two other captains, but their resignation was only recorded in the local newspaper when the commissions of their replacements were announced in the *Ipswich Journal* 28 March 1821. Collett was 74.

21 John Catt
22 William Knights
23 J Firmin Josselyn
24 William Waller
25 Samuel Webber
26 George Largent
27 Samuel Wright
28 John Wilson
29 Samuel Brewer
30 John Vertue
31 Ralph Rabbett
32 Cornelius Wilson
33 Thomas Walker
34 Charles Blake
35 James Elliot
36 John Garrod
37 John Cooper
38 William Page

Appendix 1

List of subscribers for the internal defence of the county of Suffolk, January 1795

	£.	s.	d		£.	s.	d
Abbott John		5.	0	Betts George	5.	5.	0
Ablett Nat & Son	5.	5.	0	Bigg Charles	2.	2.	0
Acton Nath	100.	0.	0	Bigg Elizabeth		5.	0
Acton Nath Lee	50.	0.	0	Bigg Samuel		5.	0
Adamson Richd	10.	10.	0	Bigg Sarah		5.	0
Adams Thos		10.	6	Bigg William		5.	0
Adkins Edward		10.	6	Biggs Nath	3.	3.	0
Afflick Gilbert	50.	0.	0	Bigsby Thos	5.	5.	0
Aldham John	1.	1.	0	Birch John Rix	20.	0.	0
Alldis Thos	3.	3.	0	Blackburn Hundred	54.	6.	6
Allen James	2.	2.	0	Blackly Charles	10.	10.	0
Allington John		10.	6	Blakely John	1.	1.	0
Amass Willm		2.	6	Blois Sir John	50.	0.	0
Amass Willm Jun		2.	6	Blomfield Robt	2.	2.	0
Amyas I	25.	0.	0	Blowers I	20.	0.	0
Amys John	5.	5.	0	Boast Baaharyes		10.	6
Arnold Ald Cha	20.	0.	0	Bobbitt John	5.	5.	0
Arnold B	5.	5.	0	Bobbitt John	1.	1.	0
Arthur George	10.	10.	0	Bodham Mrs	1.	1.	0
Ashby G	10.	0.	0	Bohun G W B	5.	5.	0
Assey I	5.	0.	0	Bohun L G B	20.	0.	0
Ayton John	5.	5.	0	Bolton Thomas	2.	2.	0
Bacon Nicholas	100.	0.	0	Bolton William	5.	5.	0
Bacon Philip	5.	5.	0	Bond J C	5.	5.	0
Badley Samuel	10.	10.	0	Bond John	5.	5.	0
Baker George	5.	5.	0	Bond W	10.	10.	0
Baker John		10.	6	Bonhote Daniel	2.	2.	0
Bantoft Thos	10.	0.	0	Boone Charles	100.	0.	0
Barber Edmund	5.	5.	0	Booth Richard		5.	0
Barclay Chas M	10.	10.	0	Borrett Mrs	1.	1.	0
Barker Joseph		10.	6	Bowness Francis	10.	0.	0
Barnard Cary	25.	0.	0	Boxted Parish	5.	17.	6
Barne Barne	25.	0.	0	Boyce Robert		2.	6
Barne Miles	100.	0.	0	Boyce Thomas	5.	5.	0
Barne Thos C	20.	0.	0	Boyden Robert	3.	3.	0
Barnes I	20.	0.	0	Brand John	21.	0.	0
Barnes Isaac	5.	5.	0	Brand John C	4.	4.	0
Barnwell Fred	5.	5.	0	Brand Wm B	50.	0.	0
Barnwell T M	3.	3.	0	Brent Eleigh Parish	7.	9.	0
Bates Revd Dr	10.	10.	0	Brett Robert	2.	12.	6
Baynes William	5.	5.	0	Brettell John		10.	6
Beales Francis	2.	2.	0	Brettingham Robt	5.	5.	0
Beales John		10.	6	Brewster John		5.	0
Bedel Thomas		10.	6	Brewster Mrs		5.	0
Belgrave G	10.	10.	0	Brice Samuel	20.	0.	0
Bennett Thomas		2.	6	Bridgman Edward	5.	5.	0
Bennington Jos	5.	5.	0	Bristol Earl of	200.	0.	0
Berners Charles	100.	0.	0	Broke Phil B	100.	0.	0
Berners H D	20.	0.	0	Bromley N W	10.	0.	0

	£.	s.	d		£.	s.	d
Brooke Francis	10.	10.	0	Coe James		10.	6
Broome William	2.	2.	0	Colchester William	5.	5.	0
Brown Chas	2.	2.	0	Collett Anthony	25.	0.	0
Brown R I	5.	5.	0	Collett Cornelius	5.	5.	0
Brown Wm Jun		10.	6	Cook James		5.	0
Brown Wm Sen		10.	6	Cook Samuel		5.	0
Browne Charles	5.	5.	0	Cooke John	3.	3.	0
Browne Willm	2.	2.	0	Cooke M & Co	2.	2.	0
Buchanan Simon	5.	5.	0	Cooper Capt	10.	0.	0
Buckle Chas	5.	5.	0	Cooper John	5.	5.	0
Bullock Henry		5.	0	Cooper Mrs	1.	1.	0
Bunbury Sir T C	100.	0.	0	Copsey William		5.	0
Burke James	5.	5.	0	Corder James		10.	6
Burke John	1.	1.	0	Corder Thomas	2.	2.	0
Burke Thomas	10.	10.	0	Cornwallis Marquis	100.	0.	0
Burman Edward	20.	0.	0	Couperthwaite John	3.	3.	0
Burroughs T C	3.	3.	0	Cousins Wm		2.	0
Burstell Nelson	5.	5.	0	Cowper Robert	5.	5.	0
Butts William	3.	3.	0	Cowper Thomas	20.	0.	0
Cadogan Lord	100.	0.	0	Cowsell Thomas	1.	1.	0
Calthorpe Sir H G	100.	0.	0	Cox John		10.	6
Camell Robert	5.	5.	0	Crick Thomas	5.	5.	0
Cantley T	5.	5.	0	Crickett Chas A	50.	0.	0
Capper Francis	10.	10.	0	Cross John	2.	2.	0
Capper George	5.	5.	0	Crowfoot W	5.	5.	0
Carss Robert	3.	3.	0	Cullum Sir T G	10.	0.	0
Carter John	10.	0.	0	Cunningham J	2.	2.	0
Carter Rev Mr	20.	0.	0	Cutting Samuel	1.	1.	0
Carter T	5.	5.	0	D'Eye Nath	10.	0.	0
Cartwright Jn	20.	0.	0	Dalton R P	1.	1.	0
Case Phil James	5.	5.	0	Dalton William	10.	10.	0
Cavendish Parish	27.	6.	0	Davers Sir Chas	50.	0.	0
Chambers P	3.	3.	0	Davie John	3.	3.	0
Chandos Dow Duch of	100.	0.	0	Davy D C	5.	5.	0
Chevalier T F	5.	5.	0	Davy E	25.	0.	0
Chevalier Temple	10.	10.	0	Davy Thomas		5.	0
Clarke J & J	5.	5.	0	Daw Maximillian	5.	5.	0
Clarke Jermyn		10.	6	Dawson Henry	10.	10.	0
Clarke Osborne	1.	1.	0	Deane Anthony	50.	0.	0
Clarke Robert	3.	3.	0	Denny Robert	3.	3.	0
Clarke Samuel	2.	2.	0	Denton John	4.	4.	0
Clarke Thomas	20.	0.	0	Dillingham B G	21.	0.	0
Clayton John	20.	0.	0	Dinsdale George	2.	2.	0
Cleares John		5.	0	Doughty George	50.	0.	0
Close Henry J	10.	10.	0	Doughty Mrs	5.	5.	0
Clubbe John	5.	5.	0	Dove Edward	1.	1.	0
Coates Henry	2.	2.	0	Dove John	10.	10.	0
Coates Valentine	3.	3.	0	Drake Nathan	5.	5.	0
Cobbold John	10.	10.	0	Dusser John	10.	0.	0

	£.	s.	d		£.	s.	d
Dyball John		10.	6	Gooch Sir Thos	100.	0.	0
Eade John	5.	5.	0	Goody Jeremiah		10.	6
Eade Peter	2.	2.	0	Goodwin Grace	3.	3.	0
Eagle John	2.	2.	0	Gosnall John	5.	5.	0
Edgar Mileson	21.	0.	0	Gould Mrs	5.	5.	0
Edge John	10.	10.	0	Grant Andrew	5.	5.	0
Edge Peter	3.	3.	0	Graves Morgan	5.	5.	0
Edwards Thomas	1.	1.	0	Greaves William	5.	5.	0
Edwards William	5.	5.	0	Green Brawn	5.	5.	0
Ele John		5.	0	Green Daniel		10.	6
Elmy William	5.	5.	0	Green Gabriel	1.	1.	0
Elwes R C	25.	0.	0	Green Samuel	1.	1.	0
Euston Earl of	100.	0.	0	Griggs Nath		15.	0
Ewen I	5.	5.	0	Grimwood William		2.	6
Ewer I	5.	5.	0	Grizby George	3.	3.	0
Ewer Thomas		10.	6	Gunning Jos	3.	3.	0
Farr John Junr	5.	5.	0	Gurdon Philip	25.	0.	0
Farr T	5.	5.	0	Gusitt John	25.	0.	0
Favre John	5.	5.	0	Gusitt Rev Mr		5.	0
Fenner James		10.	6	Gwith Edward	20.	0.	0
Fenner John		10.	6	Hailstone William	1.	1.	0
Fenner Juliana		10.	6	Halward John	5.	5.	0
Fenner William		10.	6	Hammond Thomas		1.	0
Finiham John	2.	2.	0	Hanmer Lieut	10.	10.	0
Fiske John	5.	5.	0	Harrington John	5.	5.	0
Ford John	21.	0.	0	Harrington Jos	5.	5.	0
Fowke William	30.	0.	0	Harrison Charles	20.	0.	0
Frampton Dr	10.	10.	0	Harrison Chas Jun	5.	5.	0
Frank Dr Richard	50.	0.	0	Harrison Henry	5.	5.	0
Freeland John	5.	5.	0	Hartest Parish	10.	10.	6
Freere John	25.	0.	0	Hasell Edward	10.	0.	0
Frere Edward	5.	5.	0	Hawes Robert	1.	1.	0
Frere Mrs Eleanor	20.	0.	0	Haws Thomas	5.	5.	0
Fuller Osborn	10.	10.	0	Hayward John	2.	2.	0
Fuller Robert	3.	3.	0	Heigham Henry	3.	3.	0
Fuller Thomas	2.	2.	0	Heigham John	21.	0.	0
Gage Sir Thomas	20.	0.	0	Heigham John	2.	2.	0
Gamble D	5.	5.	0	Heigham Rev Jn	3.	3.	0
Garnham T	10.	10.	0	Henniker Sir Jn	50.	0.	0
Gibbon Dr	5.	5.	0	Hibble Philip	2.	2.	0
Gibbs I	5.	5.	0	Higgs John	50.	0.	0
Girling Daniel		2.	6	Hill Henry	10.	0.	0
Goate Edward	31.	10.	0	Hill Thomas	3.	3.	0
Godbold John	30.	0.	0	Hilliar Nath	25.	0.	0
Golding George	100.	0.	0	Hinchman William	3.	3.	0
Golding Mary		10.	6	Hingeston John	10.	10.	0
Goldsmith J Jun	1.	1.	0	Holden I W	1.	1.	0
Goldsmith Thomas	1.	1.	0	Holden Rev Mr	50.	0.	0
Gooch John		10.	6	Holt Thomas	100.	0.	0

	£.	s.	d		£.	s.	d
Hopton Parish of	6.	14.	0	Le Grice John	3.	3.	0
Horrex Edmund	10.	0.	0	Leake F G Y	5.	5.	0
Howes Thomas	5.	5.	0	Leake I B Jun	10.	10.	0
Hubbard James	2.	2.	0	Leakey J	2.	2.	0
Hunt Joseph	2.	2.	0	Lehurp Michael	20.	0.	0
Hurrell Thomas	1.	1.	0	Leman R	10.	0.	0
Hyde John	25.	0.	0	Leman Robert	5.	5.	0
Hyldyard John	5.	5.	0	Leroo John	10.	10.	0
Isaacson William	3.	3.	0	Liancourt Duc de	5.	5.	0
Ives Mrs	5.	5.	0	Lilley William		2.	6
Ives Mrs T	6.	6.	0	Lillistone S	10.	10.	0
Jacob George	5.	5.	0	Lingwood Thomas	5.	5.	0
Jarvis William		10.	6	Lloyd Richard S	25.	0.	0
Jeaffeson Chris	10.	10.	0	Lock John	5.	5.	0
Jeffreis A Sen	1.	1.	0	Lofft Capel	5.	5.	0
Jenkin Abraham	5.	5.	0	Long John	5.	5.	0
Jenney Edward	5.	5.	0	Long William	20.	0.	0
Jennings George		5.	0	Lukin Robert	10.	0.	0
Jennings William	50.	0.	0	Lungley H	2.	2.	0
Jermyn George	2.	2.	0	Lynch William	25.	0.	0
Jermyn Peter	5.	5.	0	Lynn James	3.	3.	0
Jermyn Peter Jun	5.	5.	0	Lynn James	5.	5.	0
Jesup Devereaux		2.	6	Maber Peter	5.	5.	0
Johnson Joseph	5.	5.	0	Macklim William	10.	0.	0
Jones Rev W B	3.	3.	0	Maltyward Robert	5.	0.	0
Josselyn John	5.	5.	0	Mann Gibson	5.	5.	0
Jourdan I Kemp	2.	2.	0	Mann Thomas	3.	3.	0
Keddington Roger	20.	0.	0	Mann William	5.	5.	0
Keddington W	10.	10.	0	Manning A	10.	0.	0
Kay Arthur	1.	1.	0	Manning John	1.	1.	0
Keer George B	5.	5.	0	Mannock William	25.	0.	0
Kerridge John	10.	0.	0	Marriot Robert	3.	3.	0
Kerrison Matthew	10.	10.	0	Maulkin I	5.	5.	0
Kett William	5.	5.	0	Mayhew Samuel		5.	0
Kett William C	3.	3.	0	Maynard Thomas	100.	0.	0
Key Mary		10.	6	Melford Parish	36.	9.	0
Kilderbee Sam C	10.	0.	0	Mercer Bernard	5.	5.	0
Kilderbee Samuel	20.	0.	0	Methold Thomas	21.	0.	0
Kilgour Rev Dr	10.	0.	0	Midson R Jun	3.	3.	0
King Benjamin	5.	5.	0	Miles Francis	2.	2.	0
King George	3.	3.	0	Miller Thomas	2.	2.	0
King Mrs		10.	6	Mills Edward	10.	10.	0
Kingsbury M B	1.	1.	0	Montagu Gerard	20.	0.	0
Kirby John	10.	10.	0	Moore Christmas		2.	6
Knowles Dr	5.	5.	0	Moore Richard	30.	0.	0
Lathbury John	21.	0.	0	Moore Robert		2.	6
Lawton Henry	5.	5.	0	Moore Robert	2.	2.	0
Lawton Robert	20.	0.	0	Morest James	5.	5.	0
Le Blanc Thomas	25.	0.	0	Morgan Humph		10.	6

279

	£.	s.	d		£.	s.	d
Morris William	5.	5.	0	Pooley Mrs.	3.	3.	0
Mortlock Thomas		5.	0	Potter John	1.	1.	0
Mosely John	30.	0.	0	Powell I H	10.	0.	0
Mosely Richard	21.	0.	0	Powell Richard	5.	5.	0
Mullett Samuel		5.	0	Poyson John	10.	0.	0
Mumford John	3.	3.	0	Preston Parish	6.	7.	6
Mumford William	1.	1.	0	Preston Rev D	10.	10.	0
Murrills Thomas		5.	0	Price Matthew	1.	1.	0
Nassau George	50.	0.	0	Pritchett Richard	10.	0.	0
Nesfield William	5.	5.	0	Pugh Edward	5.	5.	0
Newson Thomas J	3.	3.	0	Purvis Charles	50.	0.	0
Nicholls Mr	10.	0.	0	Purvis Richard	10.	10.	0
Nolinn Mary		5.	0	Purvis Robert	5.	5.	0
Norgate Dr	5.	5.	0	Pytches John	5.	5.	0
Norton Nicholas	10.	0.	0	Quilter Samuel	2.	2.	0
Notcutt Thomas F	5.	5.	0	Rabett Reginald	20.	0.	0
Oakes James	20.	0.	0	Randall Nath	5.	5.	0
Oakes O R	5.	5.	0	Rawlinson Sir Wm	50.	0.	0
Oldham John	1.	1.	0	Ray James	2.	2.	0
Oldham Rev O	5.	5.	0	Ray Orbell	10.	10.	0
Ord Dr	10.	0.	0	Ray Richard	25.	0.	0
Orgill N T	5.	5.	0	Rede Robert	5.	5.	0
Osborn William	2.	2.	0	Rede T	25.	0.	0
Oswald W	5.	5.	0	Reed James		10.	6
Paddon Rev George	5.	5.	0	Reed Stephen	1.	1.	0
Paddon Rev Thos	1.	1.	0	Reeve A	5.	5.	0
Page John	5.	5.	0	Reeve James	5.	5.	0
Page John Jun	3.	3.	0	Reeve Richard	2.	2.	0
Palgrave William	20.	0.	0	Reeve Thomas	5.	5.	0
Palmer George	5.	5.	0	Revans William	2.	2.	0
Palmer Matthias		1.	0	Revens Stebbing	5.	5.	0
Parker John		10.	6	Revett John	25.	0.	0
Parker Sir Harry	50.	0.	0	Revett John C	10.	0.	0
Pattison Henry	20.	0.	0	Rhudde Dr	50.	0.	0
Peake James	5.	5.	0	Richardson Thomas	2.	2.	0
Pearson William	5.	5.	0	Riches Philip	5.	5.	0
Peterson Benj	1.	1.	0	Rissour C T	5.	5.	0
Pettitt John		10.	6	Rissour Robert	3.	3.	0
Pettitt Jonathan		2.	6	Roberts John	10.	10.	0
Phillips Robert	5.	5.	0	Roberts Thomas	2.	2.	0
Philpot William	5.	5.	0	Robinson Col	10.	0.	0
Pizzey William		2.	6	Robinson Francis	5.	5.	0
Plampin George	5.	5.	0	Robinson John	5.	5.	0
Plankin John	5.	5.	0	Rodwell Josiah	4.	4.	0
Plankin Rev I	10.	10.	0	Rogers James		10.	6
Plestow Rev I D	10.	0.	0	Rooke William	20.	0.	0
Pomfrett Elizabeth		10.	6	Rous Sir John	100.	0.	0
Pomfrett John		10.	6	Routh P	5.	5.	0
Pooley John W	10.	0.	0	Rowley Sir William	25.	0.	0

	£.	s.	d		£.	s.	d
Ruggles Thomas	25.	0.	0	Stone George	5.	5.	0
Rush George	50.	0.	0	Streett William	5.	5.	0
Rushbrooke Mrs	20.	0.	0	Sturgeon Reubin	5.	5.	0
Ruson James	10.	10.	0	Sulyard Edward	10.	10.	0
Rye John	1.	1.	0	Sumner Dr	10.	0.	0
Rye Samuel		10.	6	Syer I Neville	1.	1.	0
Safford James	10.	10.	0	Syer Rev B B	3.	3.	0
Schutz William	20.	0.	0	Syer Rev Dr	5.	5.	0
Scotman Thomas	5.	5.	0	Symonds John	10.	10.	0
Scott Jn & Samuel	5.	5.	0	Symons A	10.	0.	0
Scott Mrs	2.	2.	0	Taylor John		5.	0
Scott N L	2.	2.	0	Taylor John		2.	6
Scott Thomas	2.	2.	0	Taylor Robert	5.	5.	0
Scrivener John	100.	0.	0	Temple T W	10.	0.	0
Sewell James	10.	0.	0	Thelnetham Parish	17.	15.	6
Sharpe John	3.	3.	0	Thelwall Major	10.	10.	0
Sharp Martin	5.	5.	0	Theobald I M	40.	0.	0
Shave & Jackson	5.	5.	0	Thomas George	21.	0.	0
Sheldrake Robert	2.	2.	0	Thompson I	5.	5.	0
Sheppard John	30.	0.	0	Thorowgood Sir T	20.	0.	0
Sheppard John J	1.	1.	0	Thurkettle John		2.	6
Sheriff Rev Thos	5.	5.	0	Tipple William	5.	5.	0
Sherman Samuel		2.	6	Tolbott William	21.	0.	0
Sherman Widow		1.	0	Tozer Aaron	5.	5.	0
Short Henry	26.	5.	0	Trotman Robert	21.	0.	0
Shrive William	5.	5.	0	Truelove William	10.	0.	0
Simpson Thomas	10.	6		Turner Charles	2.	2.	0
Simpson William	3.	3.	0	Turner John		5.	0
Slapp Thomas	5.	5.	0	Turner George	5.	5.	0
Smear Chris	5.	5.	0	Turner Thomas	2.	2.	0
Smith George	5.	5.	0	Turner Zach	2.	2.	0
Smith I	5.	5.	0	Tweed Joseph	5.	5.	0
Smith John	3.	3.	0	Tyrell Charles	10.	0.	0
Smith John	1.	1.	0	Tyrell Edmund	40.	0.	0
Smith Joseph		10.	6	Upcher Peter	25.	0.	0
Spalding Susan	3.	3.	0	Vankamp J	2.	2.	0
Sparke John	10.	10.	0	Vanneck Sir Jos	100.	0.	0
Sparrow Robert	100.	0.	0	Vernon J G	21.	0.	0
Spink John	20.	0.	0	Waddington R	10.	0.	0
Spurgeon I G	5.	5.	0	Wade John		10.	6
Squire Charles	10.	0.	0	Wade William		10.	6
Stamford John	5.	5.	0	Wales Isaac	5.	5.	0
Stammers Edward	1.	1.	0	Walford William	3.	3.	0
Stammers Joseph		10.	6	Walker Thomas		2.	6
Stammers Thos	2.	2.	0	Walker William C	1.	1.	0
Stebbing George	3.	3.	0	Walpole Robert	5.	5.	0
Steel George	3.	3.	0	Warren Robert		1.	0
Steggall John	3.	3.	0	Wastell John	20.	0.	0
Steward Chas Ed	10.	10.	0	Watson Dr	5.	5.	0

	£.	s.	d		£.	s.	d
Watson J Sen	5.	5.	0	Wollaston Dr	5.	5.	0
Wayth Thomas	5.	5.	0	Wollaston Wm	25.	0.	0
Webb Mary		5.	0	Woodcock John	5.	5.	0
Welton Corn	1.	1.	0	Woods Alex	2.	2.	0
Wenyeve John	21.	0.	0	Woodward T I	20.	0.	0
Westhorpe R M	5.	5.	0	Woodward T Sen	5.	0.	0
Whimper John	5.	5.	0	Woollard John	1.	1.	0
Whimper Nath	10.	10.	0	Woolnough John	3.	3.	0
Whitbread Jacob	30.	0.	0	Wortledge John	3.	3.	0
White I	10.	10.	0	Wright L	5.	5.	0
White Robert G	5.	5.	0	Wright Matthias	10.	10.	0
White Thomas	100.	0.	0	Wyatt R	10.	10.	0
Wilbrow Wm Sen		10.	6	Wythe John	5.	5.	0
Wilgress Rev Dr	10.	0.	0	Wythe Thomas	5.	5.	0
Wilkinson John	5.	5.	0	Yorke William		10.	6
Wilson Edward	10.	0.	0	Young Arthur	20.	0.	0
Wilson John	1.	1.	0	Young Susan	5.	5.	0
Winke Joseph	1.	1.	0	Young William	1.	1.	0
Wissin William	1.	1.	0				

(Source: Collett's Book, p. 20)

Appendix 2

Dates of general musters 1794–1820

	January	February	March	April	May	June	July	August	September	October	November	December
1794					14		30	26	9, 11, 12, 16, 18, 23, 25, 26, 30	7, 14, 21, 28	4, 11, 18, 25	2, 9, 16, 23
1795	6, 13		10, 17, 24, 31	10, 14, 21, 28	5, 12, 19, 26	2, 9, 19, 26	3, 10, 17, 24	14	25	2, 9, 16, 23, 30	6, 13, 20, 27	4, 18, 31
1796	8, 18, 22	5, 12, 19	11	1, 15, 29	6, 13, 20	4, 10, 24	1	5	2, 23, 30	21	4	2, 30
1797	20	3, 17	3, 17	28	19	2, 9, 16, 21, 22	28		29	27	24	29
1798	26	23	30	20, 24, 27		4, 29	27	31	28	3, 8, 26	30	
1799			29	12, 26	17	4, 14	19, 27	9	18	4, 25	15, 29	13
1800		28	14, 28	25		4, 27	25		17, 26	31	3, 6	
1801		27	12, 27	24	15	4			11, 25	30	27	18
1802				9			13, 20				9	
1803	2, 17, 31				3, 17	4, 21	26	9, 16, 19, 25	6, 13, 20, 27	4, 10, 18, 25	1, 3, 15, 22, 29	6, 28
1804		14, 23, 28	20	24, 27	10	4	23		25	2, 16, 23	6	
1805				2, 3	7, 14, 21, 28	4, 13, 18, 25	9, 16	13		16	12, 15, 19, 22	
1806			18, 25	1, 9	28	10, 13, 16, 20				14, 21, 28	4, 11, 18	
1807		17, 24	3, 10, 17, 24		5, 12, 19, 26	2, 9, 23		13		20, 27	3, 10, 17	
1808			15, 22, 29	5, 22		7, 16, 23	26		13, 20, 27		1, 8	
1809			7, 14, 21, 28		1, 2	20, 23, 27				24, 27, 30, 31		

284

	January	February	March	April	May	June	July	August	September	October	November	December
1810			5, 6, 12, 13	3	7, 8, 14, 21	4, 5				16, 19		
1811			8, 12, 15, 19		24, 28, 31	4				22, 25, 29	1	
1812			24, 26	3, 7	15, 19	4, 5				16, 20, 23, 27		
1813			9, 12, 16, 19			1, 4, 5	29, 30			22, 26, 29	2	
1814	No musters held since it was peacetime after Napoleon's abdication											
1815			9, 14				25, 27	1, 4		24, 27, 30	2	
1816			14, 15, 18, 19		20, 21					31	1, 4, 5	
1817			17, 20, 21	29	1		21, 24, 25, 29					
1818	Muster days taken together on permanent duty – dates unknown											
1819					17, 24	1, 3, 7, 8						
1820					16, 19	2, 6, 23, 30						

(Source: **Collett's Book Muster Rolls**)

285

Appendix 3

Occupations and residence of members of Captain Collett's Troop, 1804

Approximate Distance from Woodbridge (miles)	Residence	Banker	Farmer	Surgeon	Butcher	Malster	Miller	Corn Merchant	Horse Farrier	Merchant	Brickmaker	Inn Keeper	Liquor Merchant	TOTAL
9	Alderton		1											1
9	Blaxhall		1											1
9	Boyton		1											1
3	Bredfield				1									1
8	Butley		1											1
6	Charsfield		2											2
9	Chillesford		1											1
12	Cransford		1							1					2
4	Dallinghoo		2											2
4	Eyke		1											1
8	Glemham		1											1
16	Leiston		1											1
8	Marlesford		3											3
3	Martlesham		2											2
2	Melton			1										1
9	Parham		3											3
5	Pettistree		3											3
9	Ramsholt		1											1
6	Rendlesham		1											1

Approximate Distance from Woodbridge (miles)	Residence	Banker	Farmer	Surgeon	Butcher	Malster	Miller	Corn Merchant	Horse Farrier	Merchant	Brickmaker	Inn Keeper	Liquor Merchant	TOTAL
14	Saxmundham			1									1	2
5	Sutton		2						1					3
12	Sweffling		1			1								2
3	Ufford		2											2
9	Wantisden		1											1
5	Wickham Market		1				1							2
0	Woodbridge	1							1	2	1	1		6
	TOTALS	**1**	**33**	**1**	**1**	**1**	**2**	**1**	**2**	**2**	**1**	**1**	**1**	**47**

(Source: Collett's book, pp. 165–6)

Summary of distances of members of the Troop from Woodbridge
(Sources p. 165 and Google)

Distance (miles)	Number of men
0	6
1–5	17
6–10	17
>10	7

Appendix 4

Return of the 2nd Corps of Suffolk Yeomanry cavalry under the command of Major Edgar in 1804 with numbers of arms and accoutrements supplied, purchased and retained

(See Collett's book, p. 153)

Accepted strength of the Corps						Effective strength of the Corps					
	Establishment per Troop						Strength per Troop				
Number of Troops	Sergeants	Corporals	Trumpeters	Privates	Total	Number of Troops	Sergeants	Corporals	Trumpeters	Privates	Total
3	3	3	1	38	115	3	3	3	1	35	42
With 3 Officers 1 Quarter Master 1 Farrier to the Corps to each troop											

Date and place whence received	No. of Arms Accoutrements supplied by Government with the date when received and from whence						No. of Arms Accoutrements purchased by the Corps and for which Government has granted the regular allowance						No. of Arms Accoutrements purchased by the Corps for which no allowance will be claimed						No. of Arms Accoutrements retained by the Corps at the conclusion of the last war					
	Bugles	Trumpets and Strings	Belts & Knotts	Sabres	Pistols	Carbines	Bugles	Trumpets and Strings	Belts & Knotts	Sabres	Pistols	Carbines	Bugles	Trumpets and Strings	Belts & Knotts	Sabres	Pistols	Carbines	Bugles	Trumpets and Strings	Belts & Knotts	Sabres	Pistols	Carbines
With bayonets & belts in the Year 1794						12							3	2	140	140	120			1		71	71	12
April 1795 Board of Ordnance					55																			
April 1799 Board of Ordnance					16																			
7 Feb. 1804 Depot at Stowmarket			10	10	10																			
Nov. 1798 Board of Ordnance				16																				
Dec. 1794 Board of Ordnance		1																						
Aug. 1794										55														
TOTAL		1	10	26	81	12				55			3	2	140	140	120			1		71	71	12

BIBLIOGRAPHY

UNPUBLISHED SOURCES

Suffolk Record Office, Ipswich
FB220/A7/3 Haughley Returns 1798
HA11/B1/3/2 Table showing returns in the Blything hundred
HA11/B2/3 'Driving the country' plan 1803
HA247/5/10–115 Mileson Edgar papers: miscellaneous papers relating to the administration of the Suffolk Yeomanry
HA247/5/25 Mileson Edgar papers HD80/3/1, 2, 3 Cornelius Collett's Account in three volumes
HD11/475/2405 Isaac Johnson's Map of Cornelius Collett's land at Farlingay Hall
HD79/B1 Subscribers' minutes: receipt and drawing for silver epergne for Lieutenant Colonel Sharpe
HD365/1–3 William Goodwin of Earl Soham's Diary 1785–1810
HD408/4 Folio 98 Sketch 98 Isaac Johnson's sketch of Lieutenant Colonel Sharpe's epergne
P454 Copy of Lord Euston's Letter Book
P630/1 Map of the army barracks in Woodbridge

Gloucestershire Archives, Gloucester
D421/X19 General Sir Eyre Coote's Notebook and Map

The National Archives, Kew
PROB 11/17/1748 Will of Cornelius Collett

William L. Clements Library, University of Michigan
Eyre Coote Papers, 6612/14/144

PRINTED SOURCES

Dymond, David, ed., *Joseph Hodskinson's Map of Suffolk in 1783*, Suffolk Records Society, Volume 15 (1972)
Fiske, Jane, ed., *The Oakes Diaries: Business, Politics and the Family in Bury St Edmunds 1778–1827,* Suffolk Records Society, Volumes 32 and 33 (1989 and 1990)
Scarfe, Norman, ed., *A Frenchman's Year in Suffolk: French Impressions of Suffolk Life in 1784,* Suffolk Records Society, Volume 30 (1988)
Shaw, John, ed., *The Loes and Wilford Poor Law Incorporation 1765–1826*, Suffolk Records Society, Volume 62 (2019)
Stone, Michael, ed., *The Diary of John Longe (1765–1834) Vicar of Coddenham*, Suffolk Records Society, Volume 51 (2008)

Young, Arthur, *General View of the Agriculture of the County of Suffolk* [1813] (Newton Abbot, 1969)

Bury and Norwich Post
Ipswich Journal

SECONDARY WORKS

Archer, J. E., *By a Flash and a Scare: Incendiarism, Animal Maiming and Poaching in East Anglia 1815–70* (Oxford, 1990)

Archer, J. E., 'Rural Protest 1815–1851', in Dymond, D. and Martin, E., eds, *An Historical Atlas of Suffolk* (Ipswich, 1999)

Bastin, J., *The Norfolk Yeomanry in Peace and in War* (Fakenham, 1986)

Beckett, I. F. W., *Britain's Part-time Soldiers: The Amateur Military Tradition 1558–1945*, 2nd edn (Barnsley, 2011)

Bettley, J. and Pevsner, N., *The Buildings of England: Suffolk East* (London, 2015)

Blatchly, J., *Isaac Johnson of Woodbridge: Georgian Surveyor and Artist* (Dorchester, 2014)

Colley, L., *Britons: Forging the Nation 1707–1837* (London, 1992)

Dymond, D. and Martin, E., eds, *An Historical Atlas of Suffolk* (Ipswich, 1999)

Dymond, D. and Northeast, P., *A History of Suffolk* (Chichester, 1995)

Emsley, C., *British Society and the French Wars 1793–1815* (London, 1979)

Foynes, J., *East Anglia against the Tricolour, 1789–1815* (Cromer, 2016)

Glover, R., *Britain at Bay: Defence against Bonaparte 1803–1814* (London, 1973)

Harrup, V., 'Woodbridge Barracks during the War with Napoleon', Part 1, *Suffolk Review* (Autumn 2013), pp. 35–41; Part 2, *Suffolk Review* (Spring 2015), pp. 21–6

Laver, J., *British Military Uniforms* (London, 1948)

Maurice-Jones, K. W., *The History of the Coast Artillery in the British Army* (Uckfield, 2009, first published 1959)

Millward, J., *An Assessment of East Coast Martello Towers* (London, 2007)

Norrington V., 'Peace at Last: Celebrations of Peace and Victories during and after the Napoleonic Wars', *Suffolk Review* (Spring 2003), pp. 17–33

Peacock, A. J., *Bread or Blood: The Agrarian Riots in East Anglia 1816* (London, 1965)

Roberts, W. M., *Lost Country Houses of Suffolk* (Woodbridge, 2010)

Robinson, G., 'The Loyal Worlingworth Volunteers', *Suffolk Review* (Autumn 2015), pp. 20–31

Smith, R. and Satchel, M., 'Malthus, Poverty and Population Change in Suffolk 1780–1834', *Proceedings of the Suffolk Institute of Archaeology and History, Volume* 44 (2018), pp. 256–69

Stone, M., *Suffolk 1775–1845: Conflict and Co-operation* (Cambridge, 2015)

Thomas, M. and Sign, N., *The Loyal Suffolk Hussars: The History of the Suffolk Yeomanry 1794–1967* (Solihull, 2012)

Uglow, J., *In These Times: Living in Britain through Napoleon's Wars, 1793–1815* (London, 2014)

Wade-Martins, S. and Williamson, T., *Roots of Change* (Exeter, 1999)

Watson, J. S., *The Reign of George III* (Oxford, 1985)

Young, A., 'Annals of Agriculture, Volume XVII', in Bethem Edwards, M., ed., *Autobiography of Arthur Young* (London, 1898)

INDEX OF PEOPLE AND PLACES

(Military title is the most senior commissioned rank mentioned in the text)

INDEX OF SUBJECTS

THE SUFFOLK RECORDS SOCIETY

For over sixty years the Suffolk Records Society has added to the knowledge of Suffolk's history by issuing an annual volume of previously unpublished manuscripts, each throwing light on some new aspect of the history of the county.

Covering 700 years and embracing letters, diaries, maps, accounts and other archives, many of them previously little known or neglected, these books have together made a major contribution to historical studies.

At the heart of this achievement lie the Society's members, all of whom share a passion for Suffolk and its history and whose support, subscriptions and donations make possible the opening up of the landscape of historical research in the area.

In exchange for this tangible support, members receive a new volume each year at a considerable saving on the retail price at which the books are then offered for sale. Members are also welcomed to the launch of the new volume, held each year in a different and appropriate setting within the county and giving them a chance to meet and listen to some of the leading historians in their fields talking about their latest work.

For anyone with a love of history, a desire to build a library on Suffolk themes at modest cost and a wish to see historical research continue to thrive and bring new sources to the public eye in decades to come, a subscription to the Suffolk Records Society is the ideal way to make a contribution and join the company of those who give Suffolk history a future.

THE CHARTERS SERIES

To supplement the annual volumes and serve the need of medieval historians, the Charters Series was launched in 1979 with the challenge of publishing the transcribed texts of all the surviving monastic charters for the county. Since then, twenty volumes have been published as an occasional series, the latest in 2018.

The Charter Series is financed by a separate annual subscription leading to receipt of each volume on publication.

CURRENT PROJECTS

Volumes approved by the Council of the Society for future publication include *The Crown Pleas of the Suffolk Eyre of 1240*, edited by Eric Gallagher, *Monks Eleigh Manorial Documents*, edited by Vivienne Aldous, and *The Records of Medieval Newmarket*, edited by James Davis and Joanne Sear; and in the Charters Series, *The Charters of the Priory of St Peter and St Paul, Ipswich*, the second of two volumes edited by David Allen, *Bury St Edmunds Town Charters*, edited by Vivien Brown, and *Rumburgh Priory Charters*, edited by Nicholas Karn. The order in which these and other volumes appear in print will depend on the dates of completion of editorial work.

MEMBERSHIP

Membership enquiries should be addressed to Mrs Tanya Christian, 8 Orchid Way, Needham Market, IP6 8JQ; e-mail: membership@suffolkrecordssociety.com.

The Suffolk Records Society is a registered charity, No. 1084279.